A JACOBEAN COMPANY AND
ITS PLAYHOUSE

Eva Griffith's book fills a major gap concerning the world of Shakespearean drama. It tells the previously untold story of the Servants of Queen Anna of Denmark – a group of players parallel to Shakespeare's King's Men – and their playhouse, the Red Bull. Built in vibrant Clerkenwell, the Red Bull lay within the northern suburbs of Jacobean London, with prostitution to the west and the Revels Office to the east. Griffith sets the playhouse in the historical context of the Seckford and Bedingfeld families and their connections to the site. Utilising a wealth of primary evidence including maps, plans and archival texts, she analyses the court patronage of figures such as Sir Robert Sidney, Queen Anna's Chamberlain, alongside the company's members, function and repertoire. Plays performed included those by Webster, Dekker and Heywood – entertainments characterised by spectacle, battle sequences and court-room drama, alongside London humour and song.

EVA GRIFFITH is a theatre historian working on early seventeenth-century entertainment, spectacle and drama. She began acting at the age of seven, performing in many film, television and theatre productions. Owing her entire existence to the performance of Shakespeare (her parents met during an Old Vic touring production of *A Midsummer Night's Dream*), she was encouraged in an interest in literature and history through united family concerns. As an academic she has researched internationally with the help of fellowships, for example, at the Huntington Library and the Harry Ransom Center in America, gaining funding, prizes and bursaries from the British Academy, the Malone Society and the Society for Theatre Research. She has published on Red Bull-related topics in *Huntington Library Quarterly* and in Richard Dutton's award-winning *Oxford Handbook of Early Modern Theatre*. She is currently working on a book concerning the poet, playwright and masque-writer, James Shirley, having written about him for *The Times Literary Supplement* and Four Courts Press. She acted as Research Associate on *The Complete Works of James Shirley* at Durham University and is editing a play for this large-scale edition – *Changes or Love in a Maze*.

A JACOBEAN COMPANY AND ITS PLAYHOUSE

*The Queen's Servants at the Red Bull Theatre
(c. 1605–1619)*

EVA GRIFFITH

CAMBRIDGE
UNIVERSITY PRESS

CAMBRIDGE
UNIVERSITY PRESS

University Printing House, Cambridge CB2 8BS, United Kingdom

Published in the United States of America by Cambridge University Press, New York

Cambridge University Press is part of the University of Cambridge.

It furthers the University's mission by disseminating knowledge in the pursuit of
education, learning and research at the highest international levels of excellence.

www.cambridge.org
Information on this title: www.cambridge.org/9781107041882

© Eva Griffith 2013

First published 2013

Printed in the United Kingdom by CPI Group Ltd, Croydon CR0 4YY

A catalogue record for this publication is available from the British Library

Library of Congress Cataloguing in Publication data
Griffith, Eva.
A Jacobean company and its playhouse : the Queen's Servants at The Red Bull
Theatre, c. 1605–1619 / Eva Griffith.
pages   cm
Includes bibliographical references and index.
ISBN 978-1-107-04188-2 (hardback)
1. Red Bull Theatre (London, England)–History.   2. Theaters–England–London–History–17th
century.   3. Queen's servants (Theater company)   4. Theatrical companies–England–London–
History–17th century.   I. Title.
PN2596.L7R25   2013
725′.82209421–dc23
2013012186

ISBN 978-1-107-04188-2 hardback

For my mother, Doria Marguerite Jamieson Griffith

I know a bank where the wild thyme blows
Where oxlips and the nodding violet grows …
There sleeps Titania …
Oberon, in William Shakespeare,
A Midsummer Night's Dream, Act II, scene I

Contents

Illustrations

The author and publishers acknowledge the following sources of copyright material and are grateful for the permissions granted. While every effort has been made, it has not always been possible to identify the sources of all material used, or to trace all copyright holders. If any omissions are brought to our notice, we will be happy to include the appropriate acknowledgements on reprinting.

Acknowledgements

This book represents work going back to my MA and PhD at King's College London, when Gordon McMullan sent me to Shakespeare's Globe to visit Andrew Gurr with my research. First thanks should go to Professor Gurr, who put me on the road towards theatre history and its historians.

Further thanks should go to the following: Gordon McMullan, Ann Thompson and Richard Proudfoot at King's; Caroline Barron, Vanessa Harding and Julia Merritt of the Medieval and Tudor London Seminar at the Institute of Historical Research; Olwen Myhill and Matthew Davies, also of the Institute. Other invaluable historian friends include Andrew Ashbee, Helen Payne, Paul Griffiths, John Clark, Barbara Todd, Duncan Harrington and Jessica Freeman. My gratitude towards fellow literature scholars goes to Lucy Munro, John Lavagnino, Rebecca Bailey, Richard Rowland and Sue Wiseman, along with Barbara Ravelhofer, Eugene Giddens and Teresa Grant of the Shirley Project. Warm thoughts also go out to the friends I made while researching James Shirley and teaching at Durham University.

The British Academy funded all my postgraduate higher education and provided some post-doctoral funding to further the book research. The University of London helped me make my first trip to the Huntington Library, San Marino, California. At this institution I was able to follow up my researches studying C. W. Wallace's notes, housed there. Speaking of the Americas, thanks should also go to the following people for their conversation at four Shakespeare Association of America conferences and other places: Richard Dutton, Dave Kathman, Bill Lloyd, Alan Nelson, Sally-Beth MacLean (of Records of Early English Drama) and John Astington, as well as the extraordinary William Ingram. Texts from Sir Robert Sidney's papers appear by kind permission of Viscount de L'Isle from his private collection. For Sarah Stanton of Cambridge University Press, who has been unconscionably patient, I also give thanks.

Archivists who have helped me in particular include Louise Kennedy of Suffolk Record Office, Ipswich as well as Paul Evans of Gloucestershire Archives and Wendy Hawke and Jeremy Smith of the London Metropolitan Archives. Very special gratitude is due to Tim Wales, a historian, researcher and friend, as well as to the equally kind Sir Henry and Lady Bedingfeld and their family of Oxburgh Hall, Norfolk. I am also grateful to my friends among the performing fraternity who supported me during my researches: Sonia Ritter, Tamsin Lewis, Duncan Law, Rosalind Cressy and all the actors of the Lions part company, as well as all others who supported my efforts. The end of the book's preparation was supported by a Carlyle membership at the London Library.

As the mantra goes, the thanks go to these people; *all the mistakes are mine*. Most of what was achieved was managed as a single-parent student, so another kind of thanks goes to my mother, Doria Griffith, and my son, John O'Riordan. To my husband, Paul Klein, I am always grateful for the laughter he invokes to keep me on the right side of sane.

Note on transliteration

For transcriptions from original texts, italics are used to expand contracted words; carets (^) appear in order to show where inserted words and phrases begin and end; and for deletions, 'strike-through' is employed for deleted parts. Primary source transcriptions have been given for documentary evidence, yet secondary sources are also referred to for those who wish to consult these works. For early modern printed texts, with a lack of modern editions of Red Bull plays, original quartos have mainly been used and transcriptions from these have been conservatively biased. Signature numbers or 'sigs' (appearing as 'A2v' or 'E4') have been employed as the only page references available in these books.

Abbreviations

TNA	The National Archives, Kew
LMA	London Metropolitan Archives
LPL	Lambeth Palace Library
SROI	Suffolk Record Office, Ipswich
ES	E. K. Chambers, *The Elizabethan Stage*, 4 vols. (Oxford: Clarendon Press, 1923)
JCS	Gerald Eades Bentley, *The Jacobean and Caroline Stage*, 7 vols. (Oxford: Clarendon Press, 1941–68)
EPT	Glynne Wickham, Herbert Berry and William Ingram, eds., *English Professional Theatre, 1530–1660* (Cambridge University Press, 2000)
MCR	John Cordy Jeaffreson, *Middlesex County Records* (Old Series), 4 vols. (Greater London Council, 1972 [1886–92])
MSR	William le Hardy, ed., *Middlesex Sessions Records* (New Series), 4 vols. (London: Guildhall, 1935–41)
MSC	Malone Society Collections
St JPR	Robert Hovenden, ed., *A True Register of All the Christeninges, Mariages, and Burialles in the Parishe of St James, Clerkenwell, from the Yeare of Our Lorde God 1551*, 6 vols. (London: Harleian Society, 1884–94)
Int.	Interrogatory (a question put to witnesses in a court case)
sig.	signature (page reference in early modern books)

Introduction: The Red Bull playhouse, St John Street

In William Pinks' voluminous work, *The History of Clerkenwell*, the nineteenth-century historian wrote of St John Street that it was at first 'a packhorse road' that 'very soon became an important highway'.[1] It certainly was a busy place. In the early seventeenth century, the playhouse that concerns us here was built just off this street: the Red Bull.

Today as then, St John Street is a wide road, beginning close to the thoroughfare of 'the Angel', where you can still find transport to and from the north. Instead of going west today – in order to get into central London – the early modern traveller might have journeyed down St John Street to get into the *City* of London. At that time the City was the central area for work and domestic life (see figure 1) rather than what it represents now – London's financial district.

When the Red Bull was built, St John Street was the direct route to the place where many would want to go and, in truth, where many would not want to go at all. It was St John Street that led into Smithfield Market and then beyond, if necessary, into London. It was a busy, messy thoroughfare that for unwary animals – in some numbers – meant the road to the slaughterhouse. For aberrant humans it would mean the Middlesex Sessions House and then – if found guilty – a journey onwards to Newgate gaol. Other streets, like Aldersgate and Bishopsgate to the east of St John Street, undoubtedly acted as main arteries into the City; however, it would have been this road that was most associated with the traffic of animals, in particular. Smithfield was the district where you could most easily pick up a horse for sale, for example, as well as meat-reared livestock. After a herd or flock of animals travelled down this road to Smithfield, then

[1] William J. Pinks, *The History of Clerkenwell*, ed. Edward J. Wood, 2nd edn (London: Charles Herbert, 1881), p. 294. See Eva Griffith, 'Inside and Outside: Animal Activity and the Red Bull Playhouse, St John Street', in *The Cultural History of Animals*, ed. Linda Kalof and Brigitte Resl, 6 vols. (Oxford: Berg, 2007), Vol. IV: *A Cultural History of Animals in the Age of Enlightenment*, ed. Matthew Senior, pp. 102–19.

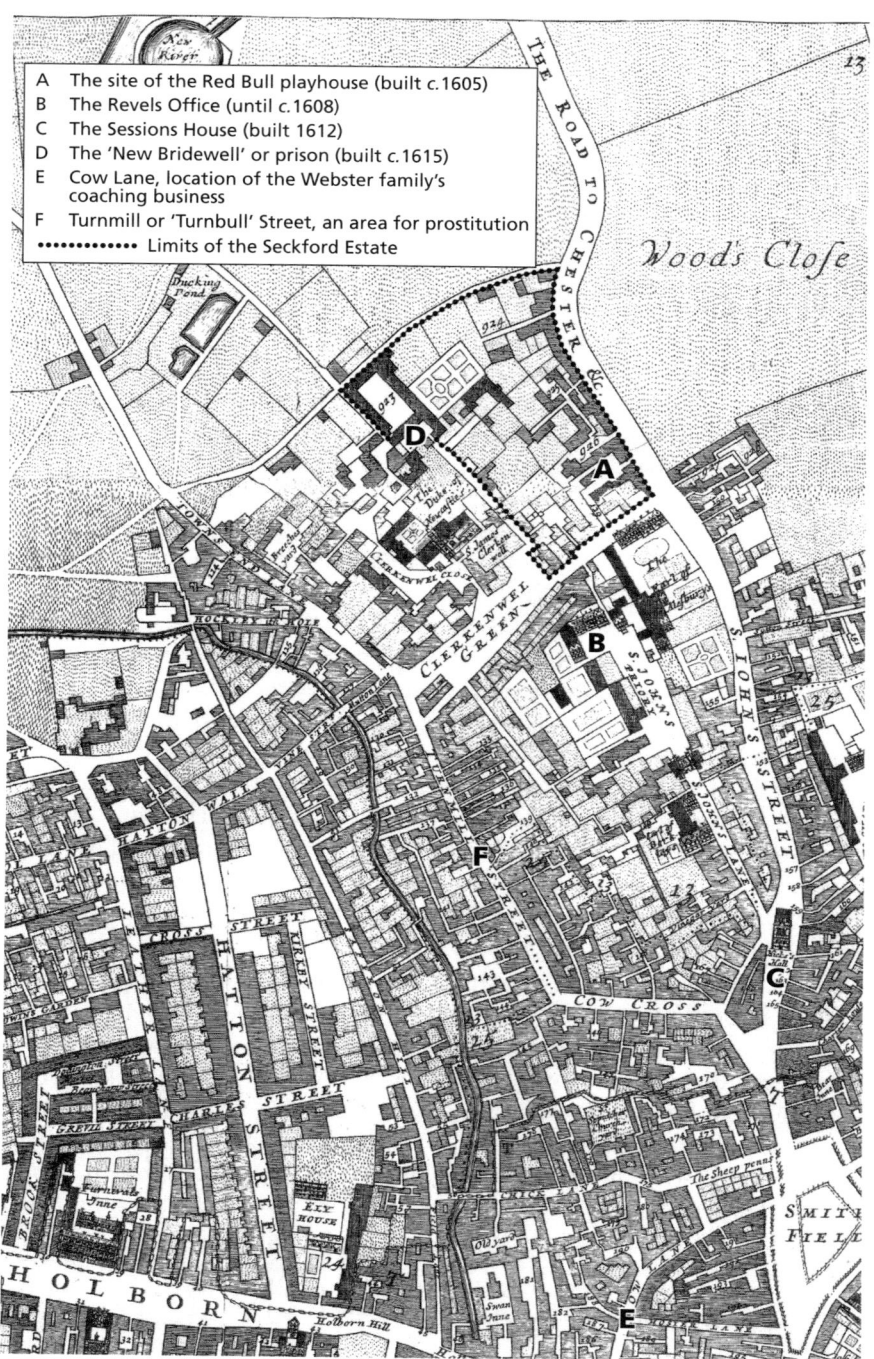

A The site of the Red Bull playhouse (built c.1605)
B The Revels Office (until c.1608)
C The Sessions House (built 1612)
D The 'New Bridewell' or prison (built c.1615)
E Cow Lane, location of the Webster family's coaching business
F Turnmill or 'Turnbull' Street, an area for prostitution
•••••••••••• Limits of the Seckford Estate

Figure 1 Map of Clerkenwell including Smithfield to the south.
William Morgan, *London &c. Actually Survey'd* (detail), 1682.

London's livestock market (presently its meat market), the produce would be penned and assessed before sale. The purchased cattle and sheep would then be led into London via the gate of Newgate where they would be slaughtered at traditional places like St Nicholas Shambles and then eventually sold on as meat.[2]

When it comes to a study of the earliest days of the Red Bull playhouse, animals are not to be taken lightly. For what this book represents is a serious study of this seventeenth-century theatre, situated in the Clerkenwell area of St John Street – a study that, in human terms, focuses on the first company that performed there, the Servants of Queen Anna of Denmark. Animals are emblematically important to our concerns here for all kinds of reasons – contextual, historical, cultural. Coming down from Islington, a seventeenth-century traveller might know that he was approaching streets known as Turn*bull* (aka Turnmill) Street, *Cow*cross Street and Cock Lane. Surrounded by a veritable cacophony of animal sounds, this traveller, making his way down this thoroughfare, would not have been surprised at all, for example, by the presence on his right-hand side, of an inn called 'The Red Bull'. He may have been intrigued by the playhouse entrance, however, and, above this, a turret or tower, and, perhaps, attached to this, the flag of the theatre, no doubt depicting a red bull, fluttering in the breeze.[3] From the size of the entrance of the playhouse, a visitor might guess that it had once been a yard where animals like horses were stalled, while their owners, perhaps drovers and farmers, stayed at the adjacent inn. Passing by, the traveller might have jumped at the roar of all-too-human sounds coming from within the venue – a noise made in response to a stage effect, a character's actions, a song or a joke. Yet, ironically, the sounds he would have heard coming from within would be just as animal in nature as those of the passing animal life moving along with him.

A study of the Queen's Servants at the Red Bull needs to address detailed matters like the animal life of St John Street because contextual detail is one factor that has been missing from any account of this company and playhouse heretofore. It could be argued that unless we perceive the fullest contexts available for somewhere like the Red Bull – contexts such as the social and cultural one of animals – we will never properly perceive either this playhouse or, indeed, the complete picture for early modern drama in Shakespeare's day. That a better understanding of the Red Bull during the first period of its existence might aid a growing understanding of early

---

[2] Smithfield has been London's 'dead meat' market since 1868. Before this, until 1855, when it was moved to Copenhagen Fields, it was a livestock and horse market. See *ibid.*, p. 105 n10.

[3] See Chapter 3 for further observations on the location, size and layout of the playhouse.

modern drama is one desired effect of this book. With any evidence of interest in the Red Bull so far, what happened outside it has never been seen as an important factor of its existence. Critics have looked down on the Clerkenwell venue for housing only riotous apprentice/citizen audiences and have had little time for it as a place of serious entertainment, a perspective I would query.

Apart from attitudes, there is also a lack of account when it comes to both the history of the company of players we know as the Jacobean Queen's Servants and the playhouse where they performed. Where available there has certainly not been much that shows any detailed knowledge prompting balanced and objective responses. What do I mean by this and why should this be? Surely by their very name, as under the patronage of the King's wife and, therefore, on the face of it, on a parallel plane with the King's Men – Shakespeare's company – they should have been worth some attention, even if only for the sake of comparative analysis? The lack of an in-depth account is certainly a situation to which this book plans to respond. This can be so in the new era when much to do with 'Shakespeare Studies' has found courage to look afresh at many neglected, misperceived or previously fixed areas for study.

As I write this, English Literature scholars might experience a little sense of irony when contemplating my planned efforts, in that – apart from the scale of the project – challenges have been mounted that would question the very notion of a successful 'narrative' account of anything. In the last decade there have also been calls for some kind of regulation, or an addressing of a situation, when it comes to the field of 'Theatre History' – the very 'discipline' employed for this book. 'Theatre History', emanating out of English Literature departments, would appear to represent a methodologically amorphous area that, it seems, has not borne comparison with history methodology from 'straight' history departments. One of theatre history's great mentors, William Ingram, has spent much time questioning what our internal rules could or should be.[4] Moreover, a whole book series has appeared claiming, with its many different perspectives, to interrogate this matter.[5] From the outset of this study, I will be challenging theatre history approaches of the past to this particular playhouse and company,

---

[4] William Ingram, 'Narrative Concerns: Prologue', in *The Business of Playing: The Beginnings of the Adult Professional Theater in Elizabethan London* (Ithaca, NY: Cornell University Press, 1992), pp. 1–11. See also 'Introduction: Early Modern Theater History: Where We Are Now, How We Got Here, Where We Go Next', in *The Oxford Handbook of Early Modern Theatre*, ed. Richard Dutton (Oxford University Press, 2009), pp. 1–15.

[5] Peter Holland, W. B. Worthen and Stephen Orgel (eds.), *Redefining British Theatre History*, 3 vols. (Basingstoke: Palgrave Macmillan, 2003–6).

while also, as occasion arises, interrogating a perceptibly less than flexible approach when it comes to theatre history in general.

The truth of the matter when it comes to a concern about theatre history amounts to two main areas with one overarching problem. The two areas of concern are the lack of evidence when wanted (and the easy misinterpretation of it when found) alongside the fact that human beings need stories. They need them simply in order to structure their comprehension of people, places and events. Because of this need for stories, some kind of consecutive narrative will always be the best form of communication for the twentieth- or twenty-first-century reader, particularly when it comes to a new or neglected story, however sparsely or oddly aligned the evidence appears to be.[6] It is the mode of presentation or interpretation that is the overarching problem. Interpretation of what we have – setting aside the all-too-probable event of completely misreading what we see – will always be multiple in possibility. Therefore, within a responsible field of early modern scholarship, the 'ifs' and 'buts' and 'maybes' are intrinsic to the narrative enterprise. With the subject of this study, not only an offering of a story, but the strange *perceptions* affecting the story need to be addressed, and that, too, will be broached here, in this Introduction, paving the way for an unapologetic previously non-existent narrative.

The rest of this Introduction will do several things. Firstly, it will describe the most basic history of the Queen's Servants at the Red Bull playhouse. It will then outline something of how the Queen's Servants at the Red Bull have been perceived in the past, lending context to largely pejorative perceptions with reference to the recontextualising effort current within general Shakespeare studies. As it continues, it will describe more Queen's Servants/Red Bull history as we have it, indicating the ways in which this book will provide a first detailed account using as yet unpublished research. The Introduction will then give one historical example – one that shows the importance of animals in St John Street – to demonstrate how we can readdress old attitudes concerning the Queen's Servants at the Red Bull. What I am about to do now involves outlining something of the previous outlook on the subject, illustrating this with a selection of the work of past historians and critics.

The basics that we have received so far are these. The Queen's Servants were a company of players who, before James Stuart came to the throne in 1603 as King James I, worked under the patronage of Edward Somerset,

---

[6] For further observations on theatre history, biography and evidence see Eva Griffith, 'Christopher Beeston, his property and properties', in Dutton, *The Oxford Handbook of Early Modern Theatre*, pp. 607–22, esp. pp. 621–2.

fourth earl of Worcester. While working as servants in his name they performed at venues including the Boar's Head in Whitechapel and the Rose
on the Bankside, as well as venues around England when on tour. After
the death of Queen Elizabeth, the last Tudor Queen, and the accession of
King James, they became the players of the King's consort, Queen Anna
of Denmark, generally known to the populace as Queen Anne. To the
best of our knowledge, some time prior to 1605, an associate of the company, Martin Slatiar, teamed up with an inn-holder called Aaron Holland,
to convert a yard to an inn called the Red Bull into a playhouse. Building
work was apparently stopped during 1605, but the playhouse must have
been finished – at the very latest – by late March 1606, most probably
before.[7]

The company moved to their new theatre on St John Street, therefore,
sometime during 1605–6. Various pieces of evidence exist as to who held
what size of share in both the company and the playhouse. Apart from a
period when they briefly played at the indoor theatre called the Cockpit
near the Strand (built in 1616), they were to go on performing at the Red
Bull as their main house until 1619, the year when Queen Anna died.
What was left of them, after some disagreements and divisions, became
the Revels Players.

We are fortunate that we live in an era when almost everything within
the broad area of 'Shakespeare Studies' has been re-examined. It has
become a mantra to claim that in the last fifth of the twentieth century
our focus on the very subject of 'Shakespeare' has been interrogated, and
this has opened up the opportunity to look at early modern drama and
its contexts anew. In terms of the wider study of the entertainment of this
time, through the good auspices of hard-working – if questioned – theatre
historians, we are certainly now allowed to see Shakespeare as simply one
amidst a crowd of actors struggling to make theatre work as an economic
enterprise. Shakespeare was an actor among a mass of other actors –
friends and rivals at concurrent moments – pursuing their entertainment
objectives in commercially orientated playing companies. One of the
ways in which the actor Shakespeare effected this success, for example,
was by writing for his company. Recent studies emphasising commercial
playhouse companies of actors have, in part, sought to redress a balance
where it seemed that the study of the work of *playwrights*, rather than the
contribution of a company's whole *repertoire* of plays, had resulted in misunderstandings. These misunderstandings, once analysed, reduced down

---

[7] See Eva Griffith, 'Martin Slatiar and the Red Bull Playhouse', *Huntington Library Quarterly* 74
(2011), 553–74.

to the all-important *material conditions* within which such textual work was achieved. Because of the evolving dominance of 'the author' – with Shakespeare as the most dominant – critics of former times have given too much importance to a particular author's collected works, and too little to the financially motivated working environment within which those works were produced.[8] Thus it is that a study like this book, which attempts to detail an individual company and its conditions, represents a worthwhile contribution towards redressing a balance.

The obvious company-centred groundwork was addressed in the 1990s by Roslyn Knutson, for example, working on the King's Men's repertoire (all the plays, not just Shakespeare's), and the Records of Early English Drama (REED) project and its acolytes – Scott McMillin and Sally-Beth MacLean – on the Elizabethan Queen's Men (a large and significant earlier company).[9] Taking, perhaps, a cue from this kind of one-by-one company approach, more general work of most recent times, laying down direction for detailed actor-and-company research, has been widening in scope. I would mention Andrew Gurr's *Shakespeare's Opposites* on the Admiral's company, and John H. Astington's *Actors and Acting in Shakespeare's Time*, as two examples of the recent generalised trend: one looking at a specific non-Shakespeare company, the other looking at the 'Art of Stage Playing' with particular actor and actor-experience examples from the time.[10]

The total effect of much of this flowering is a useful multiplicity when it comes to the kinds of concentrated recording of early theatre. These range from transcriptions of documents; to the narratives constructed around the complexities of an actor's life; to further studies on particular companies, their venues, their touring practice and their repertoires in books both cohesive and of the essay kind. I would mention Mary Bly and Lucy Munro as both company-interested, producing work on the Children of the King's and Queen's Revels respectively, unafraid to introduce critical approaches such as queer theory and Derridean deconstruction into the

---

[8] Many works that have recently sought to challenge 'author centrality' were founded on Michel Foucault, 'What is an Author?', trans. Josue V. Harari, in *Textual Strategies: Perspectives in Post-Structuralist Criticism*, ed. Josue V. Harari (London: Methuen, 1980), pp. 141–60. See also, however, Gerald Eades Bentley, *The Profession of Dramatist in Shakespeare's Time 1590–1642* (Princeton University Press, 1971); and *The Profession of Player in Shakespeare's Time, 1590–1642* (Princeton University Press, 1984). Also Roslyn Lander Knutson, *The Repertory of Shakespeare's Company, 1594–1613* (Fayetteville: University of Arkansas Press, 1991); and Scott McMillin and Sally-Beth MacLean, *The Queen's Men and Their Plays* (Cambridge University Press, 1998).
[9] McMillin and MacLean, *The Queen's Men and Their Plays*.
[10] Andrew Gurr, *Shakespeare's Opposites: The Admiral's Company 1594–1625* (Cambridge University Press, 2009); John H. Astington, *Actors and Acting in Shakespeare's Time: The Art of Stage Playing* (Cambridge University Press, 2010).

equation of particular company/theatre/repertoire history accounts.[11] I would forefront Richard Dutton's *The Oxford Handbook of Early Modern Theatre* as a particularly useful example of the essay-collection kind of approach, taking us at one moment through different time periods of early theatre, while at another juncture becoming detailed about all kinds of areas of focused importance to early drama as a whole. Cambridge University Press's *English Professional Theatre, 1530–1660* (*EPT*), edited by Glynne Wickham, Herbert Berry and William Ingram and published in 2000, seems central to a concerted effort to improve our documentary knowledge in the most straightforward of ways. This it did mainly by offering transcriptions of documents from the period of early theatre history. The editors, however, did not avoid interpretations of the material they offered, even if told within given topic areas (three parts: documents of control, the players' lives, the playhouses) rather than with any attempt at an overarching chronological form.

The growing body of work by Dave Kathman, centring on details concerning the lives of actors and their playhouse associates, alongside his new interests in early modern inn-yard performance, is derived from ranges of documents, civic and national in nature. Kathman shows how complex such lives can be, and therefore, by default, the complexities of theatre history itself.[12] Susan Cerasano's long-awaited works on the Rose/Fortune/Alleyn/Henslowe enterprises are anticipated, and we are glad to see Grace Ioppolo's work with the Dulwich College manuscripts, digitising Henslowe's papers, and her new interest in a complete works of Thomas Heywood, which this study can only applaud.[13] For others I would invoke names like Alan Nelson, Richard Dutton and Anne Lancashire, simply as scholars also interested in seeking answers for dramatic literature, not just about the use of the literature itself, but in the context of the historical conditions within which it was produced. William Ingram, in his book *The Business of Playing*, goes further than any: he interrogates our understanding and is detailed about specifics. Somewhere in the mix – if

---

[11] Mary Bly, *Queer Virgins and Virgin Queans on the Early Modern Stage* (Oxford University Press, 2000); Lucy Munro, *Children of the Queen's Revels: A Jacobean Theatre Repertory* (Cambridge University Press, 2005).

[12] Recent David Kathman works include: 'Alice Layston and the Cross Keys', *Medieval and Renaissance Drama in England* 22 (2009), 144–78; 'Inn-Yard Playhouses' and 'Players, Livery Companies, and Apprentices', both in Dutton, *The Oxford Handbook of Early Modern Theatre*, pp. 153–67 and pp. 413–28 respectively; 'London Inns as Playing Venues for the Queen's Men', in *Locating the Queen's Men, 1583–1603*, ed. Helen Ostovich, Holger Schott Syme and Andrew Griffin (Farnham: Ashgate, 2009), pp. 65–75; 'The Rise of Commercial Playing in 1540s London', *Early Theatre* 12 (2009), 15–38.

[13] Available online at www.henslowe-alleyn.org.uk/index.html.

lucky – we catch a glimpse of the complex nature of what we study, and are exhorted to remember just how diversely structured early theatre was and – in truth – how we should always regard it as such.

Perhaps the most daring points I have to make about the Queen's Servants concern their not only having the Red Bull in which to perform their plays but the Curtain playhouse as well. This thought is backed up with a considerable body of evidence that others have only occasionally acknowledged and put into print in record form. It is, however, indicative of Queen's Servants/Red Bull difficulties in the minds of theatre historians that, despite knowing of patents for the company including the Curtain and acknowledging how Queen's Servants players owned parts of the Curtain estate, critics have not taken this company seriously as wide-ranging in any kind of multi-venue way. We are permitted to view Shakespeare's company, the King's Servants, as responsible for two theatres at one time, but contemplating similar conditions for the Queen's Servants seems harder to admit. Attitudes like this, and described here, are hangovers of an old-school way of thinking where, unfortunately, Shakespeare-associated company histories insistently lead scholars to believe that business was only manageable, and success only achievable, by particular companies for particular reasons.

Back in 1998, when McMillin and MacLean published their important book on the Elizabethan Queen's Men, their sense of our lack of familiarity with an 'Elizabethan theatre that had never heard of Shakespeare or Marlowe' made them suspect the whole area of their company had 'not been studied firmly enough'.[14] Roslyn Knutson's 1991 comments, on skewed views of Shakespeare's part in the Chamberlain's Men and the nature of company competition, are now accepted, and studies have widened. Today we look at whole areas, not lopsided parts. Sadly, however, the suspicions of recent decades are still recognised by the scholar of the Jacobean Queen's Servants/Red Bull history. In truth, the situation with the Clerkenwell company and its playhouse has always been much worse. At least in the case of the Elizabethan Queen's Men there was a cogent body of scholarship to draw from, much of it received first-hand through ongoing work completed Britain-wide for the Records of Early English Drama; at least, with Shakespeare's company, 'every scrap of information' has been treated 'as priceless treasure'.[15]

The problems for the Jacobean Red Bull company scholar are of a different order in comparison with the difficulties of others. Not only is there a

[14] McMillin and MacLean, *The Queen's Men and Their Plays*, p. xii.
[15] Knutson, *The Repertory of Shakespeare's Company*, p. 2.

scarcity of accounts from which to draw a coherent history of the Queen's Servants, but lying alongside what exists is a strange set of warped, subjective perceptions. These perceptions were brought about a long time ago but supported, I would suggest, in order to focus attention on Shakespeare. Published works that may be termed 'histories' of the Queen's Servants are, as I say, few and far between. Original, transcribed sources that have helped with such accounts are also sporadic and disparately spaced when it comes to publication. A valuable list of such histories and sources could begin with, for example, Frederick Gard Fleay's nineteenth-century transcriptions of the bill and answer to the *Worth* v. *Baskervile* case of 1623–6.[16]

This was a case where a Queen's Servants player called Ellis Worth, among other players of the company, took the widow of their one-time leader and clown, Thomas Greene, to court, and it contains much information that is useful to an understanding of the company and, in particular, its share-owning systems. When a company of actors was formed at this time, the core members involved would put, in effect, equal *shares of money* into a pool to meet their basic needs for performance – costumes, props and scripts, etc. This portion of the money to start their enterprise was known as their *share*. Because you had a share of the company's economic beginnings, it was understood that you would reap the rewards through access to a pre-agreed proportion of profits at the door. There are instances where traditional playing company values meant a dead actor's estate might retrieve the value of a share, and instances where a non-actor might be offered sums equivalent to a share, yet generally shares were only accessed by active, share-committed players in a company.[17]

A company could only benefit from further funds being put into it by people wishing to invest in its good fortune to gain a return. As my research will show, Susan Greene, the widow of Thomas Greene, was a much more important part of the monetary infrastructure of the company – with an attendant interest in its playhouse – than has been previously thought. Formerly married to the actor Robert Browne, a lessee-actor of the Boar's Head playhouse who died in 1603, she married her second husband, Greene, the leader of the Queen's Servants and sharer in the Curtain theatre as well as investor in Red Bull shares, soon after.[18] When,

---

[16] TNA C2/JASI/W2/67; Frederick Gard Fleay, *A Chronicle History of the London Stage, 1559–1642* (London: Reeves and Turner, 1890), pp. 270–97.

[17] See Chapter 7 for matters concerning the estate of the actor George Pulham and the nature of some company agreements with Susan Baskervile.

[18] Greene held the tenure of the Curtain sometime during and/or before 1611. See TNA C54/2075, no. 17; *EPT*, p. 416. The Queen's Servants were allowed to use the Curtain from after the plague of 1603–4. See Dulwich, MS I, fo. 54; John Payne Collier, *Memoirs of Edward Alleyn, Founder of Dulwich*

in turn, Greene died in 1612, she became the sole owner of their Red Bull playhouse shares. After this she was partnered for a third time to a James Baskervile, who bought into the company's fortunes. The legality of their marital status, however, was queried by an actor giving evidence in the court case.[19] Up until now, all we knew of this *Worth* v. *Baskervile* case was that it concerned a claim for the *company shares* that Susan Baskervile inherited from Thomas Greene – that is, the part that Susan felt she was owed from her husband's original input into their work. From evidence in this case and from that in another, later, rediscovered suit, it would appear Susan Browne-Greene-Baskervile possessed even more than this from her and Greene's investment in the *playhouse*, and this fact informs analysis of the 1623 case.[20] *Playhouse shares* were different from company shares in that they represented money that was ploughed into the fabric of the building. Some of the profits from playhouse performance could be accessed through owning company shares. A good portion of the money available, however, could only be derived from having a share in the theatre itself. In this way, although the players in the company would have derived some profits taken, for example, during their time at the Rose, it would have been Philip Henslowe – the builder and manager of this playhouse – who benefited significantly from box office returns.

Fleay's work was followed up much later by C. J. Sisson's article, 'The Red Bull Company and the Importunate Widow', which used the witness depositions of the *Worth* v. *Baskervile* case to draw conclusions about the company.[21] However, Sisson's language in this piece takes the opportunity to put forward pejorative perceptions about the company. 'When we think of what is sordid, self-seeking, or petty or cunning, in these people', he concludes about the Red Bull players, 'we should not forget that in the

---

College: *Including Some New Particulars Respecting Shakespeare, Ben Jonson, Massinger, Marston, Dekker etc.* (London: Shakespeare Society, 1841), p. 66; *EPT*, p. 414. Their continued allowed use of the playhouse is recorded in both their draft patent of *c.* 1604 and the official one of 1609.

19   TNA C24/500/9, Thomas Basse, Int. 22. The text of his answer claims that 'Baskervile [deleted: 'having taken up diuerse commodityes in & about London upon Creditt, and being taxed for hauing two wieues lyuing both at one tyme did'] about vij yeares agone did goe into Ireland as this deponent hath heard where he yet liueth for any thing yet this deponent knoweth to be contrary.' Other actors were more circumspect: Richard Perkins, for instance, stating that Baskervile left 'upon some private reasons'.

20   TNA REQ2/709. Eva Griffith, 'Playhouse, Company, Repertoire: The Queen's Servants at the Red Bull Theatre, Clerkenwell (*c.* 1605–1619)', Ph.D. thesis, University of London, 2003, p. 40; Eva Griffith, 'Baskervile [*née* Shawe], Susan (*bap.* 1573, *d.* 1649)', in *Oxford Dictionary of National Biography* (Oxford University Press, 2004), www.oxforddnb.com/view/article/74435?docPos=1, accessed 9 April 2013.

21   Charles J. Sisson, 'The Red Bull Company and the Importunate Widow', *Shakespeare Survey* 7 (1954), 57–68. See TNA C24/500/9 and C24/500/103.

year in which the actors and Susan joined battle in Chancery, in 1623, the great First Folio of the works of Shakespeare was published'.[22]

When it comes to an account of the individuals among the Queen's Servants who will be alluded to in this book we are certainly looking at a range of exciting people, accused or accusing in cases ranging from assault and battery to theft, rape and manslaughter. However, inciting arbitrary divisions among a mass of London actors who at one time knew and worked with one another and at another time regrouped as economic rivals while still, basically, friends, lacks the useful objectivity at which this study aims. We should, perhaps, applaud a critic like Sisson for his use of the depositions of this particular and obscure (to most eyes of the time) court case, therefore alerting our attention to the information they provide. As no complete transcription has ever been published of the *Worth* v. *Baskervile* depositions, which contain valuable things about the company coming out of the mouths of the actors themselves, I have returned to these papers from The National Archives, using them to reveal a range of facts.

Between Fleay's transcriptions and Sisson's article, Charles William Wallace found and published material that was relevant to a history of the Queen's Servants. As a publication of materials that were already disintegrating at the beginning of the twentieth century, Wallace's transcriptions of two cases concerning the Queen's Servants are invaluable.[23] The two cases were the *Smith* v. *Beeston* case of 1619–20, in which proof of the actor Christopher Beeston's particular command over the company becomes evident, and the *Woodford* v. *Holland* case, concerning the then sole information we had about the Red Bull playhouse's share structure. This latter case stretched from 1613 to 1620 – or so Wallace thought. Leslie Hotson's *The Commonwealth and Restoration Stage* appended transcriptions of further documents in the *Woodford* v. *Holland* suit, which, in fact, finally ended in 1624.[24] Hotson managed to correct some of Wallace's assumptions that were unfortunately carried through to E. K. Chambers' account, where it was thought that the playhouse share belonging to an actor called Thomas Swinnerton comprised a one-seventh, rather than the correct one-eighteenth, part.[25] This latter case is also of particular use for

[22] Sisson, 'The Red Bull Company', 66.
[23] Charles William Wallace, 'Three London Theatres of Shakespeare's Time', *University of Nebraska Studies* 9 (1909), 291–397.
[24] TNA C3/390/47 (bill and answer); and TNA C33/146, fo. 948 (court result). Leslie Hotson, *The Commonwealth and Restoration Stage* (Cambridge, MA: Harvard University Press, 1928), pp. 82–7, 327–47.
[25] *ES*, Vol. II, pp. 445–8. The mistake originated in Woodford's 1619 proceedings. See *EPT*, p. 594.

the study of the Red Bull as a playhouse that comprised only part of an inn going by that name.

So much else has, for a long time, lain undiscovered among the unpublished transcriptions of Wallace, held at the Huntington Library in California. After a three-week visit there researching my thesis, I made use of Wallace's transcriptions, following them up with my own renderings of the documents he saw at the beginning of the twentieth century once the originals were found at The National Archives at the beginning of the twenty-first. These include the case that tells us about Susan Greene's playhouse shares, and the various power struggles in the company involving Martin Slatiar, a wayward but important member of it, and Robert Leigh, a long-term member of the troupe. Also discussed is evidence of Christopher Beeston's further involvement with the company and its playhouse into the 1630s. Further to this, new evidence has been forthcoming demonstrating Beeston's involvement in a Shoreditch inn property stretching back to the early 1600s. This inn was quite possibly acquired with an eye to other inn-yard projects.[26]

Gerald Eades Bentley's contributions in *The Jacobean and Caroline Stage* and Chambers' entries in *The Elizabethan Stage* should also be included in this list of sporadically mentioned Queen's Servants/Red Bull materials.[27] Problems may arise when looking to these bibles; however, nothing can take away the scale of these works and the invaluable facts they donated to us.

Chambers stated, as if it were a fact, that Anne Bedingfeild, the leasehold-owner of the Red Bull Inn who sublet to Aaron Holland the builder, was the widow of a *Christopher* Bedingfeld. In fact she was married to one *Eustace* Bedingfeld, whose family comprised the famous recusant Bedingfelds of Norfolk. In an article published in 2001, much evidence was presented about the full contexts of Anne Bedingfeild's leasehold-ownership as the daughter of a brewer, John Draper; the playhouse's situation on a charitable estate; and much more that will be elaborated upon in this book.[28] Chambers' mistake was small but significant; however, at least he did not feel he should offer an *opinion*. Bentley began his section

---

[26] TNA C54/3060, no. 3. See Griffith, 'Christopher Beeston', pp. 620–1.

[27] *JCS*, Vol. I, pp. 158–75 (Queen's Servants/Revels companies). See also *ES*, Vol. II, pp. 220–40, 445–8; *JCS*, Vol. VI, pp. 214–47 (Red Bull playhouse), 47–77 (Cockpit playhouse); and relevant actor entries in *JCS*, Vol. II.

[28] Eva Griffith, 'New Material for a Jacobean Playhouse: The Red Bull Theatre on the Seckford Estate', *Theatre Notebook* 55 (2001), 5–23. This book will divide the identification of members of the Bedingfeld family by using the spelling 'Bedingfeld' for the noble family from Norfolk; 'Bedingfeild' for Anne Bedingfeild, Eustace's wife; and 'Bedingfield' for their daughter, who was active on the Seckford Estate during the later seventeenth century.

on the Red Bull with the true statement that 'less is known of the building
of the Red Bull theatre at the upper end of St John's Street, Clerkenwell,
than of the Fortune or the Globe or the Hope'.[29] Perhaps this statement
represents enough of an excuse for this present venture, for there has certainly been little written about it since. Contexts such as the Drapers and
the Bedingfelds, and that of the Seckford charitable land where the playhouse was located, are important to the fullest understanding of the Red
Bull, as well as in terms of access to relevant documents.

Bentley went on to quote Martin Slatiar's petition to King James concerning a stoppage to building work on the playhouse in 1605, which provided a basis for understanding approximately when work began on it,
who was involved in its setting up and something of what it was like. It
gave a description of the site as 'a square court in an inn' previously consisting of 'stables and other rooms' that were being turned into galleries.
He covered the *Woodford* v. *Holland* material about the eighteenth part
shares in the theatre and drew upon evidence to indicate its size, growth,
etc. Discussing the actor Christopher Beeston's management of the company after the death of Thomas Greene, he also mentioned the *Smith* v.
Beeston suit, Beeston's construction of the Cockpit and the famous riot
there.[30] He puts the Company of the Revels at the Red Bull after the death
of Queen Anna and discusses their succession, during the period 1622–3,
by Prince Charles' company. In fact, he covered many of the materials that
will be described in this book.

After this first section, however, Bentley decided to include a special
extra part entitled 'The Reputation of the Red Bull Theatre'.[31] 'Though
Londoners of the seventeenth century were scarcely inclined to treat any
theatre with undue respect', he began, 'the Red Bull was the subject of
more sneers than any other playhouse of the time.'[32] Admitting the fact
that it was often put together with the Fortune theatre, he qualifies this
admission by saying that 'there are more admiring or non-committal references to the Fortune than to the Red Bull, and fewer condescending ones'.
Going on to describe how the Red Bull reigned 'supreme in ignominy'
and how 'violence and vulgarity' was the usual province of the playhouse
hardly helps the current endeavour towards detailed objectivity. Moreover,
what Bentley described for the most part was a much later Red Bull play-

---

[29] *JCS*, Vol. VI, p. 215.
[30] *Ibid.*, pp. 219–20.
[31] *Ibid.*, pp. 238–47.
[32] *Ibid.*, p. 238.

house, unfortunately tarring the earlier life of the theatre with the same brush as the later one.

As we know that the Red Bull continued activity throughout the Civil War into the Restoration period, the project to put what it was into a few pages of one volume was a hard one and, as with Sisson, the current scholar must appreciate the scope of the challenge involved. An instance of Bentley's use of valuable sources would include mention of the Middlesex Sessions records.

These nineteenth-century transcriptions of fragments of county crime were edited by John Cordy Jeaffreson and were first published in four volumes between 1886 and 1892 (*MCR*). Compared with Surrey crime (i.e. court records covering Bankside offences) a surprising amount of evidence from Middlesex is published and readily available; but perhaps this ready availability has not afforded the Red Bull's reputation many favours. Among the Red Bull-related cases found there are legal records such as 'a notable outrage att the Playhowse called the Redd Bull'. This is a case that involved Edward Purfett, feltmaker; William Tedcastle, 'yeoman'; Thomas Williams, feltmaker; John Fryne, feltmaker; and Edward Brian, feltmaker, who together committed some undisclosed felony – 'a notable outrage' – at the playhouse in 1610.[33] Also recorded from Jeaffreson's transcriptions in Bentley is another Red Bull case of March 1613, where one Alexander Fulsis is accused of picking the pocket of another man at the theatre, Robert Sweete.[34] Bentley then goes on to describe the case of the audience member called John – sometimes known as Richard – Gill, a feltmaker of Clerkenwell, who threatened a player called Richard Baxter in 1623.[35] Baxter accidentally wounded Gill with his sword while playing on the stage and Gill was eventually to organise 'one hundred persons' to assemble 'riotously at Clerkenwell aforesaid to the terror and disquiet of persons dwelling there'.[36] The former two cases indicate reprehensible behaviour by a group in the audience, and the last case, it should be emphasised, lay outside the time when the Queen's Servants performed at the theatre and during the period when the Revels Players – or some other company – were performing there. However, those who have mistakenly associated this time with that of the original company have unfortunately come under the influence of disputes like these to extrapolate a distasteful situation all round. Claims are made from such instances that not only fix

[33] LMA MJ/SR/0489, 9, 11, 101, 103, 105; *MCR*, Vol. II, pp. 64–5; *JCS*, Vol. VI, pp. 238–9.
[34] LMA MJ/SR/0519, 53; *MCR*, Vol. II, 86.
[35] LMA MJ/SR/0616, 89; *MCR*, Vol. II, 165–6. See *JCS*, Vol. VI, 239.
[36] LMA MJ/SR/0617, 30; *MCR*, Vol. II, 175–6

ideas about rowdiness among the Red Bull's clientele but seem to throw shadows, too, on the effect of the entire group of individuals who first performed there. Edmund Gayton's observations of 1654, which could refer to either the Red Bull or the Fortune – mentioning actors only associated much later with Clerkenwell, therefore – and which allude to the bickerings of unhappy, elite 1630s writers, are all instances that provoke unfortunate confusions for a reader coming to Red Bull scholarship, unaware of the significance of precise contexts and time periods.[37]

From the legal references in particular, it becomes obvious that perceptions of audience in association with playhouse, which have also dogged interpretations of the Queen's Servants at the Red Bull, cannot be uniformly interpreted from evidence. Most of Bentley's attack on the reputation of the Clerkenwell playhouse is, in fact, taken from remarks made about it after – sometimes long after – the Queen's Servants/Revels company had gone. Moreover, he takes them from a time when – it would seem – public (and some private) playgoers were paying good money to see the more noisy, spectacle-driven kinds of drama that the Queen's Servants and the Red Bull engendered and supported, over the more intellectually driven, poetically astute kind of entertainment.

At this point, not meaning to upset anyone, let me assure the reader that my scholarship must make a priority of avoiding any legend-defacing. Let us hope this work does not deface the 'legend' of the Red Bull, as rigour while engaged in historical endeavour can seem depressing to readers who wish to see things in more satirical ways. Critics, for a long time, have loved to see this playhouse, its company, its repertoire and its audience within a certain mindset. This has been so from right back within the seventeenth century itself to our own era – preferring overall to draw extreme distinctions between theatres, auditors and sets of plays – the Red Bull representing the most distinctive set of all. To be more cheery from this point of view, let me confirm that this Clerkenwell playhouse was always an exciting and excitable place. True it is (for example) that in the Revels Players' play, *The Two Merry Milkmaids*, first published in 1620, close to the Queen's Servants' time there, the Prologue issues a warning

---

[37] See Edmund Gayton, *Pleasant Notes on Don Quixot* (London, 1654), p. 271, referring to Cane and Fowler from both the Fortune and the Red Bull. See *JCS*, Vol. II, pp. 399–401; and also John H. Astington, 'Playing the Man: Acting at the Red Bull and the Fortune', *Early Theatre* 9 (2006), 130–43 (p. 137). Coupling the Red Bull with the Cockpit, as the embittered Thomas Carew's address for Davenant's *The Just Italian* (London, 1630) shows (A3v–A4r), meant acknowledging economic success for these Middlesex playhouses. See also Leonard Digges' remarks: 'Vpon Master WILLIAM SHAKESPEARE, the *Deceased Authour, and his* POEMS', in William Shakespeare, *POEMS: WRITTEN BY WIL. SHAKESPEARE. Gent.* (London, 1640), *3v.

for audiences that people will be disappointed if they expect the noise of 'Guns, Trumpets' and 'Drum', and 'lowd Clamors' that there was 'wont to bee' in the theatre. What is promised in this play is much more intellectual 'Sence and Words' appropriate to the drama. However, the author of *The Two Merry Milkmaids* never had to confirm for us, here in the twenty-first century, what was already evident in the Red Bull's early seventeenth-century texts. With reference to 'Guns, Trumpets' and 'lowd Clamors' etc., the Queen's Servants' repertoire always possessed a martially noisy interest, presented in the bang and clash of battle.

There may have been more immediate reasons for this than has yet been properly recognised. The Queen's Servants' period at the Red Bull coincided with a renewed interest in the martial, embodied in a national admiration for heroes like Sir Philip Sidney and Prince Henry, but also taking in the Stuart prince's European family and the effect of their visits, for example. This interest took in the impressive magnificence of 'Dansk drummers', Danish fireworks experts and the new foreign order that Queen Anna represented. A European flavour was associated in many minds with readiness for Protestant military action, and early Red Bull/Queen's Servants auditors, many of them practising their skills with the trained bands, must have relished the 'Sword and Targuet' practice exercised on stage with the many large-scale battle and sword-fight scenes.

These were particularly but not exclusively evident in Heywood's classical plays performed at the venue, including, for instance, all the plays of the *Ages* cycle (often only given away in one-sentence stage directions), and the civil war scenes in *The Rape of Lucrece*. Alongside these there are, for instance, the pikestaff skills displayed by the young Giovanni in Webster's *The White Devil*, and the manner in which Heywood's *The Foure Prentises of London*, published in 1615 and acknowledging performance at the Red Bull, displayed a woodcut title-page showing four men engaged in feats of arms (see figure 2).[38]

Heywood's play is dedicated to the apprentices, honouring the martial endeavour formally restarted at the Artillery Garden in Finsbury at the time.[39] The author of the *Merry Milkmaids* goes on to advertise that his piece possesses other successful things evident in individual plays of the Queen's Servants' repertoire, such as 'a Coniurer, a Deuill, And a Clowne too' – but unfortunately no 'Squibs and Crackers at their taile' as evident

---

[38] John Webster, *The White Devil*, ed. Christina Luckyj, 2nd edn (London: A. & C. Black, 1996), II.1, pp. 30–2.
[39] Thomas Heywood, 'To the honest and hie-spirited Prentises The Readers', in *The Foure Prentises of London* (London, 1615), A2r–A3r.

Figure 2 Title-page with woodcut of Thomas Heywood, *The Foure Prentises of London with the Conquest of Jerusalem* (2nd edition, 1632 (woodcut the same as first edition, 1615)).

in, for example, Thomas Dekker's *If This Be Not a Good Play the Devil Is in It*, or some scenes in the *Ages* plays. I believe with this Prologue – as with many Prologues, certainly to comedies – the aim was to make a sophisticated and recognising audience laugh at themselves with descriptions of what they were like and what they liked, rather than to assuage 'nervousness about the Red Bull audience' for being 'badly trained' in intellectual endeavour, as one critic suggests.[40] The audience could only be as proficient in their intellectuality as the performers they liked to watch, and Thomas Heywood himself was at pains to assert in his *Apology for Actors* that 'Actors … should be rather schollers', knowing how to speak well and understand what they are saying. Where 'a good tongue & a good conceit both faile, there can neuer be good actor', he wrote, not without some veracity.[41]

With textual evidence alone we understand that early monetary success for the playhouse was mainly achieved through its comedy, its probable jigs, its above-mentioned fights, alongside its famed and extraordinary spectacle. In the last century, George Fullmer Reynolds ventured into the Red Bull's repertoire in order to describe the playhouse through analysing stage directions in its plays, this helping us to imagine, for example, in what physical context various effects might have been produced at the venue.[42] A variety of capabilities are certainly evident in the dramas belonging to the playhouse's earliest time and were part of its long-term durability. The spectacle was something other theatres were to try and emulate. Yet intellectual challenge is also evident in Red Bull texts. If it were not, why would the author of the 1620 play risk the danger of referring to his audience's enjoyment of the demonstrative right from the start of the play? Surely without a witty outlook all round on their love of such things, this would be a very foolish thing for the author to do, inciting unappreciative responses. For this work in hand, we have to remember that it is the redressing of a balance through historical detail that is engaging us here, hopefully inspiring us to greater endeavour to read all of these plays in as many of their historical contexts as possible, without wishing to patronise any of the audiences to whom they were meant to appeal.

With reference to Bentley and the above thought, much of the material he uses refers to a perceived differentiation of audiences, indicating a particular kind of entertainment needed for a particularly noted clientele. After quoting Edward Howard's reminiscences of the theatre's 'Drums, Trumpets, Battels, and Hero's', acknowledging, in fact, some pointers to the success of the playhouse if only in satirically critical terms, Bentley quotes James Wright's 1699 summary of the citizen and poorer sort of

---

[40] I write in response to Lucy Munro's article, 'Governing the Pen to the Capacity of the Stage: Reading the Red Bull and Clerkenwell', *Early Theatre* 9 (2006), 99–113.

[41] Thomas Heywood, *Apology for Actors* (London, 1612), E3.

[42] George Fullmer Reynolds, *The Staging of Elizabethan Plays at the Red Bull Theater 1605–1625* (New York: Modern Language Association of America, 1940).

auditors that the Red Bull and Fortune playhouses attracted, demonstrating how the perception of the playhouse and company under discussion
developed even within its own century.

> Before the Wars, there were in being all these Play-houses at the same time.
> The *Black-friers*, and *Globe* on the *Bankside*, a Winter and Summer House,
> belonging to the same Company called the King's Servants; the *Cockpit* or
> *Phoenix*, in *Drury-lane*, called the Queen's Servants; the private House in
> *Salisbury-court*, called the Prince's Servants; the Fortune near *White-cross-
> street*, and the *Red Bull* at the upper end of St *John's-street*: The two last were
> mostly frequented by Citizens, and the meaner sort of People. All these
> Companies got Money, and Liv'd in Reputation, especially those of the
> *Blackfriars*, who were men of grave and sober Behaviour.[43]

This last account among all of them had, perhaps, the most pervasive
effect on attitudes towards the Red Bull (and the Fortune). However
impressively summary it is, and weighty in feel, it represents very *late*
observations concerning, for instance, when Queen Henrietta Maria's
men resided at the Cockpit. What we should remember best, perhaps,
from Wright's account, is the first part of his last sentence as a statement
of useful fact: '*All* these Companies got Money, and Liv'd in Reputation'
(my emphasis).

Bentley wanted to finish his piece on the Red Bull with the thought
that the Red Bull was 'the least reputable' of 'all the Jacobean and Caroline
theatres in London'. Yet during the ban on playing during the Civil War
and Interregnum, records indicated for him that the Red Bull continued
successfully in a way the other playhouses did not. 'One is tempted to
speculate on the relationship of these two conditions', he wrote.[44]

This specific judgement on both the daring Interregnum audience and
this playhouse, and the effect that the whole may have had on attitudes to
the Red Bull and its original, earlier company, gives pause for thought all
by itself, and perhaps cues in the endeavour to challenge such overarching

---

[43] Edward Howard, *The Six Days' Adventure; or, The New Utopia* (London, 1671), A4v–a; *JCS*, Vol.
VI, p. 246; James Wright, *Historia Histrionica: An Historical Account of the English Stage, Shewing
the Ancient Use, Improvement, and Perfection of Dramatic Representations in this Nation* (London,
1699), B3r.

[44] *JCS*, Vol. VI, 247. With reference to these arguments, I agree with Andrew Gurr when he writes
that it was probably between the mid 1620s and 1640s when the Fortune and the Red Bull achieved
their reputations as 'citizen' playhouses (although Thomas Heywood had aimed at the citizen market previously). I also agree with him concerning Bentley and the Red Bull's reputation as stated
in his book on *Playgoing in Shakespeare's London*, 2nd edn (Cambridge University Press, 1996).
However, I may take issue with him when he describes the plays of the later northern playhouses as
being of only 'minority interest, unimportant on the social scale compared with the preferences of
the Blackfriars audiences'. See *ibid.*, p. 188; and Andrew Gurr, *The Shakespeare Company, 1594–1642*,
3rd edn (Cambridge University Press, 2004), p. 12.

interpretations with the use of detailed examples. Going back to the Queen Anna's men period at the Red Bull, perhaps it is time to return to those legal documents of the Middlesex sessions.

I wrote at the beginning of this Introduction that just as many who wanted to enter the City via the thoroughfare did not want to travel down St John Street, and by this I meant to draw attention to another kind of activity that was centred on the area. This is also where we begin to imagine important contexts for the Red Bull that come into play with the initial chapters of this book. These are the kinds of context that all histories of theatres deserve to have – including the history of the ground beneath the theatre's feet and the people who gave meaning to that ground, and therefore the ongoing context of the theatre.

Many of the earlier records John Cordy Jeaffreson took for his volumes were originally created at the Castle Inn, situated in St John Street, which for a long time acted as a Sessions House for the hearing of criminal cases for the entire Middlesex area. Such was the volume of county-wide crim-inal activity investigated there that in 1612 a whole building was erected for the purpose of hearing cases. It was called Hicks Hall and it was built in the middle of St John Street, not far from the Smithfield Bars that divided Middlesex and the London suburbs from the City's jurisdiction. The whole area of which we are speaking was, therefore, associated with the preven-tion of crime by virtue of its having a site for prosecuting the criminally accused. With the benefit of newly acquired knowledge we also know that the playhouse was situated on a piece of charitable land, administered by heavyweight legal governors. These included, later in its history, top-notch governmental figures such as the Chief Justice of the Court of Common Pleas and the Master of the Rolls – not the kind of human being who was ignorant of the law and its relationship with the land. Perhaps we should remind ourselves that in the case of the threatening of the actor Baxter by the feltmaker Gill, the latter organised 'one hundred persons' to assemble 'riotously at Clerkenwell aforesaid'. This was 'to the terror and disquiet of persons dwelling there'.[45]

Now undoubtedly, when looking at Clerkenwell, we observe an area of diverse social mix. However, what is likely is that many of the people living in or around the charitable estate and, indeed, in the rest of Clerkenwell beyond, were probably just the sort of elite set to complain and to appeal to the law in a way in which – perhaps – the residents of the Globe's Bankside were not. Clerkenwell was the kind of area where a diverse

---

[45] LMA MJ/SR/0617, 30; *MCR*, Vol. II, p. 175.

social mix could and did exist side by side – from the bawdy houses to the west along Turnmill Street, to the bureaucratic Revels Office buildings to the east. The area, set around two one-time monastic communities, was not perceived as an unpleasant situation for many residents, and the kind of well-to-do person living in Clerkenwell was very much akin to those embodied in the group that were the estate's governors. Mentioned in Clerkenwell records of the time, knights and members of the nobility would include Sir John Andrewes, Sir Thomas Holte, Sir Francis Coningsby, Lady Burleigh, the Chaloner family, the earl of Shrewsbury (the Talbots), the Cavendishes, the Westons and the Woodhouses, to name but a few.[46] The point to be made is that the Red Bull was very much built in an atmosphere that was indeed mixed with less salutary aspects, but was also very respectably neighboured, and with reference to suburban playhouse building the motivation may not have been, as some have suggested, about locating venues in less than salubrious areas, but more about having the same space to breathe that these well-to-do residents also found attractive.[47]

These better-miened neighbours would not tolerate lawlessness if confronted with it, including the so-described 'rowdy' behaviour of the playhouse's audience used in evidence against it. Even the actor Baxter was aware enough to put the threatening letter from Gill immediately into the hands of the authorities.[48] For Clerkenwell was the kind of place that would quickly act upon reprehensible activity for a number of reasons expanded upon early in this book. These reasons might include both the legally charitable nature of the site upon which the playhouse was built and the regulatory factor of the old Revels Office, situated nearby until 1607–8, when it was sold on.[49] These factors would also include the continuing residency of Sir Henry Seckford and Thomas Bedingfeld, both

---

[46] See, for example, Pinks, *The History of Clerkenwell*, pp. 46–9. According to the *Survey of London*, seventeenth-century residents also included William Cecil, second Earl of Exeter (St John's Priory from 1612), Francis Thynne (d. 1608, antiquary and herald), Sir Ferdinando Gorges and Dame Elizabeth Bullock (Clerkenwell Green), and many more significant Clerkenwell figures will come to the fore in this book. See Philip Temple, ed., *Survey of London Vol. XLVI: South and East Clerkenwell* (New Haven: Yale University Press, 2008).

[47] See Steven Mullaney, *The Place of the Stage: License, Play, and Power in Renaissance England* (University of Chicago Press, 1988).

[48] In *EPT*, Herbert Berry points out that when Gill sent his threatening letter to Baxter, the actor immediately gave it 'to the Middlesex authorities, whose offices were nearby in St John Street' (p. 581).

[49] According to E. K. Chambers, the St John's site was handed on to Ralph Freeman in 1607, with the Revels Office buildings going to Esmé Stuart, eighth Lord Aubigny (*ES*, Vol. I, pp. 101–2); however, the *Survey of London Vol. XLVI* believes that King James granted the land to Martin Freeman, a City fishmonger, who quickly sold the freehold to Sir Thomas Fowler the Elder of Islington, who parcelled it out for leases and sales in 1608.

associated with the site and Masters of the Tents and Toils, and the nature of the street where it was located – a focal point for legal activity against crime – not an area that would ever want to be seen to house or encourage misdemeanour by the actors or anyone else.

To consolidate this perspective, a few years after the institution of Hicks Hall, i.e. in 1615, the 'Clerkenwell Bridewell', a house of correction, was built not far from the playhouse.[50] This prison catered to the needs of both Middlesex as a county and Middlesex as including the ever-burgeoning suburbs of London north of the City's ward structure. The prison and its area, the function of which developed and extended over time (the 'New Prison'), were built on the same charity's land as the playhouse.[51] From this legal and criminal perspective therefore, and in terms of Middlesex juris-diction, perhaps it is no surprise that there is more material concerning the response to felonious activity by audiences at this playhouse, found at such a centre for the identification and punishment of crime, than there may be for other playhouses – although other playhouses certainly expe-rienced crime. In the instance of the Red Bull, both Hicks Hall and the New Bridewell were built during the Queen's Servants' period at the Red Bull playhouse, which was in close proximity, and they both bore witness to a desire for lawfulness in that specific area. Correct activity by audiences at the Red Bull, however, is not the only matter concerning legal records that is relevant when it comes to theatre history's perspectives on the com-pany. In the first volume of Bentley's *Jacobean and Caroline Stage* where he concentrates on the companies, he mentions documents describing how the Queen's Servants were punished for not keeping the highways in good repair.[52] The original passages describing this situation are given here.

Firstly, a list made in October 1616 notes that 'Christofer Beeston and the rest of the players of the Redd. Bull are behinde five pounds, being taxed by the bench 40s. the yeare by theire owne consentes'.[53] On 2 October 1617 they were forgiven for not keeping up with repairs:

> Forasmuch as a peticion preferred to this Court by Christofer Beeston Thomas Heyward Richard Perkins Thomas drew Richard Harrison & Ellis

---

[50] See Pinks, *The History of Clerkenwell*, p. 179.

[51] See *ibid.*, pp. 183–6. A brief descriptive record of the estate (undated), putting it at 7 acres and worth £1,000 per annum at the time of writing, states that 'The Mr of the Rolls and the Lord Chief Justice of the Common pleas for the time being are the Trustees for the almes Houses', and later, 'New Prison in clarkenwell is part of it which tis said pays the rent to the Justice of the peace who cannot receive it legally for they have not nether naturall nor politick – Capacity to receive it.' See SROI HD21/480, with a rough drawing of the estate sketched on the other side.

[52] *JCS*, Vol. I, p. 163.

[53] LMA MJ/SB/P/001, fo. 90 (microfilm X071/003); *MSR*, Vol. IV, p. 37.

Worth players at the Redd Bull in the upper end of St Johnstreet wherby
they shewed that they stood seuerall presented at seuerall Sessions of peace
for not repayring the high wayes in the parish of Clarkenwell in the County
of Middlesex and that they had latelie bestowed great charge in amending
& new rayling the foote way leading towards woods Close in the upper end
of St Johnstreet ~~and all alonge the churchwaietowards Woodes close in the
upper end of St Johnstreet~~ and all along the Churchway leading all alonge
to the parishe Church of Clerkenwell afore said at their owne charge. And
therefore prayed that they might be releived by the favour of the Court
against the proces issuing upon these presentments Whereupon in respect
that the Court took notice of the Charge they had bene at in repaire of the
Footwayes aforesaid It was ordered that further proces upon the said presentments shold be stayd.[54]

In 1617, then, the actors had, at their own expense and endeavour, seen to
the needs of the footpaths near their playhouse, and were therefore forgiven for not attending to the highway.[55] Despite the actors' best endeavours, however, on 3 October 1622 – when many of the people named had
ceased to be the Queen's Servants but were still perceived as responsible –
another order was made with reference to them. Noting the sympathetic
response of those previous 1617 sessions, a 'proces de Nouo' was awarded
against Beeston, Heywood, Perkins, Drew, Harrison and Worth, who had
been 'hertofore presented at severall Sessions of the peace for not repayringe the highwayes' because 'forasmuch as the footewaies neere the said
Red Bull, which ought to be repaired by the persons aforenamed are nowe
very farre out of repayre, and they doe obstinatelie refuse to amende the
same, It is therefore ordered that proces de Nouo be awarded against them
vpon the former presentments'.[56]

   Five years had passed since the actors' last attempt to see to footpaths
near to the playhouse, but where a successful playhouse existed there was
bound to be a great deal of wear and tear. The fact is, however, that a lot of
people who were not players were reprimanded over their contribution to
the state of St John Street. As we have seen, the thoroughfare, on its way
into the City via Smithfield, was a busy place, and was therefore destined

[54] LMA MJ/SB/R/002, 461a–462 (microfilm X071/24); *MSR*, Vol. IV, p. 285.
[55] A long-term confusion has been caused because lists of highway maintenance defaulters have
    been mistaken for similar-looking lists of recusants in Middlesex sessions records, and because
    Christopher Beeston's family and household occur regularly as recusants. Beeston's name only
    occurs on highway lists as an individual about to be outlawed in 1617, which must relate to neglect
    of the road outside his home in Clerkenwell. It appears that Beeston was a long-term defaulter, as
    the record listing many people refers to a previous session of April 1612. See LMA MJ/SR/0561, 30;
    MSR, Vol. IV, p. 273.
[56] LMA MJ/SB/R/003, p. 479 (microfilm X071/25).

to need constant maintenance. With animals going one way down it and horses and carriers parading both ways, it was the very worst road for keeping up with local community expectations. William le Hardy describes the highways problem for the early modern suburban resident in his first volume of *Middlesex County Records* thus:

> Several troublesome liabilities were placed on the inhabitants of the County, and perhaps the most irksome of these was the repair of the highways, for which every freeholder had to provide men or wagons for so many days, according to the proportion laid down by the Justices. Those failing or refusing to provide the necessary quota were naturally brought before the Court, and either bound over or fined.[57]

Le Hardy observed that 'defaulters' included 'members of the nobility, knights, esquires and gentlemen, and as many as twenty-five of them appear at one sitting'. On the previous page where the players' fines are considered in October 1616, the following people appear in a list of those who failed to provide carts for the road work, all of them distrained for six days: 'Lady Burley [Burleigh] of Clerkenwell, Sir John Butler, Sir Francis Anderson' and 'Rebecca, Lady Sackford [Seckford] of the same, widow'.[58] The list is informative in a number of ways. The fact that many of these Clerkenwell residents of 1616 were titled indicates, for example, to what extent the actors' neighbours were not just criminals and prostitutes. It also demonstrates the simple truth that St John Street was a thoroughfare that was hard to maintain, and that nobody should be judged – including the players – for not attending to its difficult demands. The last-named of the titled defaulters of 1616 is significant. Rebecca, Lady 'Sackford' was the widow of someone associated with both the site of the Red Bull and the administration of the early modern entertainment world in London. Sir Henry Seckford, her husband, had died in his house at Clerkenwell and was buried in the south aisle of the parish church of St James on 15 October 1610.[59] We will discuss both him and his family in the next chapter of this book. Lady Seckford died in Clerkenwell in 1631 and was buried in the chancel of St James'.[60]

The presence of Lady Seckford on the list of defaulters – someone who was part of the Seckford family and therefore associated with the estate upon which the playhouse was built – goes to prove, if further proof

[57] *MSR*, Vol. I, p. xxiii.
[58] *MSR*, Vol. IV, 37; LMA MJ/SB/P/001 (microfilm X071/003), fo. 89v.
[59] A. Daly Briscoe, *A Tudor Worthy: Thomas Seckford of Woodbridge* (Ipswich: East Anglian Magazine, 1979), p. 86. See *St JPR*, Vol. IV: *Burials 1551 to 1665*, p. 113.
[60] 8 June 1631; *St JPR*, Vol. IV, p. 202.

were needed, that troublesome local duties were felt across the board in Clerkenwell society. They therefore cannot be interpreted as further indicators of the bad reputation of the actors, as they only prove that the same statutes that troubled the players were 'irksome' to everyone else.

That the company came to an arrangement with the courts concerning extra yearly fines for their neglect in 1616 and again successfully appealed in 1617 indicates to what extent the courts understood the tremendous expense of the maintenance of the ways around the playhouse. As the judgement of 1622 stated, the court had previously taken notice 'of the great Charge they had bene at in repayringe the said waies'. That the people perceived to be involved in the Red Bull in 1622 would not pay these fines may show something of the financial difficulties of the company over time – complex difficulties that this book will discuss. These things involved other issues however, both concerning simple economics and to do with the expectations of individuals. There is no evidence that they had anything to do with the social or moral quality of the company overall.

The point I would confirm with reference to the two accounts of Bentley and Sisson concerning the Red Bull is that in important ways, over many years, a dichotomy has been created to which they bear witness. This dichotomy has been between theatres, companies and selections of plays that are deemed worthy of note, and other companies, theatres and repertoires – like that of the Queen's Servants at the Red Bull – who have been placed as something distinctively different from them. It has, perhaps, been an important part of the development of Shakespeare studies to ensure that more marginal companies to that of Shakespeare were perceived as worse in order to privilege the material conditions of that centrally important author. That the Queen's Servants may well have had a different approach to company life and activity in comparison to the King's Men is a truth that will emerge throughout this book without any effort to point it out. I believe, alongside McMillin and MacLean in their book, that 'each company would have had its own style, its own textual procedures, its own sense of purpose, and its own impact on audiences and other acting companies'.[61] In terms of theatre history interest so far, perhaps it is needless to say that by privileging one or two sets of company conditions, none of which were the Queen's Servants company's conditions, a lopsided effect has resulted as far as the whole picture for early modern drama is concerned.

---

[61] McMillin and MacLean, *The Queen's Men and Their Plays*, p. xi.

I have really only scratched the surface of an account of perceptions of this company and playhouse. In 2006 a set of articles on Red Bull-related subjects was published in Volume IX of the journal *Early Theatre* under their 'Issues in Review' banner, which emanated from a conference on playhouse history north of the City walls. This group have afforded the Red Bull some welcomed serious attention, with subject matter including medieval contexts for Clerkenwell plays, detailed narratives given for the 1630s players at the playhouse and work done respecting the readership for published Red Bull plays.[62] With reference to this last, which feeds into a much needed understanding of how the audience was perceived in relation to the drama, a lot more repertoire work needs to be done in the future. Apart from the playhouse and the plays en masse, I could discuss the strange perceptions of other critics towards its audience as 'bourgeois' and 'middle-class'. This obviously stands in odd relation to the 'rowdy' sort of interpretation they have received.[63] I could describe the even odder perceptions of Thomas Heywood down the centuries – a writer catering to a perceived 'citizen' market and therefore only worthy to be disparaged by many. He was an actor and a playwright for one company at one time, like Shakespeare, but certainly he has never been perceived as on the same level as William S. It is gladdening to note that Richard Rowland is carrying out the same style of detailed appreciation of Heywood that I am trying to achieve with a theatre history associated with him.[64] The first job here, as I have indicated, is to give time and attention to the ground beneath the feet of the players. In doing this I hope to put ground beneath the feet of their plays, thus giving their repertoire real context as an economic entity.

It is my argument that it is only by giving a detailed and thorough account of the earliest time at the Red Bull, using the materials only now made available to us, that we can best approach an already seriously affected attitude to its drama. In chapters to come, therefore, there will be detailed examinations of the site of the Red Bull playhouse; how the people behind it were related to it and the clues they give us through

[62] The conference was called 'Beyond Shakespeare's Globe'. It was held at the London Metropolitan Archives and was organised by myself and the Centre for Metropolitan History at the Institute of Historical Research. The three essays from the collection were: Anne Lancashire, 'Multi-Day Performance and the London Clerkenwell Play', *Early Theatre* 9 (2006), 114–29; Astington, 'Playing the Man'; Marta Straznicky, 'The Red Bull Repertory in Print', *Early Theatre* 9 (2006), 144–56.

[63] See, for example, references in Louis B. Wright, *Middle-Class Culture in Elizabethan England* (Ithaca, NY: Cornell University Press, 1958).

[64] See Richard Rowland, *Thomas Heywood's Theatre 1599–1639: Locations, Translations and Conflict* (Farnham: Ashgate, 2010); as well as Thomas Heywood, *The First and Second Parts of King Edward IV*, ed. Richard Rowland (Manchester University Press, 2005).

its Clerkenwell contexts – the location, environment and proportion of the site; how the same people were involved in other playhouse sites; the agency of the earl of Worcester in the development and support of the company; the company itself, actor by actor; the history of the company before the Red Bull; the Curtain playhouse as another licensed venue for them; the European contexts for the company; pleasing the Stuart Queen (from Denmark) and her circle; the beginning, middle, and end of the company.

Repertoire analysis that will be attempted here will be flagged up in section titles and will only be ventured in order to achieve a more comprehensive understanding of the Red Bull's beginnings. What the tenor of it and its company's business might have been like, and the ambience of both company and playhouse, will be evinced within different contexts. The repertoire was, in fact, mixed, with tragedy, comedy and forms of tragicomedy in the blend, as well as citizen-interested drama. The Thomas Heywood plays that will help us with the analysis include *If You Know Not Me*, Part I; *The Foure Prentises of London*; *The Rape of Lucrece*; and his spectacle-enhanced *Ages* cycle. Other plays of the company analysed will include, for instance, *Swetnam the Woman-Hater, Arraigned by Women* and *Greene's Tu Quoque; or, The Cittie Gallant*. When studying the repertoire to help us understand the Red Bull, a particular interest may be how the plays responded or related to other repertoires – 'rival', or otherwise interpreted.

In doing all this it is not my object to take away the 'fun' that the Red Bull has represented for early modern theatre studies. The Red Bull, its audiences, its players and the entertainment through which all three became famous were – I can assure the reader – successfully 'fun' all by themselves. It is for another study – one to which I hope I will contribute – to come to the full repertoire of the Queen's Servants afresh, bolstered by the confidence of having an acceptable history to contextualise it.

CHAPTER I

Elizabethan contexts for a Jacobean playhouse: Clerkenwell, East Anglia, the Strand and the Liberty of the Clink (1586–1603)

Our historical topography of the Red Bull playhouse so far has centred on St John Street, the important thoroughfare that cut a swathe through Middlesex to one side of Clerkenwell proper. St John Street was situated to the east of the hub of St James' parish, no doubt centring on Clerkenwell Green. The Green was, and still is, the open space below and in front of St James' Church. This was located a little to the north of the old Priory of St John of Jerusalem, where the Knights Hospitaller were once based, and which is now represented by an area called St John's Square that extends to both sides of Clerkenwell Road. The roaring traffic of this thoroughfare now ploughs its way through what had once been a range of ex-monastic buildings in the Red Bull's day.[1]

During that post-Reformation period, the site where monastic brothers had once walked and practised their faith became buildings given over to the sixteenth-to-seventeenth-century Masters of the Revels.[2] St James' too had once been a site for religious life in its pre-Dissolution guise as St Mary's nunnery. Therefore when speaking of Clerkenwell we are speaking of a place that must have been associated in many minds with the old forms of belief and worship. The fact that much of early seventeenth-century Clerkenwell was post-Reformation land is important to this study, as the rest of this chapter, and indeed a whole understanding of the true contexts for the Red Bull, will make clear.

---

[1] The Metropolitan Board of Works, replaced by the London County Council in 1889, created, among other thoroughfares, Clerkenwell Road. According to English Heritage's recent study of *South and East Clerkenwell*, the road was built in 1874–8 as the 'cross-capital arterial road, linking West End and East End'. See *Survey of London Vol. XLVI*, p. 385.

[2] According to E. K. Chambers, the locations of the offices of the Revels and Tents were moved from the Blackfriars to St John's after the death of Sir Thomas Cawarden on 29 August 1559 (*ES*, Vol. I, p. 74); the Revels Office removed again to the Whitefriars in 1608, when Esmé Stuart, eighth Lord Aubigny, was given the Office's part of the property (*ibid.*, pp. 102, 103).

When writing of Clerkenwell, however, we are also contemplating a place that had been associated with drama for a very long time. Reading accounts of early Clerkenwell is like reading about something akin to the City of London's own 'parish green', and indications reveal it as being a venue for citizen entertainment well before either Thomas Heywood was born or his company moved there. John Stow records the earliest mention of the area in terms of the young people of the City who enjoyed walking there:

> There are (saith Fitzstephen), neare London, on the North side, special wels in the Suburbs, sweete, wholsome and cleare, amongst which Holywell, Clarkes wel, & Clements well, are most famous and frequented by Scholers and youthes of the Citie in sommer euenings, when they walke forth to take the aire.[3]

By defining Clerkenwell visitors as people 'of the Citie', Stow is referring to the people who lived or worked or derived their status within the walls/ward-structure of London. It was these people who would value the wider space that Clerkenwell had to offer at that time. The Tudor historian goes on to record the theatrical activities of the clerks of the City with the subheading 'Playes by the parish Clarks at Clarks well'. It was because of the entertainment that took place in the area, associated with the clerks, that the village got its name:

> The third [well] is called *Clarkes well*, or *Clarken well*, and is curbed about square with hard stone, not farre from the west ende of *Clarken well* Church, but close without the wall that incloseth it: the sayd Church tooke the name of the Well, and the Well tooke name of the Parish Clarkes in London, who of old time were accustomed there yearely to assemble, and to play some large hystorie of holy Scripture.[4]

Parish clerks were lay parish assistants who led responses in church and assisted the priest, and near the Clerks' well was the Skinners' well where, as Stow describes, plays were also performed. The Issue Rolls of Richard II record a payment for 11 July in the fourteenth year of the reign:

> To the clerks of the parish churches and to divers other clerks in the city of London. In money paid to them in discharge of £10 which the Lord the King commanded to be paid them of his gift on account of the play of the 'Passion of our Lord and the Creation of the World' by them performed at

---

[3] John Stow, *A Survey of London: Reprinted from the Text of 1603*, ed. Charles Lethbridge Kingsford, 2 vols. (Oxford: Clarendon Press, 1909), Vol. I, p. 15.
[4] *Ibid.*

Skynnerwell after the feast of Saint Bartholomew, last past. By writ of privy seal amongst the mandates of this term – £10.[5]

The reason, then, that Clerkenwell got its name had everything to do with the entertainment value derived there from earliest times, and so, in terms of history, it was an oddly appropriate place for a 'citizen playhouse' like the Red Bull.[6] The days of specifically City-supported biblical entertainment in Clerkenwell were gone by the time that is the focus of this book, however. Entertainment had not quite gone, but was passing, according to John Stow, who wrote of the sporting skills of the late-sixteenth-century citizen displayed at the August feast of St Bartholomew:

> In the Moneth of August about the feast of S. *Bartholomew* the Apostle, before the Lord maior, Aldermen, and Shiriffes of London placed in a large Tent neare vnto Clarken well, of olde time were diuerse dayes spent in the pastime of wrestling, where the Officers of the Citie: namely the Shiriffes, Sergeants and Yeoman, the Porters of the kings beame, or weigh house, now no such men, and other of the Citie, were challengers of all men in the suburbs, to wrestle for games appointed … of late yeares the wrestling is onely practised on *Bartholomew* day in the after noone …[7]

Whether entertainment continued to be associated with the area or not, the religious associations with Clerkenwell must have turned sour in the minds of many who remembered those times. The last prioress of the nunnery was Isabel Sackville, a relative of Thomas Sackville, Lord Buckhurst, earl of Dorset: Lord Treasurer and Queen Elizabeth's Privy Councillor at the end of her life. Dorset was to carry on in that office into the first four years of King James' reign.[8] John Weever, Clerkenwell resident, friend of Thomas Heywood and the author of the book *Ancient Funerall Monuments* of 1631, recorded her epitaph, finding that she was a nun at St Mary's from the early sixteenth century, leaving a will naming Dorset as overseer. It was dated 19 February in the twelfth year of Queen Elizabeth's reign (1570), the year Isabel died.[9] She was buried near the high altar of what had once

---

[5] Frederick Devon, *Issues of the Exchequer: Being a Collection of Payments Made out of His Majesty's Revenue, from King Henry III to King Henry VI Inclusive* (London: John Murray, 1837), pp. 244–5; Pinks, *The History of Clerkenwell*, p. 5.

[6] See Lancashire, 'Multi-Day Performance', esp. p. 122.

[7] Stow, *A Survey of London*, Vol. I, p. 104.

[8] Robert Cecil took over as Treasurer after Sackville died on 19 April 1608. In his mid twenties Thomas Sackville was co-author of an important play to Renaissance drama studies called *Gorbudoc*. He wrote this with his Inner Temple colleague, Thomas Norton. See Rivkah Zim, 'Sackville, Thomas, first Baron Buckhurst and first earl of Dorset (*c.* 1536–1608)', *Oxford Dictionary of National Biography*, www.oxforddnb.com/view/article/24450, accessed 23 January 2008.

[9] John Weever, *Ancient Funerall Monuments Within the United Monarchie of Great Britaine, Ireland, and the Islands adjacent …* (London, 1631), p. 429. According to Weever, Isabel Sackville was a nun

been the church of the convent under her leadership. It became and is now the Church of England Parish of St James.

From hereon, much of our story concerns what happened both to the buildings that made up the Priory of St John and to the lands that once belonged to Isabel Sackville's nunnery, St Mary's. This part of the Red Bull's history involves another bureaucrat and not inconsiderable man of the law, who was a great servant to the Crown and a significant charitable giver: Thomas Seckford.

Thomas Seckford and his almshouses

Something less than thirty years before the first known transaction concerning the site of the theatre between Eustace Bedingfeld's widow, Anne Bedingfeild, and Aaron Holland, the builder of the Red Bull, Queen Elizabeth gave one of the government's 'men of business', Thomas Seckford (1515–87), a gift of land.[10] In 1573, she conveyed some property she held in three acres on the west side of St John's Priory near Clerkenwell, called Bocher – or Butt – Close, to Seckford, one of her Masters of the Court of Requests.[11] This part of Clerkenwell did not include the site where the theatre came to be located, but was one area, among a few, that the Seckford family was to hold in the parish, situated on the two religious sites.[12] On

---

as far back as 1506. See also John Stow, *A Survey of the Cities of London and Westminster: Containing the Original, Antiquity, Increase, Modern Estate and Government of Those Cities*, ed. John Strype, 2 vols. (London, 1720), Vol. II, p. 64.

[10] The term is used by Patrick Collinson to denote those who facilitated 'the interests and objectives of the privy council', who were 'secondary political figures whose identities were less important than the fact that they looked after everything admirably'. See Patrick Collinson, 'Puritans, Men of Business and Parliaments', in *Elizabethan Essays* (London: Hambledon, 2003), pp. 59–86 (p. 65).

[11] Briscoe, *A Tudor Worthy*, p. 38; Carol Weaver and Michael Weaver, *The Seckford Foundation: Four Hundred Years of a Tudor Charity* (Woodbridge: Seckford Foundation, 1987), p. 8. Pinks, *The History of Clerkenwell*, p. 288, describes the location of this ground in his section on 'Red Lion Street' as that:

extending from the site of the west wall of the hospital court nearly to Turnmill-street … formerly an open plot of ground belonging to the hospital, and which was subsequently called Bocher, or Butt Close, and afterwards Garden Alleys. It has been conjectured that from the vicinity of this plot to Cow Cross and Smithfield Market Bocher Close is a corruption from Butcher's Close, and that it was for some time used either for the slaughtering or turning out of cattle.

[12] Although we cannot, at this time, discern how Seckford acquired rights to the property he used to fund his almshouses (the 'Seckford Estate' where the Red Bull was built), we know that among the offices he was granted by the Queen, he became, in 1575, 'bailiff, collector and receiver of rents of all manors, messuages, and lands which had belonged to the Priory or Hospital of St John of Jerusalem but were now in the possession of the Crown in the City of London and County of Middlesex'. This may have enabled him to come to terms with those with rights over land in the area. See Briscoe, *A Tudor Worthy*, p. 43.

THOMAS SECKFORD ESQVIRE.

MASTER OF REQVESTS AND
SVRVEYOR OF Ŷ COVRT OF
WARDS AND LIVERIES.

FOVNDED YᵉE

ALMS-HOVSES
AT WOODERIDGE
ANNO DOMINI.
1587.

Figure 3 Likeness of Thomas Seckford. Drawn in 1792 by Isaac Johnson of Woodbridge
and published by Robert Loder in the same year.

land he acquired over time, Thomas Seckford was to build property, either
for his own domestic use or in order to lease it out to others.[13]

---

[13] The following is mainly a synthesis of information found in Briscoe, *A Tudor Worthy*, and in the
entry on Seckford in P. W. Hasler, ed., *The History of Parliament: The House of Commons 1558–1603*,
3 vols. (London: HMSO, 1981), Vol. III, pp. 362–4.

Seckford came from an eminent Suffolk family, the Seckfords of Seckford Hall, Woodbridge, near Ipswich. Born in 1515, he was well educated, entering Gray's Inn in 1540. His name is found on the students' register next to that of William Cecil, later Lord Burghley, and it is alongside his lifelong association with Cecil – that extraordinary Privy Councillor whose son Robert was to continue to serve during the next reign – that we should put Seckford's life.[14] After being called to the bar in 1542 and becoming Lent Reader in 1556, Seckford, along with one Walter Haddon, was appointed a Master of Requests in December 1558, during the Queen's accession year. He was granted an annuity of £100 for his counsel and attendance on the Queen's person, which was to be paid from 1561.[15]

Cardinal Wolsey named the main court over which Seckford presided 'the Court of Requests' in 1529. Its previous manifestation had been as a fifteenth-century committee devolved from the Privy Council known as the Court of Poor Men's Causes. It dealt with the pleas of poor men in the form of petitions to the Crown, and much of what we have gained of Queen's Servants/Red Bull history is derived from Court of Requests cases. Seckford was given many great responsibilities, including acting as temporary Keeper of the the Great Seal (as part of a commission); Surveyor of the Court of Wards and Liveries; MP for several constituencies over time; Steward of Marshalsea Court; and Justice of the Peace, for Middlesex and Suffolk from about 1559, and for Essex from 1569.[16] He sat on the commissions seeking adherence to the Acts of Supremacy and Uniformity to further the development of the Church of England (in 1559 and 1576), and others, for example dealing with the counterfeiting of money and one concerned with the enclosure of land around London that had been used for the practice of archery. (This was one issue that caused John Stow such dismay with regard to the erosion of citizen pastimes.) These are just a few of the jobs Seckford accepted as an officer for the Crown, especially before 1573 when the Queen gave him his first property in Clerkenwell from the Priory of St John.

In 1573, then, we know that the Queen gave Thomas Seckford some Clerkenwell property, and we know something of the service that made him worthy of such a gift. The exact extent of his building work in Clerkenwell is not known, although what he did with his property was

---

[14] Briscoe, *A Tudor Worthy*, p. 13.
[15] Hasler, *History of Parliament*, Vol. III, p. 363.
[16] MP for Ripon in 1554, Orford in 1555 and 1558, Ipswich in 1559 and 1563, Suffolk in 1571, and Ipswich again in 1572. *Ibid.*, 362.

far-sighted and permanent. It would seem, crucially, that the land he acquired extended beyond the bounds of St John's onto the neighbouring religious site of St Mary's nunnery – land that was to become known as St Mary's Close. Here were built a number of houses, including a family residence noted on some maps as 'Seckford's Seat'.[17] We know about Seckford's property on the old nunnery site because of the characteristic efficiency and sense of responsibility that he demonstrated towards the end of his life.

After his wife, Elizabeth, died in 1586 and was buried in Clerkenwell, the following year – the year of his own death – Seckford sought to settle his estate, attempting properly to found his almshouse for the poor in his home village of Woodbridge in Suffolk. For this he would use the rents gained from his Clerkenwell estates. Seckford died on 19 December 1587, but by Letters Patent granted by the Queen on 23 May 1588 permission was granted to establish the almshouse.

> KNOW YE, that We upon the humble Petition of Our well beloved and faithful Thomas Seckford, Esquire, who has faithfully served us from the first day of February, in the Third Year of Our Reign, for Our Counsel about our Person:– For the founding, erecting and establishing one Hospital of the Poor, or Almshouse, in the Town of Woodbridge – will, grant and ordain that it shall be lawful …[18]

Seckford had set out the structure of the government for what was to become the charity bearing his name, as well as its 'Ordinances and Statutes'. One governor was to be the Chief Justice of the Court of Common Pleas, and the other the lord of the manor of Seckford Hall, Woodbridge. Thomas was not the eldest in his family. Francis, the older brother, died before Seckford, but it was Francis' son Charles who inherited the estate, and became the lord of the manor. If the male line ended, the Master of the Rolls was to take over the running of the charity in partnership with the Chief Justice, as governors of the almshouse. In his will of 1 August 1587 Seckford outlined his provision for his charity, giving the almshouse to the governors

> for ever to thintente that there shalbe in the said howses or dwellinges contynuallie resident either in the Lief or after the deathe of me the said

---

17 See SROI HD21/480. It is also likely that he built property on the St John's site too; Briscoe, *A Tudor Worthy*, p. 39. Rebecca, Lady Seckford, his sister-in-law, certainly built property there in 1610 or 1620 according to the *Survey of London Vol. XLVI* (Clerkenwell Green).

18 Weaver and Weaver, *The Seckford Foundation*, p. 16. The original document is written in contracted Latin. TNA C66/1291, mm. 37–9.

Thomas Seckforde thirtene poore men or some of them that is to saie in everie of those six howses of the said seauen howses or dwellinges that be westwarde twoo poore men unmaried And in the seauenth howse or dwellinge towardes theast one onlie pore man which shalbe called the principall of the poore aforesaide according to the tenor of hir Maiesties said Licence to me graunted beringe date the xxiijth daye of Maye last past and accordinge to my true meaninge expressed in certen Ordinaunces and statutes by me made deuised and sett downe in writinge under my hande for the better gouernement and order of the said xiij poremen[.][19]

He also outlined how the charity was to be funded, and as this describes the site on which the Red Bull theatre came to be located, a large part is quoted here.

And whereas I stand seased to me and to my heires of and in all theese parcelles of grounde hereafter mencionned Lyinge within the Close heretofore called St Marie Close in the parishe of Clarkenwell in the Countie of Middlesex, which now to my greate Chardges I haue enclosed with a brickwall that is to saye of and in all that principall new builded howse or howses next to St Johns wherein I now dwell with the broode walke under the Sowthwall of the saide close Latelie called St Marie close, with one pece of grounde set forth appointed and laide out to belonge to the saide house which saide pece of grounde besides the saide walke and the walke at the west end of the same conteyneth halfe an acre which said howse and howses and other the premisses I purpose to demise and Lett for diuers yeares for the yerelie rente of thirtie and six poundes and of and in one other newe builded howse conteyninge a hall a parlor a kytchin three Chambers twoo garrettes and a Sellor under the same hall to the saide principall howse adioyninge with the gatehowse washhowse and other Buildinges and of and in a garden plott and one pece of grounde set out and appointed to belonge and apperteine to the said new builded howse conteyninge by estimacion halfe an Acre and xj perches besides the Walke at the west ende of the same which last recited premisses are nowe demised together to one _____ for the yerelie rente of twentie six poundes thirteen shillinges and foure pence And also of and in one stable with the yarde belonging to the same and of and in one pece of grounde conteyninge by estimacion twoo acres and xxxij perches appointed for the makinge of xij gardens as the same be now demised to gether to William Bowes esquier and Thomas Hall gent for the terme of lx yeares for the yerelie rente of thirtie twoo poundes. And also of and in certen grounde or gardens as the same is now seuered and enclosed with a brick wall on theast and north partes And with a Timber wall and quick sett on the west parte and with a ditche and quick set on the South parte conteyninge by estimacion _____ acres as the same be

---

[19] TNA PROB 11/72/51, fos. 25–26v (fo. 25).

now demised to one Will*ia*m Goulde for the terme of thirtie yeares for the yearelie rente of eightene ponndes, The whole yerelie revennew of all w*hi*ch said premiss*es* as the same are or maye be letten for amounteth to the some of Cxijli xiijs iiijd I geue and bequeathe all the saide new builded howses gardens Stables groundes and all other the premisses before recited and the rentes reuersion and reuersions and inheritannce of the same and everie p*ar*te and p*ar*cell thereof unto the governors of the said howse of poore or Almeshouse called Sekfordes Almeshowse in Woodbridge in the Countie of Suff. To have and to houlde to them and their Successors for ever. (fos. 25–25v)

The property described thus far in Seckford's will was to become part of the present history of a charitable foundation; therefore documents concerning this site exist, not in the records for the Clerkenwell area, but in those concerned with the Woodbridge almshouse that the Clerkenwell property funded, at the Suffolk Record Office, Ipswich. It is because of the charitable nature of this Clerkenwell site, located on the west side of St John Street, north of what is now Aylesbury Street and near Clerkenwell Green, that local historians readily recognise it as the 'Seckford Estate'.[20] Because of this ready recognition, one is able to define the locality of the theatre, derived from published maps, such as Ogilby and Morgan's of 1677, naming it 'The Red Bull Yard', or William Morgan's of 1682, as situated on the charity's property.

Somewhere in Seckford's will of 1587 is described the site location of the Red Bull playhouse before it was built. We know this because of established scholarship that demonstrates how Anne Bedingfeild gave the lease of the Red Bull Inn to Aaron Holland, Clerkenwell inn-holder there by 1602; how Anne Bedingfeild's (or her husband's) relationship with the Seckford Estate stretched back to at least 1591; how title-page ascriptions located the Red Bull playhouse as either in Clerkenwell or St John's Street; and how maps of the 1670s and beyond describe a yard off St John Street as 'Red Bull yard'. All this information sits alongside much other evidence gathered besides, including a picture of the outside of the playhouse, complete with a likely tiring house (where actors changed costumes), labelling it 'Red Bull play house' and showing it precisely in the location where seventeenth-century maps place it.[21]

---

[20] The dark boundary line imposed on the William Morgan map reproduced in the Introduction to this book outlines the Clerkenwell Seckford Estate.

[21] Gloucestershire Archives, D1799/P12 is reproduced in full in Griffith, 'Martin Slatiar and the Red Bull Playhouse', p. 565. The sketch of the Red Bull with tiring house tower is found in Chapter 3 of this book.

The obvious question to put to the evidence so far, however, would be: which part of Seckford's 1580s will describes the land on which the playhouse was to be built? Seeming to start the description of the charitable gift at the south end of the property where the 'Red Bull yard' was, the part of the will relating to that part may well represent the area. In the will, the part of the property to the south is not apportioned to a particular person or set of persons – there is an obvious blank line inserted where this should be. This part of the description concerned a property with 'a hall a parlor a kytchin three Chambers twoo garrettes and a Sellor under the same hall ... with the gatehowse washhowse and other Buildinges', along with a garden plot etc. of 'halfe an Acre and xj perches' in size. According to the will, this was leased out to this undisclosed person for 'twentie six poundes thirtene shillinges and foure pence' per annum. Along with this piece of property was 'one stable with the yarde belonging to the same' – an ideal area for playhouse conversion – the only such yard area mentioned in the will.

This was, indeed, the kind of land that we know was used for the Red Bull playhouse from the one description we have of its erection – Martin Slatiar's petition to the Privy Council of 1605. In his petition Slatiar describes how he and Aaron Holland altered 'some stables and other rooms beinge before a square Court in an Inne' to make the playhouse – and in Seckford's will these are the only stables mentioned on the whole estate. The Red Bull property – including an inn with a stable and yard attached – was probably already let or sublet to Anne Bedingfeild in 1587. This can be stated because she was given property in both St John Street and the nearby Turnmill Street (at the west end of Clerkenwell) by her father, John Draper. This was itemised in Draper's will made in 1576.[22]

With the aid of an as yet unpublished image (Figure 4), we can illuminate further – by a process of elimination – how this southern portion of the charity's land was what Anne Bedingfeild owned by 1591. To do this we must compare Seckford's will text with this image, which shows how the sections of land were apportioned by Seckford as laid down in his will.

[22] See John Draper's will, TNA PROB 11/58/119, fos. 56v–57v. The possible scenario is that Seckford, when writing his will, remembered the lease belonged to a man called Draper but, conscious that this man had died and the daughter to whom he had left the land was married, left the portion blank in order to ascertain the new name. In saying this we must allow for the possibility that it was another property in St John Street that Anne acquired from her father; we only have real evidence that she had a relationship with this piece of land from 1591, four years after the institution of Seckford's gift.

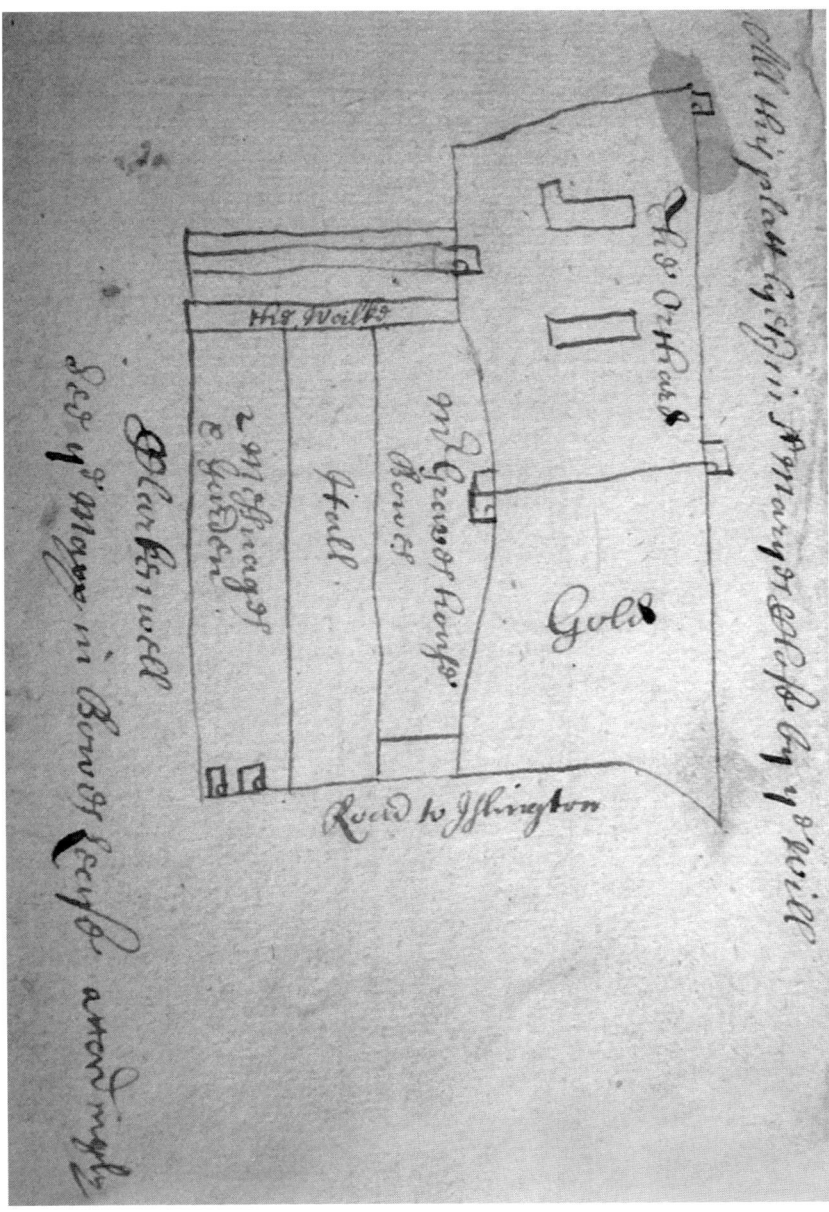

Figure 4 Small sketch of Seckford Estate, Clerkenwell, with owners of parts, as in Thomas Seckford's will. Seventeenth century.

The document where this image is found concerns matters on the estate pursued in the later seventeenth century, and has nothing to do with the specific part where the Red Bull was located, but with a confusion over the part that was leased 'to Will*ia*m Bowes esquier and Thomas Hall gent' in the will.[23]

In the top right-hand corner of the first page of this document is a drawing entitled: 'All this platt lyeth in St Maryes Close by ye will'. The drawing shows the Hall part immediately above the undisclosed lease-holder's part, with Bowes' part above this. William Gould – in the case of the drawing 'Gold' – holds the part to the north-east of the upper por-tion, and there was also an orchard section, belonging to the Seckford family and described later in the will, located to the north-west. Because all except the southern part are allocated to individuals (or, in the case of the orchard, simply 'seased' of Seckford's family), the most southerly part of the estate – which allies itself with where the Red Bull playhouse was located in all other representations of it – must be the portion that Anne Bedingfeild owned and that she sublet to Aaron Holland.

Anne Bedingfeild, Eustace Bedingfeld, Francis Naylor and the Seckford Estate

In 1587, when Thomas Seckford died and left his Clerkenwell property to his almshouse charity, Anne Bedingfeild née Draper may well have been the leasehold landlady-owner of the Red Bull Inn for eleven years. For the first three of those years she had been a single young woman, who had come into the property at the age of sixteen.[24] On 4 June 1579, at eighteen years old, she married Eustace Bedingfeld, and for the next

---

[23] SROI FC25/L3/3/11. A Thomas Hall is mentioned in Seckford's will in association with a Seckford house in Clerkenwell 'now occupied by the Countesse of darbie or by hir assignes'. This Hall inherited houses and gardens in unison with Humphrey Seckford, another Seckford brother, and one Simon Mawe. On this second occasion that 'Thomas Hall' is mentioned he is described as Seckford's 'oulde' servant along with Mawe, despite being a 'gent' the first time. According to the will, William Bowes is Seckford's 'Lovinge frinde' and 'Late sonne in Lawe', who is later men-tioned again in the will as nominated to look after a relative in his minority. He is also a witness to the will. William Bowes is recorded answering an appeal for money to aid defence against the Spanish in 1588. He gives £25 and is 'of St John-street, gent'. See Pinks, *The History of Clerkenwell*, p. 305.

[24] On her burial brass her age at death is noted as '80 YEARES & 7 MONTHES' in late March 1641, making her birth in the latter half of 1560 (Figure 5). See Alfred Suckling, *The History and Antiquities of the County of Suffolk with Genealogical and Architectural Notices of Several of Its Towns and Villages*, 2 vols. (London: John Weale, 1846–8), Vol. II (1848), after p. 224.

Figure 5 Anne Bedingfeild of Darsham. Sketch taken from the burial brass in Suckling's *History and Antiquities of the County of Suffolk* (London, 1848). The lozenges show heraldic symbols with elements of the Bedingfeld arms and the Draper family's symbols combined.

twenty years, until his death in 1599, her property would have been his responsibility.[25]

Eustace Bedingfeld is mentioned in Anne Bedingfeild's lease histories only as a husband giving her the status of widow. He is talked about quite specifically, however – and in quite an unexpected way – as a builder and developer in the Seckford Estate papers. In evidence made during a suit of 1633, Anne Bedingfeild was to describe how, in May 1591, Henry Seckford, Thomas's brother, came to a sixty-year lease arrangement with Charles Seckford, the then head of the household, for certain 'Edifices and buildings' on the estate and 'one parcell of grounde' beyond these buildings.[26] In the same year it was her husband, Eustace, along with one William Pope on the one part, and Henry Seckford on the other, who came to a further arrangement about these sublet properties.[27] The 'parcell of grounde' beyond the buildings could have been the orchard part that Thomas Seckford left to his relatives, and Bedingfeld and Pope put a £700 house on it.[28] In June 1594, Pope relinquished his interest to Bedingfeld, and according to Anne, her husband continued to pay £40 per annum to Charles Seckford or his representatives forever afterwards.[29]

Apart from the revelation that Eustace Bedingfeld of the Norfolk Bedingfelds became a building developer on the Seckford Estate, there are two other pieces of information from this court case that are worthy of note. One is that the new house that Bedingfeld built at this time was the only one where he secured a lease that had not yet expired in 1633. This was for 'the Ladie Elizabeth Hatton Widdowe', who took on the fifty-three-year lease on 13 June 1597, the same year her husband, Sir William Hatton, died.[30] This means that a significant member of Queen Anna's circle who took part, for example, in some of her early masques, possessed a residence local to the Red Bull playhouse.[31] The other piece of

[25] They were married on 4 June by general licence. See *Allegations for Marriage Licences Issued by the Bishop of London 1520 to 1610*, 2 vols. (London: Harleian Society, 1887), Vol. I, p. 88. Anne Bedingfeild, the widow, is mentioned in the court case where Aaron Holland's tenure of the inn is described – i.e. she is 'Anne Beddingfeild late wyeffe and administratrix of the goodes and Chattelles' of her husband, Eustace Bedingfeld. The record is TNA REQ2/411, Box 2, 149, which is the bill. The answer is REQ2/411, Box 2, 148. Both are mostly now unreadable but were transcribed by C. W. Wallace (See Griffith, 'New Material', 10–11); Eustace's Inquisition Post Mortem, TNA C142/261/51; TNA C142/269/56.

[26] SROI FC25/L3/3/8, pp. 2–3.

[27] *Ibid.*, pp. 8–9.

[28] *Ibid.*, pp. 9–10.   [29] *Ibid.*, pp. 10–11.   [30] *Ibid.*, pp. 11–12.

[31] The *Survey of London Vol. XLVI* also reveals that her brother, William Cecil, second earl of Exeter, bought the Prior's Hall on the St John's site in 1612. This was two years after a previous resident, Sir Henry Seckford, Master of the Tents, had died and was buried in the parish.

information, extraordinary to note at first, is that when she gave evidence, the seventy-three-year-old Anne Bedingfeild claimed that neither she, nor Henry Seckford, nor her husband ever knew that this land had anything to do with a charitable estate. This was probably true in the case of the property of Elizabeth, Lady Hatton, if on the orchard part, but not with reference to Bedingfeild's own part of the estate, and she denied knowledge of the charitable foundation altogether. In the case of the two men, it is impossible to believe that they did not know of the charitable status of 'the Seckford Estate'. However, it is, perhaps, imaginable that Anne Bedingfeild never took in the change of status of the land between when she was married in 1579 and when her husband died in 1599; for the charitable change happened in 1587 when her husband was in charge of her properties.

Because of a much later indenture of lease of 9 February 1679/80, we know that the first traceable arrangement between Anne Bedingfeild (with her husband in charge) and the charity (as opposed to Thomas Seckford, possibly before that) occurred in 1591.[32] This late-seventeenth-century document gives a whole history of this portion of the estate once the periods of previous leases are worked out. From this we know, then, that in 1591, Anne Bedingfeild had been given a sixty-year lease with Seckford's charity, taking her family's rights over it to 1651. It also explains how, in 1635, another indenture had been made that would have furthered their tenure up until 1707. Lastly we learn that by 1651, the good working order of the estate had become the responsibility of Francis Naylor, Anne Bedingfeild's grandson.[33] Because of some improvements he had made on the land, the lease was again extended for another thirty years in 1669, and another lease was granted in this last of 1679/80, bringing the final year of the lease up to 1767.

In 1641, the year of Anne Bedingfeild's death, the picture becomes complicated, as it is recognised that Anne Bedingfeild's spinster daughter, also called Anne Bedingfield, must have come into this portion of the estate.[34] We know this because of a royal patent she acquired in May 1663,

[32] SROI HB10/427/214.
[33] Griffith, 'New Material', pp. 8–10.
[34] On a memorial tablet in the old St James' Church, the following was engraved: 'M. S. *Juxta heic sita est* Anna Bedingfield, *Filia e trinis* Eustasii Bedingfield *de* Holmehale *in agro* Norfolciae, &c. 1664.' On the same tablet, for another daughter of Anne Bedingfeild Sr: '*Hic prope* Sara, *Relictu* Thomae Naylor, *Gen. perantiqua prosapia* Bedingfeldorum *In Com.* Norfolciensi *prognatu*, &c. 167'; Stow, *A Survey of the Cities of London and Westminster*, ed. Strype (1720), Vol. II, p. 65. Anne Bedingfield Jr was buried on 4 November 1664; 'Mrs Ann Beningfield, an antient maid, burd in ye Chancel'; *St JPR*, Vol. IV: *Burials* (1891), p. 358.

a year before both her own death and the last known entertainment at the Red Bull. It was a patent entitling her to make changes on the land.[35] The daughter is never mentioned in the indenture of 1679/80, although her mother is alluded to as 'the mother' as if it were worth making sure that a distinction be made between two people bearing the same name. This entitlement of 1663 is as intriguing as it was wide-ranging. In it Charles II gave full permission for Anne Bedingfeild Sr's appropriate relatives and assignees 'to alter take downe and rebuild all or anie the messuages houses or buildings With theyr appurtenances nowe standing and already built upon the said percell of ground as she or they shall thinke fitt'. This permission would extend 'from time to time and at all tymes as often as neede shall require'. The patent also gave permission to Anne Bedingfield Jr and her associates to 'frame erect newe build and sett upp such and soe manie newe messuages dwelling houses stables Coachouses and other edifices and buildings in or upon the said peece or percell of ground or anie parte thereof in such manner and at such times as shee or they shall thinke fitt'.

This means that from 1663 onwards, Francis Naylor – who as Anne Bedingfield Jr's nephew, Anne Bedingfeild Sr's grandson, was the one to be most actively involved in the building work – could change anything he liked on their leaseheld land – including the site of the Red Bull. There was also text in the patent that covered any difficulties about existing laws concerning new building in the suburbs – laws that may have dogged building work on the playhouse in the past. Anne Bedingfield, her friends and 'their servants labourers or Workmen'

> shall not be impeached lett or hindred in erecting setting upp and finishing the said buildings or anie of them or in anie other matter or thing hereby graunted or intended to be graunted contrary to the true intent and meaneing of these presents Although the said messuages houses edifices and buildings or anie of them shall be erected upon newe foundacions Anie Act Statute lawe ordinances proclamacion provision or restreint whattsoever to the Contrary notwithstanding[.]

In other words, with the old timber buildings existing on the Bedingfield portion as its main concern, this patent overrode any laws about having to build on old foundations to prevent the spread of building in the suburbs, thereby giving the family permission to found new buildings.

In the year 1664, when Anne Bedingfield Jr died and when entertainment on the site stopped, Francis Naylor must have completely taken over

---

responsibility. Between the previous year when they gained the patent, and the survey and text of the later indenture of 1679/80, we realise he was very active, for the text of the patent reveals that over half of the site was vacant in 1663.[36] By the time of the drawing of the survey attached to the indenture of 1679/80, the land was covered with buildings. The two areas itemised as recently developed in the indenture are small by comparison, and can be identified with the use of the survey's scale in feet.[37] These parts must have been developed very recently, inviting the charity's approval.

Anne Bedingfeild née Draper and her sixteenth-century family

Anne Draper, the woman who owned leasehold property on part of the Seckford Estate, probably from the age of sixteen and certainly at thirty-nine – including the site of what was to become the Red Bull playhouse – was born into a wealthy brewer's family. She was the daughter of John and Margery Draper of the parish of St Dunstan-in-the-West, where the Drapers' main brewery was situated. This was in the ex-monastic Whitefriars area of London, south of Fleet Street. According to his will, John Draper also owned various properties in the Blackfriars precinct, as well as in the Barbican and in Middlesex.[38] Eustace Bedingfeld, too, had dealings with Blackfriars property, as did his father Anthony. He is also present in correspondence with William More, one day to be Sir William More, whose voluminous property affairs at the Blackfriars may be traced in the Loseley manuscripts held in Surrey.[39] William Pope, the other man involved in the Seckford Estate development, is also present in these documents.

As soon as her father had died and left her property, it seems that Anne Draper may have become a dangerously viable property herself. Records exist of Margery Draper being taken to court by one Thomas Hobson, one-time clerk to John Draper, for unfair dismissal because, according to Margery, Hobson had 'most shamefully, wickedly and horribly' tried to

---

[36] Griffith, 'Martin Slatiar and the Red Bull Playhouse', pp. 566–8.

[37] The itemised areas were described as: 'One hundred foote front South towards the way leading from St John=Streete to Clarkenwell Greene and upon the ffortie foote or thereaboute Easttowards St John=Streete'. The likeliest spot for one of these two areas, once one tries to identify them on the survey attached to the indenture of 1679/80, would seem to be to the south-west of the playhouse site on the 'Road from Clarkenwell to St John street'. The other spot could be a small portion on part of the Red Bull site fronting St John Street; however, there is another place where this could be, also on the 'Road from Clarkenwell to St John street'.

[38] TNA PROB 11/58/119, fos. 56v–57v.

[39] Surrey History Centre, Woking, Loseley MSS SHC LM/348/125 (19 August 1578; a Eustace Bedingfeld property); SHC LM/COR/3/707 (an Anthony Bedingfeld letter).

marry her daughter.⁴⁰ Whether the accusation of attempted and enforced marriage was true or not, Margery Draper's family, the Wilkeses, were not averse to intelligent marriages. Margery's sister Alice – one day to be known as Dame Alice Owen – became a serial wife, widow and consequent wealthy woman of her age, endowing her own charitable activity with funds resulting in a school, still in existence. Hence it is no surprise – while no straightforward event – that a parentally blessed marriage for Anne was soon forthcoming in the shape of Eustace Bedingfeld.

The general licence for Anne's marriage on 4 June 1579 puts Eustace down as 'Eustace Bennefelde of the City of London, Gent.', and his funeral certificate of 1599 describes him as 'of the new Temple of London' and his dying on 19 May 'at his house without Temple barr'.⁴¹ Apart from his newly discovered building activity, however, nothing is currently known of how he came to be in London. What is known is he was the son of Anthony Bedingfeld, whose seat was at Holme Hale, Norfolk, near to that of Anthony's brother, Sir Henry (d. 1583), at Oxburgh Hall, Oxborough.⁴² Sir Henry Bedingfeld was a well-known recusant, a Privy Councillor in Queen Mary's reign, and the famous 'gaoler' of the Princess Elizabeth before she became Queen, according to John Foxe's version of events. We will examine the whole issue of the wider Bedingfeld significance to the Red Bull's story later in this chapter, but also in relation to our first foray into the Heywood/Worcester's company/Queen's Servants repertoire, within somewhat curiously embarrassing contexts. For now I would like to describe a little more of the most immediate significance of the Draper/Bedingfeld family in Tudor/Jacobean London.

Eustace Bedingfeld was not the first son to the Holme Hale Bedingfelds, and was therefore someone who would have had to make his own way in the world. He and Anne had a number of children, but it would appear that they were well supported by Margery Draper.⁴³ We do not know where

⁴⁰ TNA REQ2/78/56 (Court of Requests: Pleadings, 1558–1603); Judith M. Bennett, *Ale, Beer and Brewsters in England: Women's Work in a Changing World 1300–1600* (Oxford University Press, 1996), p. 91. Although Margery Draper had at least one other daughter, called Susan (who was named in John Draper's will along with Henry, Robert, Jasper, Thomas and John), Anne would have been the likeliest candidate for any unwanted marriage bid in view of her enhanced financial circumstances. Susan was left £200 by her father, which was either to be given to her on her marriage or when she reached twenty-one.
⁴¹ College of Arms MS I16/416 (funeral certificates; I series, Vol. XVI).
⁴² We know of Eustace's parentage and family because of a variety of evidence including, for example, the Bedingfeld arms incorporated on Anne Bedingfeld's brass at All Saints' Church, Darsham in Suffolk. See Griffith, 'New Material', p. 22n21.
⁴³ In 1581, a couple of years after their marriage, a baby, also called Anne, was buried 'at the chardge of Margery Draper widow, late wyfe of John Draper, Citizen and bere brewer of london – her

the family were living at the time or what their circumstances were – only that the couple were resident in the Strand as an independent entity by 1591, as from that year until his death eight years later, Eustace was paying poor rates for the parish of St Clement Danes. As a widow, Anne continued to be recorded as making these payments, more intermittently, up until 1614.[44] Where the family were living from 1579 until 1591 is open to speculation; the Strand parish is not far from the Whitefriars, where the Drapers' church of St Dunstan's is situated. John Draper, however, privileged his property interests in the Blackfriars precinct in his will, leaving most of what he owned there to his wife in order to help with bringing up a younger son. Anne and Eustace may have lived near the future site of the Blackfriars theatre, therefore, until 1591, at least.[45]

With regard to the Strand, it is interesting that Aaron Holland, the man to whom Anne Bedingfeild gave the lease of the Red Bull by 1602, was also a resident there in 1594, where he was indicted for keeping a bowling alley in Drury Lane with 'dicing Tabling and Carding'. However, his parish is the neighbouring one of St Mary le Strand, or the Savoy.[46] Holland is also recorded as keeping an inn in the Savoy in 1598 when he promised to appear at a gaol delivery on 7 July that year.[47]

When he died in 1599, Eustace left Anne Bedingfeild a widow after twenty years of marriage.[48] She never married again. The year 1576, when Anne Draper had come into her Clerkenwell property – one day to include the Red Bull playhouse within its boundaries – was the same year in which the Burbage family erected their first purpose-built amphitheatre, the Theatre, in Shoreditch. As is well documented, in 1599 – owing to rental problems – the Burbages were forced to remove the timbers from the Middlesex suburbs of London to the Bankside in Surrey. Here they adapted what they had, and refitted them as the Globe. Just opposite this old venture built on new foundations was another playhouse, the Rose,

---

Graundmother'. Jim Golland, 'Anne Bedingfeld: The Brasses in Pinner Church', *Pinner Local History Society Newsletter: Silver Jubilee 1972–1977*, 25. Although the brass describing these details is to be found in Pinner Church, it may have been removed to this site from a place unknown.

44 Westminster City Archives, St Clement Danes Parish Records B1, Surveyors' Accounts, 1581–1621.

45 According to some Chancery papers of 1605–11, Alice Seckford, formerly Karvile, née Bedingfeild, entrusted some substantial property in Great Wood Street, London, to her cousin Eustace, Anne Bedingfeild's husband. This was so that after Alice's death they would convey the property to her then young son, Henry, the now adult complainant. The papers relate how Eustace Bedingfeld held on to the property even after Alice Seckford's death. It may be, therefore, that the Bedingfelds lived in Wood Street. See TNA C3/278/53, *Henry Kervill v. Anne and Anthony Beddingfeild*, Bill and Answer.

46 TNA KB9/685/14; Mark Eccles, 'Elizabethan Actors IV: S to End', *Notes and Queries* 238 [n.s. 40] (1993), 165–76 (p. 171).

47 LMA MJ/SR/0355, 38; *MCR*, Vol. I, p. 245.

48 Inquisitions Post Mortem, TNA C142/261/51 and TNA Ward 7/24/153.

erected on the Bankside in 1587. This business enterprise was owned by Philip Henslowe, a figure whose theatre plays a part in the company history, given later in this book, of the Earl of Worcester's Men, the actors who were eventually to inhabit the Red Bull.

Philip Henslowe's non-performing neighbours are also part of a network that connects Anne Bedingfeild to the theatrical community, for her brother, Henry Draper, was a high-achieving member of the brewer fraternity and can be proved to have been an associate of Henslowe's on the Bankside.[49] His brewery was located near the Rose from evidence in the Records of the Surrey and Kent Sewer Commission, which recorded instances of the need to maintain the 'gulleys' and 'wharfs' of householders in particular areas, including Maid Lane, where the Globe and the Rose were located.[50] We know he was Anne Bedingfeild's brother because he left her a ring, giving her married name, in his will dated 13 August 1614, and he is recorded in Henslowe's documents, where he borrows from him in the early 1590s.[51] He also, perhaps more significantly, lent his name to a petition that the watermen put forward through Henslowe's auspices.[52]

It is a danger to over speculate, but we might imagine a situation where, on hearing that part of her Clerkenwell property might be converted into a playhouse, Anne Bedingfeild may not have felt completely averse to the idea of her inn-yard as an entertainment venue. This may have been especially so in view of her brother's association with a playhouse builder and owner.

---

[49] He was made a freeman of the company in 1585, a warden in 1604, and a Master in 1606 and 1608. Guildhall Library, Brewers' Company, Court Minute Books, CLC/L/BF/B/001/MS05445/007 (1582–6). He was accepted as a freeman apprenticed by Robert Wilkes (a relation of his mother) on 26 or 29 August 1585. See also CLC/L/BF/B/001/012 (1604–12) for evidence of Henry's wardenship and his masterships, the first beginning on 18 August 1606 with the last meeting on 11 August 1607, the second from 10 January to 5 September 1609.

[50] LMA SKCS/018 (microfilm X067/001), fos. 372v and 381v – named address. He is always in trouble in these records for the bad upkeep and smell of his arrangements. Folios that mention Draper include 130v, 143, 146, 158, 160, 197, 201v, 212, 221, 266, 274v, 279v, 353v, 381v, 402, 404v, 407 (fined), 413 (two entries), 415 (two entries), 420, 422 (seven entries), 425v, 426v (three entries), 432. His entries in this document extend from 1587 to 1606, when the record ends. Records where he is mentioned as adjacent to Philip Henslowe occur at fos. 239 (1596, with one 'Robert Miles' mentioned in between), 398 (1604, with three entries in between), 416–416v (1605, five entries between), 422–422v (1605, no entries between), 426v (1605, no entries between), 437v–438 (1606, seven entries between).

[51] TNA PROB 11/125/67, fos. 42–3. In this will he asks the St Saviour's churchwardens to make payments from the proceeds of a 'Brew House called the Red Hinde' already in the possession of his son, Thomas, which was 'scituate in the saide parrish'. For Henslowe's loans see Philip Henslowe, *Henslowe's Diary*, ed. R. A. Foakes, 2nd edn (Cambridge University Press, 2002), pp. 7, 8.

[52] Henslowe, *Henslowe's Diary*, ed. Foakes, pp. 284–5. Henry Draper signs his name with no need of a mark.

REPERTOIRE 1   EUSTACE BEDINGFELD AND
HIS UNCLE HENRY: THE STRANGE CASE OF *IF YOU
KNOW NOT ME YOU KNOW NOBODY*, PART I

As mentioned earlier, Eustace Bedingfeld, Anne Bedingfeild's husband, was the son of Anthony Bedingfeld of Holme Hale, Norfolk. Eustace, therefore, was the nephew of Sir Henry Bedingfeld of Oxburgh Hall: the famous 'gaoler' of the Princess Elizabeth before she became Queen. This was during the reign of Mary I, and the whole story was recorded in John Foxe's *Book of Martyrs*, making the brave Elizabeth a Protestant heroine of the first order. Thomas Heywood saw the economic virtue of this story when told in the immediate aftermath of the death of the old Queen. It is therefore the case that, sometime during 1603–4, Heywood wrote a play that put the company's soon-to-be landlady's relative on the stage.[53] This play was to become a highly popular staple of the Queen's Servants' repertoire; however, what has to be stated from the outset is that this representation of the most important of Bedingfelds was not written in the most flattering of ways.

If You Know Not Me You Know Nobody is a two-part play by Heywood, who was the main actor-playwright of the Queen's Servants. Part II was first published in 1606 and would be one of the best repertoire excuses to call the Queen's Servants company and theatre 'citizen-orientated' entities, as it was a play that tackled the life and times of Thomas Gresham, a Tudor London hero. Part I, published in the previous year, 1605, was a very different kind of drama from its counterpart, focusing on the earlier life of Queen Elizabeth just prior to her accession. It impressively ran into many editions in relatively quick succession – in 1606, 1608, 1610 and 1613 – meaning that it must have become a 'must-see' at the Red Bull, the company's flagship playhouse. It achieved editions outside the Queen's Servants' period too – in 1623, 1632 and 1639 – bearing witness to its significantly nostalgic popularity.[54]

---

[53] Certainly a Queen's Servants' play, it may have received a first performance at the Curtain or the Boar's Head. It is the case that the only true evidence of a play belonging to a particular company at a particular playhouse is a title-page statement giving the facts. Both parts of *If You Know Not Me* carry no such title-page information. Because the plays are by Thomas Heywood and published during the period when the Red Bull became an entity, it has been assumed that they were originally Red Bull plays; however, according to strict repertoire scholarship, we cannot be certain of this, as, for example, Roslyn Knutson believes the general idea that a play would have been presented 'about eighteen months before its appearance in the hands of the stationers' (Knutson, *The Repertory of Shakespeare's Company*, p. 10). What we can be certain of is that they must have been written after the death of the Queen, who could be sensitive about impersonations of her. Part II could have been the first play performed at the Red Bull.

[54] Such was this popularity that it is known to have been produced during the Restoration period too. See Teresa Grant, 'Drama Queen: Staging Elizabeth in *If You Know Not Me You Know Nobody*', in

John Foxe's account of Henry Bedingfeld's relationship with the Princess Elizabeth, upon which much of the play is based, is illustrated by Foxe's martyrology, which enjoyed a success unique to itself. Published in 1563, it was regarded as so important that copies were put into every parish throughout the nation.[55] Giving graphic, pictorially illustrated accounts of the Protestant movement in England through its many stories of the men and women who gave their lives to their religious cause, it included the young Princess Elizabeth, who is depicted as one who survived her sister's reign to bring Protestantism back to the country. As mentioned above (p. 46), the story tells of how she was looked after by Sir Henry Bedingfeld, a Privy Councillor to Queen Mary, covering the period from Elizabeth's sojourn at the Tower of London to her stay at Woodstock.[56] The story of *this* period in the life of Elizabeth – popularly known as her 'Troubles' – was promoted through Foxe, and it was this account that Heywood chose for his successful retrospective of recent times in dramatic form. Bedingfeld did this job so well that, according to Foxe, Elizabeth later stated that if she wanted anyone 'sharply and straytly kepte' then she would send for him.[57]

Now it is an obvious fact of this particular story that the Bedingfeld custodianship narrative could not have been written without prejudice. In Foxe's tale of the Princess just prior to her accession, he gives the impression that an overbearing Sir Henry managed his job of protective work too harshly, without the manners to allow people to treat her with the respect befitting her station, and with 'a company of rakehels' in attendance. At Lord William of Thame's house, a beautiful chair was provided for the Princess with a 'fote carpet, very fayre and princelike'. Here Bedingfeld sat himself down and asked 'one Barwicke his man to pull of his botes' – behaviour that was deemed 'undiscrete' by the ladies and gentlemen in attendance. Another incident recounted how a certain 'mery conceited man' took a goat that had been seen in the vicinity of the Princess to Sir Henry, reporting the animal to be a suspicious Welshman.[58]

Foxe's work became widespread, and such popularisation of recent history did nothing to hurt a growing 'cult' of Queen Elizabeth. This cult could only have been seen as beneficial to the nation at the time, and it is

The Myth of Elizabeth, ed. Susan Doran and Thomas S. Freeman (Basingstoke: Palgrave Macmillan, 2003), pp. 120–42 (p. 120).

[55] Thomas S. Freeman, 'Providence and Prescription: The Account of Elizabeth in Foxe's "Book of Martyrs"', in Doran and Freeman, *The Myth of Elizabeth*, pp. 27–55 (p. 46).

[56] John Foxe, *Actes and Monuments of these latter and perillous dayes...* (London: John Day, 1563). The work is oddly paginated. Princess Elizabeth's story is to be found on pp. 1713(1)–1716. In Foxe's text Bedingfeld's name is invariably spelt 'Benifield' or 'Benifielde'.

[57] *Ibid.*, p. 1004.   [58] Both incidents, *ibid.*, p. 1713.

likely that Foxe, knowing this, also wittily depicted how, on acceding to the throne, the Queen referred to Bedingfeld as her 'Gaoler'.[59] Foxe also wrote of how, with great grace and regal foresight, the Queen declined to punish Bedingfeld in any public way for his control of her.

Heywood's play, as we have seen, was to continue being published while the Queen's Servants were at the Red Bull. Looking for a repertoire success on a par with Foxe's feat of popular history, Heywood certainly upped the ante in the extreme in the story, making Elizabeth even more 'put upon' than in the Foxe version.[60] Instead of Bedingfeld's rudeness to Elizabeth, Heywood's particular slant on the incident of Sir Henry and his boots involves scene-participation for the Clown, where the character pulls the throne away from Sir Henry as he sits to remove his boots, sending him crashing to the floor.

> *Enter Beningfeild and Barwick, his man.*
> BENING: *Barwicke*, is this the chayre of state.
> BAR: I, sir, this is it.
> BENING: Take it downe, and pull of my boots.
> BAR: Come on Sir.
> *Enter Clowne.*
> CLOWN: O monstrous, what a sawcy companion's this?
>   To pull of his boots in the chayre of state,
>   Ile fit you a penyworth for it.
> BENING: Well sayd *Barwick*, pull, knaue.
> BARW: A ha Sir.
> *The Clowne pulls the Chayre from under him.*
> BENING: Well sayd: now comes.[61]

The Clown gets a beating for his pains.

Heywood retells the goat story by again giving the part of the 'mery conceited man' to the clown of the company. Among the Queen's Servants at the Red Bull, this part would most probably have been played by Thomas Greene, their leader from *c.* 1604.

> *Enter Clowne.*
> CLOWNE: O Sir *Harry*, you looke well to your office,
>   Yonders one in the garden with the Princesse.
> BENING: how knaue, with the Princesse? she parted euen now.
> CLOWNE: I sir thats all one, but shee no sooner came into the
>   Garden, but he leapt ore the wall, and there

---

[59] *Ibid.*, p. 1715.   [60] Grant, 'Drama Queen', p. 137.
[61] Thomas Heywood, *If You Know Not Me You Know No Bodie; or, The Troubles of Queene Elizabeth* (London, 1605), Part I, E1–E1v. In Heywood's play the Bedingfeld name is spelt 'Beningfeild'.

They are together busie in talke Sir.

BENING: Heer's for thy paynes, thou art an honest fellow:
   Goe take a Gard, and apprehend them straight.

Exit Clowne.

Bring them before me,
O this was well found out,
Now will the Queene commend my diligent care,
And prayse me for my seruice to her grace.
Ha, traytors swarme so neere about my house,
Tis time to looke into't:
O, well said, *Barwick.*
Wher's the prisoner.

Enter Clowne, Barwick, and souldiers: leading of a Gote, his sword drawen.

CLOWNE: Here he is in a string my Lord.

BENING: Lord blesse vs, knaue what hast thou there?

CLOWNE: This is he I told you was busie in talke with the Princesse;
   What a did there, you must get out of him by examination.

BENING: Why knaue, this is a beast.

CLOWNE: So may your worship be for any thing that I know.[62]

The Clown gets another beating.

   The scenes represent supreme slapstick, with Sir Henry situated as the butt of the play's jokes. How this drama could have been received by Anne Bedingfeild (if she ever saw it) as a representation of her husband's family, we can only leave to the imagination. What it did to any Bedingfeld associates' perceptions of Thomas Heywood is yet another curious thought. For Anne Bedingfeild was not the only person going by the name who had business dealings in the Clerkenwell area, and whom it may have been unwise to cross with Heywood's/the Queen's Servants' drama. To understand the roots of yet more embarrassment that could have been caused by *If You Know Not Me* Part 1 we must understand what really happened when Sir Henry Bedingfeld looked after Elizabeth Tudor.

The true story of Princess Elizabeth's custody and Thomas Heywood's play

With more empirical evidence available, taken from correspondence between Sir Henry and Queen Mary and her Council, we are told of a much more family-orientated affair surrounding the protection of Elizabeth.[63] With regard to the Bedingfeld family, it is noted that Anthony

---

[62] Heywood, *If You Know Not Me*, Part 1, E4–E4v.

[63] BL, Additional MS 34563, which was published in 1855. See C. R. Manning, 'State Papers Relating to the Custody of the Princess Elizabeth at Woodstock, in 1554', *Norfolk Archaeology* 4 (1855), 133–231.

Figure 6 Portrait of Sir Henry Bedingfeld 'The Gaoler',
Oxburgh Hall, Norfolk.

Bedingfeld – brother to Sir Henry and the father of Eustace, Anne
Bedingfeild's husband – is named many times in these papers.[64] Other
members of the Bedingfeld family are also mentioned as involved in
looking after the soon-to-be Queen, along with associates. These include
at least one and – it is possible – two, who were directly relevant to the

---

[64] *Ibid.*, fos. 6b, 7b, 43 and five times subsequently.

history of entertainment, the topic of gentry residents in Clerkenwell, and to the site of the Red Bull playhouse itself.

Sir Henry Bedingfeld recorded events of interest to the Privy Council in his letters to them, careful to report any strange anomalies in day-to-day events. In one letter he reported a situation that occurred in 1554 concerning a servant of his and one of his own sons.[65] The servant's surname specified is pointedly familiar as being the same as the founder of 'the Seckford Estate' where the Red Bull was built. Henry Seckford was, at this time, Sir Henry Bedingfeld's servant, and the brother of Thomas Seckford, future Master of the Court of Requests and founder of the almshouse charity. During his middle years, after his time serving Sir Henry Bedingfeld, this Seckford gained repute as a ship builder and privateer. He was knighted at Charterhouse, becoming Sir Henry Seckford soon after King James came to the throne in 1603.[66]

Far from being one of a company of 'rakehels', as John Foxe would have it in his account, or being in any way reprimanded or demoted for his participation in Elizabeth's so-called 'protection', Henry Seckford was made Groom of the Privy Chamber in 1558 soon after her accession as Queen, and was rewarded for his services to her in 1562.[67] By then Sir Thomas Cawarden, Master of the Tents and Revels, had died, and Seckford was made Master of the Tents, 'Halls' (or 'Hales') and 'Pavilions'. This meant that he was engaged in a Revels-related job to do with looking after and keeping stuffs necessary for the monarch's progresses outside the court: tents, temporary horse stalls, but also – pertinently – things needed for entertainment at court.[68] Because of this post, Henry Seckford was given a work-related residence in Clerkenwell among the Revels Office buildings on the St John's Priory site. Among the Revels Office papers, a number of entries mention him, including a description of his residence in 1572/3 and an account with a note of his general kind of activity:

> Henri Sekeforde esquier for mony by him disbursed for Rushes in the hall & in the greate chambere where the *workes* were doone & the playes Rezited – xxs for ij greate tables in the hall – xxxiijs iiijd for hanging vp Tent*es* to keepe away the wynde & snow from dryving into the hall & taking downe the same agayne – vjs viijd/ Two long peec*es* of Tymber of xx foote appeece to

[65] *Ibid.*, fo. 42b.
[66] He was knighted on 11 May. See Briscoe, *A Tudor Worthy*, pp. 65–81 (p. 81).
[67] See Susan M. Maxwell, 'Seckford, Sir Henry (*d*. 1610)', *Oxford Dictionary of National Biography*, www.oxforddnb.com/view/article/61385, accessed 25 January 2008.
[68] Banqueting stuffs and temporary stages, etc. By 1576 he was also Master of the Toils (or 'toyles') – that is, hunting nets – and evidence exists of his being engaged in the care of the royal deer.

make A frame for the paynters – xs./ and for ij M of Billett*es* & Coles where the playes were rezited in the greate chamber – xxvjs viijd[.][69]

Henry Seckford's work was directly associated with the Revels Office activity of hearing plays for the purpose of 'perusing', 'perfecting' and 'correcting' drama likely to appear at court. Put alongside Henry Seckford in this work, however, was Thomas Bedingfeld, the son of the famous recusant and 'gaoler', Sir Henry Bedingfeld, and therefore cousin to Eustace Bedingfeld, the husband of Anne Draper. This Bedingfeld may well have been the 'son' referred to in Sir Henry Bedingfeld's letter concerning events that took place in 1554. If so, he must have become a lifelong associate of Henry Seckford, for Seckford become brother-in-law to Thomas when he married Alice Bedingfeld, Thomas's sister.[70] Like Henry Seckford, Thomas Bedingfeld was honoured by Queen Elizabeth, but this time he was made not a Groom of the Privy Chamber, but a Gentleman Pensioner – in 1567.[71]

A cultured gentleman of some standing, Thomas Bedingfeld was accomplished in Italian and Latin, a fact borne out by the publication of a number of translations, including a rendering of Gerolamo Cardano's work on grief.[72] This English translation of Italian is seen by many to be one of Shakespeare's sources for Hamlet's thoughts on suicide. Bedingfeld's translation, called *Cardanus Comforte*, was first published in London in 1573, and, it is therefore thought that Bedingfeld may well have supplied much inspiration for 'To be or not to be' – the most famous dramatic speech written in the English language.[73]

---

[69] Albert Feuillerat, *Documents Relating to the Office of the Revels in the Time of Queen Elizabeth* (Louvain: A. Uystpruyst, 1908), p. 179. The items that he looked after were kept in the converted church or chapel of the Priory. He had a thirteen-room residence with the office (See BL, MS Lansdowne 86. Art. 60, fo. 47). It included a kitchen, a larder, a coalhouse, a washing yard, a chamber, a still house, a 'fayer' garden with an orchard, a cellar, a hothouse, a buttery and a hall that included a dining chamber. He also had a door that could take him 'through the wall leading to Clerkenwell and Iselington'.

[70] They were married by the 1570s. Throughout a period of difficulties concerning the family recusancy, when Sir Henry refused to adhere to government orders concerning the new Church, there is evidence of Henry Seckford's defence of his father-in-law, begging leave for consideration of the state of his health, for example. See Katherine Bedingfeld, *The Bedingfelds of Oxburgh* (Privately printed, 1912), p. 46.

[71] TNA E179/69/82, m. 11; E407/1, 4–35; William Joseph Tighe, 'Gentlemen Pensioners in Elizabethan Politics and Government', Ph.D. thesis, University of Cambridge, 1983, p. 323

[72] Gerolamo Cardano, *De consolatione*; or, *De utilitate ex adversis capienda*, written to console himself after the loss of his son, who had been executed after a conviction for poisoning his wife (Venice, 1542). Bedingfeld also translated Machiavelli's *History of Florence*, which was published in 1595. This was dedicated to Sir Christopher Hatton.

[73] See William Shakespeare, *Hamlet*, ed. Harold Jenkins (London: Methuen, 1982), pp. 277–80, 484–92. At the beginning of *Cardanus Comforte*, Bedingfeld addressed a letter to the earl of Oxford, who wrote a reply, also contained in the prefatory material. Bedingfeld was sent to retrieve Oxford from his flight to Flanders in 1574. See Alan H. Nelson, *Monstrous Adversary: The Life of Edward de Vere, 17th Earl of Oxford*, Liverpool English Texts and Studies 40 (Liverpool University Press, 2003), pp. 77–9, 109, 112–13, 205.

Aside from this philosophical work, Bedingfeld published *The Art of Riding*.[74] This was a translation of Book II of *Il cavallarizzo*, written by one Claudio Corte. It is also known that at one time Bedingfeld held a share of the playing cards monopoly in England with Ralph Bowes, to whom he gave up his share in 1585.[75] He was probably born in Oxburgh: in a 1585 inventory of the goods and property included in the Bedingfeld estate, one of the rooms mentioned at Oxburgh Hall is 'the Chamber called Mr Thomas Bedingfeldes chamber'.[76] Helpfully, and noted immediately before it, is a room listed as 'the Chamber late Mrs Sackfordes' – meaning it had belonged to Alice Bedingfeld, who had become Henry Seckford's wife.

Also included in the 1585 Bedingfeld inventory is a list of things noted from a property in London. It is entitled 'Goodes and Plate at London viz St Bartholomews there'. This is intriguing because of the proximity of St Bartholomew's in Smithfield to Clerkenwell.[77]

Wherever Thomas Bedingfeld's living quarters were from 1603, we know that both he and Henry Seckford lived, died and were buried in the parish of Clerkenwell, and therefore the set of chambers on St Bartholomew's Priory land would have suited him well. Both men were engaged in property and parish affairs in the area, noted in the parish vestry minutes of the time. In this record a 'deed of ffeofment' is listed that concerned a property arrangement made between Henry Seckford and his in-law, Thomas:

> Item a deed of ffeofment dated the xuiijth of december 1595 made by the said henry Sackford esquier and others to Thomas Bedingfeild esquier and others of the said Tenemente in Turnmillstreet and of diuers Tenementes in Snt Johnes street in the tennor of william Golde and others to hold to them and their heires to the use of the poor as aforsaid/[78]

The location for the Revels Office, and therefore, presumably, the site that kept the materials of the Masters of the Tents and Toils, changed in 1608, this coming relatively soon after the Red Bull playhouse was up and running. Both Henry Seckford and Thomas Bedingfeld died and were buried

[74] Thomas Bedingfeld, *The Art of Riding, Conteining diuerse necessarie instructions, demonstrations, helps, and corrections apperteining to horssemanship, not heretofore expressed by anie other Author* (London, 1584).

[75] This may be a relative of 'William Bowes', discussed earlier, who held a lease of property on the Seckford Estate; TNA C66/1137, mm. 32–3; Tighe, 'Gentlemen Pensioners', pp. 246–7.

[76] Oxburgh Hall, Norfolk, Wooden Box, Household Inventories. I am grateful to the current Sir Henry Bedingfeld, Bt. of Oxburgh Hall and his family for letting me look through their documents, and for extending such generosity and friendship towards me.

[77] Because of Thomas Bedingfeld's interest in horses, Smithfield would have been a useful place for him to live. This is the case for a number of people living adjacent to the Red Bull. See Griffith, 'Inside and Outside'.

[78] Islington Local History Centre, Finsbury Library, St John Street, Clerkenwell, St James' Parish Vestry Book, 1590–1683, fo. 8.

in St James', Clerkenwell, however: Sir Henry in 1610 and Bedingfeld in 1613.[79] Bedingfeld's memorial stone was placed 'in a comely Chapel by the Pulpit', describing him as son of Sir Henry, 'one of the Privy Councel to Queen *Mary*', a Gentleman Pensioner to Queen Elizabeth and Master of the 'Tents and Pavillions' to King James.[80]

The Bedingfelds' seat was and still is the beautiful Oxburgh Hall, which is today maintained by the National Trust. The citizen status of the Drapers was in no way comparable to that of the Bedingfelds. The Bedingfeld family was included among the upper echelons of the gentry – some would call them *nobilitas minor*. This status was tempered historically, however, by the fact of their recusant beliefs, which, with the change-around to a Protestant state denomination, means that they would have attracted extreme taxation if they held onto it. Many of them did indeed hold on to their faith, as do the current family; however, it is believed that Thomas Bedingfeld, with his status at court, did not.[81] We cannot tell the Bedingfeld family's response to the play about Sir Henry, which was, quite probably, performed at the Red Bull playhouse. If they saw it, the experience could only have been strange for both men who were part of the familial retinue associated with the events depicted. For both knew the truth behind the fictionalised account.

Thus far, and as far as the Red Bull playhouse is concerned, we have a situation where we know this particular theatre was converted out of an inn-yard on a charitable estate. The freehold-owner of the estate was a heavyweight bureaucrat of the court of Queen Elizabeth who died in the 1580s; however, his brother, Henry Seckford, possessed an entertainment-related office with a brother-in-law whose relative had married the lease-hold-owner of the site.

There were other members of England's elite, however, who were found to be living in Clerkenwell a little time before the building of the Red Bull in a period just before the change in reigns. These people were of an even higher social order than either the Bedingfelds or the Seckfords. With these people, discussed in the next two chapters, come questions to do with Elizabethan and Jacobean patronage, the cutting-edge political history of the period and the subject of the company that became the Servants of Queen Anna, the wife of James I.

---

[79] For Sir Henry's burial see *St JPR*, Vol. IV, p. 113; Bedingfeld's is recorded as taking place on 1 August, 'in the bodye of the Churche' (p. 124).

[80] Stow, *A Survey of the Cities of London and Westminster*, ed. Strype, Vol. II, p. 65. Stow's editor here, John Strype, records the placing and wording before the original church was demolished and a new one was built. The tablet notes Bedingfeld's death as 11 August, not 1 August, however.

[81] Tighe, 'Gentlemen Pensioners', p. 177.

CHAPTER 2

The earl of Worcester, the Essex circle, the Queen's Servants and their playhouses (1589–1607)

The company of actors that were to take up residence at the Red Bull in c. 1605 were those who originally worked under the patronage of Edward Somerset, fourth earl of Worcester, during Queen Elizabeth's reign. His continued support of them after King James I's accession in 1603 is somewhat demonstrated through dedications by the company's main playwright and fellow actor, Thomas Heywood. These dedications include those found in *Troia britannica* (London, 1609), *An Apology for Actors* (1612), an elegy for Prince Henry (1613) and an elegy for King James (1625). Heywood also dedicated his large-scale history of women – *Gunaikeion; or, Nine Bookes of Various History Concerninge Women; Inscribed by the names of the Nine Muses* – to the earl in 1624, and his *Conspiracy of Catiline* and *War of Jugurtha* to Sir Thomas Somerset in 1608. Sir Thomas was Worcester's third son and the Master of the Horse to Queen Anna, the company's patron.[1]

Edward Somerset became earl on 22 February 1589, upon the death of his father, William. The latter died, significantly, at the family's then home at St John's, Clerkenwell, which seems as if it had been sublet from either Thomas or Henry Seckford, and was on the Priory site.[2] Of particular interest, in view of our account of the Bedingfeld family, is the fact that William Somerset was a reputed Catholic, as was, apparently, his son, Edward, who was anecdotally described by Queen Elizabeth as someone

---

[1] This younger Somerset was an official person chosen to tell King James of Queen Elizabeth's death and of his succession, and he was made a knight in January 1605. He subsequently became a close associate of Prince Henry. See Michael G. Brennan, 'Sir Charles Somerset's Music Books (1622)', *Music and Letters* 74 (1993), 501–18, esp. p. 503n.

[2] We know that Thomas Seckford owned property on the St John's site as well as on St Mary's nunnery. Margaret, countess of Derby writes letters describing being sent to her 'cosen Sackford', 'his house at St Joneses' and to her kinsman's house, the Queen's 'graue officer the master of Requestes'. For a full account of the third earl, stretching back to Henry VIII's reign, see W. R. B. Robinson, 'Somerset, William, third earl of Worcester (1526/7–1589)', *Oxford Dictionary of National Biography*, www.oxforddnb.com/view/article/26015, accessed 3 February 2008.

who '*reconciled* what she believed *inconsistent, a stiff Papist to a good subject*'.[3] Both William, the third earl, and Edward, the fourth, were involved in the patronage of dramatic playing companies, and E. K. Chambers suggested that there may have been some historical confusion between the two.[4] The elder Somerset's company has been most associated with provincial touring, and these actors may well have come into contact with Shakespeare's father when John Shakespeare was Stratford bailiff during 1568.[5] So far the inference has been that the third earl's company never played in London, but his son's most certainly did, performing at the Boar's Head, the Rose, and the Curtain during Queen Elizabeth's reign, as well as at the Red Bull during that of James I.

Worcester formed links with the coming Jacobean court early on, sent, as he was in 1590, as envoy from England to the Scottish court to mark the King's marriage of the year before. This was to Anna, now consort queen of James VI of Scotland, later the new patron of Worcester's old acting company. A good huntsman, Worcester was made deputy Master of the Horse to Queen Elizabeth in 1597 when the Master of the Horse at that time was Robert Devereux, earl of Essex. When Essex was questioned during his detention at York House, Worcester was among those sent to hear the charges against him on 5 June 1600. He was also one of those held prisoner by Devereux at Essex House on 8 February 1601 when Essex marched on the City on that notorious day. Worcester was even selected to try Essex and, after he was condemned, Worcester replaced him as the official Master of the Horse.

On 29 June 1601, the earl was made a member of the Privy Council and grew in favour to the end of the old Queen's reign.

Several residences of the earl in and around London are recorded, including those in Bishopsgate Street and Anchor Street in Vintry Ward (at the foot of Garlick Hill), as well as others in Tower Street, Stepney, Southwark, Acton, Ewell Park and Enfield.[6] When his father William died at their house at St John's, Clerkenwell in 1589, Worcester inherited the earldom. He continued to live in Clerkenwell, the parish where his

[3] David Lloyd, *State Worthies. Or, The States-Men And Favourites of England Since the Reformation ... During the Reigns of King Henry VIII, King Edward VI, Queen Mary, Queen Elizabeth, King James, King Charles ...* (London, 1670), p. 582.

[4] *ES*, Vol. II, pp. 220–1.

[5] Albert Frederick Pollard, 'William Somerset, Third Earl of Worcester (1526–1589)', in *The Dictionary of National Biography*, Vol. XVIII (London: Smith, Elder, 1897–8; repr. Oxford University Press, 1921–2), pp. 655–6 (p. 656); *ES*, Vol. II, pp. 220–1.

[6] Sidney J. Madge, 'Worcester House in the Strand', *Archaeologia or Miscellaneous Tracts Relating to Antiquity* 91 (1945), 157–80 (p. 157).

company's theatre was to be located fifteen years later. Roger Manners, who was constantly moving around London and its suburbs with his brother John, was staying in the early 1590s at 'my lord the Erl of Worseter's howse that was Mr. Sacford's at Sainct Johnes'.[7] While the earl was in Clerkenwell, a son, Christopher, was born to him in 1590 by his wife, the daughter of Francis Hastings, second earl of Huntingdon. When Christopher died four years later in 1594, he was buried in the aisle of St James' Parish Church.[8] By 1604 it would seem that Worcester had moved to Russell House on the Strand. This was renamed Herbert House or Worcester House when it came into his family's hands after the marriage of Henry Somerset, Worcester's second son (who later took the title) in the year 1600.[9]

Worcester's rise, within a court context, went hand in hand with vigorous participation in the activities of playing companies and the action of regulating them. He was one of the Privy Councillors who signed the letter of 31 March 1602, asking the Lord Mayor to let the merged Oxford/ Worcester's company play at the Boar's Head as the third company allowed in the London area, thereby breaking the duopoly that had existed for some time.[10] He also co-signed that order in April 1604 to the Lord Mayor and the justices of Surrey and Middlesex authorising the three companies of the time – the King's Men, the Prince's Men and the Queen's Servants – to play in their respective houses in the London area. For the Queen's Servants, the Curtain is specified at this time.[11] No doubt these

---

[7] Historical Manuscripts Commission Twelfth Report, Appendix, Part IV, in *The Manuscripts of His Grace the Duke of Rutland, G.C.B., Preserved at Belvoir Castle*, 4 vols. (London: HMSO, 1888–1905), Vol. I (1888), p. 287; Lawrence Stone, *The Crisis of the Aristocracy 1558–1641* (Oxford University Press, 1965), pp. 395–6.

[8] *St JPR*, Vol. I (1884), p. 23; Vol. IV (1891), p. 55. Edward Somerset had five sons who lived into manhood: William (who predeceased him); Henry (fifth earl and first marquis of Worcester); Thomas (Viscount Somerset of Cashel in 1626); Sir Charles; Sir Edward.

[9] To clarify further, the Somerset Clerkenwell residence may have been one of several Seckford-related houses in Clerkenwell. It could have been, for example, the residence of Henry Seckford as Master of the Tents and Toils at the Revels Office that is referred to. The marriage of Worcester's son was to Anne Russell and was celebrated on 16 June 1600 (Madge, 'Worcester House in the Strand', p. 161). The ceremony took place at St Martin's, Ludgate with the Queen present, and a picture was painted for the occasion. See Penry Williams, 'Shakespeare's *A Midsummer Night's Dream*: Social Tensions Contained', in *The Theatrical City: Culture, Theatre and Politics in London, 1576–1649*, ed. David L. Smith, Richard Strier and David Bevington (Cambridge University Press, 1995), pp. 55–67 (pp. 58–9).

[10] *Remembrancia*, 9 vols., Vol. II: LMA COL/RMD/PA/01/002, no. 189. See E. K. Chambers and W. W. Greg, eds., *Dramatic Records of the City of London: The Remembrancia*, MSC 1.1 (Oxford: Malone Society, 1907), pp. 43–100, (p. 85); Andrew Gurr, *The Shakespearean Playing Companies* (Oxford: Clarendon Press, 1996), p. 317.

[11] Dulwich College MS 1, fo. 54; Edward Alleyn, *Memoirs of Edward Alleyn*, ed. John Payne Collier (London: Shakespeare Society, 1841), p. 66; *EPT*, p. 414.

manoeuvres were successful in view of the fact of the earl's development as a leading light within emerging court politics – arranging itself around members of the new royal family.

After his carefully planned advances towards the Stuart family from King James' marriage onwards, in July 1603, Worcester was made Earl Marshal for the coronation of King James on the 25th of that month. Evidence shows that the King favoured the previously mentioned pro-Essex circle, which included Penelope Rich neé Devereux, Essex's sister. Her lover, and then husband, Charles Blount, earl of Devonshire was also included in the group.

The Essex circle and their well-placed status at court during King James' reign (alongside the Cecils and the Howards) are not without significance when it comes to Elizabethan contexts for Clerkenwell, the Queen's Servants or the Red Bull, where the acting company came to play. One reason for this is Penelope Rich's lover, Blount, and the particular set of circumstances in which Rich found herself immediately after her brother's rebellion. With Essex's trial and execution in 1601, his sister was implicated in the plot and was put under house arrest at Seckford's house.[12] The earl of Devonshire – Blount – a friend of Essex and father of six of Rich's children, must have seen it as obvious that his familial interests had been forcibly moved to the Clerkenwell area, and we find that by 1602, his servant, Aaron Holland, had become a Clerkenwell resident.[13] He is described as part of Devonshire's retinue in Martin Slatiar's 1605 petition concerning the Red Bull, as the builder of the theatre, and someone who was to go on to profit from the inn site for some years.[14]

The earl of Worcester and the formation of the Queen's Servants company

When Worcester was made Earl Marshal for the coronation of King James in July 1603 at the height of a dreadful plague year, decisions must have been made quickly concerning what to do about the City procession, which was to be postponed to March 1604. He may have felt some sense of pride when it came to those listed to have cloth for the procession, as no

---

[12] TNA PC2/26, fos. 84v and 90v.

[13] In a controlment roll requiring him to appear by the first week of January 1603 he is described as a Clerkenwell inn-holder in relation to an incident of June 1602; TNA KB29/242, m. 25d. Five of the Rich–Blount children survived; previously, with her husband Robert Rich, four had survived.

[14] Petition: Cecil Papers (Hatfield House), MS 197, fo. 91(2), also available on microfilm at the British Library: BL microfilm M485/52/91(2).

longer Worcester's Men, but the 'Officers to the Queene'. He had assured them, by then, a firm standing both within their professional community and the court of which he was a part.[15] Since the letter of 1602, asking the Lord Mayor to let the merged Oxford/Worcester's company play at the Boar's Head, consolidation and status were what Edward Somerset had set out to achieve.[16] The group so listed for the postponed procession, which took place on 15 March 1604, were: 'Christopher Beeston', 'Robert Lee', 'John Duke', 'Robert Palante', 'Thomas Haward', 'James Houlte', 'Thomas Swetherton', 'Thomas Grene' and 'Robert Beeston'.[17]

This procession list was quickly followed by Worcester acting as co-signatory to the order of April 1604 authorising three companies to perform in the London area, with the Queen's Servants at the Curtain.[18] Worcester's pride of 1604 chimes with another document dated, by The National Archives, to an even earlier time. This was a draft patent for the company, and the fragment licenses and authorises:

> Thomas Greene, Christopher Beeston, Thomas hawood, Richard Pyrkins, Robert Pallant John Duke, Thomas Swynerton, James Hoult, Robert Beeston: & Robert Lee: servannts unto our dearest ~~and welbeloved~~ wyfe ^the^ Queene <u>Anna</u>: with the rest of there associates, freely to use and exercise the art and faculty of playinge Comedies, Tragedies, Histories, Enterludes, Morralls, Pastoralls, Stage plaies, and such other lyke as they haue already studied …[19]

It was addressed to 'all Justices ^of peace^ Maiors Sherifes, vicechanncellors ^as of any our unyuersities, Bailiffes^ ~~Constables~~, headboroughes, ~~and other our~~ ^Constables^ ~~officers~~ [marginal insertion:] and to all other our Officers', and allowed the company to play 'publikly, when the infecion of the plague shall decrease to the Number of thirty Weekly'. This decrease should seem to be so 'within ^oure Citie of^ London and the liberties ^therof^ … Aswell within there now usuall howsen, Called the Curtayne, And the Bores head, within our County of Midd*lesex*, ~~or~~ ^as in^ any other

[15] They had already performed before Prince Henry on 2 and 13 January. John Duke was the payee; TNA E351/543, m. 116.
[16] *Remembrancia*, Vol. II.
[17] TNA LC2/4/5, p. 84.
[18] Dulwich College MS 1, fo. 54; *EPT*, p. 414.
[19] TNA SP14/2, fos. 246v–247, in a group dated by The National Archives to between 1 June 1603 and 31 July 1603. However, Richard Perkins, present here, does not appear in the procession list precisely dated to 1604. This draft document should therefore be dated after March 1604, when Perkins must have joined them. This transcription strikes through deletions and puts carets around interlinear additions. See also MSC 1.3 (Oxford: Malone Society, 1909), pp. 260–84 (pp. 265–7); *ES*, Vol. II, pp. 229–30.

playhowse not used by others, by the said ^Thomas^ Greene, elected, or by hym hereafter to be builte'. Any speculation on the dating of this document (which is not physically dated) must centre on the appearance of the name of Thomas Greene in Worcester's Men/Queen's Servants history, as he was never previously an Elizabethan performer with the company (or any other) to the best of our knowledge. Greene also plays a significant role in another document of 1604: that of payee for a sum of money given to 'himselfe and tenne of his Fellowes' as 'groomes of the Chamber'. This was during the negotiations of the Somerset House conference, attempting to achieve peace with Spain, when they attended the 'County Arrenbirgh and the reste of the Com*m*yssioners at Durham Howse' between 9 and 27 August of that year.[20]

Charles de Ligne of Arenberg, a Habsburg, was an important ambassador for Philip III of Spain and took a leading part in the delegation to the conference. Greene seems to have replaced a member of the old Worcester's company who disappears from central playhouse records at this time, and would have acted as clown to the company as Greene came to do – Will Kemp. Thomas Greene became an important figure in relation to the developing history of the Queen's Servants and, indeed, of their playhouse. We can see at this point to what extent – not content with options to play at the Boar's Head and the Curtain in the draft licence – this company was aiming to include another theatre, one that was to be 'elected' by Thomas Greene and one that, in *c.* 1604, was about to be built.

Aaron Holland and Martin Slatiar

Aaron Holland, builder of the Red Bull, was born in 1556.[21] In the year 1589 we know that a man going by his name was living in Gray's Inn Lane, where he was taxed 'iijli vs', a low amount in comparison to those of most of his neighbours for the subsidy roll of October that year.[22] In the churchwardens' accounts for St Mary le Strand for 1600–1 however, while

---

[20] Greene was paid 'xixli xvjs' on behalf of the players; Augustine Philips and John Hemings were paid 'xxjli xijs' for the King's Men. TNA E351/543, m. 113v; David Cook and F. P. Wilson, eds., *Dramatic Records in the Declared Accounts of the Treasurer of the Chamber, 1558–1642*, MSC 6 (Oxford: Malone Society, 1962 [1961]), p. 38.

[21] TNA C24/497 (*Bingham* v. *Bonham*). See Sisson, 'The Red Bull Company', p. 67n.

[22] The subsidy was a tax payment for military activity. Gray's Inn Lane would now be recognised as the Holborn end of Gray's Inn Road, London. TNA E179/269/41; Mark Eccles, *Christopher Marlowe in London* (Cambridge, MA: Harvard University Press, 1934), p. 62; Eccles, 'Elizabethan Actors IV', p. 171.

he was keeping another inn in the Savoy on the Strand, Holland paid 6s
8d towards the parish poor rate – a lower-to-middling amount.[23]

Had Aaron Holland come up in the world? In the petition of *c.* 1605
made by the actor Martin Slatiar, directed to the Privy Council and concerning the building of the Red Bull theatre, Holland was described as a
'servaunt of the right Honorable the Earle of Devonshire'. It may have
been this status, perhaps acquired in the interim between his time at Gray's
Inn and his period at the Savoy, that had resulted in his seeing slightly
better days. A rented residence in the early seventeenth century has been
traced for Charles Blount, eighth Baron Mountjoy and earl of Devonshire,
in Little Salisbury House on the Strand, not far from Holland's inn in
the Savoy.[24] But as we know, Holland was holding the lease of the inn in
Clerkenwell by 1602, where Mountjoy also had possessed interests in view
of its proximity to his one-time detained paramour, Rich.

The Clerkenwell/Strand/Aaron Holland connections do not stop with
these, however. During the time that Holland was working in the Strand
in the later 1590s, we should also remember that Anne Bedingfeild, the
leasehold-owner of the Red Bull site, and her husband Eustace, were also
living there in the parish of St Clement Danes. They may well have been
acquainted with the inn-holder who was to convert the yard of the Red
Bull Inn into the playhouse in the next decade. Anne was thirty-eight in
1598 when Holland is recorded as living in the Strand, and she had been
married to Eustace Bedingfeld for nineteen years.[25]

The petition of the actor, Martin Slatiar to the Privy Council of King
James concerning his alliance with Aaron Holland to convert an inn-yard
to a playhouse – dated to 1605 – has been discussed many times before by
theatre historians.[26] The petition was written in response to an attempt to
stop the building of the playhouse, and one of the references that dates

---

[23] The poor rate was money collected by the parish to aid its poor. Westminster City Archives: St
Mary le Strand Churchwardens' Accounts; William Ingram, 'Playhouses Make Strange Bedfellows:
The Case of Aaron and Martin', *Shakespeare Studies* 30 (2002), 118–27.

[24] Stone, *The Crisis of the Aristocracy*, p. 395. See also Griffith, 'Martin Slatiar and the Red Bull
Playhouse', pp. 560–1.

[25] The burial brass in the chancel of All Saints, Darsham, puts her death precisely at 29 March 1641,
'BEING OF AGE 80 YEAES & 7 MONTHES' (Suckling, *History and Antiquities*, Vol. II, after
p. 224); see also Eva Griffith, 'Bedingfeild [*née* Draper], Anne (1560–1641), *theatre landlord and
benefactor*', *Oxford Dictionary of National Biography*, www.oxforddnb.com/view/article/74436,
accessed 18 April 2013. For the marriage licence, see Joseph Foster, ed., *London Marriage Licences
1529–1869* (London: Bernard Quaritch, 1887), p. 115. The licence is dated 4 June 1579.

[26] For example, Leeds Barroll, 'Defining "Dramatic Documents"', *Medieval and Renaissance Drama
in England* 9 (1997), 112–26; Ingram, 'Playhouses Make Strange Bedfellows'; Herbert Berry,
'Building Playhouses, the Accession of James I, and the Red Bull', *Medieval and Renaissance Drama
in England* 18 (2005), 61–74; Griffith, 'Martin Slatiar and the Red Bull Playhouse'.

the petition is to Ulrik, duke of Holstein, who, Slatiar claimed, wanted a group of actors who needed the playhouse. Holstein was the brother of Queen Anna, the patron of the Queen's Servants. He felt he had to leave England in May 1605 owing to a number of faux pas he had made during his stay. This is what dates the petition and all that the text implies. We know Aaron Holland held the tenure of a Clerkenwell inn by 1602 – presumably the Red Bull – because of the data contained in a controlment roll of that year. We also know that it was Anne Bedingfeild who gave Holland the lease sometime by this year from a 1619 bill for a case where a plaintiff, Thomas Woodford, described the arrangement between them.[27] In later documents we hear that one 'John Waintworth' was also associated with the inn as well as other parts of the estate, and one John Attree is also mentioned in papers.[28] It would seem that responsibility for the inn shifted between many people, but both Aaron Holland and Anne Bedingfeild remained a constant throughout.

In the petition, Slatiar describes himself as 'one of her Maiesties servaunts', the status of which may be proved by a court case of 1607, where he is shown to have been a sworn member by December 1604. Given that the March 1604 list of Queen's Servants who were given cloth for the celebratory procession of that year did not include Slatiar, and the draft patent dated to approximately that year did not include him either, we can speculate that he joined the company in about August 1604, because both lists name ten men including Thomas Greene, whereas the payments for the company's involvement in the Somerset House conference were made to Thomas Greene plus ten of his fellows, equalling eleven men. Slatiar, therefore, is likely to have been the eleventh. With reference to the playhouse and the petition, he described converting 'some stables and other roomes, beinge before a square Court in an Inne' to house Holstein's men. Moreover, he, together with Holland, with whom he held the lease of the 'howse' associated with the converted space, had already sought the Privy Council's approval for the conversion.

Who were the duke of Holstein's men supposed to be? Something of the answer to this question may be given in Chapter 5 of this book, where

---

[27] TNA REQ2/411, Box 2, 149, now mostly unreadable. See Wallace, 'Three London Theatres of Shakespeare's Time', p. 303.

[28] John 'Wentworth' or 'Waintworth': TNA C3/390/47 (1623 bill); SROI FC25/L3/3/8, pp. 14–15 (1630s document of events of 1601). Attree: TNA C24/500/9, Robert Leigh's answers, Int. 31. Here Leigh mentions Attree as 'part owner of the *said* play howse called The red Bull'. On 14 February 1627, a William Beeston is recorded as having been given permission to sue Sir John Wentworth. There is no current evidence that this Beeston was the actor or that this involved a dispute over the Red Bull, however.

we contemplate the European version of the Queen's Servants company under John Green, Thomas Greene's likely brother. In whatever way the situation developed, the theatre that Slatiar and Holland were building in 1605 became the Red Bull playhouse of Queen's Servants fame, not the playhouse of a company given patronage by a disgraced foreign duke.

From the text of the petition we understand that they had leased a 'howse' with 'stables and other roomes' set around a 'square Court'. It was these stables that they had changed – or 'framed and sett vp' for theatre galleries – before the stoppage. Holland held the entire inn complex or, in his words from legal documents, 'the said messuage or tenement nowe comonlie called or knowne by the name or signe of the Redd Bull ... with the courts gardens Cellars wayes and libertyes thervnto belonginge'.[29] It was 'to his great charge and expences' that he did 'erect & sett vpp in and vpon *parte* [my italics] of the said premises divers buildinges and Galleryes for a Play howse'.

There are all sorts of ways of understanding why Slatiar, so much maligned by the company when they took him to court in 1607, was a good person to have among them in 1604. In 1596, he was involved with Edward Alleyn and the Admiral's Men, paid for performances at court in that year.[30] By 1599, he was performing with Lawrence Fletcher before the royal family in Scotland and may well have met Ulrik, duke of Holstein at that time if he had been in Edinburgh the year before.[31] Before his petition of 1605, he was involved in many activities, most significantly as a payee for the Earl of Hertford's Men at the beginning of 1603.[32] This is an important factor as we consider the circle set around Anna into the next reign, which included the countess of Hertford as one of two Ladies of the Queen's Bedchamber. It could be that Martin Slatiar was a significant signing to the Queen's Servants in the context of the new group of women gathering around Queen Anna, including Hertford.

---

[29] TNA C3/390/47; Hotson, 'Holland's Answer', in *The Commonwealth and Restoration Stage*, Appendix I, *Woodford* v. *Holland*, pp. 327–47 (p. 336).

[30] TNA E351/543, m. 12b; Cook and Wilson, *Dramatic Records*, p. 29; *ES*, Vol. IV, p. 165; Eccles, 'Elizabethan Actors IV', p. 169.

[31] Historical Manuscripts Commission, *Calendar of the Manuscripts of the Most Honourable The Marquess of Salisbury Preserved at Hatfield House Hertfordshire*, ed. S. R. Scargill Bird, R. A. Roberts, E. Salisbury, M. S. Giuseppi and G. D. Owen, 24 vols. (London: HMSO, 1883–1976), Vol. VIII (1938), p. 43; *ES*, Vol. II, pp. 269–70; Ethel Carleton Williams, *Anne of Denmark* (Harlow: Longmans, 1970), p. 60; Eccles, 'Elizabethan Actors IV', p. 170.

[32] TNA E351/543, m. 95b; Cook and Wilson, *Dramatic Records*, p. 37; *ES*, Vol. IV, p. 167; Eccles, 'Elizabethan Actors IV', p. 169

Slatiar was also a citizen and a member of the Ironmongers' Company, active among them from Guildhall records.[33] He was also associated with Philip Henslowe, from whom he borrowed £5 in July 1604, shortly before the start of his Queen's Servants involvement.[34] He was obviously a confident man endowed with experience and many contacts. It is quite likely that Slatiar – who both knew the Stuart court in Scotland before it came to England and knew members of the new Queen's English circle prior to this time – was the player who was given the job of choosing a company for the Queen's brother. It is equally possible that, with the loss of favour towards Duke Ulrik, the theatre was redirected towards the actors who were intending to embark on another theatre venture anyway – the Queen's Servants themselves. Favoured on the Privy Council at the time was Worcester, who had been himself living on or adjacent to the Seckford Estate where the theatre was built, and who undoubtedly knew of his old company's desire for their own theatre. Aaron Holland's patron, Charles Blount, earl of Devonshire, also had experience of the Clerkenwell area. All kinds of interests and associations converged to create a situation whereby the new theatre for the Queen's Servants could have been refashioned out of a somewhat dubious plan for a company/playhouse for the duke of Holstein.

The theatre must have been finished by late March 1606. We know this because a share of the playhouse was sold to a Queen's Servants actor called Thomas Swinnerton by this time.[35] The share was an 'eighteenth part' of profits from the galleries and stage for which Swinnerton paid £25.[36] Crucially, in the *Woodford* v. *Holland* court case whence this information is derived, Holland said that Swinnerton gained his lease in 1605–6, *after* the event of 'having erected and made' the 'buildinges and galleryes' that formed the Red Bull playhouse. This would accord with what Slatiar claimed by the middle of 1605 – that it was all but finished.[37] We do not know when in 1605–6 Swinnerton's lease began, nor how long it was for or when it was to end. What we can glean from this share information is

---

[33] See, for instance, LMA COL/CC/01/01/027, fo.143v (LMA microfilm X109/67) [CLRO Journal (of the Court of Common Council), 26]; Eccles, 'Elizabethan Actors IV', p. 170, where he is shown to be party to a bond in support of a dead man's son.

[34] He needed money from Henslowe, possibly associated with a sojourn in prison at this time. See LMA MJ/SR/0416, 55; Eccles, 'Elizabethan Actors IV', p. 170. See also Griffith, 'Martin Slatiar', p. 558.

[35] King James acceded to the throne when Elizabeth I died (24 March 1603). The relevant text refers to the 'regnal year' which began on 24 March 1605 and ended a year later on 23 March 1606. See C.R. Cheney, ed., *A Handbook of Dates for Students of British History*, 2nd edn, rev. Michael Jones (Cambridge University Press, 2000).

[36] A summary of the share-selling situation may be found in *EPT*, p. 565.

[37] TNA C3/390/47; Hotson, 'Holland's Answer', pp. 336–7.

that the duration of the same share, once bought by one Philip Stone in February 1609, was for twenty-five years and three-quarters of a year from the Christmas before the date of his indenture. This would have taken him up to Michaelmas 1634, and there are various pieces of evidence to show that the whole leasehold structure of this part of the estate entered a hiatus period during the mid 1630s.[38]

March 1606 was a month that could be said to be important to the company for another reason, for on the 7th of that month Queen Anna quite possibly put her hand to a warrant allowing 'Robert Lee, Martin Slatier, Roger Barfield with theyr fellowes and associates' to 'travell' throughout the King's dominions in order to play. Although we only have this warrant copied out in the archives of Southampton, intriguingly the document also said they could perform in the City of London, apparently side-stepping edicts forcing companies into the suburbs. However, given that Slatiar and Swinnerton in particular were to find themselves in difficulties while touring using copies of Queen's Servants patents, and that Slatiar himself was taken to court in 1607 for performing without enough of the other actors, the evidence of this copied-out warrant could remain questionable.[39]

Further evidence of Holland's residence in the Clerkenwell area prior to 1605 comes in the shape of his attendance at St James', Clerkenwell vestry meetings. He first appends his name to such a meeting convened to disadmit a preacher called Johnson on 29 June 1604. Given that it would take time for a new man in the area to demonstrate his means enough to allow community acceptance as a vestryman, Holland's signature, in initial form (he always signed his name this way, indicating illiteracy as other court cases confirm) would help us gain a sense of his arrival some years before this date. He would go on to attend or to be mentioned at vestry until 1629, either listed as taking up duties or putting his name as attending thirteen times. The vestry attendance signed in 1604 also included the signature of Thomas Bedingfeld at the top of the list.[40]

[38] One of Anne Bedingfeild's durations of lease ended at this time, and from what we know of Thomas Greene's half of the tiring house from 25 December 1606, his rights to this finished on Christmas Eve 1633.

[39] The warrant, from the Southampton *Book of Remembrances*, is quoted in *ES*, Vol. II, pp. 234–5. A modern English transcription is printed in 'The Manuscripts of the Corporations of Southampton and King's Lynn', *Report of the Historical Manuscripts Commission* 11 (1887), appendix, Part III, p. 26. For Slatiar's company troubles, see Griffith, 'Martin Slatiar', pp. 561–2.

[40] Islington Local History Centre, St James' Parish Vestry Book, 1590–1683.

New playhouse-ownership: Thomas Greene and Christopher Beeston

So Martin Slatiar, with his maverick association with the Queen's Servants – not included in the procession list or draft patent, both of 1604; a sworn member by 1605 according to the petition; taken to court by the company during 1607 – *may* have owned half the house associated with the Red Bull yard in 1605. However, half of the tiring house and yard belonged to an altogether different figure among the Queen's Servants by the beginning of 1607.

From a set of recently rediscovered 1632 Court of Requests proceedings moved by Susan Baskervile against Christopher Beeston, we know that both she and her deceased husband, the clown of the company, Thomas Greene, possessed half the tiring house and yard from Aaron Holland. This ownership was acquired from an indenture of lease agreed with Holland on 23 December 1606, and it was to last from Christmas Day 1606 to Christmas Eve 1633. They were also entitled to 'certaine Roomes being *pa*rte or *pa*rcell of the Messuage and Tenement … called or knowne by the name of the signe of the Red Bull then or late in the tenure and occupation of the saide Aron Holland or of his assignes'. In other words, in 1607, they were in possession of rooms that had belonged to Holland on the inn site itself, as well as a large part of the playhouse – probably, in some way, buying out Slatiar.

Apart from the fact of Greene and Baskervile's playhouse share-ownership, the *Baskervile* v. *Beeston* case also informs us that in August 1607, Thomas Greene concluded an agreement with Christopher Beeston for an eighth- or ninth-part share of Greene's half of the tiring house and yard. Christopher Beeston is not only an important figure for Queen's Servants history, but he is increasingly recognised as important to the development of British theatre as a whole. His career spanned a period that involved acting, as a young man, with the Chamberlain's Men (alongside Shakespeare); building, after the Blackfriars, a second indoor public playhouse for London, the Cockpit; and becoming a more recognisably entrepreneurial figure in the Caroline period as he developed and expanded his powers as owner and manager. The most important thing to recognise about Beeston from a wider, British theatre history perspective, however, is that the Cockpit, renamed the Phoenix when it had to be rebuilt after a riot, was the first theatre in the Drury Lane area of London. The success of the Cockpit marks the beginning, indeed, of what we now call 'West End' theatre, and converges with everything we are learning about the expansion to the west of London that was happening at the time.

Despite how we may immediately interpret Beeston's entrepreneurial ways, the fact that Beeston held on to his open-air public playhouse share in the Red Bull until at least 1632 (he would have been entitled to it, we imagine, until 1633) is significant. This long-term ownership means that Beeston continued his involvement with the Clerkenwell playhouse and therefore the Queen's Servants/Revels company for a long time after either his separation from the company around Christmas 1618, or the important *Worth* v. *Baskervile* case of 1623.[41] This fact was never understood until relatively recently.[42] It has always been believed previously that after he commandeered the Cockpit in 1617, the break with his old company was final and irrevocable. This and other evidence would indicate that the opposite was true, and that he had an investment in this company's future over a longer period than was originally thought.

In many ways this chapter has brought to our attention all that was threaded through the company's history from before Elizabeth I died into the new Stuart age for playhouse drama. In doing this it has set the scene for us to look at the company itself through a similar period. In effect the easily defined nobility, the bigger personalities of the playhouse and obvious gentry influences are left behind as contexts as we look at the roots of the Queen's Servants themselves, approaching their brand new playhouse. In doing this we try our best to recreate the Elizabethan Worcester's Men as they became their Jacobean counterparts, ready to engage with audiences at the Red Bull theatre.

---

[41] Hotson, *The Commonwealth and Restoration Stage*, pp. 83–4, 327.
[42] See Griffith, 'Christopher Beeston', pp. 619–20.

CHAPTER 3

Who were the Queen's Servants? What was the Red Bull like?

This book has begun to talk about some of the main 'players' of the company both in the performance sense and in the business sense – the seemingly central clown, Greene; the entrepreneurial actor, Beeston; and the ubiquitous Martin Slatiar. The best possible contexts for this company can now be given as we start to imagine their new theatre, beginning with an investigation into their earlier development as a group of players. This account will be given within the context of one play associated with three of the company's theatres. The play in question, Heywood's *Foure Prentises of London* (London, 1615), had a particular audience appeal that was apportioned to this company, and this appeal is traceable from the period of its Elizabethan, known and original performance period onwards. It was a drama freely acknowledged as a long-term winner for early modern London audiences, beginning as a Heywood play some time before it entered the Queen's Servants' repertoire.

The Earl of Worcester's Men are difficult to recreate completely. So much is not known of how actors moved among companies – only that they could and did move.[1] Many of the probable members during the period before the change in reigns may be construed from records such as the Jacobean procession list for 1604. However, because of the amalgamation of 1602, we do not know which actors listed were originally from the earl of Oxford's company, and which were Worcester's Men before this time. Indeed, we may be dealing with shifting sands, as the impetus to bring them together may have been more to do with persuading the City to accept new companies and outlets for drama than about formalising a united troupe.[2] The personalities that were in place to form the Jacobean

---

[1] There are many examples of this pre-1603 which are discussed – less so for actors into the Stuart era. Thomas Basse spoke of William Rowley, John Newton, Thomas Hobbs, 'Hamlett' (probably Robert Hamlen), Mathew Smith, Anthony Smith and Richard Baxter moving into the Red Bull company after 1617. See TNA C24/500/9, Int. 40; Griffith, 'Christopher Beeston', p. 619.

[2] *Remembrancia*, Vol. II; LMA COL/RMD/PA/01/002, no. 189.

company included the famed clown, Will Kemp, as well as John Lowin, Christopher Beeston, Robert Pallant, John Duke, Thomas Heywood, Robert Leigh and Richard Perkins. This part of the chapter will briefly put in place the main members of the company during Oxford's/Worcester's Men's time at the Boar's Head and the Rose (from 1601 to 1604).[3]

The undoubted leader of the company at the earlier time must have been Will Kemp, the one-time clown of the Chamberlain's Men, who can be shown to have joined Worcester's company after September 1601. This was when he returned from one of a number of trips abroad.[4] His trips may have prompted the company to think of touring abroad too, and Chapter 5 explores the Queen's Servants' touring. While with the Chamberlain's Men, Kemp may have played such parts as Peter in *Romeo and Juliet* and Dogberry in *Much Ado about Nothing*.[5] One can only guess under what conditions he left the company that was to become the King's Men, turning down his chance to access playhouse profits at the Globe. Kemp, John Duke and Thomas Heywood are the only actors who we can be certain were Worcester's Men before the company's amalgamation with the earl of Oxford's company. In the Christmas period 1601/2 Kemp and Heywood were both payees for the company for performances at court.[6] Duke is known to have been involved in court proceedings moved by Robert Browne of the Boar's Head against the company in 1601, and therefore his allegiance to Worcester is assumed for that time.[7] However, he was a Chamberlain's Man with Christopher Beeston and Will Kemp at

---

[3] Alan Nelson, in his book on the Earl of Oxford, identifies Thomas Greene, James Holt, John Lowin, Robert Pallant, Richard Perkins and Thomas Swinnerton as actors who 'cannot be traced to companies active before 1601, and may have belonged to Oxford's Men – but there is no proof' (*Monstrous Adversary*, p. 392). Richard Perkins is now known to have started as a child actor with Henslowe's company. See David Mateer, 'Edward Alleyn, Richard Perkins and the Rivalry between the Swan and Rose Playhouses', *Review of English Studies* 60 (2007), 64–77. 'R Pallant' was mentioned in the 'Platt' of 'The Secound parte of the Seuen Deadlie Sinns' along with 'Jo Duke', but there is much scholarly debate about the company who performed this. See Tarnya Cooper, *Searching for Shakespeare* (London: National Portrait Gallery, 2006), pp. 102–3, who believes it was a Henslowe enterprise play of *c.* 1592; and David Kathman's arguments for it as a later Chamberlain's Men play in 'Reconsidering *The Seven Deadly Sins*', *Early Theatre* 7.1 (2004), 13–44, and '*The Seven Deadly Sins* and Theatrical Apprenticeship', *Early Theatre* 14.1 (2011), 121–39.

[4] Martin Butler, 'Kemp, William (*d.* in or after 1610?)', *Oxford Dictionary of National Biography*, www. oxforddnb.com/view/article/15334, accessed 16 April 2012. For a trip in 1586 there is evidence that Kemp performed for the Danish court of Queen Anna's father, Frederick II. In 1601 it is believed he visited Germany and Italy.

[5] Andrew Gurr, *The Shakespearean Stage 1574–1642*, 3rd edn (Cambridge University Press, 1992), p. 89.

[6] TNA E351/543, m. 83; MSC 6, p. 33.

[7] *EPT*, pp. 479–80.

a period immediately before this, as all three actors were in Ben Jonson's cast list for *Every Man in His Humour*, performed in the late 1590s.

From late summer 1601 to late summer 1602 – the period when Kemp must have joined them – Worcester's Men were performing at the Whitechapel theatre, the Boar's Head.[8] By Michaelmas 1601, however, Robert Browne, the lessee of the theatre, was suing the company for defaulting on their payments to him as actor-manager there, and, subsequently, the amalgamated company of the following year moved to Henslowe's Rose.

Thomas Heywood, actor and City dramatist

Thomas Heywood, who belonged to this company before the amalgamation, was the chief playwright of the troupe at this time and was to remain so into their Jacobean Queen's Servants period. In the case of Heywood, there is no evidence of a professional contractual arrangement with the company, as in the case of Richard Brome, for instance.[9] This was because, just like Shakespeare, Heywood was an actor-sharer who accessed profits through returns – not with any independent payment, as far as is known. He needed no separate arrangement. This can be proved not just with his naming on the licences of 1604 and 1609, or with his language of 'friends and fellows', or with his *Apology for Actors* all about his profession published in 1612, but with the *Worth* v. *Baskervile* case of 1623. In this case Heywood admitted to being a party to a company agreement with the Baskeriles in 1617 over financial arrangements needing bonds and incurring debts, and if he had been in possession of a separate, independent arrangement with the company, it is doubtful he would have had to do this.[10] Having stated this, it may well be the case that Heywood was put under certain constraints when it came to, for example, presenting plays he had written for other companies at other places once he became a Queen's Servant at the Red Bull. He would have had to be careful about publishing his plays at a moment that hurt no other company,

---

[8] Herbert Berry, *The Boar's Head Playhouse* (Washington, DC: Folger Library, 1986), pp. 51, 124, 192.

[9] G. E. Bentley uses the term 'ordinary poet', extrapolating data from Brome's contract in his published paper, 'The Profession of Dramatist in Shakespeare's Time', *Proceedings of the American Philosophical Society* 115.6 (30 December 1971), 480–3. For extracts of Richard Brome's contract at the Salisbury Court playhouse (TNA REQ2/662, Box 1 and TNA REQ2/723), see *EPT*, pp. 657–64.

[10] TNA C24/500/9, e.g. Ints. 12, 19, 24 about other agreements, but especially no. 25 where evidence of Heywood's involvement was produced in court. William Winstanley wrote in his book on writers that Heywood was said to have 'acted himself almost every day'. See Winstanley, *Lives of the Most Famous English Poets* (London, 1687), p. 96.

for instance. A play like the first part of *If You Know Not Me You Know Nobody*, published in 1605 soon after the first production, complete with intricate woodcut picture of Elizabeth on its title-page, must have been a highly saleable item and should have helped to promote further performances. It does not possess a playhouse or company ascription, however, perhaps because of moves from one outfit or playhouse to another. Similarly, although stretching over a much longer period of time, with *The Foure Prentises of London*, published in 1615, evidence from Heywood himself suggests that this was a play originally performed 'fifteene or sixteene yeares agoe [when] it was in the fashion' – outside his time as a Worcester's Man or a Queen's Servant therefore – probably dating it to an original period he spent at Henslowe's Rose.[11] The title-page of the 1615 publication also possesses an intricate woodcut that is, again, of high quality, together with a firm playhouse/company ascription: 'As it hath bene diuerse times Acted, at the Red bull, by the Queenes Maiesties Seruants'. It also possesses an epistle to its intended purchaser: 'To the honest and hie-spirited Prentises The Readers'.

The sense of the affinity between Heywood, the company and the citizenry is confirmed by satirical responses to these plays in Francis Beaumont's *The Knight of the Burning Pestle*.[12] Many known or assumed Heywood/Derby's/Worcester's/Queen's Servants plays are put into a citizen context in this Children of the Queen's Revels play. These include the lost drama, *The Bold Beauchamps* (Induction, 53), and the provable Heywood plays specifically alluded to in *The Knight* include *If You Know Not Me You Know Nobody*, Part II (Induction,19); *Edward IV* (Induction, 51); *The Foure Prentises of London* (IV.49); and *The Rape of Lucrece* (II, Interlude, 2.14). Beaumont's play was a satire on the citizenry, and as such certainly poked fun with these works, at least three of them Queen's Servants plays. He was, in fact, rewarded with an abject rejection on a first performance of *The Knight*, recorded in the preliminaries of the publication.

In *The Knight*, a citizen Grocer called George has taken his wife and apprentice to see a play at an indoor theatre. Unfortunately for the actors, they set about changing the plot with reference to their favourite parts of other plays – dramas that make reference to the City and its people. In the relevant scene, George is informing a boy-player that it is perfectly possible for a grocer's apprentice to court a king's daughter:

---

[11] Heywood, 'To the honest and hie-spirited Prentises The Readers', A2v.
[12] See Francis Beaumont, *The Knight of the Burning Pestle*, ed. Michael Hattaway (New York: Norton, 1995). References to scenes in this play will be made in brackets with the aid of this edition.

CITIZEN ... I pray you, what was Sir Dagonet? Was not he prentice to a grocer in London? Read the play of The Four Prentices of London, where they toss their pikes so. I pray you, fetch him in, sir, fetch him in.

(IV.49)

It is clear, for this 1613-published play, dated to 1607 through internal, further Queen's Servants-related references, that the character, George, has seen a production of *The Foure Prentises*, which may – in fact – have been first produced as far back as 1594. This was the year when a drama Henslowe noted in his accounts as '2 p*artes* of godfrey of bullen' was entered in the Stationers' Register. Godfrey of Bouillon or Boulogne was the subject of Heywood's play.[13] George's adjuration to 'Read' the play would be problematic in both 1607 and 1613, as *The Foure Prentises* had not yet been published as far as can be proved, and this is perhaps a note to the actor playing George that the character thinks, rather than knows, it must be published. With reference to this it is again interesting that when it *was* published in 1615, the wood engraver of the title-page chose to show the story's apprentices in action, just as George described, with their pikestaffs.[14] The seventeenth-century children's companies produced many types of plays, usually recognised as more satirically bent than most when humorous, with satire on the citizens predominating as the most memorable comic plays they presented. Heywood was to hint at something of his frustration concerning the use of young people acting in drama in this way, particularly when the plays they performed directed their venom at living people: 'The liberty which some arrogate to themselues, committing their bitternesse, and liberall inuectiues against all estates, to the

---

[13] See Philip Henslowe, *Henslowe's Diary*, ed. R. A. Foakes and R. T. Rickert (Cambridge University Press, 1961), pp. 22, 23, 24, 25; Stationers' Register, 19 June 1594. John Danter 'Entred for his Copie vnder th[e h]ande of master Cawood an enterlude entituled *GODFREY OF BULLOIGNE with the Conquest of Jerusalem*'. Along with another interlude the cost was 12d. Edward Arber, ed., *Transcript of the Registers of the Company of Stationers 1554–1640*, 5 vols. (London, 1875–94), Vol. II (1877), fo. 309v.

[14] There were four lances bought at the time Worcester's Men were at the Rose (Henslowe, *Henslowe's Diary*, ed. Foakes and Rickert, p. 215). If the reference alludes to *The Foure Prentises*, the entry concerns a 'comody' that is a 'mr smythes' as well as Heywood's. Another Red Bull play, *The Hector of Germany*, was authored by a 'W. Smith', and was published in 1615 too. This play was not written for the Queen's Servants, however, but 'a Companie of Young men of this Citie', who performed it (he stated) at both the Curtain and the Red Bull. Until recently it was believed that both Smiths were Wentworth Smith, writer of several Henslowe-associated plays. However, Dave Kathman has divided the two W. Smiths, identifying the author of *The Hector of Germany* as a herald called William Smith. See David Kathman, 'Smith, Wentworth (*bap.* 1571)', *Oxford Dictionary of National Biography*, www.oxforddnb.com/view/article/25919, accessed 20 January 2008. Heywood and Wentworth Smith were paid on 4 September 1602 for 'albe[t/l]re galles', thought to be *No-body and Some-body*, and were also paid together, along with Chettle, Dekker and Webster, 'in earneste of a playe called Ladey Jane'. See Henslowe, *Henslowe's Diary*, ed. Foakes and Rickert, pp. 215, 218.

mouthes of Children, supposing their iuniority to be a priuiledge for any
rayling, be it neuer so violent, I could aduise all such, to curbe and limit
this presumed liberty within the bands of discretion and gouernment.'[15]
The Foure Prentises certainly contains no topical reference to any living
person known of, only to City ideals. This was particularly present, it may
be believed, in order to quell any cross-status difficulty that might have
existed in London in its time.

REPERTOIRE 2   *THE FOURE PRENTISES OF*
LONDON AND THE QUEEN'S SERVANTS'
CIVIC COHESIVENESS

Heywood's address prefacing the published play of 1615 was, as we have
seen, made directly to the 'hie-spirited Prentises The Readers', indicating a clear citizen bias, just as portrayed in *The Knight of the Burning
Pestle*, when it came to an intended readership. The troubling topic of
having dual status – of being both a gentleman and a citizen in the context of the City – is addressed from the beginning of the play, however,
and this status tension can be traced as a topic in later Queen's Servants
plays.

The opening scenes show four brothers – Godfrey, Guy, Charles and
Eustace – joining the crusades under Robert of Normandy. They are
London apprentices, each working for a different livery company – four
of 'the twelve great' companies: Godfrey for the Mercers, Guy for the
Goldsmiths, Charles for the Haberdashers and Eustace for the Grocers.[16]
Before we see them, the apprentices' father, the earl of Boulogne, explains
to his daughter, Bella Franca, how the family's situation has been brought
about. In the past, while the earl had been aiding the exploits of William
the Conqueror, the King of France had seized Boulogne's lands, giving
them to someone else. Norman William was too busy keeping his own
lands to protect anyone else's kingdom – hence, according to Boulogne,
with the loss of his domain:

---

[15] Thomas Heywood, *An Apology for Actors* (London, 1612), G3v.
[16] The twelve 'great' companies were the Grocers, Mercers, Fishmongers, Drapers, Goldsmiths,
Skinners, Vintners, Ironmongers, Merchant Taylors, Haberdashers, Salters and Clothmakers.
These guilds were to dominate the Court of Aldermen, the elite body that controlled the 'muni-
cipal authority' overall. See Frank Freeman Foster, *The Politics of Stability: A Portrait of the Rulers
in Elizabethan London* (London: Royal Historical Society, 1977), p. 44. The title-page of the play,
shown in the Introduction to this book, shows the arms of the four companies to which the noble
apprentices belonged.

> And I am forc't to loose the name of Earle,
> And live in *London* like a Cittizen.[17]

In early modern London, to be both a gentleman and a citizen was to carry a kind of stigma perceived by both of your in-bred communities, and this was expressed in other early modern plays. In Thomas Dekker's *The Shoemakers Holiday* (London, 1599), an Admiral's Men/Rose play, the character Hammon becomes an object of moral ineptitude and derision because of his dual status, and Quicksilver in Ben Jonson's *Eastward Ho!* is full of scorn for the tradesman's life he and his fellow gentleman apprentice, Golding, have been forced to enter.[18] Fired up by the boredom of doing whatever their master, Touchstone, tells them, Quicksilver attempts to bring the virtuous Golding into the life of a gallant: 'We are both gentlemen, and therefore should be no coxcombs; let's be no longer fools to this flat-cap Touchstone.'[19] The intricacies of the problem in the real world are perhaps best exemplified in a work of 1629 by a friend of Ben Jonson, Edmund Bolton, called *The Cities Advocate*, subtitled *Whether Apprentiship extinguisheth Gentry*. Bolton's work as a whole is a refutation of the gentry anxiety that becoming a citizen puts a man's gentle status at risk. A letter is included at the beginning of the tract from a gentry-born citizen who had worked an apprenticeship. He is concerned for his son, his eldest, who therefore could claim his citizenship through patrimony. To some extent it would appear that his son has been bullied concerning his citizen status by fellow gentlemen youths of the City:

> *He hath beene disgraced as no Gentleman-borne, when yet not hee but I his Father was the Apprentise, thankes be to God for it. They cannot object to him want of fashion, they cannot object to him the common vices, badges rather of reprobates then of Gentlemen: They cannot object to him cowardise for it is well knowne that he dares defend himselfe: nor any thing else unworthy of his name, which is neither new, nor ignoble: But mee his poore father they object unto him, because I was once an Apprentise.*[20]

These gentry-citizen concerns, bound up with fears of a blurring of one estate with another, have never been made central to critical perceptions of *The Foure Prentises* in the past, but once aware of how important the social problem became for the citizenry, it becomes apparent that Heywood's

---

[17] Heywood, *The Four Prentises*, B1v.
[18] Ben Jonson, George Chapman and John Marston, *Eastward Ho!*, ed. C. G. Petter (London: Black; New York: Norton, 1994).
[19] *Ibid.*, I.i.108.
[20] Edmund Bolton, *The Cities Advocate: Whether Apprentiship extinguisheth Gentry* (London, 1629), K1r.

play not only presents it, but puts across the social mix in a determinedly
positive way. Boulogne's apprenticed sons are all 'high borne', yet, as he
proudly tells Bella Franca, 'of the Citty-trades they have no scorne'. He,
determined to go to Jerusalem, describes how he has left things.

> And hauing plac't my sonnes in such a sort,
> The little wealth I haue left, I leaue to thee:
> My selfe will trauaile to the holy Land;
> And ere I lie within the earths vaste wombe,
> Pay my deuoute vowes at my Sauiours Tombe.[21]

Before he goes he wants to bless them. They enter 'like Apprentices', and
when they speak to their father they each describe their situations in terms
that not only convey their individual character, but encapsulate the way in
which they view their status. Godfrey, the eldest, is representative of the
response to the father when he asks them how they can 'brooke to be as
thou art now?', meaning how do they view their bound apprenticeship,
which was usually for the duration of seven years.

> GODF. Bound must obey: since I haue vndertooke
> To serue my Maister truly for seuen yeares,
> My duty shall both answere that desire,
> And my old Maisters profite euery way.
> I praise that Citty which made Princes Trades-men:
> Where that man, noble or ignoble borne,
> That would not practise some mechanicke skill,
> Which might support his state in penury,
> Should die the death; not sufferd like a drone,
> To sucke the hony from the publicke Hiue.
> I hold it no disparage to my birth,
> Though I be borne an Earle, to have the skill
> And the full knowledge of the *Mercers* Trade.
> And were I now to be create a new,
> It should not grieue me to haue spent my time
> The secrets of so rich a Trade to know,
> By which aduantage and much profites grow.[22]

City pride is central to the energy behind an audience sympathy for
this play; and it was obviously something the company was proud to see
printed as its own. There is a great deal that could be said regarding the
intended civic cohesiveness about *The Foure Prentises*, the subtlety with

---

[21] Heywood, *The Foure Prentises*, B1v.
[22] *Ibid.*, B2.

which this is put across and how much it may have attempted to contribute to the calming of a perceived social problem. As the company's repertoire life continued, this kind of motif can be seen to have been repeated and with growing confidence, particularly with the instance of *Greene's Tu Quoque; or, The Cittie Gallant* by 'Jo: Cooke' (London, 1614). This is a play interested in the specific social mobility issue of when a servant suddenly becomes a gentleman, swapping places with his hard-up master, and deriving laughter thereby.

The company at the Rose, 1602–1603

When the company fled from the troubles at the Boar's Head to come to the Rose, Henslowe made them welcome with a celebratory supper at the Mermaid Tavern in August 1602, noted in his accounts.[23] Costume and props arrangements were soon under way, including the procurement of 'tafetie & other stuffe to macke ij wemens gownes' and 'buckram to macke a payer of gyente hosse'. Also noted were 'a clocke of chamlett lined wth crymsen tafetie pinked' and 'a sewte for wm kempe'. Four lances were also bought, possibly for *The Foure Prentises*.

The core members of the company at the Rose recorded in Henslowe's accounts include Will Kemp, Christopher Beeston, John Duke, Thomas Heywood, Richard Perkins and Robert Pallant. Those that are among the core member lists from 1603 onwards but are not mentioned in Henslowe's accounts include Thomas Swinnerton, James Hoult, Robert Leigh and Robert Beeston (reputedly related to Christopher). E. K. Chambers noted that there were names recorded in Henslowe's accounts that were not present on later documents, which might help to indicate the particular makeup of the company at this earlier time. These include John Thayer, John Lowin, 'Catanes' and a tireman.[24]

Although Chambers mentions John Thayer as someone appearing in Henslowe's records who was not a later 'core member', Thayer actually became a half-sharer of the Queen's Servants during the period 1608–9, dying in 1612. We know this from evidence given in the *Worth* v. *Baskervile* case of 1623.[25]

---

[23] Henslowe opened the account with them on 17 August; the supper was accounted for on the 21st. It cost 9 shillings. Henslowe, *Henslowe's Diary*, ed. Foakes and Rickert, pp. 213, 214.

[24] *ES*, Vol. II, p. 226. In the *Smith* v. *Beeston* case of 1619, a Merchant Taylor called William Freshwater gave evidence, describing himself as a 'workman' for the company. He had been working for them since at least 1612 and is mentioned in Henslowe's records. He could also be the 'tireman' suggested here.

[25] TNA C24/500/103, Thomas Heywood and Richard Perkins' evidence.

Thayer also comes into the story of the European version of the company, told in Chapter 5. The name of John Lowin evokes the very strongest of associations with the King's Men, as he was to become the longest-serving actor among them. This was after he left the Worcester's Men/Queen's Servants with the change in reigns. The son of a currier, he was apprenticed to a goldsmith from Christmas 1593; however, some time before 1602 he became an actor and went on to be remembered as a fine Volpone and Falstaff, and the original Bosola in Webster's *The Duchess of Malfi*.[26] From observation, Thomas Blackwood, who is also mentioned in Henslowe's accounts, is also very active at the time when the company were at the Rose, but is not heard of again in association with the others according to documents available. A Robert Blackwood is heard of on the Continent, however (see Chapter 5).

Robert Leigh was born in 1569 and was therefore the oldest player associated with the Worcester's Men/Queen's Servants group.[27] Leigh, thought to have been an Admiral's/Strange's man performing at the Theatre in 1590–1, continued to have associations with the Alleyn/Henslowe group during the following ten years.[28] Around 1594 we know he met a crucial character to the story of the Queen's Servants who was not a member of the company: Susan Browne, née Shawe, was the daughter of Edmond Shawe of St Botolph, Aldgate.[29] In 1592 she married Robert Browne, who became the actor-lessee of the Boar's Head by 1599, and with whom Worcester's Men had difficult dealings in 1601–2.[30] Francis Langley, one of the landlords of this inn-yard playhouse, paid hired men to stop performances at the theatre in the autumn of 1601 in order to enforce payments from the actors.[31] Consequently, Worcester's Men had to go back on an arrangement they had made with Robert Browne, Susan Shawe's husband. The result was a suit against the company by Browne, and the

---

[26] Martin Butler, 'Lowin, John (*bap.* 1576, *d.* 1653)', *Oxford Dictionary of National Biography*, www.oxforddnb.com/view/article/17096, accessed 15 February 2008.

[27] In the *Worth* v. *Baskervile* case of 1623 he described himself as '54 yeares, or thereabouts'; TNA C24/500/9, Int. 1; Sisson, 'The Red Bull Company', 59; C. J. Sisson, 'Notes on Early Stuart Stage History', *Modern Language Review* 37 (1942), 25–36, (p. 28); Mark Eccles, 'Elizabethan Actors III: K–R', *Notes and Queries* 237 [n.s. 39] (1992), 293–303 (p. 296).

[28] Gurr, *Shakespearean Stage*, p. 36.

[29] LMA P69/BOT2/A/001/MS09220: baptisms, 1558–1625; christenings, 1572, p. 20.

[30] The marriage is recorded in LMA P69/BOT2/A/019/MS09234/002, St Botolph, Aldgate, memoranda book, 1591–2, fo. 18.

[31] The other landlord was Oliver Woodliffe. Records of the proceedings include TNA REQ2/466, Box 2 (bill and answer in *Woodliffe* v. *Browne* suit) and TNA C24/304/27; Berry, *The Boar's Head Playhouse*, pp. 51–2.

company's counter-suit, ending with the amalgamated troupe's flight from the Boar's Head.[32]

Susan Browne, soon after the death of her husband in 1603, would become Susan Greene, the wife of the Queen's Servants' clown, Thomas Greene; and later than that, after the death of Greene, she would become Susan Baskervile, married to James Baskervile, bigamously – it is inferred – on the part of Baskervile. James Baskervile was to be a further investor in the company.[33] But Susan Greene's association with Robert Leigh at this earlier time when she was Susan Browne is important because of the later court case of 1623, brought about in order to hear her arguments concerning Thomas Greene's share in the company. Leigh's sympathy towards her during this case may have come about through his earlier acquaintance with her, starting in the 1590s.

We first hear of James Hoult in December 1602, when Robert Browne bailed him out along with Thomas Pope, a friend of Will Kemp, and William Mago, the son of John Mago who built the stage and galleries of the Boar's Head.[34] This was in order that they should keep the peace towards Oliver Woodliffe, the co-landlord of the Boar's Head, who, with Francis Langley, was responsible for the difficulties between Browne and Worcester's Men. Hoult was named a member of Worcester's Men/the Queen's Servants in the draft licence of 1604, and was on their official 1609 patent.[35] He was to live in the parish of St James, Clerkenwell while the company played there, and he was also included on the list of mourners for Queen Anna in 1619, but after this time he apparently disappears from the records of early English actors.[36]

Thomas Swinnerton, discussed before with reference to the playhouse-owning element of the company, also appears on official documents concerning them: namely, the patents of 1604 and 1609 (see below) and the funeral lists of 1619. He was also to occur in records to do with the nominal company while on tour in England. Richard Perkins was to leave one day for other companies, but not before he had been a long-term Queen's

[32] According to Berry, Browne was suing the company for defaulting on their payments to him by Michaelmas 1601 (*The Boar's Head Playhouse*, p. 52). Many of the documents relating to the case are dated May–June 1602 (*ibid.*, p. 206n15).

[33] TNA C24/500/9; Sisson, 'The Red Bull Company', 65.

[34] LMA MJ/SR/0410, 3, 4, 9, 10. Mark Eccles, 'Elizabethan Actors I: A–D', *Notes and Queries* 236 [n.s. 38] (1991), 38–49 (p. 41); 'Elizabethan Actors III', p. 297.

[35] TNA SP14/2, fos. 246v–247; *ES*, Vol. II, pp. 229–30. TNA C66/1827, no. 29; *ES*, Vol. II, p. 231.

[36] *St JPR*, Vol. I (1884), 59; Mark Eccles, 'Elizabethan Actors II: E–J', *Notes and Queries* 236 [n.s. 38] (1991), 454–61 (459); *ES*, Vol. II, p. 236.

Servant, becoming one again under the patronage of Queen Henrietta Maria by 1626–9.[37] He is included among Henslowe's records of the Rose time for the company and interesting data has been discovered about his origins from November 1596 as a young actor with Henslowe. The information emanates from a court case describing a dispute over him between Henslowe, to whom Perkins was contracted at the Rose, and Langley, for whom Perkins had been working at the Swan. Perkins was contracted to Henslowe for three years; therefore he would have been at the Rose until at least 1599.[38]

Actors like Leigh and Lowin could have been members of Worcester's company before the period at the Boar's Head and the Rose, as could Thomas Swinnerton, but there is no evidence of this. The only evidence of Hoult's prior relationship to the company is when Robert Browne bailed him out in 1602, which is tenuous proof. Alternatively, all these men could well have come from the Earl of Oxford's troupe. Another, long-term associate of the amalgamated company would be John King, who claimed in 1623 that he was first hired by them in 1593 when he was eighteen years old.[39] He describes this thirty-year working period as the time he was attached to 'the companie of Sharers of the players of the redd Bull'; therefore we cannot say which part of the amalgamation he was originally linked to. Whichever one it was, he was only a hired man, never a sharer. He stands as possibly the only provable candidate for longest surviving member of the combined troupe.

With new beginnings at the Rose and with a newly arranged company, some things might have been said to be coming together in a positive way for the players. At this point, however, other things began falling apart.

To begin with, Henslowe's entries for 1603 appear to end with a note of debts and a promise of payment from Thomas Blackwood on 'xvj of mrche 1603', and the reader takes this to be a mistaken modern-style dating eight days before the end of the old-style year, as previous entries on the same page are for March 1602.[40] There are two and a quarter inches left blank according to Greg, and then on the next page is written:

---

[37] He is in the cast list of James Shirley's *The Wedding* (London, 1629).

[38] See Mateer, 'Edward Alleyn, Richard Perkins and the Rivalry'.

[39] TNA C24/500/103, Int. 5.

[40] 'F. 120ᵛ', in Philip Henslowe, *Henslowe's Diary*, ed. W. W. Greg, 2 vols. (London: A. H. Bullen, 1904–8) Vol. I, p. 190. See also Henslowe, *Henslowe's Diary*, ed. Foakes and Rickert, p. 225.

In the name of god amen
Begininge to playe agayne by the kynges licence
& layd owt sense for my lord of worsters men
As folowethe 1603 9.of maye.[41]

In November 1603, 'Kempe a man' was buried at St Saviour's, Southwark. In the past it has been taken that this was the famous clown, who was no doubt the centre-piece of the company for the short time he was with them, and who lived at Langley's rents.[42] However, according to new scholarship, it may be that this was another Kemp, as one going by that name turns up later in the documents of Lady Hunsdon.[43] Either way, Kemp was in the company no more. Robert Browne of the Boar's Head was buried in his parish in October 1603, leaving his widow Susan and his several children.[44] With the turnabouts in fortune that occurred with the change of reign – including the devastating plague that put an end to London playing – Worcester's Men also lost John Lowin to the King's Men. Subsequently, however, the players gained another member, and Susan Browne another husband, in the shape of the actor who was apparently to lead the Queen's Servants as a Kemp-like figurehead, taking up managerial positions within the company structure while he lived. Tellingly, it was Thomas Greene who was put down to attend the delayed coronation procession with the company in March 1604, and not Will Kemp.

A new start *c.* 1604: Thomas Greene, and all the Queen's Servants' theatres

As we know, the undated draft licence for the Jacobean Queen's Servants is one document – alongside the list of players given cloth for the 1604 procession – that specifies the shape of the company after the change in reign. They were: 'Thomas Greene, Christopher Beeston, Thomas Hawood, Richard Pyrkins, Robert Pallant Iohn Duke, Thomas Swynerton, Iames Hoylt, Robert Beeston: & Robert Lee', and their theatres included 'there now vsuall Howsen, called the Curtayne, and the Bores head, within our County of Midd*lesex*', as well as 'any other play howse not vsed by others, by the said ^Thomas^ Greene, elected, or by him hereafter to be builte'.[45]

[41] 'F. 121', in Henslowe, *Henslowe's Diary*, ed. Greg, Vol. I, p. 190.
[42] LMA P92/SAV/3001.
[43] Katherine Duncan-Jones, 'Shakespeare's Dancing Fool', *Times Literary Supplement*, 11 August 2010.
[44] LMA P93/MRY1/001, fo. 54 (microfilm X024/090).
[45] TNA SP14/2, fos. 246v–247.

At least half of the actors listed have just been described as probable members of the Worcester's/Oxford amalgamation. But one of the theatres – and the name of Greene, singled out to choose or possibly build a theatre for the company – was new to Worcester's company from the sparse records we have of it.

The history of the Curtain theatre, built in Shoreditch in 1577, a year after the erection of the original Theatre of 1576, and located in the same area, north of the City's walls, is sketchy. At one time, according to Chambers, the land on which it was built was in the possession of the Mountjoy family, belonging, as it did, to an ancestor of Charles Blount, earl of Devonshire.[46] In 1567 it was sold to Maurice and William Longe, clothworkers, and in 1581 it was sold on to one Thomas Harberte of Cheapside who was a girdler. Then a string of people owned it, according to research, until 1611, when the playhouse was said to be 'in decay'. It is believed that in 1585 Henry Lanman, a yeoman of the Queen's Guard, was gaining profit from the estate, so it has been assumed that he built the playhouse, and he is even mentioned as one of the tenants as far back as 1581.[47] According to Chambers, Lanman made arrangements with the Burbages that indicate they pooled resources from 1585 to 1592, with the Chamberlain's Men probably using the Curtain from 1597 while preparations for the Globe were under way.[48] Thomas Pope, Will Kemp's friend, who was with the Chamberlain's Men until his death in 1604, owned a share of the playhouse, as his will shows.[49]

The Queen's Servants could have used the Curtain when playing resumed after the plague of 1603, which interrupted their performances at the Rose.[50] This may explain its inclusion in the 1604 patent alongside the Boar's Head. However, both the Boar's Head and the Curtain are firmly associated with Thomas Greene, the named leader of the company at this time, which means that either theatre – or even both theatres – was probably employed.

---

[46] *ES*, Vol. II, p. 401.
[47] Ingram, *The Business of Playing*, pp. 219–38; *EPT*, pp. 404–6.
[48] *ES*, Vol. II, p. 402.
[49] TNA PROB 11/103/138, fos. 95–7; E. A. J. Honigmann and Susan Brock, eds., *Playhouse Wills 1558–1642: An Edition of Wills by Shakespeare and His Contemporaries in the London Theatre* (Manchester University Press, 1993), pp. 68–72.
[50] Indeed, a Privy Council order of that time instructs the Lord Mayor and justices to allow 'the three companies of players to the King, Queen and Prince publicly to exercise their several and usual houses … the Globe situate in Maiden Lane … the Fortune in Golden Lane, and the Curtain in Holywell'. See *EPT*, p. 414.

The name of Thomas Greene, the company member who is cited as responsible for the choosing or building of a new playhouse, is the feature of the text that helps to date the 1603–4 draft, along with the appearance of Richard Perkins after his non-appearance in the procession lists. From subsequent history and documents, we know that Greene became a member of the company and received payments from court on its behalf. Greene is first officially mentioned on the procession lists of March 1604.[51] He was also given a primary status among the company when, in the Chamber accounts, he 'and tenne of his Felowes' were given money as 'groomes of the Chamber' for attending on 'Countye Arrenbirgh and the reste of the com*m*yssione*r*s at Durham Howse'.[52] This was for an eighteen-day period between 9 and 27 August, during the signing of the Treaty of London, when the King's Men were likewise paid for attending on the Spanish Ambassador at Somerset House. John Duke was paid for performances by the company as Worcester's players on 20 April 1603. He was also paid on 19 February 1604, again on 19 February 1605 and again at the end of April 1606, on these occasions as representative of the Queen's Servants.[53] Thereafter, however, from 1608 onwards until the year before his death in 1612, Greene is the payee.[54] In the draft patent he is named first in the list of members, before Thomas Heywood, who is named third and who had, up until 1604, been the other payee-representative with Kemp. Christopher Beeston further superseded Heywood in significance (if order of writing is important), as he is named second in the patent (Beeston is named first in the procession list, Heywood fifth, Greene second to last). Thomas Greene was also to be the clown of the company, and it is clear that he took over from Kemp in this capacity. Because the patent document does not name the Red Bull, it is dated to *c.* 1604 because Greene is named in it instead of Kemp, and because subsequent history we have now explored has shown that this playhouse – the one 'hereafter to be builte' or chosen by Greene – is likely to have been begun and finished in 1604–5. Chambers described the original manuscript of the draft patent well: that it was a 'rough draft full of deletions'. What happened to the licence after its draft was written is not known. The only official

[51] TNA LC2/4/5.
[52] TNA E351/543, m. 113b. It is not clear whether they were mentioned as grooms to the chamber of Queen Anna or the King; they are certainly described as 'the Queenes Players' as well, given the job of waiting on 'Arrenbirgh' and the other commissioners. The King's Men were to look after the Spanish Ambassador at Somerset House specifically as 'his ma*j*esties' grooms of the chamber.
[53] TNA E351/543, mm. 95b, 116, 137b, 163b.
[54] TNA E351/543, mm. 214, 235, 249b, 267b (twice paid for two separate sets of performances).

fair-scripted and properly authorised licence for the Queen's Servants is dated 1609. It names the same members, but by this time it includes the Red Bull in its playhouse stipulations alongside the Curtain alone as the allowed fixed venues.

Greene was born in 1573. We know this because there is a record of a Thomas Greene's baptism on 27 September 1573 in Romford, and this Essex town is where the clown claimed he was born.[55] This was during a defamation case of June 1607 when Greene, then aged thirty-four, said that he had lived for the last three years in Whitechapel and the previous six at the Tower of London.[56] With him we have a pronounced beginning to the Jacobean story of the Queen's Servants, for, to some extent, it must have been Greene who gave the company its distinct flavour.

Greene's three years in Whitechapel from 1604 put him in the Boar's Head vicinity shortly after Susan Browne had been made a widow. Although Robert Browne, Susan's husband, 'dyed very pore' in Mrs Alleyn's words, his wife was still able to access his interests in the Boar's Head early in that year and she would have been able to keep these until c. 1615.[57] It is likely, then, that Thomas Greene married Susan Browne sometime in 1604, becoming the owner of rights in the Boar's Head through his marriage to Browne's widow. By the time of his marriage, or soon after, he joined the company that was to record their association with the Boar's Head on their licence. Greene's prominence as leader on the licence, and the Boar's Head's inclusion on it as a venue, are no doubt factors that are interrelated. He must have come into the company holding considerable financial reins.

Tracking back through records concerning Thomas Greene, the draft licence cannot be said to be the first one associated with this clown and property issues. In the Audit Office accounts for 1602 and for 1603 – a time before Greene's sojourn at Whitechapel – he is named.[58] He goes on appearing in these 'hanaper' accounts, five times in 1603/4 and regularly between 1605 and 1609.[59] Thomas Greene is a common name, but

[55] Essex Record Office, Chelmsford, St Edward the Confessor Parish Registers, Romford, D/P 346/1/1.
[56] LMA DLC/2/7 (photocopy R1098).
[57] Browne died mid October 1603 and his wife acquired the administration of his goods on 9 January the following year (See TNA PROB 6/6, fo. 183v). After 1615 the Boar's Head would have come into the hands of whoever owned Oliver Woodliffe's share of the 'grand lease' (Berry, *The Boar's Head Playhouse*, pp. 70, 76).
[58] TNA AO3/377/3 and AO3/377/4. He paid 20s 4d in 1601–2 and two sums of 20s 4d and 6s 8d in 1602–3.
[59] 1603–4: 6s 8d in February, another 6s 8d on 10 July, another on 18 July and a final occurrence on 20 July.

Figure 7 Title-page of Io: Cooke, *Greene's Tu Quoque; or, The Cittie Gallant* (London, 1614), showing a bearded Greene with two feathers in his cap, wearing a jacket like a backgammon board with pieces for buttons. In the part of 'Bubble', a money pouch hangs from his belt, holding the cash bequest that has made him a gentleman.

during the earlier period, two sets of amounts were paid that referred to alienation of land between him and one Robert Dawes. Bentley notes that Dawes was a member of the Duke of York's company in 1610 and of the Lady Elizabeth's in 1614, and so these records are intriguing.[60] His name comes into view again as someone who gave bail concerning an assault on a waterman. The money was for both Dawes and Martin Slatiar to attend a hearing about the assault on the man, Edmund Chambers, who had caused 'an affray and a tumult at the curtayne dore', and all were enjoined to keep the peace. The bail was given over on 27 July 1613, but the following year, both Slatiar and Dawes were outlawed, it would seem, for lack of attendance at proceedings.[61]

The Audit Office accounts involving Dawes and Greene are dated at about the time when Greene was living at the Tower of London, the most curious portion of his life as an inhabitant in and around the City. What specific arrangements he was coming to with Robert Dawes, within a system similar to the 'land registry' today, is so far a mystery. However, in C. W. Wallace's notes, where he transcribes these documents, he mentions a consultation with 'Mr Giuseppi' of the Public Records Office, the writer of the PRO's guide, where Giuseppi said that the two entries of 1602/3 concerned 'the delivery of land to Thos. Grene the heir to them'.[62]

A picture builds up of a more and more pronounced pre-eminence for the leader and 'clown', Thomas Greene. The Curtain is a theatre that is stipulated on the patent, that was a venue where we also know he held rights, and perhaps, indeed, the hanaper accounts were to do with his ownership there. In 1611, the freehold of the land where the Curtain was built changed hands, and in the documents describing this event Greene is named as holding the theatre's interests within the Curtain estate: 'all that large mesuage or tenemente built of Timber and thatched now in decay called the Curtaine with a parcel of ground adioining thereto wherein they use to keepe Stage playes now or late in the tenure and occupacion of Thomas Greene his assignee or assignes'.[63]

---

[60] *JCS*, Vol. II, p. 422.

[61] LMA MJ/SR/0523/219, 220 and 221; TNA KB29/255, m. 84d.

[62] Wallace papers, Huntington Library, Box 2, File B1, 11.

[63] TNA C54/2075, no. 17, my transcription. See also *EPT*, p. 416 where Berry transcribes this document, correcting the English of 'they use to keep stage plays' to 'they use[d] to keep …'. Berry notes further that the contract states that Greene was also one of three men who held the lease of the entire Curtain estate. Christopher Beeston also held land on or around the estate but not the theatre itself (p. 405 and note).

Perhaps of interest in relation to all this is how, during the seventeenth century, an area for drama in Shoreditch came to be known as 'the Green Curtain'.[64]

With the new knowledge that Greene (and his wife) owned half of the tiring house and yard of the Red Bull by 25 December 1606, we can say that all three theatres stipulated on the draft patent of 1604 – the extant two and the one that was planned – were either linked to Thomas Greene or soon were to be. This means that he was a substantial owner of play-house shares, independent of his importance to the company. His seem-ingly efficacious involvement in playhouse ownership makes it pertinent to suggest – as with the later and similar playhouse-ownership issues with Christopher Beeston – that it was always in Greene's best interests to see that his company used all the theatres he owned, for as the person hold-ing shares in these sites, he would have been entitled to playhouse profits from them as well as company shares.[65]

With further reference to the Curtain, Francis Beaumont's *The Knight of the Burning Pestle*, with its satirical references, has more to offer, as this play has been dated to 1607 because of a particular comment made in it concerning *The Travails of the Three English Brothers* by John Day, William Rowley and George Wilkins, dated to this year. Where the pertinent speech states that *The Travails* was 'stale' from performances at the Red Bull, the Stationers' Register, in fact, places the text as belonging to the Curtain playhouse. Greene would have seen the sense of performing the Queen's Servants' repertoire at both venues.[66] William Smith's description in his 1615 *The Hector of Germany* says that *The Hector* was certainly both a Curtain and a Red Bull play, and this now makes more sense in the con-text of his association with the company and Greene's two theatres. On the title-page of this play – written in honour of the Princess Elizabeth's new husband, Frederick V, Elector Palatine – the herald, Smith, says that it was published as it was 'publikely Acted at the Red Bull, and at the Curtaine, by a Companie of Young men of this Citie'.

We do not know exactly when *The Hector of Germany* was presented, nor by whom (the 'Young men' of the City may not refer to the Queen's

---

[64] John Aubrey, writing of Ben Jonson's return from the Low Countries, *c.* 1592, and of where he 'acted and wrote'. See Ian Donaldson, 'Life of Ben Jonson', in Ben Jonson, *The Cambridge Edition of the Works of Ben Jonson*, ed. David Bevington, Martin Butler and Ian Donaldson, 7 vols. (Cambridge University Press, 2012), Vol. I, pp. lxxxvii–cxv (p. xci).

[65] See Griffith, 'Baskervile [*née* Shawe], Susan (*bap.* 1573, *d.* 1649)'; 'Christopher Beeston', pp. 611–12.

[66] This puts dating Beaumont's play in some confusion however, as *The Travails* need not have been played at both the Curtain and the Red Bull in the same year at the same time.

Servants – that does not mean they were not performing under the
Queen's Servants' auspices), but while Greene could put on plays simul-
taneously at more than one venue with which he was associated, he and
others could access much more profit. Moreover, continued performances by the Queen's Servants at the three theatres spread out beyond the
City walls would explain why there is no evidence of the actors moving
their domestic arrangements quickly to Clerkenwell from 1605 onwards.
Thomas Greene is the first recorded resident in St James' parish among
the actors, attending a vestry meeting there in November 1607.[67] We also
know, however, that he was in possession of Aaron Holland's rooms from
Christmas 1606 (according to the Court of Requests proceedings of 1632),
while still a Whitechapel resident in 1607, according to the defamation
case. Christopher Beeston stayed in the Curtain parish of St Leonard's,
Shoreditch until 1611, as did his friend from the Chamberlain's Men,
John Duke.[68] Like Greene, we also know that Beeston held interests in
the Curtain estate even if he did not provably have a stake in the Curtain
theatre.[69] When they moved, Beeston stayed in Clerkenwell only until the
building of the Cockpit in 1616. Duke died in 1613 in Clerkenwell. Robert
Pallant, who, it is suggested, may only have acted as a Queen's man in a
satellite capacity, always remained on the other side of the river.[70]

In the defamation court case of June 1607, during which Greene
claimed he was still living in Whitechapel, he spoke up for a woman called
Mary Phillips.[71] She had been engaged as a doorkeeper for the playhouse.
At one point he describes an event that happened 'in the winter time last
at suche time as playes wear vsed to be played and acted at the bores head
without Algate'. Mark Eccles cites this as proof that the Queen's Men were
still using the Boar's Head in 1606, even though Greene is only indicating
that all players – not necessarily the Queen's Servants – had stopped using
the playhouse after this time.[72] However, as I have indicated, it would

---

[67] 27 November 1607; Islington Local History Centre, St James' Parish Vestry Book, 1590–1683,
fo. 28.

[68] *JCS*, Vol. II, p. 364; Eccles, 'Elizabethan Actors I', 47.

[69] TNA C54/2075, no. 17; *EPT*, p. 405 and note.   [70] *JCS*, Vol. II, pp. 518–19.

[71] LMA DL/C/0217, pp. 216–19, fos. 108–10: 16 June 1607 (Eccles, 'Elizabethan Actors II', 456). Phillips
was an associate of the company over a longer period. She appears in a bill of Thomas Woodford's
issued during the *Woodford* v. *Holland* case of 1613–23. There Woodford says she was paid 'tenn shillinges' to bring Philip Stone into a conspiracy concerning shares in the playhouse. This connects her
with the Red Bull *c.* 1613–14, as well as with the Boar's Head in 1607. See Wallace, 'Three London
Theatres of Shakespeare's Time', p. 310; Hotson, *The Commonwealth and Restoration Stage*, p. 334.

[72] Berry cited evidence in his *Boar's Head Playhouse* (pp. 74–5) to show that the Prince Charles' Men
were performing in Whitechapel in 1609 (see *EPT*, pp. 486–7).

have been beneficial to Thomas Greene for his players to have used his playhouse, and therefore it could be that it was the Queen's Servants who played there. Described as a gentleman in this suit, Greene was charged at £3 in goods in the subsidy, which means his income at the time was not bad, although not as great as Aaron Holland's had been in 1598.

Susan had brought five children of Browne's to her marriage with Greene, four of whom were baptised at St Mary's, Whitechapel: Susan (23 December 1600), William (25 April 1602), Elizabeth (13 February 1603) and Anne (born after her father's death and baptised on 22 January 1604).[73] The other child, Robert, was probably the eldest, born *c.* 1599–1600.[74] He was later described as a 'Habberdasher' in his brother William's will.[75]

The adult company that was put under the patronage of Queen Anna had by now taken shape with Thomas Greene leading it and Thomas Heywood acting as putative company playwright. Their draft patent of 1604 stipulated two up-and-running playhouses for the company to perform in, both financially associated with Greene: the Boar's Head and the Curtain. The patent also provided a window on another opportunity, however, that was clearly taken up by the players. Stating that Thomas Greene could be responsible for choosing any other theatre 'not vsed by others … or by him hereafter to be builte', it would seem that the person responsible for drawing up the document was already aware that the company hoped to have its own playhouse. Responsibility for a theatre where more members of the company could benefit financially meant freedoms that, for a long time, the Worcester's Men/Queen's Servants company could only envy in others. Owning their playhouse as a group (rather than bits and pieces of the Curtain as individuals) would mean that shares could be apportioned in a style akin to the King's Men at the Globe. After their experiences at the Rose, where Philip Henslowe had received considerable profits from their work, and previously at the Boar's Head, where they had encountered landlord difficulties from Langley and Woodliffe, the desire for a company playhouse must have been urgently felt. The Red Bull playhouse was an answer to a prayer.

[73] LMA P93/MRY/001 (microfilm X024/090).
[74] Berry, *The Boar's Head Playhouse*, pp. 196–7.
[75] Dated 23 October 1634, TNA PROB 10/530; Honigmann and Brock, *Playhouse Wills*, pp. 179–82.

Figure 8 Interior and exterior of Hayward's Place, London ECI, site of the Red Bull yard (the playhouse). The entrance underneath the buildings measures the same today as the entrance shown on the 'Plott or Survey' of Anne Bedingfeild's part of the estate.

How big was the Red Bull playhouse? What was it like?

From the few materials we have, suggestions can be made towards what the Red Bull may have been like for the Queen's Servants as they entered into it for the first time, having endured so many playhouse adventures. There are some texts about the content and size of the piece of land that Holland leased from Anne Bedingfeild, yet there are difficulties about specifics. One of the problems is not just about the passage of time since the Red Bull existed, but the changes the playhouse underwent during its long lifetime. These known changes are likely to prevent firm answers about the *first* set of theatre buildings, because there exist only later surveys and plans that could help us with them. There is some map and further drawing evidence, with one sketch of the outside to give us clues, but the three early plans of the Seckford Estate that we have here are, for example, drawn later than the Queen's Servants' time at the Red Bull.

A second problem is to do with evidence from the plays. As the first, long and detailed part of this chapter goes to show, the Red Bull was not the only venue where new dramas were performed, and it would have shown a lack of common sense if the company had not used all the venues available to them for their repertoire.[76] Moreover, as has also been demonstrated, the older plays began in yet other venues before the Red Bull's time, and therefore the texts we have may have been designed for them.

George Fullmer Reynolds, who wrote the book often invoked for the purpose of imagining the Red Bull based on the stage directions given in the plays, called it *The Staging of Elizabethan Plays at the Red Bull Theater* – not *The Staging of* Jacobean *Plays* – conscious as he was (one imagines) of the good number of dramas employed at the playhouse pre-dating the building.

Reynolds was very careful to grade the dramas he explored, giving 'A' grades only to the plays with evidence showing original first performances at the Red Bull. He discounted plays I would not discount – *Greene's Tu Quoque*, for instance, which receives a 'B' grading because the title-page advertises the published text as the one performed at court. This made Reynolds suspect that the stage directions said more about Whitehall or other palace venues than the Red Bull. The text of the play, however,

---

[76] George Fullmer Reynolds alludes to Adams on this issue, believing the company 'could hardly use two big public playhouses at the same time'. He thought they played 'intermittently at both'. Reynolds himself thought they would have used the newer, inferring that the company would have stopped using the Curtain *c.* 1609, but there is no evidence of this. See Reynolds, *The Staging of Elizabethan Plays*, p. 7.

makes a joke specific to the Red Bull – 'meta-theatrical' in the extreme –
when the clown, Greene, playing 'Bubble', the main character, makes a
quip about the clown Greene at the Red Bull. This kind of humour would
have worked most immediately if the audience had been in the playhouse itself. *The Silver Age* was similarly given a 'B' grade because of its
court performance record, this despite both dramas either side of it in the
Ages cycle (*The Golden Age* and *The Brazen Age*) being given an 'A' grade.
Only *The Golden Age* notes the Queen's Servants and the Red Bull as the
play's company and playhouse on the title-pages, however – *The Brazen
Age* (London, 1613) is assumed. On the other hand, Reynolds gave John
Webster's *The White Devil* an 'A' grade – many would say quite rightly – as
Webster's comments about the first playhouse that premiered his work are
so vivid that critics have assumed they were about the Red Bull, despite
the fact that the title-page does not have a playhouse ascription, meaning,
technically, that the first performance *could* have been produced at the
Curtain.[77]

Once it is decided what plays can and cannot be used for evidence,
larger questions can be asked – alongside more kinds of evidence. These
questions might include: (1) What was the playhouse physically like?, and
(2) What was the ambience? Other types of evidence possible for the first
of these questions are the aforementioned maps and plans (at least one
with a scale in feet – see figure 9). These can be used in order to learn
something of the size and shape of the Red Bull: straightforward draw-
ings may be observed to discern its orientation (there is one of the 1660s);
title-page illustrations may represent something of the interior; evidence
from plays from the Queen's Servants' repertoire (where we can be certain
the Red Bull was the primary venue) may lend us clues for the interior
staging capabilities of the early playhouse (e.g. stage directions involving
machinery, doors, pyrotechnics, etc.); petitions, bills and witness depositions lend further data – its gates, entrances and flag, for instance. For the
ambience we can look to these latter kinds of record too, and also to personal accounts of the playhouse from people who visited, such as Kirkman
and Pepys – which although from a later time might lend us something.

[77] Reynolds published his work, recording things like possible numbers of entrances, clues given as
   to any upper area, and indications of special effects and prop needs etc., in 1940. His work will be
   of particular use in a book that aims to focus on repertoire issues, which this book does not. When
   using Reynolds, moreover, the scholar has to be aware that his theatrical thinking can be shown to
   be somewhat specific to his own time – 1940 – and place, where elements of staging were dependent on believing in immoveable areas of performance space, for example. His work was scrupulous
   in intention, and if not used intensely here, in an early company and playhouse history, it should
   be referred to more widely in a follow-up book to this concentrating on the plays.

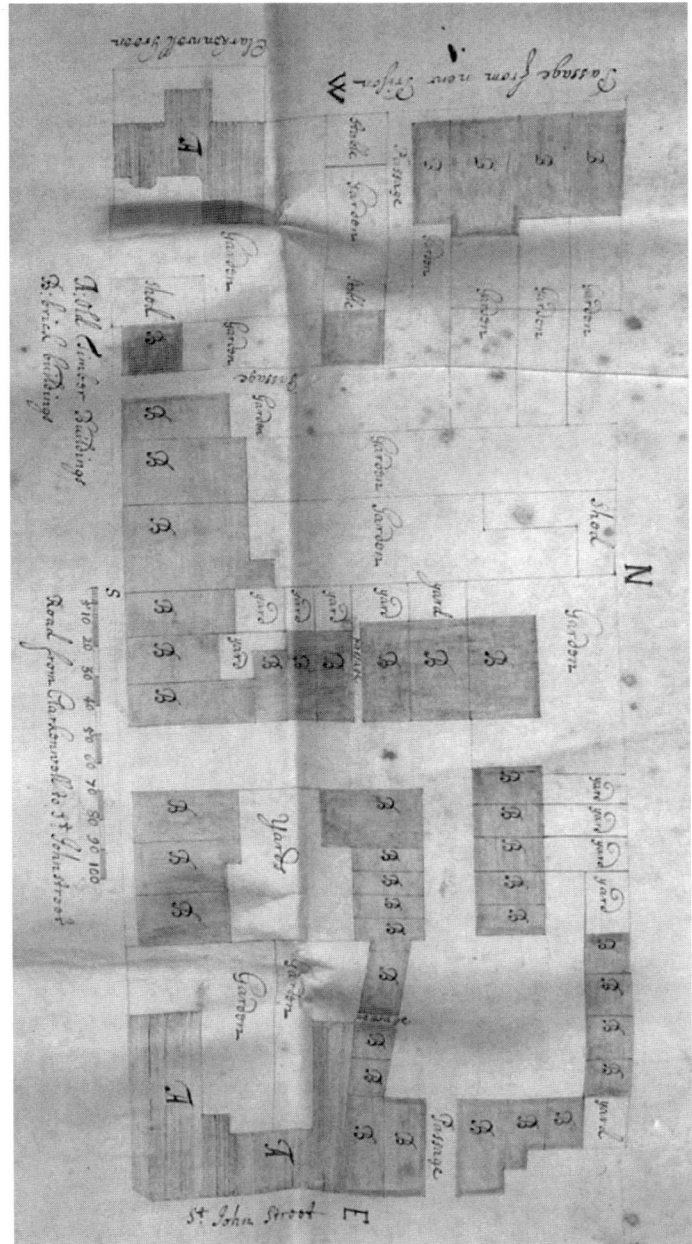

Figure 9 'Plott or Survey' attached to the Naylor indenture of the lease of 1679/80, showing the site of the Red Bull yard to the north-east, and complete with a scale in feet.

Similarly, there are 'accounts' from poems and plays from other repertoires that may be profitable.

For this section I will primarily look at possibilities concerning the most physical of issues, such as the size, shape, orientation and capabilities of the Red Bull, always remembering that much of the information we have is from a later time and should therefore be believed with a large measure of caution.

From the one careful survey we have – which comes complete with the scale in feet – we can say the following about a playhouse space that had been closed, and probably developed for other uses, over the fifteen or so years before it was drawn.[78] Indeed, what makes up the perimeters of the Red Bull yard space on the survey of 1679/80 – which is in the north-east corner of Anne Bedingfeild's land – is made up of rectangular brick units: quite possibly buildings that had been developed over that fifteen-year period, although we cannot be certain that the original 1605 theatre was not converted to brick from indications drawn here.[79] The yard space (by which is meant the area where paying audience members could stand before the stage) was quadrilateral in aspect, square – in the sense of having 90° angles implied to the north – yet set on the diagonal, or 'canted', to the south.[80] This brings about the unusual feature of seeing a wider space allowed on the part of the yard fronting St John Street than on the part of the yard space to the west of the map. When it comes to the St John Street side, it is as well to bear in mind the Gloucestershire Dyrham papers sketch, which clearly shows a tower-like elevation (see figure 10). This was the likely tiring house of the playhouse – where the actors 'attired' (changed costumes) and 'retired' off the stage (waiting within it, no doubt, for the next entrance). Here on this paper it is located at the St John Street end, making the orientation from the point of view of where the stage was, as on this eastern part of the yard.

The tiring house building, perfunctorily drawn on the Dyrham papers sketch as a local landmark in the 1660s, but undoubtedly of a different

---

[78] The following includes measurements taken from my 2001 'New Material', pp. 13–15. The late John Orrell, to whom I was introduced by Andrew Gurr, kindly undertook to make the measurements, cagey as he was about the 1679/80 survey. As I wrote then (p. 19), major questions can only be answered once 'an archaeological survey on the site' has been achieved. All indications as to the directions north, south, east or west refer to the survey's orientations 'N', 'S', 'E' and 'W' for this discussion. They do not refer to the true orientation in London geographical terms.

[79] See *ibid.*, pp. 18–19 for speculation concerning a brick Red Bull of 1605.

[80] In 2001 the situation was described thus: 'The irregularly formed building on the south-west corner of the yard veers the south side away from the west at a 100 degree angle, in other words creating an 80 degree angle where it meets the east side'; *ibid.*

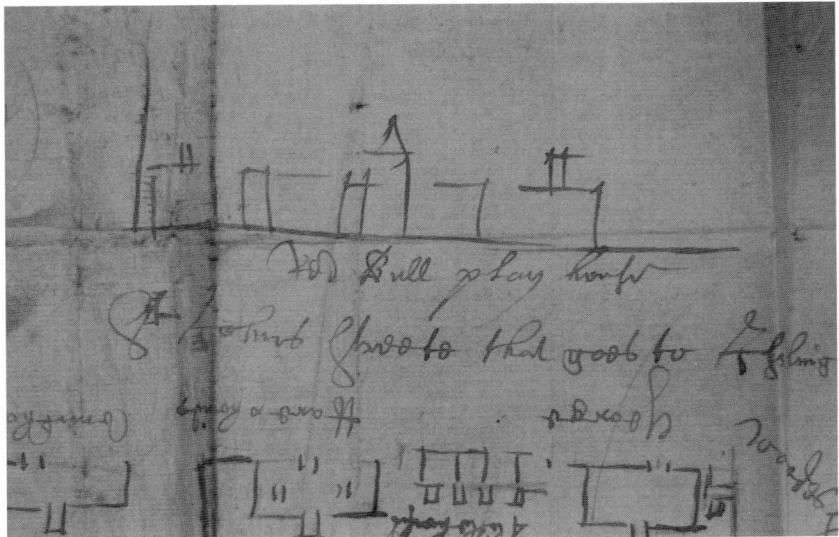

Figure 10 Gloucestershire Archives, D1799/P12. Sketch of the exterior of the 'Red Bull play house' (detail from larger drawing of St John Street property, 1660s). The sketch shows an elevation akin to a tower on the location, which may have been the tiring house of the theatre in its final years.

order to the squarer chimney or hearth-side elevations elsewhere on the sketch, may be compared to the 1679/80 survey in order to detect the locality and size of the house on that map. Where this likely tiring house must have been, once aligned to the survey, is where a larger building than the others exists on the north side of a passage coming in from St John Street. This building juts out into St John Street in comparison with these, the near twin of the other (narrower) on the opposite side of the passage. This same 'Passage' running between the yard and St John Street is the entrance to modern-day 'Hayward's Place', and measures the same today, length and breadth, in 2013, as it did then – approximately 10 feet wide and 35 feet long. That best candidate for the location of the tiring house measures 16 feet by 33 feet on the 1679/80 survey.[81]

[81] The other buildings on the survey were also measured in 2001: four buildings on the north side coming to about 15 feet square with rectangular yards at either end, and the three buildings to the north of the 'Passage' getting smaller and smaller to the north with the most northerly one 12 by 18 feet, the one to the south of this a six-sided irregular building, 14 by 18 feet on its north side and 24 feet on its south. Beyond the passage to the south the buildings were regular, with the southernmost a slightly irregular rectangular shape as it continues the canted formation of the south side's

On the 'canted' side of the drawing, another passage leads to the yards and gardens of a largely timber building to the south. It would not be over-speculative to suggest that this could have been the Red Bull Inn as Aaron Holland described it, 'with the courts gardens Cellars wayes and libertyes thervnto belonginge'.[82] This area, together with its 'court', as Martin Slatiar described it, would have been – very approximately – 170 feet long by between 140 and 165 feet wide.

To the west of the yard space are five brick buildings, each measuring 22 by 12 feet, and these may once have stood as candidates for where an early Red Bull tiring house could have been, particularly as we know it was changed in the 1620s – 'reedified' or 'magnified' and 'enlarged' (see below, pp. 99–100). Changing the location of the tiring house to the St John Street side from another location would have naturally enlarged it because the bulk of the open property was to the west. Such a development would have opened up the yard to its greatest possible capacity.

Because of the description of the site in the 1663 patent granted to Anne Bedingfeild's daughter, any possible tiring house placement opposite the St John Street side becomes unlikely.[83] This description indicates that a larger than hitherto imagined area of Anne Bedingfeild's leaseheld property was *not* built on at all in the 1660s – an area, namely 'from East to West one hundred and eightie foot of Assize and from North to South one hundred sixtie five foot of Assize together with a peece of ground on the West side thereof percell of the premises conteineing from East to West ninety three feet of Assize and from North to South seaventie six feet of Assize'. This means that, at that earlier time, a large proportion of what we see on the survey (perhaps around half of it) was undeveloped, and this makes the possible capacity of the yard, in audience terms, a very large one indeed. It is also possible and, indeed, the favoured scenario by some, that an earlier tiring house could have been placed to the north of the square yard, leaving what we have in public yard entrance terms more *behind* the audience, which scholarship has taken to be a more practical layout for theatre inception and development.[84]

---

exterior walls. It was not a building that would have overlooked the yard, but would have abutted the (suggested) north end of the timber Red Bull inn.

[82] See above, p. 66.

[83] TNA C66 3040, no. 10.

[84] Actors taken to the site seeing the 1679/80 survey instinctively feel that with the passageways into the yard placed to the west, east and south, the tiring house and stage should have been placed to the north, so that the audience members could enter facing the stage.

Even without the possibility of changing the tiring house situation, perhaps in the 1620s, and going back to the measurements we have taken from the 1679/80 survey, by looking at this yard within the perimeters made by the brick buildings alone, the audience capacity would have been larger than, for instance, that of the Globe. Taking all measurements into consideration, the yard created by the buildings would have been 57 feet on the north side, 57 on the west side, roughly 56 feet on the canted side and 67 on the east side. This, together with the greater audience capacity possible in square galleries as opposed to polygonal ones means that if, as Herbert Berry claimed, these public playhouses could hold 3,000 upwards, the Red Bull would certainly have managed the upper limit – based on what we can speculate about it from the survey of 1679/80.[85] On the evidence of this late drawing, it would have been larger than the Fortune theatre, which we know, from texts, was 55 feet square.

For those interested in traditional orientations, and where the sun would have been directed during the afternoon at different times of year, the true bearing of the point 'N' for 'north' on the survey would have been orientated more round to the north-west once one makes comparison with, for example, the Ogilby and Morgan map of 1677, or even the William Morgan 1682 map, the relevant detail of which is given in this book with the location of the yard situated at 'A' (Figure 1). This means that if the five buildings jutting into the yard facing the passage from St John Street ever represented the location of a tiring house, the orientation of the stage would have been facing the north-east; if the tiring house was where the Gloucestershire sketch suggests (at least, that is, by the 1660s) it would have faced to the south-west. Or if the tiring house was to the north in terms of the 1679/80 survey, it would have been facing south-east.

With reference to a mid-1620s period for the Red Bull, and the changes that may well have happened at this time, a different kind of document comes into play – the kind that E. K. Chambers dubbed 'Documents of Criticism'. It is a truism that much theatre history is only derived from when things go wrong – crime, civil suits or, in the case of William Prynne's *Histrio-mastix*, when theatre is despised. Without Prynne's anti-acting work we would not know that in the mid 1620s the Fortune and the Red Bull (by the 1633 publication described as '*two olde Playhouses*') had been 'lately reedified, enlarged'.[86] Prynne's dating confirms

---

[85] *EPT*, p. 288.

[86] William Prynne, *Histrio-mastix* (London, 1633), 'Epistle Dedicatory', *3–3v. Prynne discusses the situation of seven years before, which takes it back to Crashaw's time. The names of the playhouses are given in the margins.

the observations of William Crashaw who, in his anxiety over the soul of London in his *Londons Lamentation* of 1625, mentions that while the Godly prayed, the theatres were 'magnified, and enlarged'.[87] When we look at later seventeenth-century representations of the Red Bull site, therefore, we are looking at something that had already changed since 1605 – tellingly changed because of theatre's need for *growth* in the 1620s. Despite what some company members claimed – for understandable reasons – in the *Worth* v. *Baskervile* case of around the same time, the Red Bull was a successful economic venue, and needed to consolidate its position as a 'reedified' structure, at the same time creating greater audience capacity. Indeed, the fact of the *Worth* v. *Baskervile* case taking place at around the time of these possible building changes may inform us further about company division and the more sporadic playing by different companies at this time (described in Chapter 7 and the Conclusion to the book).

In the 1670s, when Francis Kirkman wrote about the playhouse, the Red Bull was no more; however, Kirkman was only just in his forties, and was remembering the theatre from decades previously, recording the drolls, or short entertainments, that proved practical for the playhouse, particularly during the Interregnum: *these small things were as profitable, and as great get-pennies to the Actors as any of our late famed Plays. I have seen the* Red Bull *Play-House, which was a large one, so full, that as many went back for want of room as had entred.*'[88] Kirkman, when he knew the Red Bull, remembered it as a theatre that was large but, even so, could not hold the numbers of entertainment-starved people who attended.

Included among the Seckford Estate papers, a sketch exists, currently thought to be of the 1650s and relating to an erroneous claim of one John Gibbon Seckford to the estate (figure 11).[89] Divided in two, the northern half shows, for example, where 'Seckfords Seat', the family London residence, was located – the southern part is marked 'This part for the Charity'; however, other titles show other residences present on both parts. To the east of the southern half are indicated 'New buildings', and further into the area 'Two Old Houses' are marked. It is within this southern part where the inn and inn-yard were located: Martin Slatiar's 'square court in an inne'. In an article of 2011 I showed how the 'New buildings', to the east of this map, could not have been 'ruinous and decayed' as described in the 1663 permission to rebuild, indicating that some building work had

---

[87] William Pryyne, *Londons Lamentation* (London, 1625), B2v.
[88] Francis Kirkman, *The Wits; or, Sport upon Sport* (London, 1673), A2v.
[89] SROI HD21/480.

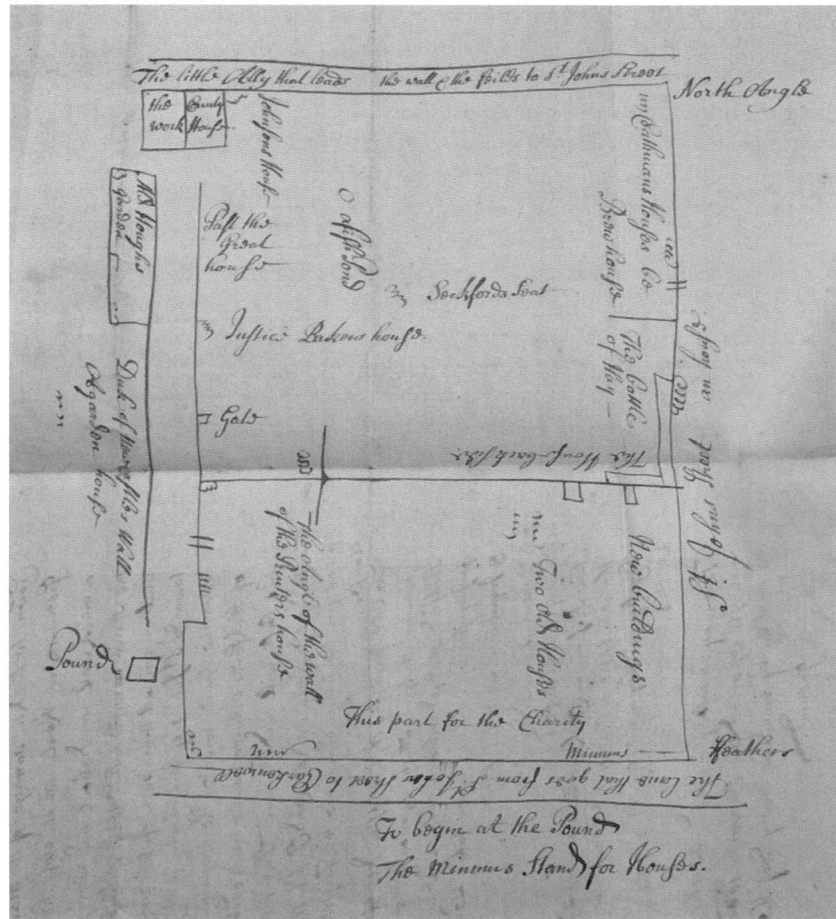

Figure 11 Sketch of the estate showing two halves, with 'New buildings' to the east and the 'Duke of Newcastle's wall' to the west of the estate, *c.*1650s[?].

already taken place at the St John Street end by that time and was regarded as 'New'.[90] It would seem these buildings were made of brick.

With reference to size and entrances, the late Glynne Wickham, when thinking about the Red Bull in his *Early English Stages*, suggested something along the lines of a Spanish 'corral'-type playhouse in its original

[90] Griffith, 'Martin Slatiar and the Red Bull Playhouse', pp. 566–70.

form. If anything like the surviving one of the kind – the 'Corral de Comedias' at Almargo, built in 1629 – such a style, generally betokened, might well fit the bill for the Red Bull.[91] The descriptive verb 'to corral', as in 'corralling', holds the real appeal however, for there is evidence that at least one entrance to the playhouse may have been a wide one, allowing as much public access into the space as possible.

There were probably two entrances, somewhat awkwardly aligned in terms of both the orientation evidence we have and experience of other playhouse public entrances. To back this up, however, where stated on title-pages, the location of the playhouse is described between two landmarks. One early title-page to a Red Bull play locates the playhouse as 'neere Clarken-well' (to the west of the inn and yard, in other words) and another, later, one as '*in S. Iohns streete*' (to the east); it would seem that there were – and with reference to the 1679/80 survey – two entrances reflecting these two situations, the larger one more towards Clerkenwell Green.[92] In Hotson's transcription of the *Woodford* v. *Holland* case, 'The Great Gate' is recorded as the place where transactions concerning shares took place.[93] It has been tempting to see this gate as that fronting on St John Street, although this is not a particularly large or 'Great' entrance as it stands today, and it was probably closer to the other location. For when Ned Ward lived on the site in 1712, he described the place where he lived exactly, not at the Red Bull in St John Street, but somewhere further west: 'At the Great gates *in* Red Bull Yard, *between* St John Street and Clerkenwell Green' (my emphasis).[94] If the same location, as sounds likely, this would place the site for these financial transactions as off modern-day Aylesbury Street, either somewhere near the beginning of current Woodbridge Street intersecting with Aylesbury, or further along, where it meets with Hayward's Place. This would have been a much quieter situation for money to change hands.

[91] Glynne Wickham, *Early English Stages*, 4 vols. (London: Routledge, 1959–2002), Vol. II (1972), pp. 106–9.

[92] The two title-pages are those of *The Rape of Lucrece* (London, 1608) and the 1622 production of Marlowe's *Edward II*. See SROI HB10/427/214, with the 'Passage' into the yard from 'St John Street' to the east, and the larger entrance from the 'Road from Clarkenwell to St Johnstreet' to the south. These entrances are equivalent to the entrance of the passage called Hayward's Place and the start of current-day Woodbridge Street respectively.

[93] Hotson, *The Commonwealth and Restoration Stage*, p. 329.

[94] Pinks, *The History of Clerkenwell*, p. 196. Ward opened an ale-house on the site in 1712; James Sambrook, 'Ward, Edward [Ned] (1667–1731)', *Oxford Dictionary of National Biography*, www.oxforddnb.com/view/article/28682, accessed 24 October 2012.

Having two entrances placed like this would mean, logically, and in comparison with other theatre sites that others have already analysed, that the stage should have been to the north, so that the entrances were placed towards the back of the yard space. However, the one drawing of the exterior of the playhouse from St John Street that we have – the Dyrham papers sketch, which cannot be placed before 1664 – shows a likely turret to a tiring house placed to the St John Street side at this time.[95] A strong tiring house on this side would make sense in terms of the 'New buildings' stipulated on the Ipswich sketch, and the extra space there should have been for the yard noted in the 1663 patent; however, a passage into the yard on the stage/tiring house side seems odd to minds accustomed to more discreet placements of public entrances.[96]

There is a certain aspect we can state without question about the Red Bull. It must have had a good, strong tiring house, with ambitious 'heavens', braced with winching machinery. This is because of the demands of the *Ages* plays in particular, where many stage directions require such technology. Take for instance the end of *The Golden Age*, an 'A' graded Reynolds play published in 1611 and described as 'sundry times acted at the Red Bull by the Queenes Maiesties Seruants'. Here we find the following descent and ascent of Iris and Jupiter:

> Iris *descends and presents him*
> [Jupiter] *with his Eagle, Crowne and*
> *Scepter, and his thunder-bolt.* Iupiter
> *first ascends vpon the Eagle, and after*
> *him Ganimed.*[97]

Only a speech later, a seahorse appears for Neptune to mount, given a robe and trident by the Fates. How the Fates placed a burning robe and

[95] Gloucestershire Archives, Dyrham papers (Blathwaite family), D1799/P12. Although previous archivists have dated this drawing to the 1620s, perhaps with reference to texts from an earlier time, it can be quite precisely dated to 1664, as the building to the left of 'Clerken well' (Aylesbury St) is marked 'Earle of Alisburyes house' and there was no earl of Aylesbury until Robert Bruce was made one on 18 March 1664. This time also marks the last entertainment occasions at the Red Bull playhouse.

[96] The Dyrham papers drawing, roughly sketched to show the location of a piece of property across the road from the playhouse, may well have been outlining a half-hearted gable structure. It might also be imagined that the indication of a tiring house was intended to give the impression of a theatre building *with* a tiring house, not necessarily attempting accuracy about the feature's precise location. It is also possible, and has been discussed, that the first theatre's tiring house and stage were on the west side of the yard (see Griffith, 'New Material', 14–15). However, again there would have been an entrance, this time directly to the left of the stage from the audience's perspective.

[97] Thomas Heywood, *The Golden Age* (London, 1611), K2v.

crown on Pluto is left to the imagination; however, the topic of fire and fireworks at the Red Bull will be returned to later in this book.

Reynolds refers to entrances and exits of an ascending/descending nature, yet not always with theatrical 'heavens' or winching in mind. Some of his observations, at that time innocent of the possibility of a castle-tower-like tiring house, led him into thinking about perplexing staging mysteries that the Dyrham drawing may go some way to solve. For instance, again with *The Golden Age*, Reynolds points out a particular staging dilemma where we supposedly see both sides of a gate in the scenes where Jupiter seduces Danae. Danae is kept in a tower of brass by her father, King Acrisius. She is guarded by four old women or 'beldams'. Here Reynolds shows himself to be a little fixed in his thinking, as throughout the book he wants to believe in a constant discovery space involving a curtain, and imagines the beldams starting this part of the play in this curtained area.[98]

When a bell rings and the beldams believe it is the King, they refer to a 'gate' to let him in by, which Reynolds imagines is a door on the side of the rear stage. Danae's door is a central one, so that when she comes on to meet her father she exits the same way, and the beldams show how they are guarding her by settling at the centre. 'So far', Reynolds writes, 'the scene is clearly supposed to be within the tower. Whether the gate is in sight or not is not clear but I have assumed that it is.' But immediately after this there is an outside scene with Jupiter arriving with 'the Clowne his man', and they ring the bell as if they are *outside* the tower. This puzzles Reynolds without his really understanding how the stage can operate as all kinds of in-between spaces.

In today's post-structuralist critical climate, perhaps, we find it easier to conceive of a multiple, plurally invented imaginative world where, in the words of Samuel Taylor Coleridge in his *Biographia Literaria* (1817) an audience, just as a reader, has an unwritten contract with the writer to enjoy 'a willing suspension of disbelief' in order to enter new worlds. In the case of the Danae scenes there are two staging factors about the Red Bull that help us to understand how such a willing suspension was made possible. Firstly, when Jupiter – at the gate – asks the beldams what he should call this 'rich and stately tower', he may well have had a tower tiring house

---

[98] There is certainly a large discovery space employed in Red Bull plays, and certainly a curtain was used, such as at the end of Dekker's *If This Be Not a Good Play the Devil Is in It*, revealing the tortured souls. However, there is no reason to believe that it was a constant curtain space; it may have been a door, for instance, where a curtain was put up now and again when needed.

above them to refer to, of the kind indicated in the later Dyrham draw-ing. 'This is the rich and famous *Darreine* Tower', the beldams explain (H3). Also, as Reynolds shows with the help of another 'A' play, Dekker's *If This Be Not a Good Play the Devil Is in It*, there are entrances in Red Bull plays that start offstage or 'at the corners'. While this was the case, it was always possible for the four beldams to occupy the central stage quite comfortably; for Danae to make her entrance from her room, which was in the tower tiring house behind them; and for King Acrisius, Jupiter and the Clown to enter from offstage – from the yard, even – ringing the bell there, and for the beldams and Danae to engage with them onstage.

With the visual aid of the tower tiring house, if such a construction existed from the beginning of the Red Bull's existence, the Darreine tower illusion is made very easy. By the time we get to the seduction scene with Jupiter inside Danae's room in that tower, we are ready to be a party to the new interior venue on stage. This is particularly so bearing in mind the decisive action of the beldams' physically drawing on the bed, bringing us squarely to the heart of the love-scene action:

> Enter the foure old Beldams, drawing
> out Danae's bed: she in it. They place
> foure tapers at the foure corners. (11v)

When it comes to the tiring house we have a number of pieces of evi-dence, particularly regarding its ambience. This feature in the 1660s, for instance, along with its 'Musique-room', was described by Samuel Pepys when he visited in 1661 for a performance of *All's Lost by Lust* by William Rowley. He was brought into the tiring room 'by a seaman that knew me' and observed 'the confusion and disorder' that were evident among the players. He then went into what he called 'the pitt' for a badly attended performance, 'poorly done', and saw a boy-singer beaten by the master for bad singing.[99] Although Pepys does not mention any machinery, it is interesting that he was invited backstage by a seaman, as it is known how land-bound sailors found employment at theatres because of their expert-ise in pulling ropes.

This later, 1660s allusion to a music room certainly points to an upstairs area for performance and, indeed, Reynolds spotted a variety of moments where this space 'above' or 'aloft' was used. With *The Rape of Lucrece*, for instance – an early Red Bull play – at one moment the area functioned

---

[99] Samuel Pepys, *The Diary of Samuel Pepys*, ed. Robert Latham and William Matthews, 11 vols. (London: Bell, 1970), Vol. II, p. 58.

as a hill outside Rome, at another the City walls. Two characters, at one point, use the 'above' area to enter 'in several places'. What is absolutely imperative when imagining these venues for entertainment is just how little could be 'fixed' at all (as with Reynolds' wished-for 'discoverable space' involving a curtain) for the very reason that fixed aspects of the stage would have prevented many of the multiple and free-wheeling features of the playhouse demonstrated by the Red Bull's play-texts. There was no notion of what we would term 'Health and Safety' in the Red Bull's day, so the performer would have to be careful on a variety of occasions. Imagining, for instance, *one* set of boards covering the stage for the duration of the time the company spent in Clerkenwell stifles possibilities. If there were a trapdoor for one play, why should there not be multiple trapdoors for another play for instance? All that would be necessary for multiple trapdoor effects were a saw, some extra wood, some hinges and a willing workman, and then the boards could be completely replaced for another production, if it were important, at not that much extra cost.

Dekker's play, *If This Be Not a Good Play The Devil Is in It*, has multiple below-stage entrances by devils, and he prefaces the text by mentioning his gratitude for the company's 'Cost, Counsell, and Labour' in his address. With typically cryptic Dekker-like references to 'Fortune' in her 'blind pride' (meaning the Fortune playhouse as much as the personification of luck) rejecting his play as a badly designed building, he acknowledges the Queen's Servants' endeavours for what proves to be a challenging play to present. In another chapter, a scene setting from the anonymous play *Swetnam the Woman-Hater, Arraigned by Women* will be analysed, dependent, as it was, on slots in the stage into which a post might be placed along with, perhaps, further slots for a wooden stall area standing for a court.[100] With no rules for protecting actors against tripping up over such holes, flaps and enhancements, companies could do whatever seemed necessary to bring off effects. Alongside strings of fireworks set up in whatever fashion seemed feasible, the Red Bull presented entertainment that saw actors in contraptions coming down from the 'Heavens', then ascending again; characters and objects coming up from below the stage; actors appearing in the balcony area; and others entering from the corners of the stage. Red Bull noise included drums and trumpets, but also the bang and clash of

---

[100] Similarly, for Cooke's *Greene's Tu Quoque; or, The Cittie Gallant* – a 'B' play for Reynolds, a certain Red Bull play for me – a whole mercer's shop is set up from the beginning that may well have been similarly inserted into the stage boards.

fights; storm scenes; fire-cracker effects; and songs, melodic and of the tub-thumping, drinking variety too.

To crown the playhouse, there was a flag. We know there was a flag because of a comment made in the *Worth* v. *Baskervile* case, where Thomas Drewe describes how depressed the company were getting over Susan Baskervile's financial demands:

> It is true, That the *sa*id Company did pr*e*sente them selves greved, ffor that ^their Gettinge*s* were but small, and yet^ the s*a*id def*endan*t Susan, fro*m* the tyme of the Entering, into the s*a*id later Cov*e*raunte*s* and Bonds, by the compl*ainan*tes and their fellowes, untill Ch*r*istmas, in the yeare of or Lord god one thowsand, six hundred & eighten, receiued the s*a*id three shillinge*s* eight pence a [deleted: 'weeke'] day, ^without any abatemt^ And would haue put downe the fflag, being weary of the s*a*id paym*ent* ...[101]

We can only imagine that such a flag would have sported an eponymous, and St John Street-appropriate, bright red bull.

This has been a chapter that has set up many matters worthy of consideration – some of them multiple and alternative, fit for further exploration. In whatever ways such multiple and alternative historical contexts are understood, the book has certainly begun to give detail to this theatre's generalised history, drawing material from documentary proof where before, for the most part, it was only granted perceptions taken from opinion.

Thomas Heywood's company certainly catered to a citizen audience, and in 1612 Heywood was at pains to dedicate, for example, his *Apology for Actors* to the 'the Citty-Actors', which was an indication, perhaps, of his knowledge concerning Clerkenwell's longer-term entertainment past, catering to the citizens of London. However, Queen's Servants plays were directed at more than one sector of society. Everything had settled into the right niche as far as the old Elizabethan earl of Worcester's company was concerned. They had even founded a new and distinctive playhouse to sell their wares. It is now time to think about the company in terms of their appropriateness to their new Jacobean task – catering to a Danish queen – and what the fullest implications of this task suggest.

---

[101] TNA C24/500/9, Drewe's evidence, Int. 31.

CHAPTER 4

The court and its women: Queen Anna, her circle and some women-centred plays

Up to this point in this book much, in the way of a story, has been started and contextualised. We know something of the Queen's Servants' Elizabethan manifestations as the Earl of Worcester's Men and how the company's makeup developed towards a Jacobean future. We know of its late Elizabethan playhouses and the main personnel involved at that time (e.g. the actor-playwright, Thomas Heywood; the clown, Will Kemp; the managerial Philip Henslowe of the Rose; the Boar's Head's Robert Browne); we know something of its Jacobean playhouse beginnings (the continuing Thomas Heywood; the clown and leader, Thomas Greene; the uncomfortably peripheral Martin Slatiar; and the builder of the Red Bull, Aaron Holland). Another stratum of understanding has been broached in the form of the land on which the Red Bull was built (Thomas Seckford, Anne Bedingfeild), and the bureaucratic and local contexts available to us through the related personalities in the Revels Office (Thomas Bedingfeld, Henry Seckford, Masters of the Tents and Toils). In terms of the nobility, we know Aaron Holland was nominated 'servaunt' to Charles Blount, earl of Devonshire.

With reference to the nobility and its relationship with companies, we also know that the Queen's Servants, set up to please the consort Queen, did indeed have provable – mainly patronage – relationships with some of the courtiers gathered around Queen Anna. Thomas Heywood, in particular, maintained such relationships with the Somerset family, demonstrable through his dedications to both Worcester and his son, Thomas.[1] A further subject for discussion is the extent to which records exist that establish the

---

[1] Dedications by Heywood to Worcester include the seventeen-canto narrative poem, *Troia britannica* (London, 1609); *An Apology for Actors* (London, 1612); and his large-scale history of women, *Gunaikeion; or, Nine Bookes of Various History Concerning Women; Inscribed by the names of the Nine Muses* (London, 1624); as well as funeral elegies to both Prince Henry and King James (London, 1613 and 1625 respectively). He also dedicated his *Conspiracy of Catiline* and *War of Jugurtha* to Sir Thomas Somerset, Worcester's third son, in 1608.

Figure 12 *Anne of Denmark*, by John de Critz the Elder.

company's relationship with the Queen's Chamberlain, Sir Robert Sidney, earl of Leicester from 1618, and also Sir George Carew, Vice Chamberlain as well as Receiver General to the Queen.[2] The evidence concerning these relationships with the nobility and their associated bureaucracy is sparsely recorded, but what is available should be elaborated upon. It needs to be stated here to what extent it is a mistake to pretend that this company, with its long-term reputation for citizen-orientated work within the public playhouse domain gained over many years of criticism, was not chosen as Queen Anna's company for specific reasons, and did not develop *as* her company. I would make the case that the Queen's Servants, chosen for their appropriateness to the task, attempted to cater to Anna of Denmark as well as those with whom she was associated, all this while bearing in mind her family's culture, and that of her circle.[3]

Who was Queen Anna? And what of the significance of herself, her family, and her courtly circle to the newly named Queen's Servants acting company with its smart new north-of-the-walls theatre?[4]

Queen Anna of Denmark: her family and her culture

Anna of Denmark – the consort queen of James VI of Scotland, who became James I of England in 1603 – was born at Skanderborg Castle in Jutland, Denmark, on 12 December 1574. Her father was King Frederick II; her mother, Queen Sophia. Anna was the second child among a family of seven who were all to make their mark on Europe. Her elder sister, Elisabeth, was to marry Duke Heinrich Julius of Braunschweig-Lüneburg at Wolfenbüttel; her younger sisters, Augusta and Hedevig, Duke Johann Adolf of Schleswig-Holstein at Dottorf and Christian II of Saxony, respectively; Anna's brothers were Christian (later Christian IV of Denmark and Norway), Ulrik and Hans (both dukes of Schleswig-Holstein).[5]

---

[2] Carew was made Baron of Clopton in 1605.

[3] Care has to be taken when using the word 'court' in the context of the Stuart queens. This is because a legal court was developed for them dealing with affairs of their property. See N. R. R. Fisher, 'The Queenes Courte in Her Councell Chamber at Westminster', *The English Historical Review* 108.427 (April, 1993), 314–37. I will mainly use the term 'circle'.

[4] The following early biographical material is mainly taken from the *ODNB* entry by Maureen Meikle and Helen Payne, 'Anne [Anna, Anne of Denmark] (1574–1619)', *Oxford Dictionary of National Biography*, www.oxforddnb.com/view/article/559, accessed 14 May 2013. Where other sources are used, they will be footnoted.

[5] For the Danish royal family I generally use the spellings of Mara R. Wade in her invaluable essay, 'Duke Ulrik (1578–1624) as Agent, Patron, Artist: Reframing Danish Court Culture in the International Perspective c.1600', in *Reframing the Danish Renaissance: Problems and Prospects in a European Perspective*, ed. Michael Andersen, Birgitte Bøggild Johannsen and Hugo Johannsen, Studies in Archaeology and History 16 (Copenhagen: National Museum of Denmark, 2011).

Both of Anna's parents were interested in learning and learning development in Denmark, and her mother Sophia, daughter of Duke Ulrich III of Mecklenburg, was noted for taking a personal interest in the education of all her children. As proof of their forward-looking stance when it came, in particular, to science, the son of Queen Sophia's mistress of the wardrobe became the famed astronomer Tycho Brahe, who discovered the nova in Cassiopeia in 1572. King Frederick furnished Brahe with a castle called Uraniborg, which came complete with a laboratory. It was located on the island of Hven, and James I (when he was James VI of Scotland) visited it on 20 March 1590, apparently giving Brahe Scottish copyright over his material for thirty years and continuing to correspond with him afterwards.[6] In Leeds Barroll's words, Brahe's data, taken from his astronomic observations, which were developed later by Johannes Kepler, 'laid the groundwork for Newton's law of gravitation'.[7] Brahe's tutor and friend, Anders Sörensen Vedel, a historiographer and canon of the cathedral at Ribe in Jutland – with the support of Queen Sophia after a meeting at Hven – was one day to publish a book of ancient ballads, or *Kjæmpeviser*.[8] An interest in the ballads of the native country was no doubt passed to Anna of Denmark, and such cultural engagements, embodied in local song, are also traceable in Worcester's Men/Queen's Servants work, such as Thomas Heywood's *A Woman Killed with Kindness* and, in particular, *The Rape of Lucrece*, discussed in the next chapter.

Giving further details about the court at Denmark and its far-reaching family associations across Europe at an important time in the continent's development would begin to take this book into a complex realm far beyond company/playhouse history. It would not be too glib to say, however, that these European ramifications could be of some importance to the acting company under discussion. We have already seen the relevance of Duke Ulrik of Holstein, Anna's brother, to the beginnings of her company in the Jacobean age while contemplating the petition of Martin Slatiar and the Red Bull playhouse. Further to this, however, a sufficient understanding of how important Anna's Danish roots may have been to English masque, spectacle and drama is relevant to the study at hand. Denmark will also be considered in the next chapter, when we look at the European touring group associated with the Queen's Servants.

[6] J. L. E. Dreyer, *Tycho Brahe: A Picture of Scientific Life and Work in the Sixteenth Century* (Edinburgh: Adam and Charles Black, 1890), pp. 203–4.
[7] Leeds Barroll, *Anna of Denmark, Queen of England: A Cultural Biography* (Philadelphia: University of Pennsylvania Press, 2001), p. 16.
[8] Dreyer, *Tycho Brahe*, pp. 138–9.

From an early age Anna spoke a number of languages, including the vernacular Danish, German (as the formal court language in Denmark) and French (which was useful as a language of the Scottish court on her 1589 marriage to James Stuart).

Thomas Heywood wrote in his *Apology for Actors* concerning Frederick II that 'the King of *Denmarke*, father to him that now reigneth, entertained into his seruice, a company of *English Comedians*, commended vnto him by the honourable the Earle of *Leicester*' (E). The clown Will Kemp did indeed visit the Danish court in 1586 in just the way Heywood describes.[9] This would have occurred at a time prior to Anna's marriage to King James in 1589, and she would no doubt have remembered the time when the proposed clown for her new company had visited the family court.

Foundations that encouraged learning from all the arts including drama were laid for Anna of Denmark from her earliest years. From later Danish history it may be observed how an interest in the performative continued and developed in her native country. According to observations about entertainment in Denmark and its associative courts in the duchies and northern Germany, spectacle-orientated Red Bull-like elements of entertainments, using, for example, fireworks, were much in evidence. This was from a time long before the idea of the Clerkenwell playhouse, noted by critics as a venue for fire-related displays.

Danish fireworks

Denmark was in advance of the rest of Europe when it came to pyrotechnic shows.[10] During the occasion of the teenage Christian IV's tour before his coronation, there were fireworks set off to greet him at the castle at Güstrow, for example. This was in November 1595, when a 'flying dragon bearing a man on his back' set off an impressive fiery castle entertainment.[11] There were also devices created for the coronation of Christian,

---

[9] See Butler, 'Kemp, William (*d.* in or after 1610?)'. It should be noted that the 'Earle of *Leicester*' referred to here is Robert Dudley – not Robert Sidney, who gained the title in 1618.

[10] See Mara R. Wade, 'Pyrotechnic Splendor', in *Triumphus nuptialis danicus. German Court Culture and Denmark: The 'Great Wedding' of 1634* (Wiesbaden: Harrassowitz, 1996), pp. 120–46. Many motifs found in these German and Danish displays are also matter for Red Bull plays, such as the vanquishing of Turks (pp. 121, 123, 128, 132), which might compare with scenes from *The Travails of the Three English Brothers*; or classical themes such as Neptune, Mercury and Amazonian women, etc. (pp. 122, 124, 132), which compare with elements in Heywood's *Ages* plays. Devils and mythical animals also feature in these displays, just as in the Red Bull's repertoire.

[11] Wade, 'Duke Ulrik', pp. 246 and 247.

which took place at Copenhagen in August 1596. This occasion was most extraordinarily elaborate and ambitious, and there are engravings of the pageant in existence and 'running at the ring' events showing the extensive processions involved.[12] To mark the entry of important foreign dignitaries, the following spectacle is described:

> a plinth was made consisting of three steps standing on a tall crocodile with gaping jaws and a long tail. On this base a huge dragon stood on four feet, with five heads of different shapes and kinds and a long tail extending upwards. On top of this sat the Whore of Babylon in a red dress, with a golden crown on her head and, in her hand, a golden cup. Next to the dragon [were] a merman and a mermaid with two basilisks of *papier-maché* tournament horses on which rode two men, each with a *papier-maché* cuirass. There was also a skirmish with swords armed with fireworks and shot.
>
> The entire firework display consisted of 16,000 shooting fireworks and explosions and 300 soaring rockets.[13]

King James and Queen Anna were not present at these Danish coronation celebrations, but bearing in mind the famed scale of the event it is, perhaps, no surprise that when Christian IV came to visit his sister Anna in London in 1606, a large-scale firework display was attempted. Mara Wade records the occasion, when Christian thanked James I for his hospitality by staging this event 'superior to any seen until that time in England'. The pyrotechnics involved erecting a 'lion holding the eight capital vices in chains', and all this impressed James greatly. Those responsible were artillery masters of the Danish fleet who were with the Danish King at the time, and James persuaded Christian to leave one of these experts behind. Such a man is later said to have contributed to a Christmas event described as including 'rare fireworks contrived by a Dane'.[14]

Such new and enlivening spectacle contributions as Christian's Thames barge celebrations, put on in a public place with intentions to impress, are bound to have provided a note to the acting company now bearing the

[12] August Erich, *A Detailed and Accurate Description of the Royal Coronation …* (Copenhagen: Waldkirch, 1597); see Mara R. Wade, 'The Coronation of King Christian IV of Denmark, 1596', in *Europa triumphans: Court and Civic Festivals in Early Modern Europe*, ed. J. R. Mulryne, Helen Watanabe-O'Kelly and Margaret Shewring, 2 vols. (Aldershot and London: Ashgate and MHRA, 2004), Vol. II, pp. 245–67 (engravings reproduced on pp. 246–7).

[13] Mara R. Wade, 'Entries in Denmark and Norway', in *Speculum Europaeum [Theatre and Spectacle in Europe (1580–1750)]*, ed. Pierre Béhar and Helen Watanabe-O'Kelly (Wiesbaden: Harrassowitz, 1999), pp. 744–9. Wade comments in her appendix under 'II. Future Research' (p. 749) that 'A study of the continuous tradition of pyrotechnics in Denmark during our period would be an invaluable addition to the study of court culture, especially since Denmark was clearly an advanced centre for fireworks from an early date.'

[14] See *ibid.*, p. 748.

Danish Queen's name. This may well explain how the Queen's Servants, in their year-old playhouse, came to perform plays with such obvious special effects – noisy and bright. In 1940, when George Fullmer Reynolds published his important observations about the repertoire capabilities of the Red Bull, he made a statement speaking volumes about what the playhouse must have been like:

> There are more uses of fireworks than one would expect in a theater lighted by daylight and made of wood.[15]

As Reynolds claimed, Queen's Servants/Red Bull plays with fire-effects included, for example, the blazing star in *If You Know Not Me You Know Nobody*, Part II (London, 1606); a 'line of fireworks' set off in *If This Be Not a Good Play* (London, 1612); and Jupiter's thunder-bolt and Semele's burning bed in *The Silver Age* (London, 1613). There were also the effects in *The Brazen Age* (London, 1613) – the fury entrance 'all fire-works', and the 'Two fiery Buls', the dragon, golden fleece and 'Medea with strange fiery-workes' hanging above them, as well as Hercules' downward exit touched by Jupiter's bolt with a star ascending to take his place.[16]

The company playhouse once professing to have been built for the Danish duke of Holstein's English players was clearly engendered with demonstrative, economically successful drama in mind. The success of the company's ventures included pyrotechnic spectacle as they became, in fact, the company of the duke's sister – the much more important newly English Queen, Anna herself.

Queen Anna: made in Denmark, forged in Scotland

Going back in time, and trying to understand the personal makeup of the company's new royal patron, the scholar can find many indications of a forthright personality. This was the woman who, after all, approached Ben Jonson with the idea of an antimasque in *The Masque of Queens* – not the other way round.[17] Here was a royal person who not only dared to take part in structured entertainment which included women in the display

---

[15] Reynolds, 'Elizabethan Stage Effects', in *The Staging of Elizabethan Plays*, pp. 164–86 (p. 171).

[16] *Ibid.*, pp. 171–2. Further effects, particularly from *The Silver Age*, are described in Chapter 5 of the present volume.

[17] Jonson described the development of the English antimasque for *The Masque of Queens* in February 1609 in the following way: 'her majesty (best knowing that a principal part of life in these spectacles lay in their variety) had commanded me to think on some dance or show that might precede hers and have the place of a foil or false masque'. Ben Jonson, *Ben Jonson: The Complete Masques*, ed. Stephen Orgel (New Haven: Yale University Press, 1969), p. 122.

(masque), but who, from the first, promoted the shocking idea of her circle of women – including herself – 'blacking up' as moorish females in the Jonson/Inigo Jones production, *The Masque of Blackness*.[18]

To begin with, when the character of Anna is considered, one wonders what marriage at fifteen years old – and by proxy – could have been like. Surviving this experience on 20 August 1589 through the stand-in George Keith, the Earl Marischal, in the great hall of Kronborg, she left Denmark on 5 September, ostensibly to journey to Scotland – once she had met her husband.[19] After a lot of weather-related stop-offs, ship-leaks and even fatal explosions, they eventually converged in Oslo, Norway on 19 November, where they experienced more personal nuptials on the 23rd of that month. They went back to the Danish court where they stayed with the royal family for Anna's sister Elisabeth's wedding on 19 April 1590. The couple finally left Scandanavian waters later that month, landing at Leith in Scotland on 1 May, with Anna led in triumph to Holyroodhouse, adorned with gold and silver cloth. She officially entered the City of Edinburgh on 19 May to many celebrations.[20]

What Anna's marriage adventures can tell us from the outset is the extent to which her family operated in a different fashion from that of the Stuarts, as a seemingly relaxed and contented unit, willing to celebrate additions without hesitation or let. The experience of James VI of Scotland must have stood in stark contrast, with his life thus far a confusion of Catholic parentage alongside strict Protestant tutelage, with family assassination, murder and execution for treason seemingly written into the fabric of his life.

Despite making unwise friendships – like the one with the dangerous Francis Stewart, first earl of Bothwell – and varying mishaps in a court context, Anna's relationship with the King must have been, for a time, sexually successful. Many pregnancies, including those ending in full-term childbirth and those less viable, are recorded for the royal couple, qualifying the sense of a King who later became more interested in male favourites over his wife and family.

---

[18] Orgel, in his 'Introduction' to *The Complete Masques*, describes how Jonson related that the masquers 'appeared in blackface by the queen's own command' (*ibid.*, p. 5).

[19] Meikle and Payne, 'Anne [Anna, Anne of Denmark] (1574–1619)'; and Thomas Riis, *Should Auld Acquaintance Be Forgot … Scottish–Danish Relations c. 1450–1707*, 2 vols. (Odense University Press, 1988), Vol. I, pp. 263–4.

[20] For a more detailed and fascinating account of the romance symbolism and ritual involved during this period of Anna's life see Clare McManus, *Women on the Renaissance Stage: Anna of Denmark and Female Masquing in the Stuart Court (1590–1619)* (Manchester University Press, 2002), Chapter 2, pp. 60–96.

The children who survived early life in the royal family were all later made patrons of London's professional acting companies. Their patronage sits alongside that of their father who, as James I of England, brought these companies under royal protection when he moved south in 1603, making himself patron of the Chamberlain's/King's Men, with Anna at the head of the one-time Worcester's Men, by now the Queen's Servants. Prince Henry Frederick, duke of Rothesay (born on 19 February 1594) was to become patron of the original Admiral's – by now Prince Henry's – Men (officially patented 1606, later Palsgrave's/King of Bohemia's after the death of Prince Henry in 1612). Princess Elizabeth (born 19 August 1596) became patron of the Lady Elizabeth's/Queen of Bohemia's Men (from 1611); and Charles, duke of Albany (born 19 November 1600) was first patron of the Duke of York's Men (first patent, 1610), and then, later, of the King's Men, when he became Charles I in 1625.

Stories such as those surrounding Queen Anna's successful retrieval of her son, Henry Frederick – heir, eventually, to two British thrones – from the unwanted guardianship of John Erskine, earl of Mar and his mother (by whom James himself had been brought up), tell us more of Anna's heartfelt and strong personality. This enforced separation between mother and son is said to have caused real barriers for James and Anna as a familial unit, and it was not until 1603, when the Stuarts were to come down to England, that the Queen saw her chance to regain the prince. This, alongside the host of occurrences that took place between England and Scotland at that pivotal time in 1603, grants us a forward glimpse of both the aristocratic atmospheres and the court makeup that developed. The personalities involved in such a development embodied a number of patron-like figures for the Queen's Servants company, and the court audience for which they catered.

The Queen of Scotland, soon to be consort Queen of England, was again pregnant during the time of which we are speaking. The anticipation concerning the Stuart family at the helm of the English nation may be imagined from both a Scottish royal household perspective and that of the current English court, anxious to make headway with the new order. One of two members of the English nobility given the duty of informing King James of the death of Elizabeth was Thomas Somerset.[21] He was the third of nine sons out of at least eleven children born to Edward, earl of

---

[21] The other was Charles Percy. See John Nichols, *The Progresses, Processions, and Magnificent Festivities, of King James the First, His Royal Consort, Family, and Court*, 4 vols. (London: Society of Antiquaries, 1828), Vol. I, p. 37 and note.

Worcester, Elizabethan patron of the Queen's Servants company.[22] Under the new royal family, Thomas Somerset, later first Viscount Somerset, was made Knight Bachelor in 1604/5.[23] In 1608, fresh from publishing his long-term success, *The Rape of Lucrece*, Thomas Heywood put his prose translation of Sallust's *Conspiracy of Catiline* and *War of Jugurtha* into print, dedicating the volume to Sir Thomas. Although not the first to arrive with the news of James' accession in 1603, Thomas Somerset was made Queen Anna's Master of the Horse, as his father had been to Queen Elizabeth. Edward Somerset continued to fill the role of Master of the Horse to King James until 1616, when George Villiers took over this post.

With his wife expecting and awaiting the necessary gathering of English court ladies to go with her into England at Berwick, James went ahead of his family to England on 5 April to claim his new throne.[24] This was when Anna made her maternal move. Aware that John Erskine would not be returning to Stirling from England until 15 May, Anna travelled away from Edinburgh, arriving in Stirling on the 7th of the month. By 27 May, after much striving with the countess of Mar, and with the earl himself on his return, as well as the Scottish Privy Council, Anna left Stirling with her son, taking him back to Edinburgh. Triumphantly she took both Prince Henry and Princess Elizabeth from there, leaving Scotland for England and another kind of monarchic existence. This was on 1 June 1603.

Making new friends: Queen Anna's English circle of women

Meanwhile, gathering at Berwick-upon-Tweed were a group of women who were supposed – as far as the English Privy Council were concerned – to form the core of the Queen's circle in her new reign in the south. These women were the countess of Worcester; the countess of Kildare; Baroness Scrope; Baroness Rich; Lady Anne Herbert; and Audrey, Lady Walsingham.[25] Four of these ladies had served Queen Elizabeth before her passing (Kildare, Scrope, Herbert and Walsingham), and before leaving London they attended the Queen's funeral on 28 April, setting off for Berwick on 2 May. They arrived on the 17th of the month to meet

[22] See G. E. Cokayne, *The Complete Peerage*, 2nd edn, 13 vols. (London: St Catherine's Press, 1910–59), p. 857.
[23] Charles Mosley, ed., *Burke's Peerage and Baronetage*, 106th edn, 2 vols. (London: Fitzroy Dearborn, 1999), Vol. I, p. 221.
[24] 'A Narration of the Progress and Entertainment of the King's most Excellent Majestie…', in Nichols, *The Progresses*, Vol. I, p. 60.
[25] TNA AO1/2022/1; Nichols, *The Progresses*, Vol. I, p. 167; Helen Payne, 'Aristocratic Women and the Jacobean Court 1603–1625, Ph.D. thesis, University of London, 2001, p. 24.

Queen Anna, who eventually got there on 3 June. Elizabeth Somerset (née Hastings), countess of Worcester, married as she was to Edward Somerset (Tudor patron to the Queen's Servants), was perhaps chosen because she was the wife of the Master of the Horse. She was to be mentioned as one of Anna's Ladies of the Bedchamber – according to her husband – in a letter later discussed. Penelope Rich was singled out as someone representative of the re-emerging Essex group. As we have seen, both of these ladies – through the agency of the men with whom they were associated – had already proved significant to the history of the Queen's Servants and the Red Bull playhouse. In the case of Elizabeth Somerset, this was as the wife of the Elizabethan patron of the company; Penelope Rich is relevant as the long-term lover of the earl of Devonshire, master of the Red Bull owner. As for the others, Frances Fitzgerald, née Howard (Kildare) and Philadelphia Scrope, née Carey are certainly of theatre history interest. This niece and aunt were associated with Charles Howard and Henry Carey, the important Elizabethan patrons of drama who once gave patronage to the Admiral's/Prince's and Chamberlain's/King's Men respectively.[26] Lady Anne Herbert was the daughter of Henry Herbert, second earl of Pembroke, and the niece of Sir Robert Sidney, who is of yet more relevance to the Queen's Servants.[27] The newly made Baron Sidney of Penshurst, brother of the famed and deceased nobleman-poet Sir Philip Sidney (d. 1586), was also appointed Queen Anna's English Lord Chamberlain in 1603. Two years later he was made Viscount Lisle, and much later, in 1618, he was made the new earl of Leicester.[28] He is important to the Queen's Servants' story, in that, as her Lord Chamberlain from an early time during the first Stuart rule, he held the post most associated

---

[26] Frances Fitzgerald, countess of Kildare was a daughter of Charles Howard, Lord Admiral and the earl of Nottingham. Nottingham, like Elizabeth Somerset's husband Worcester, was patron to a company of players – the Admiral's Men – soon to become the Prince's Men. Baroness Scrope, once Philadelphia Carey, was Kildare's aunt: the younger sister to Katherine Carey, who – now dead – was the first wife of the Lord Admiral. In turn the Carey sisters, Katherine and Philadelphia, were daughters of Henry Carey, who had died in 1596. He was otherwise known as Baron Hunsdon, made Lord Chamberlain to the Queen's household in 1585 – that is, he was the Lord Chamberlain who acted as patron to Shakespeare's company during the Elizabethan era.

[27] In this identification Payne differs from Leeds Barroll. See Barroll, 'The Court of the First Stuart Queen', in *The Mental World of the Jacobean Court*, ed. Linda Levy Peck (Cambridge University Press, 1991), pp. 191–208 (p. 200). See also Barroll, *Anna of Denmark* (Philadelphia: University of Pennsylvania Press, 2001), pp. 182–3n; Payne, 'Aristocratic Women', p. 32 and note.

[28] Robert Shephard, 'Sidney, Robert, First Earl of Leicester (1563–1626)', *Oxford Dictionary of National Biography*, www.oxforddnb.com/view/article/25524, accessed 16 March 2012. Shephard writes of the long-coveted Leicester earldom and how Sidney described its attainment as '[the queen's] worck'.

with supplying entertainment for the Queen's circle and is referred to in the well-known court case relating to the company (see next chapter).[29]

History has it, however, that in whatever way these women were to figure at the beginning of the new reign, another group made it north to Queen Anna first. Not content with meeting her at Berwick – on the borders of England and Scotland – these women alighted upon the queen in Scotland itself. The happening was described thus:

> Before the departure of these personages aforesaid, divers Ladies of honour went voluntarily into Scotland to attend her Majestie in her journey into England, as the Countesse of Bedford, the Ladie Hastings, the Ladie Cecill, the Ladie Hatton, the Ladie Harington, and divers others; and also sundrie Gentlemen of good qualitie, which I here omit; so as the Queene was very honourablie attended with the English, besides sundrie of the Scottish Nobilitie.[30]

For 'the Countesse of Bedford' we read Lucy Russell (née Harrington), who, if she was the ringleader of the Scotland-bound group, certainly achieved her personal objectives through her trip to the north. A significant figure in terms of patronage of the arts, having married Edward Russell, third earl of Bedford, in 1594, she had annoyingly found herself in disgrace after the Essex Rebellion when her husband had been implicated in the plot. Like Penelope Rich, however, she was destined to be ushered into royal favour again.

The rest of Bedford's five-woman group were all related to either Bedford or to the Bedford-related Cecils. For Bedford's relations, for example, 'Lady Harington' was Anne, the countess's mother; 'Lady Hastings' was Sarah, Lady Hastings (née Harington, an aunt).[31] As for the Cecils, this was always a highly important family during this era of Tudor/Stuart politics, especially in the person of Robert Cecil – political genius, court machinator and royal adviser, who was the son of Lord Burghley. 'Lady Cecil' is likely to have been Theodosia Noel, the countess of Bedford's first cousin, who was married to Sir Edward Cecil, Robert Cecil's nephew and the son of Thomas, second Baron Burghley. Elizabeth, Lady Hatton (née Cecil)

[29] The last of this Privy Council-selected group was Audrey, Lady Walsingham, who was married to Sir Thomas Walsingham, nephew of the intelligence-gatherer, Sir Francis Walsingham (d. 1590). Audrey was said to have been a favourite of Queen Elizabeth, but was not of immediate appeal to Queen Anna. She seems to have had the least to do with drama from birth.

[30] Nichols, *The Progresses*, Vol. 1, p. 168.

[31] Barbara Kiefer Lewalski, *Writing Women in Jacobean England* (Cambridge, MA: Harvard University Press, 1993), p. 22 believes this is Lady Dorothy Hastings; Helen Payne identifies Lady Sarah as the Hastings in question. However, according to Payne, there is no evidence that a Lady Hastings gained a place at court; Payne, 'Aristocratic Women', pp. 26, 29.

was a niece of Robert Cecil – Thomas, Baron Burghley's daughter. She
had been married to Sir William Hatton, Sir Christopher Hatton's heir,
but was now married to Sir Edward Coke, the Attorney General, who
owed much to the Cecils and was close to them. It was Lady Hatton who
had owned a residence actually on the Seckford Estate since the 1590s.

The argument here with this particular set of identifications of this
second group is that the women were all involved in one intermarried
family from the Bedford/Haringtons, extending outwards towards Cecil-
associated relations. They would all have been highly conscious of their
place within a familial, yet pointedly political, milieu, centring on a combination of Cecil approval with not a little countess of Bedford excite-
ment. Moreover, they were not, as Helen Payne points out, 'women who
served Queen Elizabeth, nor did any of them attend her funeral'. Thus,
they could journey north and forge ahead of the other group without
being missed.

By pulling off this feat, Lucy, countess of Bedford, did indeed secure for
herself a premium post as Lady of the Bedchamber in Queen Anna's court
before she and the Queen had left Scotland. The countess of Kildare left
the official party at Berwick to journey to Edinburgh, and she too gained
an appointment on 5 June as governess to Princess Elizabeth, sworn in as
Lady of the Privy Chamber on the 22nd of that month.

The success of someone who did not, apparently, journey to the north –
Katherine Howard, countess of Suffolk – is not surprising in view of the
fact that she was the wife of Lord Thomas Howard, who was to be a long-
term Lord Chamberlain to King James. Evidence of this success, along
with that of the countess of Derby and Lady Walsingham, is noted from a
list the earl of Worcester drew up in 1604, where a number of names, both
recognisable from the Queen Anna welcoming groups – and as yet unrec-
ognisable – occur.[32] Elizabeth Stanley, countess of Derby, was originally
Elizabeth de Vere, daughter to the earl of Oxford, and she and her sister
Susan – also mentioned on Worcester's list – both became Ladies of the
Drawing Chamber. Susan de Vere was about to become Susan Herbert,
marrying Philip Herbert (made first earl of Montgomery in 1605).
It will be remembered that it was the Earl of Oxford's Men who combined with the Earl of Worcester's Men in 1602, thereby becoming the

[32] Helen Payne states that Katherine Howard; Elizabeth, countess of Derby; and Audrey, Lady
Walsingham were three women who successfully attained posts in the Queen's household and who
were, at the same time, Robert Cecil favourites, the latter two becoming Ladies of the Drawing
Chamber.

third company permitted in London.[33] William Stanley, the sixth earl of Derby – Elizabeth de Vere's husband – was, moreover, a one-time patron of Tudor players who had performed at the Boar's Head like Worcester's Men. Barroll notes that in 1599 Stanley was described as 'busy penning comedies for the common players', and that in 1601 he asked his wife to write to Robert Cecil, her uncle, asking for a reprieve for his players when threatened with a ban.[34] Frances Seymour, countess of Hertford, who was drawn to be another important Lady of the Bedchamber – beside Lucy Russell, Elizabeth Somerset (countess of Worcester) and Arabella Stuart – is one of whom we will hear more. She was the wife of Hertford, the one-time patron of one of Martin Slatiar's Elizabethan companies.

The earl of Worcester made the list of 1604 in an informal letter to the earl of Shrewsbury, which may be viewed at Lambeth Palace Library:

> first youe must know we haue ladyes of diuers degrees of favor some for the priva*t*e chamber some for the drawing chamber, some for bedcham-ber, and some for neyther certeyn, and of this nomber is onely my la*dy* Arbella and my wy*f*e my lady of bedford howldethe fast to the bed cham-ber my lady harford would fayn but her husband hathe Cawled her home, my lady of darbee the yonger the lady Suffolke, Ritche nottingham, Susan, walsingham, and of late the lady Sothwell for the drawing chamber, all the rest for the private Chamber when they ar*e* not shut owt, for mayny tymes the dores ar lokt but the plotting and mallice a mongst them is sutche that I thinke only hathe leyd an invisibl*e* snake abowt most theyr neke*s* to sting one another to deathe. for the presence there ar nowe 5 mayde*s*, Cary, myddellmore woodhowse, gargrave, Roper, the sixt is determyned but not Come.[35]

Obviously, highly political court manoeuvres were taking place at the time of the accession, where both noble women and important Privy Councillors saw their chance to take part – or take part by proxy – within interesting networks of power relations attendant on the consort Queen. Queen Anna herself, as final decision-maker, again defined her person-ality by mainly settling on the younger generation of the group chosen for her – many of whom had, as has been demonstrated, notable patron-age relations to do with drama. According to Helen Payne, of those who were officially sent to meet the Queen at Berwick, only Lady Scrope was an out and out failure when it came to attaining office. Audrey, Lady Walsingham, became Guardian and Keeper of the Queen's Robes; and

---

[33] LMA COL/RMD/PA/01/002, no. 189.
[34] *ES*, Vol. II, p. 127; Barroll, *Anna of Denmark*, p. 53.
[35] Lambeth Palace Library, LPL 3201, fos. 182v–183.

Lady Anne Herbert – the sister of both William Herbert, third earl of Pembroke and Philip, Susan de Vere's husband – was appointed Lady of the Privy Chamber (one of the 'all the rest' group indicated by Worcester). Of that official party, the earl of Worcester noted both Penelope Rich and Lady Walsingham as Ladies of the Drawing Chamber (with his wife mentioned as one of the elite Ladies of the Bedchamber).

Queen Anna's women-centred circle and the Red Bull's plays for women

With reference to Worcester's continued and undoubted relationship with Queen Anna and her circle, the earl was to become High Steward of Her Majesty's Revenues in 1612 on the death of Robert Cecil: an office overseeing her financial incomings and outgoings. Four of Somerset's nine daughters consistently performed roles in the Queen's masques. These, according to Leeds Barroll, were Elizabeth Guilford, Katherine Petre, Anne Winter and Catherine Windsor. All of them appeared in *The Masque of Beauty* of 1608, for instance, and all, bar Petre, in *The Masque of Queens* the following year.[36] Retrospectively therefore, it is obvious in what ways the part played by Worcester, his wife and his children demonstrates an active and proficient relationship between earl and Queen, marked out in dramatic enterprise with Worcester's old acting company becoming Queen Anna's troupe. Equally, the fact of the de Vere women's strong associations with Anna's masques marks up what had to be from the beginning a budding relationship between nobles and Queen as daughters of Oxford, co-patron of what came to be the Queen's company. Elizabeth, countess of Derby's success in being among the favoured women, recorded up to at least 1606, as wife to the earl who was writing plays at a time when both his company and that of the earl of Worcester were working at the Boar's Head, would also appear significant. But here is where an exchange of aristocratic female involvement in active entertainment may be said to take place.

Thomas Heywood, during the reign of the previous monarch, the powerfully female Queen Elizabeth, wrote a very woman-centred two-part play, misleadingly titled *Edward IV*, for it was more, in truth, about the appositely subtitled 'fayre Mistresse Shoare, her great promotion, fall and misery', than her royal lover. This play was intended for the Earl of

---

[36] See Barroll, *Anna of Denmark*, p. 204n78. All three also appeared in Samuel Daniel's *Tethys Festival* of 1610. Earlier, 'Sir Thomas Somerset' also appeared in Jonson's *Hymenaei* of 1606 (Jonson, *The Complete Masques*, pp. 475 and 476).

Derby's Men and was first published in 1599. It is likely it received a first airing at the Boar's Head, that playhouse where both Worcester's and Derby's Men are said to have played.

According to Richard Rowland, the play's critic and editor, however, it was at the Red Bull 'that the popularity and notoriety of *Edward IV* would be firmly established'.[37] This is perhaps because the first successful printing of the drama was followed by five other editions in 1600, 1605, 1613, 1619 and 1626 – the first four of these subsequent editions running right through the time of the Queen's Servants' existence with Thomas Heywood as their main playwright. Because Derby's Men had no known London venue after 1601, it has been assumed that the play went with Heywood into the Queen's Servants' repertoire.

In terms of size of role, the part of Jane Shore, as told by Heywood, is large – especially in the second part where, for example, we see her in full-blown shame, made to walk barefoot through the streets of London, covered in a sheet and holding tapers (a usual penalty for women at the time). In a speech thirty-three lines long, she readies herself for penury:

> The child, offended, flies unto the mother.
> The soldier, struck, retires unto his captain.
> The fish, distressed, slides into the river.
> Birds of the air do fly unto their dams,
> And underneath their wings are quickly shrouded.
> Nay, beat the spaniel, and his master moans him,
> But I have neither where to shroud myself,
> Nor anyone to make my moan unto.[38]

Perhaps Jane is at her strongest before this, and at her most appealing to both Elizabeth I and the consort Queen Anna, especially when she meets Queen Elizabeth, King Edward's wife. Mrs Shore appeals to the King:

> O royal Edward, love, love thy beauteous queen:
> The only perfect mirror of her kind,
> For all the choicest virtues can be named!
> O, let not my bewitching looks withdraw
> Your dear affections from your dearer queen,
> But to requite the grace that she hath shown
> To me, the worthless creature on this earth,
> To banish me the court, immediately.
> Great king, let me but beg one boon of thee,
> That Shore's wife ne'er do her more injury.[39]

---

[37] Heywood, *Edward IV*, p. 6.   [38] *Ibid.*, II.[xx].42–9.
[39] *Ibid.*, II.[x].134–43.

With this kind of drama we can perhaps begin to see how Heywood's women-centred plays could have been perceived as appropriate to Anna and – in some respects at least – to her woman-centred circle.

Other specific Thomas Heywood plays, once Elizabethan for a woman in power, now Jacobean for a king's wife, would include his play dated to 1603, *A Woman Killed with Kindness*. Again we have a woman-centred play, aiming to cater to a royal female's sympathies. Heywood does not fight shy of portraying Anne Frankford – the rural woman in this case – as caught up in a situation not dissimilar to Jane Shore's, and again a strong character through speech. Paralysed by the shame of her adultery with Wendoll, she asks her husband when the recriminations will begin:

> When do you spurn me like a dog? When tread me
> Under your feet? When drag me by the hair?[40]

As Frankford too betrays rhetorically pitched curiosity ('Was it for want / Thou playedst the strumpet? Was thou not supplied / With every pleasure, fashion, and new toy – / Nay, even beyond my calling?') he calls for their children, accusing her of bringing a stain on them, their shame growing 'in greatness as they wax in years'.[41] Dilemmas like these may have seemed to be of personal interest to intelligent women alert to the debate they suggest. At the same time it should not be forgotten that Heywood's company – a recent amalgam of two companies given patronage by important male courtiers – may well have been suggested for the Queen by male councillors preparing for her arrival, keen to feed her with male-perceived, appropriate drama. Sometimes the sentiment poured forth by female characters in this drama must have been hard for Anna's women to swallow. In *A Woman Killed*, for instance, when Frankford goes he claims that he will give her judgement on return, and Anne hopes for death:

> O me, base strumpet,
> That having such a husband, such sweet children,
> Must enjoy neither. O to redeem my honour
> I would have this hand cut off, these my breasts seared,
> Be racked, strappadoed, put to any torment;
> Nay, to whip but this scandal out, I would hazard
> The rich and dear redemption of my soul.
> He cannot be so base as to forgive me.
> Nor I so shameless to accept his pardon.
>
> (xiii.131–9)

[40] Thomas Heywood, *A Woman Killed with Kindness*, in *'A Woman Killed with Kindness' and Other Domestic Plays*, ed. Martin Wiggins (Oxford University Press, 2008), ix.91–2.
[41] Scene xiii, lines 106–9, 120–1.

Then this character goes on to do what Shakespeare's female characters, naturally played by men, would never do. She appeals directly to the women in the audience:

> O women, women, you that have yet kept
> Your matrimonial vow unstained,
> Make me your instance: when you tread awry,
> Your sins like mine will on your conscience lie.
>
> (xiii.140–3)

One pauses to imagine how a female courtly audience member – such as Penelope Rich – might have responded to these thoughts, having openly flouted original vows to a husband. I think the point can be made, from the male perspective that probably took the decision to apportion Worcester's Men to the Queen, that the company producing Heywood's overtly women-interested repertoire was probably the best one for her for all kinds of reasons, including morally directive ones. Heywood was to go on to be much associated with thinking about – and catering to – not only women in an audience but a sophisticated female readership as well. The agency of Edward Somerset, earl of Worcester, is again indicated as Heywood dedicates his *Gunaikeion or Nine Bookes of Various History Concerninge Women* to him in 1624. 'Amongst the illustrious Queenes', Heywood says, 'your Lordship may reade those whom you haue as zealously honored, as you haue been by them royally fauored, Q. *Elizabeth*, & Q. *Anne*.'[42] Heywood goes on to mention the virtues of Somerset's daughters later in his dedication, and devotes a page to both Queen Elizabeth and Queen Anna in the book, including a long funeral poem for Queen Anna.[43]

In the earlier period, many of the women gathering around the Queen at the beginning of the new reign were evidently relevant to her interests, and therefore we can perceive a coherent group ready to respond to what they read, saw and experienced as a group. Apart from theatre, the range of such interests would include language (with Anna's linguistic proficiency evident from early in her life), and, to a lesser extent, poetry, pictorial art and – in particular – the joy of the masque form. Other than a shared interest in the arts, however, it is also important to think of these women with reference to drama and the Queen's Servants in another way. The very fact that the first English Stuart Queen made sure she was surrounded by

---

[42] 'To the Right Honorable, and Most Noble, Edward Somerset, Earle of Worcester', in Heywood, *Gunaikeion*, A3.

[43] *Ibid.*, A3v; and '*Of Queenes Illustrious*', in *Gunaikeion*, pp. 122–5 (pp. 123–4).

women – high-powered, self-assured patroness-women at that – makes not just the past women characters in Heywood's plays but, in particular, the future woman-centredness of his drama a natural cause for comment.

Now, it is surely the case that, if we contemplated the extent to which not Heywood but Shakespeare has been long associated with the development of female roles in the drama of this time, we would be writing a book that has been written many times before. The images of the emotionally complex Viola, the objectively intelligent Portia, one over-hasty Juliet, another over-assured Beatrice would defeat – on one important level – any attempt to call Thomas Heywood the victor in the battle for a female auditory's heart and mind. But I would also suggest that it is with – by and large – the subtle and perceptive *characterisations* of such women that Shakespeare succeeds here, alongside the poetry that expresses their characters and character development, rather than any specific wish to explore the conflictual and/or political *situations* or narratives within which they find themselves. That they could do little about their situations with any virtue seems to be a given with Shakespeare's portrayal of many of his female characters, trapped as they are within the patriarchal societies that envelop them. Something a little different could be said to be the case with Heywood. As we have seen with Mistress Shore in *Edward IV* and Anne Frankford in *A Woman Killed with Kindness*, and from what could be observed concerning Queen Elizabeth herself in *If You Know Not Me You Know Nobody*, Part I, all these plays bear witness to the fact that their characters have something clear to say about their dilemmas, while trying – at least – to achieve active audience sympathy. Perhaps at the expense of privately observed, at times claustrophobic, Shakespearean character development, these are women in 'grande dame' drama situations whose expression in response to the politics around them is clean and straightforward, untrammelled by the overly poetic or subtle. In short, it may be argued that so many women in Shakespeare's plays appeal from a character and character-development point of view and from an internal, contemplative perspective; however, they tend to become overtly willing parties to their patriarchy-dominated situations. They tended to have, as time went on during the period, very little, if 'nothing', to say about themselves.[44] This was not the case with Heywood, who consistently gave his heroines a great deal to say, if still, much of the time, embarrassed at their shortcomings, confessional brow-beating and having to become victims of their broader-scale dilemmas in the end.

---

[44] See Cordelia in *King Lear*, I.i.

In one Heywood play where the woman certainly comes out on top, Princess Elizabeth, prior to her reign as Elizabeth I, is tested in difficult circumstances throughout. In *If You Know Not Me You Know Nobody*, Part I (i.e. that first published in 1605) the royal heroine has to show great character in order to survive. In a scene placed towards the end of the play, she confronts her fears in a meeting with her sister, Queen Mary, finding herself playing a double game – weeping for fear while pretending they are tears of joy, for instance. At this meeting she is all but interrogated by Mary, who asks her if she will 'submit' to the new order – but the characterisation of Elizabeth is one that is adamantly courageous in her doubleness, and she expresses herself as such.

ELIZ. My life madam I will, but not as guilty,
  Should I confesse
  Fault done by her, that neuer did transgresse.
  I ioy to haue a sister Queene so royall,
  I would it as much pleas'd your maiesty,
  That you enioy a sister that's so true:
  If I were guilty of the least offence,
  Madame, 'twould taint the blood euen in your face;
  The treasons of the father, being noble,
  Vnnobles all your children, let your grace
  Exact all torture and imprisonment,
  What ere my greatest enemies can deuise,
  And they all haue done their worst, yet I
  Will your true subiect and true sister dye.
                    (Part I, F3–F3v)

Perhaps Heywood's most notable achievement when it came to his woman-centred plays – one undoubtedly first performed at the Red Bull – would be his Lucrece play, first published in 1608. In this most famous story, sourced, for Heywood, through Livy rather than Ovid, a philosophical debate had long been in place when it came to questions of virtue, sex, honour and a woman's suicide. Here were found a set of issues that would have been of interest to Anna's intelligent group of friends, if, while presenting them, the playwright again took risks for a female auditory, further explored in the following chapter. At the heart of the play, however, Colatine's wife Lucrece, horrified at the thought of her impending rape by Sextus, son of King Tarquin, is emboldened to put forward arguments.

    Oh Prince of Princes, doe but weigh your sinne,
    Thinke how much I shall loose how small you winne.
    I loose my honour of my name and blood,

Lost, Romes imperiall Crowne cannot make good.
You win the worlds shame, & all good mens hate,
Oh who would pleasure, buy at such deere rate?
Nor can you tearme it pleasure: for what's sweet,
Where force & hate, iarre and contention meete?
Weigh but for what tis that you vrge me still,
To gaine a womans loue against her will?
Youle but repent such wrong done a chaste wife,
and think that labour's not worth all your strife.
Cursse your hotlust, & say you haue wrongd your friends,
But all the world cannot make me amends.
I tooke you for a friend, wrong not my trust,
But let these chast tearmes quench your fiery lust.[45]

In the next section of this chapter I would like to explore this woman-centredness further by looking at one work of the Queen's Servants period – not by Heywood, but by an anonymous writer – in relation to Queen Anna and the fact of her new, predominantly female circle. This in turn brings about an examination of two definitions that may be applied to the word 'court' when it comes to discussing the household and work-ings of the Queen, and the possibility of contemporary, women-interested topics with which the Queen's network may have engaged. One definition is to do with gatherings around royalty; the other is that to do with the legal court – an arena created not just to discuss issues, but to come to a judgement about them.

The courtly woman and her awkward situation: the countess of Hertford and the Sowernam/Swetnam pamphlets

Despite the need to take these women seriously as dispassionately intelli-gent and able to respond to female issues with zest, the fact remains that more than a few of Anna's circle could be said to be stuck within their own complex marital traps. One example of a court-bound woman of the period who, to some extent, strove for what she wanted against male hier-archical principles was Anne Clifford, countess of Pembroke, Dorset and Montgomery. Having survived parental inheritance disputes, she found herself in difficulties with her husband from 1609 – Richard Sackville, Lord Buckhurst, third earl of Dorset.[46] Sackville was supported in his

[45] Thomas Heywood, *The Rape of Lucrece* (London, 1608), G2v.
[46] Richard T. Spence, 'Clifford, Anne, Countess of Pembroke, Dorset, and Montgomery (1590–1676)', *Oxford Dictionary of National Biography*, www.oxforddnb.com/view/article/5641, accessed 15 May 2013.

desire for wealth from her estate by the King, yet she continued to fight this through the second decade of the seventeenth century. In her diaries she recorded to what extent the Queen supported her, Anna even advising Clifford against trusting the advice of James I.[47] Clifford is another recorded taking part in the 1608 *Masque of Beauty* and the 1609 *Masque of Queens*, both by Ben Jonson, and the 1610 *Tethys Festival* by Samuel Daniel (who had been Clifford's tutor before 1602), and she can therefore be shown to have had access to a structure of support in female courtly form.[48] Apart from this one example of Anna's circle – taken, in fact, from outside the specifics of the earl of Worcester's list of 1604 – Frances, countess of Hertford is another court woman who stands out. She was one of two stated Ladies of the Bedchamber, the other being Lucy, countess of Bedford. This was a post of the utmost closeness to the queen; however, Frances Seymour (neé Howard) was to be kept from much of her official duty, if accounts of her life are anything to go by.

Born Frances Howard in 1578, Seymour first married a London vintner named Henry Prannell, the son of an alderman. This was a marriage arranged by her cousin Thomas Howard (later earl of Suffolk) when she was thirteen years old. Connected to the nobility, the young Mrs Prannell formed an emotional attachment to Henry Wriothesley, the earl of Southampton. But by the time Prannell had died in 1599, Southampton had married Elizabeth Vernon, and was suffering some disgrace at court. In 1601, Frances Prannell then married Edward Seymour, the earl of Hertford, who was then sixty-two years old and had been married previously to another Frances. The newly made countess of Hertford had only married Seymour on the understanding – derived from her astrologer and medical adviser, Dr Simon Forman – that the earl would not last long. It was unfortunate then, that Hertford was to go on living until 1621, when he died at the exceptionally great age of eighty-two. During the interim, despite Frances achieving high office with Queen Anna in the new reign,

---

47 See Anne Clifford, *The Diary of Anne Clifford: 1616–1619*, ed. Katherine O. Acheson (New York: Garland, 1995), 65–6, and *Lives of Lady Anne Clifford … and of Her Parents Summarized by Herself*, ed. J. P. Gilson (London: Roxborough Club, 1916), p. 38; as well as John Chamberlain, *The Letters of John Chamberlain*, ed. Norman McLure, 2 vols. (Philadelphia: The American Philosophical Society, 1939), Vol. II, p. 63 for an outcome to the disputes; Barroll, *Anna of Denmark*, p. 153 and notes.

48 Barroll, *Anna of Denmark*, pp. 198–199n34. Clifford is also one who had links with Clerkenwell from a Seckford/early Red Bull time, stating in her reminiscences for 5 July 1647 that her youngest daughter married 'James Compton Earl of Northampton' in the 'Church in Clerkenwell', where 'my Mother & I had been parishioners for some 7 yeares together in my childhood'. See Anne Clifford, *The Diaries of Lady Anne Clifford*, ed. D. J. H. Clifford (Stroud: Sutton, 1990), p. 96.

Seymour kept a tight rein on his countess, keeping her in the country and not allowing her to come to court to take up her duties. However, it is interesting to note that this denied courtier-woman is mooted to have been the anonymous female debate-pamphleteer, Ester Sowernam.[49] 'Sowernam' was the 1617 'female' apologist for womankind who replied to an earlier misogynist tract by Joseph Swetnam called 'The Arraignment of Lewd, Idle, Froward and Unconstant Women' (London, 1615): the 'Sower' or sour pseudonym deliberately chosen to contrast with Swetnam's implication of sweetness. Sowernam's reply was also inspired by the other 1617 riposte, 'A Muzzle for Melastomus' by Rachel Speght, who happened to be a distant associate of the countess's through Speght's Godmother, Mrs Mountforde.

Although the claim that Hertford and Sowernam were one and the same has never been substantiated, if the ruralised countess was indeed as secretly cosmopolitan in tone as Ester Sowernam in her pamphlet, her possible involvement seems especially significant in view of the anonymous play of the Red Bull's repertoire, *Swetnam the Woman-Hater, Arraigned by Women* (London, 1620). In the next drama analysis section I aim to look at this play in the context of the pamphlet debate that inspired it, and as a drama meant to invoke a Queen's circle in the audience's imagination. For whether Hertford was truly Sowernam or not, the play, *Swetnam the Woman-Hater*, can only be seen as all too relevant to the subject of women's subjugation, and how 'honourable' women might have wanted to respond to the topic.

REPERTOIRE 3   *SWETNAM THE WOMAN-HATER,*
ARRAIGNED BY WOMEN

(a) The pamphlet debate

Joseph Swetnam, originally a citizen of Bristol, was a fencing master, whose professional claim to literary fame was a manual, published in 1617, called *The Schoole of the Noble and Worthy Science of Defence*.[50] His 1615 pamphlet, *The Arraignment of Lewd, Idle, Froward, and unconstant women:*

---

[49] Donald W. Foster, 'Stuart, Frances, Duchess of Lennox and Richmond [*other married name* Frances Seymour, countess of Hertford] (1578–1639)', *Oxford Dictionary of National Biography*, www.oxforddnb.com/view/article/70952, accessed 12 March 2012.

[50] Cis van Heertum, 'Swetnam, Joseph (*d.* 1621)', *Oxford Dictionary of National Biography*, www. oxforddnb.com/view/article/26828, accessed 12 March 2012.

Or the vanitie of them, choose you whether was originally written under the name of Thomas Tel-Troth and printed by Edward Allde. However, in the same year Swetnam came clean, writing under his own name, in another edition printed by George Purslowe. Both were published by Thomas Archer. Running into some sixty-four pages of quarto text, excluding title-page and preliminaries, it advertised itself as 'Pleasant for married Men, profitable for young Men, and hurtfull to none'. According to the *English Short Title Catalogue*, this book was to enjoy seventeen editions in total (including those of 1615) into the eighteenth century, eleven of these published in the seventeenth.[51] When approaching Swetnam it is as well to remember his frank confession that he 'wrote this booke with my hand, but not with my heart', and that he was 'in the rough' of a 'fury' when he wrote it.[52] He advises, moreover, that he had no intention to speak much of women 'that are good' (A2v), and it indeed looks likely to be the case, as Barbara Kiefer Lewalski states, that he wrote the pamphlet 'in the spirit of the rhetorical game' – a game that was to gain for him the reward of commercial success.[53] The pamphlet is made up of three chapters, Chapter 1 covering items like the advice of St Paul and the philosopher Socrates concerning women; nagging women; marriage; and how women marked the interrupted glories of figures like Solomon, David, Job, Agamemnon and Hercules.[54] Chapter 2 explores individual experiences further, tackling the subjects of the enticements of women, and of a woman's beauty as the 'bane of many a man' as she spends his money. With this Swetnam brings in a panoply of whores: those known to classical and biblical history, and a generalised, contemporary womanhood, who, if one takes away their clothes, hairstyles and accessories, are 'ruggedly' or just 'simple' in looks, and a danger sexually regardless.[55] The last chapter advertises advice to the young man not to marry too quickly, promoting work as the best way of taking one's mind off women, being very

---

[51] 1615 (two), 1616, 1617, 1619, 1622, 1628, 1629 (Edinburgh), 1634, 1645, 1660, 1702, 1704, 1707, 1714, [1720?], 1733.

[52] Joseph Swetnam (Tel-troth), *The Arraignment ...* (London: Allde, 1615), A3r.

[53] Barbara Kiefer Lewalski, *The Polemics and Poems of Rachel Speght* (Oxford University Press, 1996), p. xxi.

[54] 'This first Chapter sheweth to what use Women were made, it also sheweth that most of them degenerate from the vse they were framed vnto, by leading a proud lasie and idle life, to the great hindrance of their poore Husbands.' Swetnam, *The Arraignment ...*, B1r–C3r (pp. 1–13).

[55] 'The Second Chapter sheweth the manner of such Women as liue vpon euill report: It also sheweth that the beauty of Women hath beene the bane of many a man, for it hath ouercome valiaunt and strong men, eloquent and sibtill men. And in a word it hath ouercome all men, as by examples following shall appeare.' *Ibid.*, C3v–F1r (pp. 14–33).

careful of the example a prospective husband chooses if he has to choose one at all.[56] Swetnam advises men to marry at twenty-five, preferably to a maid of seventeen, far over and above a widow who may be hard to recon-figure, and at least to marry someone whose economic circumstances are beneficial. It is here in this larger chapter that Swetnam mentions a few women of virtue – Susanna, Sarah and Lucrece being three, and it is here that he goes through kinds of marriage, both advisable and ill-advised. He then includes a special section in this chapter devoted to the mistake of marrying a widow, entitled 'The Bearbaiting or the vanity of Widdowes: choose you whether'.[57]

In response, it would seem, to Swetnam's publication, a minis-ter's daughter, one Rachel Speght, was moved to publish *A Mouzell for Melastomus, the Cynicall Bayter of, and foule mouthed Barker against Evahs sex* .... This was printed by Nicholas Okes in 1617, and, tellingly, it was also published by Thomas Archer. It is obvious that Speght did not see Swetnam's topic as suitable for a rhetorical game. The subject he was tack-ling was all too serious for her. In fact, if one takes away the preliminaries to Speght's piece including prose dedications, poems, etc., the text in itself (bar the introduction of a few references towards the end) might be taken to be an eloquent, if simple, quite beautiful defence of women, drawing most thoroughly on biblical allusion, such that might be imagined from a young, intelligent woman wishing to mimic her father's sermonising in the pulpit. What begins to be important here is to whom, exactly, these pamphlets are directed, as Speght is very clear when she dedicates her work to 'all vertuous Ladies Honourable or Worshipfull' as well as 'all other of Heuahs sex', and repeats the 'Honourable and Worshipfull' direction twice in her dedicatory text. This sits alongside the indication of 'personages of so high ranke'. In her 'Preface', Speght indubitably attacks Swetnam's intentions, his blasphemous arguments and even his language, but after these preliminaries, her main text, the 'Mouzell' – or muzzle – proves itself as one tackling a subject very close to her heart. Her central concern is to put her argument for women across using mainly biblical exempla, like the minister's daughter that she was, wanting to prove her rhetoric-ally accomplished mettle. In the margins she carefully places her citations, answering Swetnam's arguments concerning the story of Adam and Eve, St Paul's and Solomon's sayings about women, St Paul on the nature of

---

[56] 'This third Chapter sheweth a remedy against loue, also many reasons not to be to hasty in choise of a Wife. But if no remedy but thou wilt marry, then howe to choose a wife, with a Commendation of the good, vertuous, and honest women.' *Ibid.*, F1r–I1v (pp. 33–58).
[57] *Ibid.*, I2–I4v (pp. 59–64).

sin, the Creation story, and the good counsels of Miriam, Sarah and even Pilate's wife. Mary Magdalene and the Virgin Mary are also invoked, and marriage lauded. If her argument comes across as naively simple, as she was all too conscious it might, this is not because she is lacking ability as a structured advocate, but rather because she shows little sign while arguing that she understands the part that the no-doubt commercially motivated and clever Swetnam employs with *humorous* intent.

After an 'Epilogue or upshut of the premises' where Speght attack's man's ingratitude, another part begins where she makes 'Certaine Quaeres to the bayter of Women', in which she quotes Swetnam page and line and gives herself away as one who accuses Swetnam of not understanding the nature of humour in the Bible. It is not certain, having read Swetnam's work, that it should not have been another way round, for it would appear that Speght does not understand Swetnam's humour. Speght makes her point with reference to Job's wife: 'In saying … that *Jobs wife counselled her husband to curse God*, you misconster the Text; for the true construction thereof will shew it to bee a *Sarcasmus* or *Ironicall* speech, and not an instigation to blasphemie' (F4, p. 31).

It would seem from this that Speght was willing to see irony and sarcasm in the Bible's texts, but not in Swetnam's. Although the inspiration behind what he wrote is clearly (according to him) a bad mood after a broken heart, the effect of Swetnam's attack itself was undoubtedly meant to be humorous. This intention would not do for Speght, however. In other words, for Speght, there is one rule for Job's wife, but quite another for Joseph Swetnam.

Ester Sowernam, thought by some to be the countess of Hertford in disguise, also dedicates her work – *Ester hath hang'd Haman* (London, 1617) – to all women, while also privileging the 'Honovrable, Noble' and gentle ones. This takes up the reins of Speght's attempt, but with a different approach and an altogether different class tone. Prompted to read Swetnam's pamphlet as the result of an after-dinner conversation, Sowernam found herself disappointed in the much-anticipated Speght work and, as she describes in her 'Epistle Dedicatory', notwithstanding Speght's 'tendernesse of yeares' she found her approach too slender 'for she vndertaking to defend women, doth rather charge and condemne women' (A2v).

After writing an exhortation to the 'young youths of Great Brittaine', whose first job, after serving their apprenticeships, is to 'looke for … a good Wife', Sowernam also centres herself on a mainly biblical defence, but taking a different tack. Where Speght takes up the position that men are the more guilty because women are weak in comparison to male strength (and therefore less perfect), Sowernam glories in the perfection of women as the chronologically second and therefore best made of the two human genders (B3v). If, as Swetnam claimed, women were bound to be flawed because they were made from a crooked rib, much rather that scenario than being made of mud, as with men in the template of Adam (B2). Moreover, she points out (agreeing with Speght), that ribs are close to the heart, and therefore the more splendid material (B3v).

From the outset Sowernam understands Swetnam's humorous twang:

> Homer doth report in his Illiads, that there was at the siege of Troy, a Grecian, called Thersites, whose wit was so blockish, he was not worthy to speake: yet his disposition was so precipitate, hee could not hold his tongue. Ioseph Swetnam in all record of Histories cannot be so likely paraleld as with this Thersites … (B1v)

Sowernam's pamphlet is made up of four parts consisting of eight chapters in all. The first part covers answers to Swetnam's accusations, giving examples of how women were honoured by God in the Creation story (through mercy and childbearing), how different individual women proved themselves in the Old Testament, and how, similarly, New Testament women understood Christ especially through grace. This takes up four chapters.[58]

The second part is prefaced by a new address to the 'courteous and friendly Reader' with a chapter on 'what estimate Women were valued in ancient and former times'. It therefore finds instances in the classical and historical world of the pre-eminence of women: mythological deities and humans – those from British history included – alike. The scope is large, including the three Graces, as well as Proserpina; Boadicea; Helen, mother of Constantine; Queen Eleanor, wife of Edward I; Queen Margaret, wife of Henry VI; and Queen Elizabeth I. Sowernam chooses to develop this central chapter by pointing out the ways in which men 'sue' to women and employ many methods of persuasion. If the devil were once a serpent, he has always since been figured as a man (E–E1v).

The third part is the 'Arraignment', and is the most directly relevant to the play. It is made up of three chapters. The first, Chapter 5, is 'The Arraignment

---

[58] Chapter 1: 'An Answere to the First Chapter of the Arraignment of Women' (B1r–B2v (pp. 1–4)); Chapter 2: 'What incomparable and excellent prerogatiues God hath bestowed upon Women, in their first Creation' (B3r–C2r (pp. 5–11)); Chapter 3: 'What choise God hath made of women to be instruments to deriue his benefits to Mankinde' (C2r–C3r (pp. 11–13)); Chapter 4: 'What excellent blessings and graces haue beene bestowed upon women in the Lawe of Grace' (C3r–C4r (pp. 13–16)).

of Joseph Swetnam, who was the Author of the Arraignment of Women; and vnder his person, the arraignment of all idle, franticke, froward, and lewd men'. There is a chapter on 'Joseph Swetnam his Enditement', and then another entitled 'The answere to all objections which are materiall, made against Women'. Swetnam entitles his piece 'The Arraignment'; Speght answers with another set of arguments seen as a 'Mouzell' to Swetnam's voice; but it is Sowernam who dares truly to 'arraign' Swetnam, using the terminology of legal procedure in her text. Putting him to the 'bar', for instance, and employing appropriate female judges – Reason and Experience – before a twelve-man jury made up of the Five Senses and the Seven Deadly Sins, she gives a true form of an indictment. This begins 'Joseph Swetnam, thou art endited by the name of Joseph Swetnam of Bedlemmore, in the Countie of …', and she includes an 'answere' to Swetnam's own charges, etc.[59] Many excellent points, relevant to the 1618/19 Red Bull drama, are made, which means that the anonymous writer of the play made full use of these pamphleteers' ideas of putting the sexes on trial.

(b) The anonymous Red Bull play

The play, then, responds to the debate by various ways and means, setting it within the framework of the tragi-comic but leaning towards comedy, for structurally, in terms of its plot and outcome, the play is a tragi-comedy. The setting is Sicily, where a king is mourning the loss of one son and fears the loss of another. His one daughter, Leonida, cannot inherit, hence the destiny of the state may lay in the hands of the man she marries. The King's other son, Lorenzo, is not dead but captured by the Turks. One Nicanor, a nobleman of the court, is given the guardianship of Leonida. He has ambitions to marry her and become King. In a new scene the imagined 'Swetnam' character, post pamphlet publication in England, muses on the response he may gain from it abroad. He has changed his name to 'Mysogynos' and has brought his lessons in fencing with him to Sicily. When another nobleman, Scanfardo, enters to join Swetnam's fencing school, Swetnam berates him because of his impending marriage:

> Marry a woman, Scholer? thou undergo'st an harder task,
> Then those bold Spirits, that did vndertake
> To steale the great *Turke* into Christendome.
> A woman! she's an Angell at ten, a Saint at fifteene,
> A Deuill at fortie, and a Witch at fourescore.[60]

---

[59] 'Bedlemmore' may well be an illusion to 'Bedlam'.
[60] Anon., *Swetnam the Woman-Hater* (London, 1620), B1v.

He cannot understand why women had to be necessary to the procreative enterprise:

> Why did not Nature infuse the gift of Procreation
> In man alone, without the helpe of woman
> Euen as we see one seed, produce another?
>
> (B2)

This is perhaps the closest we get to Swetnam's pamphlet statement concerning women being 'necessary euills' – a claim hotly responded to by Speght and Sowernam alike.[61] It is perhaps a case of the playwright rhetorically knowing and wanting to respond humorously to Sowernam's argument about childbearing. Sowernam saw it as a gift God gave women at the Creation. By putting forward a self-achieved conception by man, the playwright naturally makes Swetnam/Mysogynos look pathetic.

The play-Swetnam, Mysogynos, vows to be 'the euerlasting scourge to all their Sex' and gives Scanfardo his pamphlet, promising to give him the reason for his hatred one day:

> I haue arraign'd vm all, and painted forth
> Those Furies to the life,
> That all the World may know that doth it read,
> I was a true Mysogenist indeed.
>
> (B2v)

Of course, just as with Swetnam's pamphlet, no arraignment has taken place. But legal proceedings do occur in the play as in Sowernam's pamphlet. And there is more than one hearing for the reader or the audience to attend. Two of these legal proceedings occur in Act III. The act begins with one kind of legal court scene – initial proceedings the King is undertaking against his own daughter and Lisandro, the Prince of Naples. In an effort to see Leonida, Lisandro disguised himself as a friar and, having retired to another room with her, was discovered by Scanfardo. Atticus, the King, does not understand why the judgement against the wayward young lovers cannot be given quickly, but the judges are unable to decide between the two defendants, hell-bent on defending one another. The judges then come to the conclusion that there should be advocates brought forward to plead in 'publique disputation' – one a man and the other a woman (D4v). Hearing the proclamation given out by King Atticus in search of

---

[61] *'Epistle "To the Reader"'*, in Swetnam, *The Arraignment...* (London: Allde, 1615), A2v.

the man to speak for the 'equitie of men, against the false imputations of women', Mysogynos accepts the challenge (E2v). Lorenzo, the missing brother, escaped from the Turks, has arrived and has disguised himself as an Amazonian woman. Hearing the other proclamation made by the court of his mother, the Queen, he volunteers to speak for the 'innocency of women, against the false imputations of detracting men' (E3).

For the scene of the trial of Lisandro and Leonida, besides King Atticus there are two judges, a notary, a crier and others in attendance along with the two accused. Atticus talks in terms of a 'Session', and then Queen Aurelia leads in 'Atlanta' (Lorenzo in his female disguise), Loretta the maid and a few more women. The Crier goes about his business:

CRY. O yes! O yes! O yes! If there be any man – or woman – in this Honourable
Court – that can produce – any lawfull cause – against either of the
Aduocates – why they should not bee admitted – Let them now speake, or
for euer hereafter oald their peace –. (E3v)

The two judges are then sworn in, just as in a real trial, and the language used in the scene from thereon is shot through with legal terms and rhetorically led legal strategies. Of course, it seems a shame that the person speaking on behalf of women is, in fact, a man, but the fact of Atlanta's manhood is, on a more direct level, very funny, while it is perfectly believable that an Amazonian woman could speak proficiently in a court of law. There are two lawyers present who comment on the ongoing arguments. As Atlanta makes her points 'First …' and 'Next …', the First Lawyer exclaims 'A promising *Exordium*'. But Mysogynos comes back. It is then, at about sig. E4v, that recognisable arguments issue forth:

MYS. Did not th'inticing beautie of a woman,
　Set Troy on fire?
ATLAN. Did not man first begin
　To tempt that beautie with the fire of lust?
MYS. Beautie first tempts to lust. (E4v)

Atlanta launches into a speech all about how men 'sue' to women – just as in Sowernam's pamphlet (Sowernam, E–E1v):

　　　　　Witness the vowes, the oaths, the protestations,
　　　　　And Crocadile teares of base dissembling men,
　　　　　To winne their shamelesse purpose: Whereof missing,
　　　　　Then but obserue their Gifts, their Messages,
　　　　　Their wanton Letters, and their amorous Sonnets,
　　　　　Whereby they vent the smoke of their affections,
　　　　　Readie to blind poore women, and put out
　　　　　The Eye of Reason.

This speech continues for twenty-eight more lines, and is humorously angled in that it is delivered by a man who knows too well how men (himself) operate around women. But the women think it is wonderful, as shown by the following stage direction: '*A Plaudite by the women, with shouts, crying,* Atlanta, Atlanta, Atlanta!'. But again Mysogynos comes back:

MYS. And this is woman, who well knowes her strength,
    And trimmes her Beautie forth in blushing Pride,
    To draw as doth the wanton Morning Sunne
    The eyes of men to gaze. But marke their natures,
    And from their Cradles you shall see them take
    Delight at making Babies, deuising Christnings,
    Bidding of Gossips, calling to Vp sittings,
    And then to Festiuals, and solemne Churchings,
    In imitation of the wanton ends,
    Their riper yeers will ayme at. (F1v)

He then talks of 'the very Mother of Mischiefe', 'The mysterie of Painting, Curling, Powdring', so that the two lawyers comment on how 'The tyde begins to turn'. As Mysogynos goes on about the leading-on of men by women – 'Now to draw on, and then againe put off' –

        A *Venus* mole on euery wanton cheeke,
          To make a gracefull dimple when she laughes:
          And (if her teeth be bad) to lispe and simper,
          Thereby to hide that imperfection
                                                    (F2)

As Mysogynos's arguments develop and are appreciated by the men listening (stage direction: '*A Plaudite by the Men with shouts, crying,* Misogynos, Misogynos, Misogynos!') Atlanta (Lorenzo) loses her temper, forgetting she is a man in women's clothes, speaking in pity of Swetnam's mother.

ATLAN. Base, snarling Dogge, bite out thy slandrous tongue,
    And spit it in the face of Innocence,
    That at once all thy rancour may haue end:
    And doe not still opprobriously condemne
    Woman that bred thee, who in nothing more
    Is guiltie of dishonour to her Sex:
    But that she hath brought forth so base a Viper,
    To teare her reputation in his teeth,
    As thou hast done.
                                                    (F2–F2v)

Mysogynos responds 'O doe not scold, good woman!', and Atlanta-Lorenzo, no-doubt remembering his true sex, says, partly to himself, 'I forgot my selfe.' The two finish by hurling instances of tyrant men on the one side and whorish females on the other ('*Nero* and *Heliogabulus*'; '*Hellen* and *Cleopatra*').

After more applause for Mysogynos he is led away, and it is left to the Notary to read out the judgement that King Atticus has given him:

> NOT. That women are the first and worst temptations
>   To loue and lustfull folly: and to this
>   We are here present, ready to subscribe.
>
>   (F3)

Queen Aurelia, failing in her demand for justice, kneels to her husband. However, he is, despite her pleadings, 'obdurate':

> ATTIC. Arise; and know, A King is like a Starre,
>   By which each Subiect, as a Mariner,
>   Must steere his course. Iustice in Vs is ample,
>   From whom Inferiors will deriue example.
>
>   (F3v)

Of course, Leonida is not executed, for therein lies the tragi-comic ending – expecting tragedy but gaining a happy outcome. Her execution procession is shown in dumbshow to the accompaniment of 'While we sing the dolefull knell', a three-verse 'Song in parts' (G2–G2v). However, her brother Lorenzo (as Atlanta) asks to be present at the beheading and somehow contrives her escape. We know nothing of this until the end of the play, and before this there is yet another arraignment put on display in this Red Bull play. Queen Aurelia is distraught at the apparent death of her daughter and, indeed, the seeming suicide of her daughter's lover, Lisandro. However, Atlanta becomes aware of a comic twist that will clear a path for revenge. Mysogynos, post-trial, sends Atlanta a letter professing love to the Amazonian woman who is, of course, Prince Lorenzo in disguise. The Queen and her cross-dressed son contrive to use this situation to entice Mysogynos into his own woman-centred destiny. Mysogynos-Swetnam responds to an invitation written by Atlanta and, in a banquet scene set in an orchard, he is led on by her stand-offish attitude and says he recants his former views of women.

Alone, Atlanta suddenly becomes aggressive towards Mysogynos so that they end up in a fencing match with one another – which the Swetnam character loses. Atlanta calls the women to enter, and Queen Aurelia orders

Mysogynos to be bound. They bind him to a post threatening torture, and they gag him. Atlanta eventually intervenes, for she has other ideas:

> Forbeare your tortors yet, something is hid,
> That we must haue reueal'd, and he himselfe
> Shall be his owne accuser: you all know,
> He hath arraign'd vs for inconstancie:
> But now weele arraigne him, and iudge him too,
> This is womans counsell
>
> (I4)

Atlanta makes the Queen 'Ladie Chiefe Iustice of this Female Court', herself 'Mistris Recorder'; Loretta the maid must be 'the Notarie', another the crier, and so forth. She asks an old woman to choose a female jury with herself as foreman. A 'Barre' at which the accused can stand is called for and a 'Tree' in the orchard is used to secure it.

A 'Clarke of the Peace' is ordered to read the indictment, 'Silence in the Court' is called for and the charges read (I4v). Mysogynos denies them, pleading not guilty. His pamphlet, 'The Arraignment of idle, froward, And vnconstant women' is produced, and Swash, Mysogynos' servant, gives a long speech in evidence against him.

The judgement brings us back, not to Sowernam, but to the young Speght, as Atlanta pronounces that first and foremost he will be required to wear a 'Mouzell' (K1v) so that he will no longer be able to 'expresse / His barking humour against woman-kind'. In this way he will be paraded in the streets of cities and occasionally bound to posts or stakes, 'And bayted by all the honest women in the Parish' (K1v). The Swetnam character denies there will be such a woman, and in response further judgement is given, that he will be whipped to the coast and sent to live among infidels. All his books will be burned and his own arraignment published 'That he may liue a shame vnto his Sex' (K2).

Swetnam for women, two kinds of court, and the cross-dressed plays of the Queen's Servants' repertoire

Swetnam the Woman-Hater is, therefore, not only a play arranged around a woman-centred debate, using three pamphlets to do this – two of them purporting to be by women – but it can also be viewed as an endeavour to replicate real court proceedings. This is relevant both to the context of Queen Anna's circle – with a few of the women notably involved in proceedings or legal arguments of their own – and to the fact of the Red Bull's interest in court drama evident in the later repertoire, many of its plays

SVVETNAM,

THE

VVoman-hater,

ARRAIGNED BY

WOMEN.

A new Comedie,

Acted at the *Red Bull*, by the late
Queenes Seruants.

LONDON,
Printed for *Richard Meighen*, and are to be sold at his Shops
at Saint *Clements* Church, ouer-againſt *Eſſex* Houſe, and
at *Weſtminster* Hall. 1 6 2 0.

Figure 13 Title-page of anon, *Swetnam the Woman-Hater, Arraigned
by Women* (London, 1620).

centring on female characters.[62] The anonymous *Swetnam the Woman-Hater*, moreover, is not the only play belonging to the Queen's Servants' repertoire that employs the comic device of men dressing as women. This is a comic motif threaded through early Red Bull plays, some of them known to have been performed at court and before Queen Anna's circle. Of course, all early modern plays were performed entirely by men, so men-dressed-as-women was the norm. In Shakespeare's comedies in particular, performed by the King's Men at this period, great mileage was derived from young-men-playing-women-disguised-as-men (e.g. Rosalind in *As You Like It*, Viola in *Twelfth Night*, etc.). But it is almost as if in humorous reply that the Queen's Servants included men-playing-men-disguised-as-women, and one can imagine the comic and sexual relish employed by the company, gesturing, perhaps, to the memory of Robert Sidney's brother, Sir Philip, whose book, *Arcadia*, used this device (Pyrocles disguises himself as an Amazonian woman, Cleophila; Duke Basilius falls in love with him/her).[63]

The errant attire of Lorenzo was entirely intent on provoking laughter in an audience context. In comparison with Shakespeare's efforts, it is one comic effect to accept the convention of a woman disguised as a man struggling to maintain a manly perspective on her situation; it is quite another comic effect (funnier even?) to see – in the flesh – a man playing a woman in a dress, also struggling to maintain the appropriate perspective. Perhaps, in the case of the Amazonian Atlanta who is really Lorenzo, the actor sported large hairy legs beneath a classical tunic-dress, along with an ill-fitting wig. Heywood, in particular, was to enjoy this 'reply' to Shakespeare on several occasions, with the excuse of classical precedent set in motion long before Sidney's efforts to help him along. In his *Ages* plays Heywood invents nothing when, in *The Golden Age* (London, 1611) – 'As it hath beene sundry times acted at the Red Bull, by the Queenes Maiesties Seruants' – Jupiter disguises himself as one of Diana's nymphs in order to seduce Calisto, who promptly gets pregnant and is rejected from Diana's virgin-only group. Much comic effect is gained for the audience looking on as the god acquires his prize, Calisto puzzled at the hardness of

[62] See, for example, John Webster, *The White Devil* (London, 1612) with its court scenes involving Vittoria Corombona; and *The Devil's Law-case* (London, 1623, 'As it was approouedly well acted by her Maiesties Seruants'). This may have been presented at the Cockpit. The latter tragi-comedy is preoccupied with lawyers and contains an important, again female-interested law-case, where a mother claims her son is a bastard. These are not the only plays containing court scenes, and this somewhat challenges the impression that this company was preoccupied with citizen drama.
[63] See Sir Philip Sidney, *The Old Arcadia*, ed. Katherine Duncan-Jones (Oxford University Press, 1985), pp. 16–17.

her fellow's 'gripe', along with her too-wanton kisses (E2v). Again, in *The Brazen Age* (London, 1613), Hercules cross-dresses as he is found under the thumb of a woman, having fallen in love with Omphale, Queen of Lydia. At his first entrance in the play he is described as 'attired like a woman, with a distaffe and a spindle' (K), much to the horror of his friends, who discover him. 'How haue I lost my selfe?', he exclaims (K2v), much like Atlanta at that similarly comic moment in the *Swetnam* play.

Swetnam the Woman-Hater: the title-page

It was this play, out of the number possible, that was elected to be published in the immediate aftermath of Queen Anna's death, and in this way there is yet more to say about it, for *Swetnam the Woman-Hater* is one of a few produced at significant moments for the company choosing to display impressive title-page illustrations. The contexts for two of these, namely *If You Know Not Me*, Part I (London, 1605) and *Greene's Tu Quoque* (London, 1614) may be easily understood. With the former, Elizabethan nostalgia for Heywood's company entering the new Jacobean age could only invite playbook-selling success by producing this intricate woodcut picture of Gloriana. With the latter, the company, although professing poverty in documents emerging after the clown's death, was not shy of boasting about Thomas Greene, both through prefatory dedications to the comedy and the extraordinary picture of him on its title-page.[64]

In what context the money was found to afford these no-doubt expensive illustrations as part of the product one cannot imagine, but these quartos must have held extra commercial appeal on the bookseller's stall because of them. The *Swetnam* illustration is worthy of more than passing comment, not just because of its quality, which is of a very clear standard (the Heywood *If You Know Not Me* is very intricate; *Tu Quoque* is also clear – Greene endearingly characterised with a wink and that backgammon-board-like jacket (Figure 7)), but because of its composition and its indications of what the Red Bull's staging and even its stage may have been like.

The title-page leaves us in no doubt that it is a Red Bull play we are reading, performed by the Queen's Servants, and published after the death of their royal patron.[65] The text is unequivocal: 'SWETNAM,

---

[64] See R. A. Foakes, *Illustrations of the English Stage 1580–1642* (London: Scolar Press, 1985), pp. 91 and 102.

[65] Queen Anna died on 2 March 1619. The play was entered on the Stationers' Register on 17 October 1619, published in 1620.

THE Woman-hater, ARRAIGNED BY WOMEN. *A new Comedie*, Acted at the *Red Bull*, by the late Queenes Seruants'. The operative adjective here may be taken to be 'the *late* Queenes Seruants'. After this there is a 'framed' woodcut showing a paved floor, shaded in the appropriate places and with due care for perspective, with a large brick or stone wall rising at the back. Set into this wall are two latticed, leaded windows, in the usual Tudor style, with window-sills jutting out at the bottom as if they are exterior stone sills. Before this, placed on the paving stones, a four-sided barrier is mounted with an opening framed by a 'bar' device. This bar has been achieved by slotting two broadswords into one another, one of them stuck into a wooden 'turned' post. The post is to the left of a man standing with his back to us and seen in profile. The name 'Swetnam' is appended to the man on the woodcut, written to one side of him between the figure and the post, standing a little taller than the man. Set around the barriers are a crowd of women, all dressed similarly with tall hats and stiff neck ruffs, two with staffs in hand, again with their backs to us, like officials of the court. Centrally placed within the barriers is a large throne complete with scrolled arm-rests and canopy, and with steps up to the seat. Placed on this throne is a crowned queen with a sceptre in her left hand, her right hand held up with fingers splayed as if in control of the man below, who is clearly shown speaking. His left hand is held up as if to amplify his speech, and his right held out to the side showing further expression. To the right of the queen is a woman, dressed similarly to the others, who holds a piece of writing. She is also animated in speech as her gaze is firmly planted on the queen, her finger tracing the writing as she speaks. Outside the barrier and to the left is another woman, also speaking, with her hand stretching over the barrier raised in legal-like argument.

The setting is clearly depicting the court scene at the end of the play. This scene, described above in terms of the text, consists of Atlanta as recorder, Queen Aurelia as judge, an Old Woman in charge of the jury, the maid Loretta as notary and other women given court roles to play. One problem with regard to the way the scene is displayed in the woodcut is that it is clearly not an orchard that is depicted. The post evident in the woodcut is alluded to in the text, but so is a tree that is supposed to help with the erection of the bar at which Swetnam is meant to stand. Rather than an orchard, a kind of exterior paved area is shown. R. A. Foakes, in his *Illustrations of the English Stage*, interprets the post as doubling for a tree, which would seem to denote an acknowledged staging of the scene rather than a pictorial representation of the setting.[66] Foakes goes on to write, however, that the walls and floors shown are conventions for interiors. However, with this fine woodcut depiction of a scene that is set in an orchard in the text, showing easily reproduced staging (the post, the swords, the barriers), the drawing cannot be of an interior when it is an imagined exterior that is shown. There were certainly woodcuts for plays that depicted trees, and, indeed, trees that characters climb exist in the Red Bull texts.[67] It therefore seems strange, having gone to so much trouble with everything else, that with the *Swetnam* play the illustrative effort would not have gone the extra mile to depict a tree, were it not for the likelihood that the picture displays the scene as it was practically produced at the Red Bull, rather than as it could be imagined when read.[68] Posts and swords passing for the bar in court are easy to erect on stage: trees less so. Thus it is, I would submit, that the title-page of the Red Bull *Swetnam* play is the closest representation we have of the actual staging of a Red Bull play during the Queen's Servants' time there.[69] It was published near to the death of their own royal patron, marking, in truth, the end of their outfit as they knew it, taking the play as an opportunity to celebrate the embodiment of a queen in the full panoply of her judging capabilities, surrounded by supporting women who were both empowered and empowering.

---

[66] See Foakes, *Illustrations*, pp. 116–17 on the *Swetnam* title-page illustration.

[67] In Dekker's *If This Be Not a Good Play* there is a tree 'Blasted with Goblins, that about whose roote 5. mandrakes growe, i'th Groue by Naples', where Scumbroth the cook goes and the devils agree to meet.

[68] See title-page of, for example, *Philaster* by Francis Beaumont and John Fletcher (London, 1620) for pictorial representations of trees; Foakes, *Illustrations*, pp. 118–19. Also the Red Bull's own play by Heywood, *The Iron Age* (London, 1632), showing Hector and Ajax with a tree in Ajax's hands; Foakes, *Illustrations*, pp. 134–5.

[69] Reynolds also sees staging possibilities in the illustration. See Reynolds, *The Staging of Elizabethan Plays*, pp. 45–7, on this and important observations on 'imaginative rather than literal presentation' (p. 47).

Entities and splinter groups: the Queen's Servants companies at the courts, in England and in Europe

With the help of Jacobean records held at The National Archives in England, it is known that the Queen's Servants performed plays at court. During the first Christmas season of the new reign, for performances on 2 and 13 January 1604 – before the dating of any other of their records – they were paid for two plays.[1] Whichever plays they were, they were performed before Prince Henry, and John Duke, one-time Chamberlain's Man (of Shakespeare's company, in other words), was the payee. John Duke was again paid for one play on behalf of the company for the season 1604–5.[2] This was performed before the King on 30 December 1604. It was a Sunday, as described in the Chamber accounts' record, and according to an Audit Office document it was by Heywood and it was called *How to Larne of a woman to wooe*.[3]

In 1605–6 the company presented an unnamed play before the King on 'St Iohns Day at night'.[4] However, there is no record of court performances before anyone in the known documents during the season 1606–7 or 1607–8. During the court season 1608–9, however, no fewer than five plays were performed by the company for the King and Prince Henry 'at severall times'. For these, Thomas Greene was paid £50 for the company.[5] One play was presented by the Queen's Servants before the King on St John's Day at night 'last paste' during the 1609–10 season, for which they achieved £10.[6] For 1610–11 we learn that three plays were recorded as having been performed by the company in front of the King and the

---

[1] The following records have been taken from MSC 6, and then checked at The National Archives. 1603–4: TNA E351/543, m. 116 – John Duke was paid £13 5s 8d for 'two interludes or playes presented' on 2 and 13 January before Prince Henry.

[2] 1604–5: TNA E351/543, m. 137b – Duke was again paid £10.

[3] TNA AO3/908, Part 13.

[4] 1605–6: TNA E351/543, m. 163b – again John Duke received £8 6s 8d on 30 April for the performance.

[5] 1608–9: TNA E351/543, m. 214.

[6] 1609–10: TNA E351/543, m. 235; given to Thomas Greene on 31 March.

Prince – before Prince Henry on 10 December and before King James on St John's Day 'at night'. Thomas Greene was the payee according to both records.[7] In 1611–12, Thomas Greene is recorded receiving £20 for two performances before the King and Queen – on 27 December (St John's Day) and 2 February – and 'xiijli vjs viijd' for two plays, this time before Prince Henry and Princess Elizabeth, on 21 and 23 January.[8]

At the difficult, or even tumultuous, 1612–13 season, for both Queen and company (the former had lost her son, Prince Henry; the latter their clown, Greene), it would appear that there were no recorded court performances by the Queen's Servants, but many other plays were performed by other companies in the run-up to the wedding festivities for the Princess Elizabeth with Frederick V, the Elector Palatine. In the 1613–14 season, however, Robert Leigh received £20 for two plays performed before the King, on 24 December and 5 January (Christmas Eve and Twelfth Night).[9] The company do not technically appear in court records again for the 1614–15 season, but Leigh receives again – for seven plays in all, for 1615 and 1616. This money was given in two separate payments, both signed by the Lord Chamberlain, one for three plays dated 25 April 1615 for £30 (probably for plays performed earlier that year) and the other dated 20 May 1616 for four plays. In all, Robert Leigh was paid £70 for these unnamed plays, all performed before the King.[10] However, intriguingly, the company is not mentioned in relation to Leigh's payment in 1615, nor is there any reference to his 'fellows', and we will refer to this again when discussing the company's English touring movements in a section to come.

Ellis Worth, a new payee, also receives £10 for a play performed by the Queen's Servants company before the Queen at 'Queen's Court' on 17 December 1615. The record of this exists in the Queen's household accounts, however, where we are possessed of data for certain periods and of which we will hear more later. In two separate records for the period 1616–17 we learn that Robert Leigh was again paid, this time for three plays, performed by the named Queen's Servants before the Queen and Prince Charles.[11] This activity by Leigh from 1613 to 1617 may seem altogether

---

7 1610–11: TNA E351/543, m. 249b.
8 1611–12: TNA E351/543, m. 267b. The two performances given in December and February were of the same play according to the Revels Accounts: 'the City Gallant' (St John's Day, December) and 'Tu Coque' (Candlemas, February). The play was published in 1614 as John Cooke's *Greene's Tu Quoque; or, The Cittie Gallant.*
9 1613–14: TNA E351/544, m. 29b. The dating is wrong on this record, giving the December performance as 24 December 1614 when it should be 1613. The payment was made on 21 June 1614.
10 1615–16: TNA E351/544, mm. 65b and 66.
11 1616–17: TNA E351/544, m. 77b.

strange as, in answer to interrogatories in the *Worth* v. *Baskervile* case of 1623, he claimed he was absent from the company from at least 1611 – the year George Pulham, a half-sharer of the company, died – to Christmas 'in the yeare of or Lo: god one thowsand six hundred & eighteen'.[12] Again, this is relevant to a future discussion about the company's touring movements and to other things with regard to Leigh that were becoming an issue at the time in question.

In 1617–18, Ellis Worth is again recorded as payee. The first time, a payment is found in the Queen's household accounts – or the accounts of her Receiver General, Sir George Carew – and is 'in ye behalfe of himselfe and ye rest of ye Companie for theire attendance at Greenewich', this attendance having taken place in April 1617.[13] The second time, he is found in the main court Chamber accounts, gaining 'xixli xixs viijd' for the company for two plays performed before the King at 'xp'mas 1617'.[14] There are two things to note about these payments to Worth instead of Leigh. Firstly, the 1617 Queen's accounts' record does not state that the payment was for *plays*, and it is made by order of her 'Councell' – not by Sidney, the Queen's Chamberlain, or any of his normal deputies. Secondly, with the Christmas plays for the King, it should be understood that the sum given – somewhat over £19 – was slightly less than the £10 per play usually earned, incorporating both pay and something extra for a reward. In the last set of accounts for the Queen, another payment is made to her players, one of 'xli', which is paid out in 'ffebruarie 1618', again without an indication of a play and without a named payee. This date quoted from the record, naturally, indicates a new-style date for the sum given as in early 1619 – an 'Extraordinary' payment – which was handed over in response to a bill 'signed by the said Lord Chamberlayne' that included 'an acquittance for the Receipt thereof'. It was given in the month before the Queen died, and that is the last relevant record we have involving the players in any set of accounts before Anna's death on 2 March 1619.

What needs to be emphasised when it comes to statistics from the Declared Accounts' records of plays given at court is that the King's Men, Shakespeare's company, are pre-eminently present in them over and above all other companies. According to these records, for example, in the year 1610–11, the King's Men gave fifteen plays over the Queen's Servants' three, and in the year before that, 1609–10, thirteen plays over the Queen's

---

[12] TNA C24/500/9, Ints. 5, 7 and 31.
[13] TNA SC6/JASI/1653, fo. 29v. It is found under 'Paymentes made by Order of her Ma*jesties* Councell' and was for 100 shillings.
[14] TNA E351/544, m. 89.

one. There are ten plays mentioned in the records for the King's Men in the season 1604–5 over the Queen's Servants' *How to Larne*, and so forth. However, it would be a mistake to jump to too many conclusions about what is in and what is not in these state-kept records. For in an environment where individual royal family members (for example) also had their own resources from which to draw, the state was not the only body from whom payments were made to players.

Of particular importance when considering these statistics and, indeed, the way in which different companies performed individually and sometimes when related to one another, is the year 1611–12, when an unexpected event happens in the annals of the King's Men and Queen's Servants companies. As listed, the Queen's Servants received £20 for two 'severall' plays given on 27 December and the 2 February (on other evidence, performing *Greene's Tu Quoque*), and then received a further sum of money for two unknown plays performed on 21 and 23 January. However, we also know from another set of records that they performed two more plays IN COMBINATION WITH the King's Men – *The Silver Age* and *The Rape of Lucrece* – both plays by Thomas Heywood and of the Queen's Servants' repertoire.[15] This took place on the 12 and 13 January according to John Astington's calculations in his book on *English Court Theatre 1558–1632* (the Sunday following Twelfth Night and the day after), and they were performed before the Queen and Prince Henry.[16] Records of payment for these collaborative performances are not present in the Declared Accounts of the Treasurer of the Chamber, so when did both the King's Men and the Queen's Servants get paid for these extraordinary productions? And who paid them?

In the Introduction to the Malone Society's volume on the *Jacobean and Caroline Revels Accounts, 1603–1642*, W. R. Streitberger writes that although there were more royal companies and therefore more plays at court in the Jacobean era, 'not all were under the supervision of the Revels and not all were attended by the King'. Then he footnotes that while 'many of the plays staged at court were paid for by the King in the Chamber Accounts, he neither paid for nor attended all'.[17] In effect this means that many Queen's Servants' court performances recorded as played before the King or others in the accounts of the Treasurer of the Chamber were paid for by

---

[15] Revels Office Accounts; TNA AO3/908, Part 14, fo. 2.
[16] John Astington, *English Court Theatre 1558–1632* (Cambridge University Press, 1999), p. 244; W. R. Streitberger, *Jacobean and Caroline Revels Accounts, 1603–1642*, MSC 13 (Oxford: Malone Society, 1986), p. 49 (AO3/908, Part 14, fo. 2).
[17] MSC 13, p. xxi.

the King, and even those recorded in these accounts as performed before his wife and children could have been paid for by him – but this does not mean that some performances generally, as well as others *unrecorded* in this source, were not paid for by other individual patrons' households. Such is likely to have been the case with the two-night presentation of Red Bull/Queen's Servants plays recorded in the Revels Office Accounts – for somebody would have paid the two companies, both Shakespeare's and Heywood's – for these performances; currently, however, we do not know who this could have been.[18] Streitberger also footnotes that 'James appears to have attended those ordered through the Revels unless duties or illness kept him away.'[19] It would seem that for these Revels-listed performances outside the Chamber Accounts, the King kept away.

As stated before, accounts exist of the Queen's personal household expenses, and the Malone Society's introduction to their volume on the Declared Accounts has a section on 'Royal Entertainments Not Paid for by the Treasurer of the Chamber', citing what remains of an incomplete account for Queen Anna covering the period 1615–16.[20] This coincides with the year period when those three plays were paid for, recorded in the Declared Accounts as acted before the King, the payee being Robert Leigh where the company is not named. In the complete Queen's accounts, as well as in the incomplete ones for that time, there is one payment of £10 made to Ellis Worth 'one of her *Majesties* plaiers'. This was 'for so much paid unto him in the behalfe of himselfe and the rest of that Companie for one plaie acted before her *Maiestie* at Queenes Court', which was performed on 17 December, as already stated.[21] The King's Men received another £10 from the Queen's accounts for only one play too.

There is more to be said about the separateness of the Queen's finances and records of payments made to entertainers, however – and what is missing from these. Here the researches of Andrew Ashbee, a musician and an assiduous music historian, come to be of use. Ashbee transcribed and published Anna's own Declared Accounts by her Receiver General, Sir George Carew. When he describes what can be derived from them, he can only inform us in a limited way because, as he says, 'the picture

---

18 TNA AO3/908, Part 14, fo. 2.
19 *Ibid.*, citing MSC 6, pp. xxv–xxvii; and Martin Butler, 'Entertaining the Palatine Prince: Plays on Foreign Affairs 1635–1637', *English Literary Renaissance* 13 (1983), 319–44 (pp. 343–4).
20 Introduction to MSC 6, p. xxv, referring to Appendix B in the same volume. This is in fact TNA E101/437/8, not E101/47/8 as suggested there.
21 TNA E101/437/8, fo. 5 (incomplete accounts). For the full account reference, see TNA SC6/JASI/164, fos. 23v (Ellis Worth) and 24 (Heminges).

currently remains tantalisingly incomplete, covering only Michaelmas 1604 to March 1608, March 1615 to March 1616, and March 1617 to March 1619'.[22] It may be noted at this point that while there is a large gap between 1608 and 1615 this may well provide the answer to where the payment for the two 1612 plays at Greenwich could have been found. It might also have supplied a location where a lot more activity of the Queen's Servants could have been recorded. In relation to musicians, however, Ashbee also perceives many records that are missing – even from the Queen's accounts extant. When undertaking 'comparisons with the list of servants provided with mourning liveries at the Queen's funeral', for example, Ashbee perceives some 'unexplained omissions from the receiver general's accounts: no regular payments to trumpeters, Scottish or Dutch musicians, or to Daniell Cahill, her harpist'. So, with Ashbee's implied puzzlement, questions can still be asked: from what source did further missing payments come? When were they paid? Who paid them? The answer to the last could be a diverse mix of people, but perhaps there should be time to consider just a few.

A figure to contemplate when pondering the Queen, her circle and records of her players' performances is Sir Robert Sidney, baron of Penshurst, Viscount Lisle and one day earl of Leicester. The earl of Worcester is certainly another – one who can be seen to play both a prominent part in the development of his old company and a highly prominent part within the Queen's social environment. Robert Cecil, the earl of Salisbury, was Lord High Steward of Anna's Revenues from 1603 until his death in 1612. With his demise, Worcester took over this important position and continued in it until Anna died in 1619. According to his entry in the *Oxford Dictionary of National Biography*, Sidney was made Lord Chamberlain of the Queen's household, appointed surveyor of her revenues on 10 November 1603.[23] This was a few months after he was made Baron Sidney of Penshurst on 13 May 1603. However, the surveyor post was given over to Sir Walter Cope in 1606 (24 September), and even Cope was replaced by Sir Thomas (later Lord) Knyvett on 22 July 1609.[24] In no way does this reshuffling detract from Sidney's significant position and,

[22] Andrew Ashbee, *Records of English Court Music*, 9 vols., Vol. IV: *1603–1625* (Snodland: Ashbee, 1991), p. 196.

[23] Shephard, 'Sidney, Robert, First Earl of Leicester'.

[24] The dates for these appointments were given to me by Helen Payne, personal correspondence, August–September 2007. They are backed up by evidence in the Queen's accounts, TNA SC6/JASI/1646, fo. 17v (Sidney is surveyor general); SC6/JASI/1648, fo. 20 (Cope is surveyor general); SC6/JASI/1650, fo. 18 (Knyvett has taken the post).

indeed, he was made Viscount Lisle on 4 May 1605, at the approximate
time of the building of the Red Bull playhouse. In terms of the Queen's
Servants, as Lord Chamberlain to Anna, he was highly significant, for
in this role he was directly responsible for her entertainments. He was
another ex-associate of Essex, and the man looked to by Susan Greene, for
example, when she ran into difficulties with the Queen's company.

Sidney, who was the brother of the poet Sir Philip, chose many of the
Essex circle as godparents for his children – i.e. the earl of Southampton;
the countess of Bedford; Penelope Rich; and Rich and Mountjoy together,
on one occasion, in 1594.[25] As Lord Chamberlain and official director of
her entertainment, we find some evidence of his involvement recorded in
entries made in Anna's accounts, including those covering 1615–16. The
entry in the complete accounts already quoted – made to Ellis Worth
for the company – represents one such item of proof. The £10 was paid
'by warrant signed by the right ho*nourable* the Lord Vicount Lisle Lord
Cham*ber*laine to her M*ajestie* dated the vijth of Januarie 1615' – meaning,
in all likelihood, that a Christmas performance was paid for in January
1616.[26]

As entertainment officer at the highest level, Sidney must have had
a direct involvement with players and performers, and perhaps his own
financial records concerning the Queen's household – if there were any
known or if any, indeed, ever existed – might afford some further information about court entertainment for the Queen. The actors' evidence in
the *Worth* v. *Baskervile* case is revealing where they describe their relationship with Sidney and how they felt when Susan Greene approached this
man directly.

By the time of Susan Baskervile's answer to Worth, John Cumber
and John Blaney's bill, Sidney had achieved the title of earl of Leicester
(acquired in 1618). The then aggrieved Susan described in the suit how
she did 'peticion the Right Honorable the now Earle of Leicester, then
Lord Chamberlaine of the Howshould of the said late deceased queene
Anne, who hadd a kind of Gouernm*ent* and suruey ouer the said Players'.
Thomas Drewe agreed with this description of Sidney in his answers to
the interrogatory questions for the case that 'his L*ordshi*p:' had 'a kynde of
governem*ent* over the s*ai*d Company'. He was a little vague about Sidney's

[25] His friendship is demonstrated by the way in which Essex and his sister Penelope Rich backed
      Sidney's attempt to become Warden of the Cinque Ports in the 1590s. See Millicent V. Hay, *The
      Life of Sir Robert Sidney: Earl of Leicester (1563–1626)* (Washington: The Folger Shakespeare Library,
      1984), pp. 155, 177–8.
[26] TNA SC6 /JASI/1650, fo. [23b].

involvement in relation to Susan Greene's appeal, however.[27] Robert Leigh was clear and obsequious in his clarity:

> It is true That the *said* Susan Baskervile did exhi*b*ite hir petic*i*on, unto the right ho*nour*able the nowe Earle of Ley*cester* then Lorde Chamberlayn of the *said* late Queene Anne, to the purpose in this In*t*er*r*ogatory menc*i*oned, And his L*ords*hip was therupon pleased to wryte his L*ette*re unto the *said* Company (over whom his L*ords*hip had a kynde of Governeme*n*t) therby com*m*aunding or directing them, to satisfy hir the *said* Susan of hir right demaunds, w*i*thout trowbling his L*ords*hip with that Busines any further or to that effect.[28]

Robert Sidney is, therefore, one person we should contemplate as having a relationship with the company, and someone who may have been responsible for extra unrecorded payments for performances given by them – perhaps somehow out of the coffers of the Queen specifically, perhaps not.[29] If, from this court case account of him, he sounds a little impatient with the actors, it was not without personal cause. Robert Sidney's letters to his wife, many of them from Flushing where he was sent on England's business for a long time, betray his own financial exasperations. In one letter of 1607 he writes to her, pathetically, saying she should ask advice about his situation: 'I never was in that case in my life as I ame now. For besides mine interest debts I owe 2000 in london for most part of w*hi*ch I either ame or shall presently bee sued. The houshold debts and many of them to poor and clamorsum persons come to a thowsand pownds.'[30]

Waiting for money to 'come in from the King', Sidney is in trouble with bills for Penshurst, personal law suits and transactions over the marriage of his daughter. In other papers there is one mention of a Thomas Greene. This is in a 1610 set of accounts concerning a solicitor called William Emott. Here, under 'Law causes', is found inserted a sum of 'xxli to mr. Tho: Greene'.[31] This may or may not have been alluding to the leader and clown of the company; however, 1610 was when a 'notable outrage' by five feltmakers was recorded at the Middlesex sessions that alluded to the Red

---

[27] TNA C24/500/9, Thomas Drewe, Int. 8.

[28] TNA C24/500/9, Robert Leigh, Int. 8.

[29] Sidney and all the other officials of Queen Anna's household are paid the same amounts, year-on-year, in the accounts we have (£50 in the case of Sidney). The sums paid to him and Carew were meant to cover wages and livery.

[30] Kent History and Library Centre, Maidstone, De L'Isle papers, CKS-U1475/C81/91–165, nos. 144–5, 144.

[31] Kent History and Library Centre, Maidstone, De L'Isle papers, CKS-U1475/A62/4.

Bull, and this may have had something to do with the law costs resulting from this matter.[32]

Edward Somerset, the earl of Worcester, would be another candidate for the role of intermittent payments-maker, as would both the aforementioned Sir George Carew (baron of Clopton, Vice-Chamberlain to the Queen under Sidney and also her Receiver General) and George Hooker, Deputy Receiver under Carew. These are by far the likeliest candidates for paying for ad hoc things, possibly including performances, and gaining the money back through their own bills or resources. Both of the latter two occur in the Queen's Servants' records, particularly for 1617, when a court case involving the company talks of them. In this case, the company revealed that they expected 'Mr Houker', in his role of 'paymaster under the then right honourable, the then Lord Carewe', to pay for some hats.[33] In view of this automatic expectation it is realised that the company were more used to being paid by Hooker than by anyone else, and that therefore Hooker is a strong candidate for making unrecorded direct payments for extraneous plays and, indeed, other sorts of entertainment.

When it comes to those January 1612 performances of the King's and Queen's men combined – recorded in the Revels lists but not in the Chamber accounts – one interesting issue to note is that these were performances presented at Greenwich Palace. The reason this is noteworthy is that it is the *only* set of play performances that we can be certain were performed at this royal venue at this time. From a production perspective, it may be that the chosen hall at Greenwich was large enough for the requirements of this two-company arrangement and when it comes to these two particular plays. Both *The Silver Age* and *The Rape of Lucrece* have larger than average casts, *The Silver Age* having thirty-five named parts plus '6. Centaures', 'Seruingmen', 'Swaines', 'Theban Ladies', 'The seuen Planets' and 'Furies', and *The Rape of Lucrece* nineteen main parts plus additional senators and soldiers with civil war sword-fights presented in ambitious battle scenes.

Both plays have specific production requirements that would have suited a large-scale and capable venue well. The former *Ages* play has very many masque-like stage directions, such as '*Thunder and lightning. Iupiter discends in a cloude*';[34] more '*Thunder and lightning ... Iupiter appeares in his glory under a Raine-bow*' (Fiv); '*Iuno and Iris aboue in a cloud*' (G);

[32] LMA MJ/SR/0489, 9, 11, 101, 103, 105. Greene was also involved in an accusation against William Sayer for stealing 'goods from the redd bull' in 1611 (LMA MJ/SR/0499, 70).
[33] TNA REQ2/655, Box 2. See Griffith, 'Christopher Beeston', pp. 617–18.
[34] Thomas Heywood, *The Silver Age* (London, 1613), C3.

'*Enter* Ceres *and* Proserpine *attired like the Moone, with a company of Swaines, and country Wenches*' before they sing; '*Thunder. Enter* Pluto, *his Chariot drawne in by Diuels*' (G3v); '*Mercury flies from aboue* ... *Enter Tryton with his Trumpe, as from the sea*' (H); '*Earth riseth from under the stage*' (H1v); '*The riuer Arethusa riseth from the stage*' (H2); '*Iuno and* Iris *plac'd in a cloud aboue*' (I4); '*Thunder, lightnings,* Iupiter *descends in his maiesty, his Thunderbolt burning*' (I4v); '*As he toucheth the bed it fires, and all flyes up,* Iupiter *from thence takes an abortiue infant* ... *Iupiter taking up the Infant, speakes as he ascends in his cloud*' (K); '*Hercules sinkes himselfe: Flashes of fire; the Diuels appeare at euery corner of the stage with seuerall fire-workes. The Iudges of hell, and the three sisters run ouer the stage,* Hercules *after them: fire-workes all ouer the house* ... *Enter* Pluto *with a club of fire, a burning crown,* Proserpine, *the Iudges, the Fates, and a guard of Diuels, all with burning weapons* ... Hercules *fels* Pluto, *beats off the Diuils with all their fire-workes, rescues* Proserpine' (K2v–K3); '*Exeunt three wayes* Ceres, Theseus, Philoctetes, *and* Hercules *dragging* Cerberus *one way:* Pluto, *hels Iudges, the Fates and Furies downe to hell:* Iupiter, *the Gods and Planets ascend to heauen*' (L).

The company, as we know, were capable of pulling off spectacles like this at the Red Bull, as well as in the sharper refinements of a royal palace. That they produced this piece at court in collaboration with the pre-eminent drama-related King's company – always Revels-recorded as far as documents are concerned – leaves the known gaps when it comes to the Queen's company's presence in such documents, a subject for query.

Going on from this, and contemplating a relationship between the Queen's circle and the company – with Sidney an acknowledged member of that circle as Chamberlain – one is tempted to speculate on what other ways these actors may have served as entertainers. We know that companies could and did perform at places like the inns of court (e.g. Shakespeare's company and *Twelfth Night* at the Middle Temple); also, they could be expected to serve at special occasions, such as the Somerset House Conference of 1604.

Did the Queen's company perform at ad hoc venues at times such as these? Were they expected to help at other important events, such as the visit of the Queen's brother, Christian IV of Denmark, in 1606? Similarly, were the deaths of both Prince Henry and Thomas Greene the only reasons why the company were not recorded performing at court in the run-up to the marriage of Princess Elizabeth, or were they performing special duties, as the Queen's Servants, recorded in another way now lost to us?

The occasions listed when payments were given to players were certainly not always described as for play-performing events (e.g. the April 1615 payment to Robert Leigh and that of April 1617 to Worth, as well as the February 1619 payment to Worth). What else could the company have done for the court in entertainment terms? Were they the allotted speaking performers – perhaps with the Prince's Men – for Prince Henry's abandoned *Masque of Truth*, intended for his sister's 1613 marriage celebrations? With masque we are certainly possessed of one very obvious vacuum regarding Anna's entertainment requirements that has never been adequately addressed. At the beginning of the last chapter, I suggested that it would have taken a brave woman to suggest antimasque to Ben Jonson. With the consequent and brilliant twelve-witch antimasque for *The Masque of Queens* (February 1609) came necessary casting considerations, followed up with similar decisions concerning, for example, the twelve follies or fools in *Love Freed from Ignorance and Folly* (February 1611). In terms of player-engagement, however, the many speaking parts in the masques-proper would be probable candidates, which we know were certainly not performed by Anna's circle, who only took part silently. The King's Men are known to have taken roles in *Love Restored* (6 January 1612); however, *Love Restored* was an unusually cheap masque to produce, at £280, and the fact that specific mention was made of the company performing the speaking parts indicates, perhaps, that it was not the norm for Shakespeare's company to be doing this, rather than the opposite.[35] There are many magnificent speaking parts in Jonson's masques: Niger, Oceanus and Aethiopia in *The Masque of Blackness* (5 January 1605), for example; Boreas, Januarius and Vulturnus in *The Masque of Beauty* (10 January 1608); the witches and Heroic Virtue in *The Masque of Queens* (2 February 1609).

At this point we have to think with some critical reflection when it comes to the company who enjoyed Queen Anna's patronage. We are, after all, speaking of a troupe, previous discussion of whose repertoire has included the (somewhat patronising) phrase 'domestic drama'. Although this seems unhappily demeaning in tone, the previous chapter has covered, it is hoped, something of what the repertoire always offered in terms of a focused approach to, for example, women-centred drama, trying to explore the many traps in which the female gender could find themselves,

---

[35] Cost given in Roy Strong, *Henry, Prince of Wales, and England's Lost Renaissance* (London: Thames and Hudson, 1986), p. 174; Michael Leapman, *Inigo: The Troubled Life of Inigo Jones, Architect of the English Renaissance* (London: Review, 2003), p. 125.

while bearing in mind the intelligent courtly group for whom they may well have catered. Generally, in the past, the Queen's Servants' repertoire has been viewed as successful where the company was happy to produce entertainments that were *not* aimed at court personalities. Citizen plays; elect nation drama; and the much-loved Will Kemp, jig-extemporising kind of entertainment have certainly been associated with the Red Bull. The extra-text, improvisational kind of humour, presumably continued by Thomas Greene after Kemp, has never been seen as appropriate to the refined tastes of Anna's court and the people who visited it – particularly on such occasions as the masques. However, an alternative point of view might be offered with regard to masque on three counts: firstly, questions may be asked concerning the extent to which the Queen's men were not the more appropriate group to take part in them; secondly, where one sees evidence of the company's masque-like skills demonstrated with, for example, *The Silver Age*, one may contemplate the abilities already available to them; and thirdly, we can wonder to what extent the Queen's entertainments were truly so 'refined' – particularly when it came to the generally grotesque elements of these entertainments.

The Masque of Blackness has been seen as particularly notorious in this aesthetic respect, with the much-quoted comments of Dudley Carleton having a bearing on the matter: 'Instead of Vizzards, their Faces, and Arms up to the Elbows, were painted black, which was Disguise sufficient, for they were hard to be known; but it became them nothing so well as their red and white, and you cannot imagine a more ugly Sight, then a Troop of lean-cheek'd Moors…'[36] *Blackness* is one text that the twenty-first century critic would struggle to make politically correct for the reader today; but any political incorrectness, in early modern terms, may have had more to do with the aesthetics or cosmetics not working for the onlookers, than anything to do with our racial concerns now. It would seem 'blacking-up' for a court occasion was socially hazardous and shocking. As Carleton noted wryly, the Spanish ambassador bravely kissed the made-up hand of the Queen, 'though there was a Danger it would have left a Mark on his Lips'. Barbara Ravelhofer has made the point that makeup such as this may have seemed embarrassingly impractical in view of the expense of staining precious clothes.[37]

[36] Quoted from Orgel, 'Introduction' to Jonson, *The Complete Masques*, p. 4.
[37] Barbara Ravelhofer, *The Early Stuart Masque: Dance, Costume, and Music* (Oxford University Press, 2006), pp. 173–5.

Recently, European scholarship has recognised the idea that a black-up masque in England may have had a Danish precedent. According to John Webb, Jones's pupil, Jones had spent time in Denmark, and this is proved on the evidence of a Danish nobleman, Sivert Grubbe, who, according to Mara Wade's researches, 'locates' Jones in Copenhagen in his diaries at a garter ceremony for Christian IV in 1603.[38] While there he may well have heard of the mumming in black face that took place at Christian's coronation in 1596, pre-dating the Jonesian *Masque of Blackness* by some nine or so years. Regardless of this, Ulrik, duke of Holstein, was present at court in January 1605 when *Blackness* was performed, no doubt having communicated the style of the coronation events to his sister when he had visited her earlier in Scotland in 1598.[39]

The imagination of Anna was, it would seem, a force to be reckoned with when it came to developing the masque structure, and the idea of male-actor witches, in the *Masque of Queens* of 1609, obviously appealed. First the witches in their *'ugly hell ... flaming beneath'*, smoking *'unto the top of the roof* entered one by one, *'all differently attired'*: *'some with rats on their head, some on their shoulders; others with ointment pots at their girdles; all with spindles, timbrels, rattles or other venefical instruments, making a confused noise, with strange gestures'*.

The entrance of the Dame witch is impressive after the eleven-witch dance and their *Macbeth*-like 'Charm' speeches: *'At this the Dame entered to them, naked armed, barefooted, her frock tucked, her hair knotted and folded with vipers; in her hand a torch made of dead man's arm, lighted; girded with a snake.'*[40]

Jonson refers to rattles and 'a kind of hollow and infernall musique', which is interpreted as appropriately atmospheric and acoustic for characters of the witches' aesthetic station.[41] There were elements of the masque, it would seem, that were anything but dainty – rather reaching to the other extreme of the grotesque. Production of plays during court entertainment seasons became the main domain of the King's Men,

[38] Royal Library, Copenhagen, Udall 449, 4°, fo. 147; Mara R. Wade, 'The Queen's Courts: Anna of Denmark and Her Royal Sisters – Cultural Agency at Four Northern European Courts in the Sixteenth and Seventeenth Centuries', in *Women and Culture at the Courts of the Stuart Queens*, ed. Clare McManus (Basingstoke: Palgrave Macmillan, 2003), pp. 49–80 (p. 58 and note, p. 78). Jones was working for Roger Manners, the fifth earl of Rutland at the time, and John Dowland, the lutenist, was also in the retinue. Wade speculates that Dowland, who had been in the service of the Danish court for some time, returned to England with Jones.
[39] Wade, 'Duke Ulrik', pp. 247, 248 and 252.
[40] Jonson, *The Complete Masques*, pp. 123–5.
[41] Ravelhofer, *The Early Stuart Masque*, p. 190.

Shakespeare's company. While the King's Men were performing this function, the Queen's company, along with the other Middlesex companies
given patronage by the Princes and the Princess, for instance, would have
been fairly available for other royal entertainment needs – such as masque.
The Queen's Servants and the Prince's Men, along with the companies of
the Princess Elizabeth and that of Prince Charles (the duke of York) could
have worked alongside the 'Children of the Queen's Revels', whose very
name indicated part of their perceived function.

With regard to young people, that payment made to Ellis Worth 'in
the behalfe of himselfe and the rest of the Companie for theire attendance
at Greenewich' in April 1617 – for an occasion that does not mention a
play – comes at a significant moment.[42] This is because it coincides with
the rehearsal period prior to the performance of Robert White's *Cupid's
Banishment*, which took place at Greenwich on 4 May.[43] This masque is
one that contains a significant speech spoken by a young woman playing
Fortune, 'Mistress Ann Watkins'. The meat of the entertainment was performed, indeed, by a group of scholars of the first recorded girls' school in
England, the Ladies Hall at Deptford. Could it be that Worth and company were invited along to Greenwich for their input, perhaps to train the
young women in some entertainment technique? Their paid-for attendance at that time, with a payment sum outside the usual they gained for
drama, would seem to suggest a special job. Thinking about their possible
role as relating to court entertainments, as well as drama, it cannot be
ignored that when Anna died, the Red Bull part of her acting company
became known as the 'Company of the Revels'. A title such as this may
well have been given to them, knowing their previous function directly
relating to masquing entertainments.

Unfortunately, for some reason, probably ephemeral and historical, we
do not possess the kind of financial record that tells us what body of professional entertainers were employed for masque purposes. However, in
view of the fact of scholarship's confidence that the King's Men dominated
court-presented *drama* for most of the seasons recorded, it would surely
not be too speculative to wonder whether the other companies (e.g. the
Queen's and Prince's Men) were not ideally placed to take part in these
other presentations. Because of the knowledge we have of the Red Bull
playhouse in terms of its capabilities – the existence of its tower-like

---

[42] TNA SC6/JASI/1653, fo. 29v. It is found under 'Paymentes made by Order of her Majesties
Councell' and was for 100 shillings.

[43] See Clare McManus, 'Memorialising Anna of Denmark's Court: *Cupid's Banishment* at Greenwich
Palace', in *Women and Culture at the Courts of the Stuart Queens*, pp. 81–99.

tiring house, for example, and the staged effects we know took place in the repertoire – it would seem to be the case that the use of machinery and special effect, staples in terms of masque, was equally available to the actors in their public playhouse arena as it was while working at, for example, the Banqueting House. It is therefore not impossible to imagine that the Queen's Servants could have been capable of contributing to masquing and antimasquing scenes if it had been made a part of their remit as Queen Anna's men.

Song

From a public playhouse repertoire point of view, and to demonstrate a particular and immediate reason why this 'low-brow' company – as it has been oft-times interpreted – may have been seen as appropriate to this one-time Scandanavian royal, we could also go all the way back to Anna's early close family interests, replicated for her on a 'high culture' – but not an exclusively 'high culture' – plain. Queen Sophia, Anna's mother, had a recorded interest in the popular song of her country, and there is evidence that Anna enjoyed this too. There is one reference, for example, in a letter she wrote to her husband about the marriage of Margaret Stewart to the aging Charles Howard, earl of Nottingham and Lord High Admiral. 'I humbly desire your Majesty to tell me how it is possible', she queried, 'that I should keep this secret that have already told it, and shall tell it to as many as I speak with, and if I were a poet I would make a song of it and sing it to the tune of Three Fools Well Met.'[44]

'Three Fools Well Met' would appear to be the title of a known air of the kind referred to poetically in a number of plays in the sixteenth and seventeenth centuries. It was, in all likelihood, a 'round' type of song, and it is enlightening to imagine Queen Anna as someone to whom popular English ballad appealed. The Queen certainly enjoyed her music, and there is some evidence that it could not have been of a purely courtly nature. According to her accounts, a Scottish 'singing woman' was paid 40 shillings (in a warrant of July 1605), as were a number of other singers at people's individual houses.[45] For the summer of 1615–16, Anna's accounts include payments to the waits of Southampton, Lord Fenton's musicians,

---

[44] Quoted in Barroll, *Anna of Denmark*, p. 92.

[45] These houses, in 1605–6, included 'Lo: Mordantes' and 'Lo: Comptons', for example. TNA SC6/ JASI/1646; Ashbee, *Records of English Court Music*, 'revised and re-arranged' in 2002 in CD format. I would like to thank Andrew Ashbee for his help and advice with these National Archives references.

Welsh musicians, Christopher Hatton's musicians, Salisbury musicians, 'Thearle of Worcesters Music*i*ons that plaied unto her', Morris dancers' performances, 'Singing men upon her M*a*jesties Comaundem*ent*', a blind man playing on the virginals, 'Cowper' dancers and musicians and Marlborough musicians – to name a selected group.[46] It is unlikely that the music implied was necessarily all of the William Byrd style (although perhaps Edward Somerset's was), particularly when it came to the Scots, Welsh and 'singing men' variety of music played. Within a plainer native context, then, it is possible to indicate in what ways the Queen's Servants could be said to satisfy a proven Danish interest in the 'local' – in this case British and, indeed, European – music in their drama.

Just like Shakespeare, Thomas Heywood delighted audiences with an occasional ballad or air. The 'Shaking of the Sheets' particularly springs to mind at the beginning of *A Woman Killed with Kindness*. But in one particular play this interest was to become centrally paramount, and achieved notable success perhaps *because* of its song content.

In the next repertoire section, analysis is given of this play replete with popular song, which, from the critics' point of view, is the most puzzling item of interest about it. Much of the discomfort or challenge concerning it is in view of the juxtaposition of plot-content and musical moment. It is, after all, centred on the story of the rape of a woman.

REPERTOIRE 4 THOMAS HEYWOOD'S *THE RAPE OF LUCRECE* (LONDON, 1608)

The Rape of Lucrece stands out as an unusual entertainment venture in its time for more than a few reasons. It was a phenomenally successful Stuart enterprise for Thomas Heywood's companies, going on to be printed and provably performed many times over. Published in 1608, 1609, 1614, 1630 and 1638, the text was, for the most part, amended and extended over time, much of the additional material being centred on its song.[47] On paper it would seem to be anything but a presentation that would consolidate an incoming new royal order. The story of the rape of Collatinus' wife, Lucrece, was one that took a historian and his reader back to the first Roman republic, with its attendant anti-tyrannical points of view. The power of a represented popular rebellion in a publicly produced play

---

[46] SC6/JASI/1650, fos. 20–21v.
[47] See Thomas Heywood, *Thomas Heywood's "The Rape of Lucrece"*, ed. Allan Holaday (Urbana: University of Illinois Press, 1950), Introduction, pp. 1–44 (pp. 1–3).

of this kind could be by no means lessened through its use of ballad-style music, including a notably Scottish song and a song in the Dutch language, perhaps brought back from the Netherlands wars. The Scottish song, 'The fourth Song', is a lament for a dead king:

> *Lament Ladies lament*
> *Lament the Roman land,*
> *The King is fra thee hent,*
> *Was doughtie on his hand,*
> *Weele gang into the Kirke,*
> *His dead corpse wele embrase,*
> *And when we sea ha dean*
> *We an will cry alasse. Fala la lero la*
> *Tararara roun tarre &c.*[48]

The 'eight a Dutch song' is a drinking song:

> *O Morke gyff men eine man,*
> *Skerry merry vip,*
> *O morke gyff men eine man*
> *Skerry merry vap.*
> *O morke gyff men eine man,*
> *that tik die seine long o drieuan can;*
> *Skerry merry vip, and skerry merry vap,*
> *and skerry merry runke ede bunkh.* [etc.]
> (E4)

In seventeenth-century production, one can only imagine the subversive – perhaps, in some respects, all but 'Brechtian' – effect of the play's songs. Over its extensive publication period they did nothing but grow in number. In 1608–9 the first quartos began with thirteen songs – nine numbered, the unnumbered including a 'Catch', a little song by the Clown, and two added songs at the end – and the text remained with these thirteen songs until the 1630 edition. This was when the number was increased to seventeen, retaining the thirteen and inserting four more. The fifth edition of 1638 increased its number by five, thus making twenty-two songs in all – an increase of nine more songs since the 1608 edition. Such was the popularity of the play by 1638 that the buying readership did not have to be given the numbered titles of the old songs; the quarto simply called the five new songs 'The first new Song' to 'The last new Song', thereby ensuring the second purchase of the play by any previous buyer who wanted to collect the musical additions.

---

[48] Thomas Heywood, *The Rape of Lucrece* (London, 1608), C2 with some corrections.

Critics down the ages have not known what to make of *The Rape of Lucrece*. Arthur Melville Clark, Heywood's biographer, saw that with this play Heywood was 'debasing some of the noblest legends of Livy by the most shocking ribaldry and farce'. He continued:

> One can only shudder at the disgusting catch sung by Valerius, Brutus and the clown who has brought Lucrece's message to the camp; and even the best of the songs – 'Packe clouds away, and welcome day' [not in the first edition], or 'Now what is love I will thee tell' – beautiful in themselves, are inexcusable in their settings, while the humorous ditties of Valerius, sung by an actor who was not innocent in the matter, are for the most part rubbish.[49]

Charles Baldwyn, the early nineteenth-century presenter of the play, had it named 'a sort of dramatic monster, in the construction of which every rule of propriety is violated, and all grace and symmetry are set at defiance'. The preface even hazards a guess as to the condition of Heywood at the time of writing: 'The author, one would suppose, must have produced it when in a state of inebriety; in which a man of genius may frequently, amidst strange and foolish things, give birth to poetical and impassioned conceptions.'[50]

Richard Rowland, a convert to the play on seeing it performed in 2005, admitted his previous reluctance to approach it head-on in his previous twenty years of Heywood scholarship, because he perceived it 'with a mixture of bewilderment and distaste'. Citing Jonathan Dollimore's *Radical Tragedy*, however, and the performed production Rowland experienced, he saw ways of seeing the jarring effects of the text in an altogether different way, feeling that in performance it had demonstrated 'the ways in which Heywood's play might have similarly amused and troubled its original audiences'.[51]

What exactly were the amusing and troubling experiences that the eager seventeenth-century playgoer was put through as he or she watched this play – a play that, on one occasion, was performed at Greenwich, before royalty, by two major companies combined? One of the difficulties inherent in understanding its appeal is the fact of the songs' juxtaposition to the action. To understand this – at least a little – we have to comprehend the

---

[49] Arthur Melville Clark, *Thomas Heywood: Playwright and Miscellanist* (Oxford: Basil Blackwood, 1931), p. 219.
[50] Charles Baldwyn, in his preface to Thomas Heywood, *The Rape of Lucrece*, in *The Old English Drama*, 2 vols. (London: Hurst, Robinson, 1825) Vol. I, p. iii.
[51] Rowland, *Thomas Heywood's Theatre*, p. 5. The production he saw was by the Lions part company, produced by Rosalind Cressy and directed by Sonia Ritter at St Bartholomew's Priory Church, Smithfield in October 2005.

politically angled plot ideas, originating from the play's classical source, as context. In the play, the patrician class in Rome is depressed at the state of the nation because of the tyrannical bent of the new ruling power – King Tarquin and his family. Queen Tullia, Lady Macbeth-like, is true ruthlessness incarnate, as she not only luxuriates in the idea of the murder of her father, King Servius, but walks over his dead remains and then runs over his body in her coach.

The dissatisfaction of the Senate is expressed with unexpected and diverse spin. Brutus, a relative of the Tarquins, pretends insanity in an accurate character-rendering of the Livy story (Livy wrote about a character practising this trick *before* Shakespeare's *Hamlet*). Mutius Scevola decides to respond with laughter. Horatius Cocles expresses simple anger. Valerius does something else – and it is Collatine, Lucrece's husband, who describes Valerius' response:

> Strangely, he is all song, hees ditty all,
> Note that, *Valerius* hath giuen vp the Court
> And weand himselfe from the kings consistory
> In which his sweet harmonious tongue grew harsh,
> Whether it be that he is discontent
> Yet would not so appeare before the king
> Or whether in applause of these new Edicts,
> Which so distast the people, or what cause,
> I know not, but now hee's all musicall.
> Vnto the counsell chamber he goes singing,
> And whilest the king his wilfull edicts makes,
> In which nones tongue is powerfull save the kings
> Hee's in a corner, relishing strange aires.
> Conclusively he's from a toward hopefull gentleman
> Transeshapt to a mere balleter, none knowing
> Whence should proceed this transmutation.
>
> (C)

Valerius is prefixed 'Pub:' in the dramatis personae of the 1608 text of the play, and he is called 'publicola' in the Latin sources.[52] On his first entrance, immediately after Collatine's description of him, this 'people's' man eschews all greeting, opting to burst into song, the first two airs being the only ones that even vaguely sound like a protest:

> *When* Tarquin *first in Court began,*
> *And was approved King:*

---

[52] For the 1638 quarto, on his entrance at the start of the play, he is subtitled 'Poplicola'. See Heywood, *The Rape of Lucrece*, ed. Holaday, p. 48.

> *Some men for sodden joy gan weepe,*
> *And I for sorrow sing.*
>
> (C1v)

'The second Song', in a similar subject vein to the first, is sung to a tune of a completely different rhythm:

> *Let humor change and spare not,*
> *Since* Tarquins *proud I care not:*
> *His faire words so bewitch my delight,*
> *That I dote on his sight.*
> *Now all is gone new desires embraceing,*
> *And my deserts disgracing.*
>
> (C1v)

Songs then come in quick succession, with 'The third Song' beginning *'Now what is loue I pray thee tell'* (C1v). The lyric is reputedly by Sir Walter Raleigh and is sung in response to Horatius' observation: 'he's either mad or loue-sicke', appealing to the statesman in Valerius to respond sensibly to Tullia's cataclysmic cruelty. The Scottish song *'Lament Ladies lament'* is the fourth (C2), and is prompted by Lucretius' exhortation to lament the death of King Servius. But, as we have seen, this is no attempt at any classically derived song about an imperial king, despite lamenting 'the Roman land'. This is a Scottish song about a Scottish king, whose body is taken into a very Scottish 'Kirke'.

With this play, and its song device in particular, Heywood might be said to be sailing very 'close to the wind' – an unexpected thing for someone who in most other respects shows himself to be bending over backwards to the new ruling order. The Scottish song, in the context of the other Tarquin songs, seems particularly dangerous within the framework of a Stuart court, even though the dead king in question, in terms of the song, is not representing the sudden new tyrannical ruling order in the play (the Tarquins) but the old vulnerable one (Servius). The most straightforward significance is slipped into the whole, however, almost without one noticing, because the very act of inserting songs into this narrative – especially stylistically different songs – is so strange that it detracts or, perhaps, *distracts*, from the content of each ballad. Nevertheless, this is not completely the case, which is ultimately what is so subversive about it – a realisation of any meaning local to its period comes in fits and starts.

The effect of the popular music angle is that it immediately throws you into the world of Jacobean culture at quite an 'earthy' or 'low' level, despite the patrician setting. Because of the songs we are far more within

the realms of Henslowe's dinners at the Mermaid Tavern than we are present in the halls of Greenwich Palace. We know this play *was* performed
at Greenwich, however, with both Shakespeare and Heywood's companies
presenting it, and that with it, London's low culture, belonging more to the
drinking houses of the Bankside or Middlesex suburb areas than anywhere
else, was brought before the Danish Queen in a high-culture setting.

'This musick mads me', says Horatius. 'To heare him sing drawes riuers'
from Lucretius' eyes. Scevola, the maniacally laughing one, identifies with
Valerius' response:

> ... since the Court is harsh,
> And lookes as kaunce on souldiers, lets be merry.
> Court Ladies, sing, drinke, dance, and euery man
> Get him a mistris, coach it in the Country,
> And tast the sweets of it, what thinks *Valerius*,
> Of *Sceuolous* last councell?
>
> (C2)

To this Valerius responds with the 'fift Song' – a soldier's song: *'Why since
we souldiers cannot proue'* – all about how soldiers should, indeed, take
them *'a loue'* while there is no cause to fight, with one chorus going *'That
Ladies may say, some more of this, That Ladies may say, some more of this'*
(C2) and another chorus's lyrics crooning:

> *The Nightingale sings Iug, Iug, Iug,*
> *The little Lambe leaps after his dug,*
> *And the prety milke-maids they looke so smug,*
> *And the prety milke-maids, &c.*
>
> (C2v)

Valerius sings ten of the eleven songs in the 1608 play-text proper, including *'O Morke gyff men eine man'* ('The eight a Dutch song', E4), with the
'Catch', a three-man song with Pompie the Clown (Lucrece's servant) and
Horatius. Before this, there is a collection of songs spread throughout the
play that, in the context of a tragedy about a famous rape, seems to throw
salt into the wounds of the idea. Just before Lucrece's first appearance – an
entrance that is also memorable owing to its deliberately jarring effect –
Valerius sings 'the sixt Song', clearly a drinking song, which begins *'Shall I
woe the louely* Molly, / *Shee's so faire, so fat, so iolly'*.

> *But she has a tricke of folly,*
> *Therefore ile ha none of* Molly.
> [Chorus:] *No no no, no no no*
> *Ile ha none of* Molly *no no no.*
>
> (D3v)

Thereafter during this ditty we are treated to a list of rejected women and their traits – the '*cherry lips of* Nelly' are done with because '*too well she loues her belly*'; likewise '*bonny* Betty', whose body is too '*swetty*'. Dolly is '*pestilent holy*', Nanny '*loues not any*', Ratchel's '*cheekes hang like a satchell*' – and Biddy is too giddy (D3v–D4).

After the Molly song, Lucrece enters for the first time, with her maid and her Clown, Pompie (in all probability played by Thomas Greene), and instantly demands 'A Chaire'. It becomes obvious that Lucrece is somewhat of a puritan or, at least, our first impressions of her are of someone quite repressive:

> [To the Clown:] Sirra I ha seene you oft familiar
> With this my Maid and waiting gentlewoman,
> As casting amorous glances, wanton lookes,
> And pretty beckes, fauouring incontinence.
> I let you know you are not for my seruice
> Vnlesse you grow more ciuill.
>
> (D4)

The Clown protests his innocence, and Mirable the maid is about to support him when Lucrece steps in again:

> Nay mistres I ha seene you answere him
> With gracious lookes and some vnciuill smiles,
> Retorting eies, and giuing his demeanure
> Such welcome as becomes not modesty.
> Know henceforth there shall no lasciuious phrase,
> Suspitious looke or shadow of incontinence
> Be entertained by any that attend on Romane *Lucrece*.
>
> (D4v)

The maid tries to defend herself but Lucrece reinterrupts:

> Excuse it not for my premeditable thought
> Speakes nothing out of rashnes, nor vaine heare say.
> But what my owne experience testifies:
> Against you both let then this mild reproofe
> Forewarne you of the like, my reputation
> Which is held pretious in the eies of Rome,
> Shall be no shelter to the least intent
> Of loosenes, leaue all familiarity:
> And quite renounce acquaintance, or I here discharge you both my seruice.
>
> (D4v)

This strict moralising, threatening loss of work, seems to contrast unsympathetically and jangles with the Sweaty Betty tub-thumping singing of a few minutes before. But one can only imagine Heywood's intention as something deliberate in this as the play goes on and reaches its conclusion.

Collatine, Lucrece's husband, arrives soon with his friends, including Valerius; and then Valerius, in turn, is left onstage with the Clown. The Clown, knowing Valerius' leanings towards song, wants to sing with him and bursts into a few lines, beginning '*Iohn for the king, has bin in many ballads, Iohn for the king downe dino, Iohn for the king, has eaten many sallats: Iohn for the king sings hey ho*' (D4v). The Clown, in turn, asks for a song from Valerius that will 'teach me how to choose a wench fit for my stature and complection'. So the 'seuenth song' from Valerius, directed to Pompie the Clown, begins:

> Pompie *I will shew thee the waie to know*
> *A daintie dapper wench*
>
> (E1v–E2)

and this song continues with frank references to venereal disease, drunkenness, theft and sexual incontinence. Again, the stark contrast is marked between this imagery and the strict, refined Lucrece.

The context of the Dutch eighth song is the occasion of the senators' meal on a battlefield. Here the talk is of 'the German warres' and drinking '*upsefreeze*' (E3v–E4). But then comes 'The ninth Song' – '*There was a yong man and a maide fell in loue, | Terry dery ding, terry dery ding, tery tery dino*':

> *There was a yong man and a maide fell in loue,*
> *Terry dery ding, terry dery ding, tery tery dino.*
> *To get her good will he often did,*
> *Terry dery ding, terry dery ding, langtido dille.*
> *Theres many will say, and most will alow, terry dery, &c.*
> *Thers nothing so good as a terry dery dery dery, &c.*
> *I would wish all maides before they be sicke, terrie derie, &c.*
> *To enquire for a yong man that has a good terrie dery, &c.*
>
> (F3v)

This 'ninth Song' is sung by Valerius just as Sextus acquires a ring from Colatine that he will use to gain admittance to both Lucrece's household and her bed. Valerius sings it as Sextus leaves the camp to make his way to the city, and it is requested from Aruns as a 'merry song' to cheer them during the melancholic night. These songs are always strange in context, and often just as strange in isolation, but what comes across most oddly of all in the context of what happens to Lucrece is the last song, the 'Catch', sung by Valerius, Horatius and the Clown, Pompie.[53]

Because of the nature of this song, coming after the rape scene, I have seen the actor playing the Clown approach this mission with great care and respect.[54] But any twenty-first-century response to the dilemmas this song proposes in performance must negotiate with the tenor of its verses and its literally *laughing* chorus. To aid the actors involved, the song comes out of the Clown's delivery of a letter from his mistress after the event of the rape, and we see his desperate difficulties in telling the peers of Rome what he believes has happened to her. Pompie tries to explain this in a speech about Sextus visiting their house, his own insecurities about what truly happened, and how he had sworn to Lucrece 'that whatsoeuer I suspected I should say nothing'. However, he agrees that he could 'either laugh out my newes or sing am, and so saue my oath to my Lady'. Thus it is that Valerius, apparently suspecting Sextus all along, takes Pompie and Horatius on a sung journey – a kind of reverse 'blason' – *up* Lucrece's body, in order to ascertain what had happened:

Uale.: Did he take faire Lucrece *by the toe man?*
Clow. Toe man.
Uale. I man.
Clow. Ha,ha,ha,ha man.
Hor. And further did he striue to goe man?
Clow. Goe man.
Hor. I man. Clow. Ha, ha, ha man, hafa derry derry derry downe a, ha fa
  derry dino.
Val. Did he take faire Lucrece *by the heele man?*
Clow. Heele man.   *Val. I man.*   *Clow. Ha ha ha ha man.*
Hor. And did he further striue to feele man?
Clow. Feele man.   *Hor. I man.*   *Clow. Ha ha ha ha man, hey fadery, &c.*
Hor. Did he take the Lady *by the shin man?*
Clow. Shin man.   *Val. I man.*   *Clow. Ha ha ha ha man.*
Hor. Further too would he haue bin man? Clow. Bin man.
Hor. I man.   *Clo. Ha ha ha ha man. Hey fadery &c.*
Val. Did he take the Lady *by the knee man?*
Clo. Knee man.   *Val. I man.*   *Clow. Ha ha ha ha man.*
Hor. Further then that would he be man.
Clo. Bee man.   *Hor. I man.*   *Clow. Ha ha ha ha man. heyfa derie, &c.*
Val. Did he take the Lady *by the thigh man?*
Clo. Thigh man?   *Val. I man.*   *Clow. Ha ha ha ha man.*

---

[53] Found on G4v–H of the 1608 edition.
[54] The actor was Duncan Law of the Lions part.

Hor. *And now he came it somewhat nye man.* Clow. *Nye man*
Val. I *man.*   Clow. *Ha ha ha ha man, Heyfa dery, &c.*
Val. *But did he doe the tother thing man?*
Clow. T*hing man?*   Val. *I man.*   Clow. *Ha ha ha ha man.*
Hor. *And at the same had he a fling man.*   Clow. *Fling man.*
Hor. I *man.*   Clow. *Ha ha ha ha man, hey fadery, &c.*

(G4v–H)

The characters exit and a scene is set with a table and chair covered in black. It is the scene where the peers of Rome arrive at Lucrece's side and swear vengeance for what has happened to her, but to no avail. It is the scene where Lucrece kills herself. 'Did he take fair Lucrece by the toe man?' is the song that most exasperates the critic coming to *Lucrece*, trying to make sense of what Heywood was trying to do. However, I would suggest that it is only after this song and what it means about male desire and male helplessness in the teeth of something like rape, as well as within the play's context of desperate political tyranny, that a new response for the senators is possible. For with their promise of revenge to the suicidal yet courageous 'Romane' Lucrece, Valerius, thereafter, no longer sings, Mutius no longer laughs, Brutus no longer feigns madness and – with this new communal spirit among the men – the Tarquins are vanquished. There is no more need for coded feeling expressed in something like song: revolution is now possible. And it happens.[55]

Bearing all the above in mind, perhaps it is no surprise that the play, when presented by the King's and Queen's men combined in 1612, was only performed before the Queen and Prince Henry at Greenwich, without the King present, according to records. Publicly with this tragedy, it is important to remember how all the evidence points to it proving a tremendous success for the company. We know from accounts of his last days, for instance, that on 7 August 1628, George Villiers, the hated

---

[55] The 'new' songs that are inserted by 1638 include 'The first new Song' – 'She that denies me I would have', coming shortly before the Molly song; another 'Song', coming after this and the first scene with Lucrece about taverns in Rome (London) – 'The Gentry to the Kingshead'; the 'second new Song', coming a little after this – 'Though the weather jangles', before 'I will show thee the way to know'; 'The third new Song' – 'O yes, roome for the Cryer', during the peers' visit to Collatine's house; 'Song' – 'The Spaniard loves his ancient slop', shortly after the 'Terry dery ding' song; 'Packe clouds away', sung at the camp, after the rape; 'The fourth new Song In the praise of *Lucrece*', beginning 'On two white Collomns archt she stands'; 'Come list and harke', also at the camp after Sextus' return there; 'The last new Song' – 'I'de thinke my selfe as proud in Shackles', which comes shortly before the 'Catch'. The two songs appended to the end of the play are: 'The Cryes of Rome' and 'Arise, arise, my Iuggie my Puggie', making twenty-two songs in all by 1638. For yet more detailed scholarship and thought about the songs, see Holaday, in Heywood, *The Rape of Lucrece*; but also Rowland, *Thomas Heywood's Theatre*, pp. 4–14.

favourite made duke of Buckingham, saw this play at the Cockpit.[56] He was assassinated on the 23rd. Heywood's *Rape of Lucrece* was undoubtedly a valuable performance text that Christopher Beeston made sure he carried with him, not only to his new indoor enterprise but – eventually – to the new Queen's players under Henrietta Maria's patronage. Not only that but – after his death in 1636 – the play carried on under the management of his son, William, into the repertoire of the King and Queen's Young Company, otherwise known as Beeston's Boys.[57]

The Queen's Servants on tour – in England and Europe

(i) English touring

Whether the Queen's Servants took large-scale plays on tour with them around England we cannot say for sure, but it is certain that versions of the company toured the home country at this time. With English touring we are presented with a problem. Given that Robert Leigh and Martin Slatiar are nominated alongside the more general 'our Commedians' in the 1606 Southampton-copied patent, and given that Thomas Greene objected to Slatiar's taking 'her Ma*iesties* servantes' on tour without six of those sworn as such, a question begs: what 'Queen's Servants' company are we looking at when an entry is found for them among touring records – a questioned Swinnerton/Slatiar/Leigh-led company, or (possibly) a more 'authoritative' Greene-dominated troupe? Leading on from this, who is to say which group was the questioned outfit in early modern terms and which the more 'authoritative'? With regard to Robert Leigh we have a situation where, in the 1623 court case, he claimed that he was not with the company at the time of George Pulham's death and its aftermath in 1611, and was not to return to them until Christmas 1618.[58] However, we know from court payments that he was present in the London area to receive money for plays during this time: for 1613–14 performances, paid again in 1615, again in 1616 and again in March 1617. For the 1615 Leigh payment,

---

[56] Letter from Robert Gell to Sir Martyn Stuteville, in *The Autobiography and Correspondence of Sir Simonds D'Ewes*, ed. James Orchard Halliwell, 2 vols. (London: Richard Bentley, 1845), Vol. II, p. 210: 'On Wednesday his Grace was also a spectator of yᵉ Rape of Lucrece at yᵉ Cockpitt.' The day before he had gone to the Globe to see *Henry VIII*, 'whereat he stayd till yᵉ Duke of Buckingham was beheaded, and then departed. Some say, he should rather have seen yᵉ fall of Cardinall Woolsey, who was a more lively type of himself, having governed this kingdome eighteen yeares, as he hath done fourteen' (*ibid.*).

[57] Holaday in Heywood, *The Rape of Lucrece*, p. 29; Clark, *Thomas Heywood*, p. 48.

[58] TNA C24/500/9, answers to Ints. 5, 7 and 31.

however, there are no company or 'fellows' referred to, although he is paid
£30 for three plays. Nominated, along with Slatiar, in the 1606 paperwork
copied out in Southampton records (allowing them to travel and perform,
including in the City of London), Leigh could have used this in order to
tour with Slatiar and with Swinnerton if this warrant had been a bona
fide one.[59] If it was bona fide, perhaps it was this spin-off troupe who performed before the court, giving rise to these payments.

According to the publications of the Records of Early English Drama
(REED), Leigh, along with Swinnerton, was present in the city of Norwich
on 30 March 1616 when the Mayors' Court Books note 'A Patent' brought
in by Swinnerton. At the time the actor 'Confesseth that hee himselfe &
Roberte Lee only are here to play the rest are absent'. It was not the 1606
Southampton wording, however, that the Norwich officials noted down
in their books, but a copy of the 1609 one mentioning all the Queen's
Servants. Sticking to the letter of their received criteria, the Norfolk men
wrote that Swinnerton was 'desired to desist from playing & offered a
benevolence in mony which he refused to accept'. The city also records
how, in the event, they relented and allowed the actors to play.[60] They
may have regretted this. Ever patient yet canny, the good men of Norwich
endured further visits from the Queen's Servants that year in the persons
of both Swinnerton and Slatiar, including those on 29 May and 20 July
1616. On 29 May they reminded Swinnerton of the 30 March performances and said to him 'yf yow will play yow must doo yt at your perill
without our leaue', and he reportedly replied: 'wee will adventure the perill & we meane on Monday next to play in the Cytty'. The authorities,
despairing, 'offered him a gratuitie to desist', which 'he was content to
accept ... & promised desistance accordyngly'.[61]

On 20 July it was obviously Slatiar who 'drew the short straw' in life.
'This day Martyn Slaughter brought into this Court A Patent Teste 17
Ianuarij Anno Nono Iacobi' (1612), the Mayor's Book notes. 'This Patent
hath ben twise shewed singe [sic] Easter, this ys the Third tyme, The said
Martyn Slaughter ys not named in the Patent therefore hee hath no leaue
to play.'[62] Slatiar was indeed not mentioned in the formal patents of either
1604 or 1609. He was only mentioned in the 1606 copied-out 'permission',
which was not used, and it should be remembered that Greene had already

[59] This wording of the warrant is published in *ES*, Vol. II, pp. 234–5.
[60] Mayors' Court Books XV, NRO: 16.a, fo. 62; David Galloway, ed., *Norwich 1540–1642*, Records of Early English Drama [REED] (University of Toronto Press, 1984), p. 145.
[61] Mayors' Court Books XV, NRO: 16.a, fo, 70; Galloway, *Norwich 1540–1642*, p. 146.
[62] Mayors' Court Books XV, NRO: 16.a, fo. 81; Galloway, *Norwich 1540–1642*, p. 148.

taken Slatiar to court to query his tendency to play without enough official players. The copy of the official patent was again shown during a visit the following year on 31 May 1617, which was recorded thus: 'This day Robert Lee brought into the Court an Exemplificac*i*on of a Patent … They are licenced to play in this Cytty in whitson weeke next, Monday Tuseday & Wednesday in Powles howse & no longer.'⁶³ Ironically, according to REED, a Norwich clerk was soon to copy out a letter into their book, written by the Lord Chamberlain in the week after Leigh's visit:

> wheras Thomas Swynaerton and Martin Slaughter beinge two of the Queens Ma*iestes* Company of playors hauing sep*a*rated themselues from their said Company, haue each of them taken forth a severall exemplification or duplicate of his Ma*iestes* Letters patent*es* graunted to the whole Company and by vertue therof they severally in two Companies with vagabond*es* and such like idle p*er*sons, haue and doe vse and exercise the quallitie of playinge in diu*er*se plac*es* of this Realme to ^ [the] geat [*sic*] abuse and wronge [f] of his Ma*iestes* Subi*ec*tes in generall and contrary to the true intent and meaninge of his Ma*ie*stie to the said Company.⁶⁴

Robert Leigh

If Leigh was the person who came into the Norwich offices shortly before the instructions of the Chamberlain arrived, and he was the same man who was the main court payee for the period 1613 to 1617, it is possible that the performances for which he received treasury payment were presented by this English touring version of the company. It is not known for certain what Leigh was doing when he claimed to be away from the company, but he could have been touring, and there is a 1612 record of a man going by his name paying for an exemplification.⁶⁵ We should, however, bear in mind that the actor who visited Norwich in May 1617 may have been someone pretending to be Leigh, and wielding a Leigh-donated piece of paperwork for reasons that will become clear. Whichever way it was, we know that this was not the only activity on Leigh's mind at around

---

⁶³ Mayors' Court Books XV, NRO: 16.a, fo. 132v; Galloway, *Norwich 1540–1642*, pp. 150–1. In January 1611/12 a Robert Lee paid for an exemplification, which cost him 20s 3d. See TNA AO 3/379/3, p. 26 (fo. 14v).

⁶⁴ Mayors' Court Books XV, NRO: 16.a, fo. 133; Galloway, *Norwich 1540–1642*, pp. 151–2. The warrant also notes similar misdemeanours by William Perry (later associated with the Red Bull and other places), Charles Marshall, Humphrey Jeffes and William Parr. It was sent from Theobalds, dated 16 July 1616 and signed 'Penbrook'.

⁶⁵ TNA AO3/379/3, p. 26.

that time. C. W. Wallace once transcribed a suit made against Leigh that
the editors of *English Professional Theatre* independently found and published.[66] The document was in a poor condition in the early twentieth
century and it is in a worse condition now. The guessed date of the document is about 1618; it cannot be pinpointed to much before this time as it
is addressed to Sir Francis Bacon, who did not become Lord Chancellor
until January that year. Something that should also be taken into account
with regard to the company and its interests is that Bacon acted as Queen
Anna's legal adviser according to her household accounts.[67]

Wallace recorded the case, which concerned arrangements made and
promises broken by Leigh – at least as far as the main company were
concerned. It seems that a couple of years before the hearing of the case,
Leigh had said he wanted to leave the company, and, in exchange for
a sum Wallace surmised was £60, he had said he would give them any
'^cloaths^ booke*s* of playes, & other goode*s* belonging therunto, as he
had then, or were trusted in his hande*s* or Custody'. In the usual way in
those litigious times, three bonds were arranged whereby each committed
to paying Leigh £20 in instalments, with a £40 penalty if anything should
go awry. If Wallace's dating of 1618 is correct, the events of the previous
two years coincided with Christopher Beeston's building of the Cockpit
playhouse in 1616, which was, on 4 March 1617, unfortunately damaged
by rioters.[68] The Cockpit was to be the Queen's Servants' new indoor playhouse, but somehow, as events unfolded, Beeston found he did not need
sharers (unlike, for example, the Burbages with the indoor Blackfriars, as
playhouse-owners needing sharers among Shakespeare's company), so that
this first theatre in the Drury Lane area of London was, in effect, his.

This being the case, not long after it reopened, Beeston divested himself
of his Queen's Servants membership, and the company had to relocate
again back to the Red Bull. According to the complainants in the case
against Leigh – 'Richard Perkins, John Cumber, will*ia*m Robins, James
Holt & Thomas Hayward' – their fortunes fell with the 'Riffling' of the
playhouse in question, losing, by their estimation, '500li' in damage. An
interesting matter to note here is that on the badly damaged document,
the name of the actual playhouse is missing today. Seeing the names of the
players involved in the early 1900s, C. W. Wallace, from what he saw, wrote

[66] TNA C2/JASI/P16/14; see *EPT*, pp. 239–41.
[67] TNA SC6/JASI/1650, fo. 18v. He was made, in the year 1615/16, Anna's 'Serjeant at Law'.
[68] For this and all matters relating to Beeston's building enterprises at this time see Griffith,
'Christopher Beeston', particularly pp. 612–17 regarding the Cockpit.

that it was the 'Redd Bull' that incurred the £500 corrective costs.[69] With their knowledge about the riot, however, the editors of *English Professional Theatre* thought it must be the Cockpit. Whatever playhouse it was, the players knew they were going to struggle to pay Leigh but, undaunted, they managed £50 of the £60 expected. Leigh felt sorry for them, or, in the actors' words: '(seeming to compassionate *your* Orators losse aforesaid) rested then fully satisfyed, & [deliu]ered upp to be cancelled one of the bond*es* before menc*i*oned'. He also '*p*romised to seeke out & cancell the rest, & to deliu*er* upp unto *your* Orators, all such goode*s*, apparell, booke*s*, & other thing*es* of theirs as he or any other' possessed. The actors went on to add, however, that Leigh changed his mind. Horrified, they observed that:

> the s*ai*d Rob*er*t Lee having a p*ur*pose to ou*er*reach & defraude yo*ur* Orators & having to that end drawen & wrapt them into the Bond*es* afore*sa*id & detayned still in his hand*es* uncancelled 2 of the said Bond*es* [refuses] to giue them any security for p*er*formance of the s*ai*d p*ro*mise & agrem*ent* on his p*ar*t, & p*re*suming himself to be therby free from any daynger of suite at the Comon Law in that behalf, hath therupon of late denyed his said p*ro*mise [& agre]m*ent* & utterly refused to p*er*forme the same on his p*ar*t, but in mere breach therof hath betaken himself agayne to the practise & ^exercise of the said^ quallety of playing, & erected & sett up a new company calling them by the name of the children [of his/her] Maj*es*t*ie*s Revells[.]

Leigh, with the likelihood of gaining money from his bonds, had set up a children's company and had taken up acting again. But worse was to follow regarding this new group. Leigh had stolen the best of the Queen's Servants' own youngsters. He had:

> not only inticed & drawen from yo*ur* Orators diu*er*s of their best respected young men to the number of 7 or more whom they had trayned up & fitted for that quallety, but also deteyneth [from your] Orators diu*er*s booke*s*, apparell & other goode*s* of thers to the value of 100li or theraboute*s*, & maketh use therof to furnishe his owne new erected Company & having ^likewise^ in his custody yo*ur* Orators Lett*er*es Patent*es* afore*sa*id refuseth to [deliver up] the same unto them but hath of late offered to farme the same unto others, & soe eu*ery* way infringed & broken his p*ro*mise & agrem*ent* afors*ai*d.[70]

---

[69] Wallace papers, Box 9, File Bv, 11b.
[70] TNA C2/JASI/P16/14.

The actors estimated that they had been damaged to the tune of a further £200 because of Leigh's behaviour, with Leigh enriching himself through their ruin. Because of the missing amounts expected from them he had taken them to court for the penalties of £40 on the two remaining bonds, despite entreaties that he give up his demands for their sakes.

A set of circumstances such as these tells a story, and although we should always be careful of building narratives around bare facts, out of the evidence and characteristics of both Christopher Beeston and Robert Leigh it is possible to make a few observations.

In his evidence in the *Worth* v. *Baskervile* case, Beeston was very clear about when he left the company. This was 'before Christmas, in the yeare of or Lord, one thowsand six hundred & eighteen'.[71] As has already been stated, Leigh came back to the company at about the same time. Perhaps this is no surprise, since Leigh had been scathing over the behaviour of Christopher Beeston at the time of his management of the company *c.* 1611–18 in the *Worth* v. *Baskervile* case. 'It is true', he said, 'That both before & synce the decesse of the *said* Tho: Greene' – meaning before 1612 and after – 'the *said* Company did repose great Trust & Confidence in the *said* xxtofer hutchinson al*ias* Beeston, conce*rn*ing the Managing of their *said* playing affayers … And this dep*onen*t sayth That the *said* Hutchinson tooke upon him a power over the now Compl*ainan*tes and their then fellow Actors and toke up their Galleries money therin and accompted for yt, at his owne pleasure.'[72] Obviously there was no love lost between Leigh and Beeston – the elder actor, perhaps, believing that the younger's ability to build and own the Cockpit was suspicious in view of his management of the company's accounts. Leigh arrived back in the main company when Beeston had left, and stayed long enough to help them reduce expected payments from Susan Baskervile (see Chapter 7). One assumes therefore, that the disagreements over the sums others owed him had been settled at that point. What qualifies this, however, is Leigh's frankness about leaving the company soon after. This was due to 'some discontents falling out amongst them'.[73] The actors' other accusations – about farming out copies of company patents to other troupes – fit in with what we know of the Slatiar/Swinnerton troupe with which Leigh seems to have involved himself. Renting exemplifications out to troupes who, in the Chamberlain's words, included 'vagabond*es* and such like idle

---

[71] TNA C24/500/9, Beeston's evidence, Int. 31.
[72] TNA C24/500/9, Leigh's evidence, Int. 33.
[73] TNA C24/500/9, Leigh's evidence, Int. 34.

persons' could also have been lucrative.[74] Moreover, if a splinter group
of the company were, indeed, touring, they could have come into the
London area for both public and court performances for which Leigh,
in charge, could have afforded them as leader, and they could also have
used the 'other' venue in which the Queen's Servants were allowed to perform – the Curtain playhouse. This, indeed, was where Martin Slatiar was
accused of causing injury to a waterman called Edmund Chambers ('beating and wounding' him), who was likewise accused of causing 'an affray
and a tumult at the curtayne dore'. This was in 1613.[75] The actor Robert
Dawes, with whom Greene was to be found in those 'hanaper' accounts,
was also mentioned as a party to this event. In the following year this case
was transferred to the King's Bench, where the documents show that both
Slatiar and Dawes were outlawed, and it could be that from about that
time, touring, for Slatiar, seemed a very good idea indeed.[76]

It should be remembered, with reference to any earlier Martin Slatiar/
Thomas Swinnerton Queen's Servants touring company efforts, that
companies did sometimes divide off from one another in an authorised
fashion. If Martin Slatiar was allowed to tour as a member of a Queen's
Servants touring company as one of *six* of the patented members, then
in terms of those left there would be enough known patented residue to
make up a divided version of the company. In their book, McMillin and
MacLean point up evidence of the Elizabethan Queen's company dividing, for example, in 1583, and one assumes a similar practice could have
been taken up by the Jacobean Queen's Servants, especially with more
than one legitimate venue to return to in the London area, as was the
case.[77] Apparently it was always known that the Elizabethan Queen's men
divided after 1587, but in 1583, when they were just starting and provably successful, the evidence is that with permission to perform in two
venues on their return to London – the Bull (not the Red Bull) and the

---

[74] For instance, there is a further example of a Leigh visit to Norwich along with Philip Rossiter, 'william Percy' and Nicholas Longe on 29 August 1618, showing 'A Commission' signed in October
1617. But was it the real Robert Leigh who came, or someone in possession of paperwork Leigh had
allowed them to use? See NRO, Mayors' Court Books XV, 16.a, fo. 204; Galloway, *Norwich 1540–
1642*, p. 157. Longe came back later to Norwich on 9 June 1619 with a bill allowing the Children of
the Queen's Revels to perform (fo. 240v).

[75] Chambers, of St Olave's, Southwark, came and submitted a fine to the court on 27 July 1613. He
was bailed by a yeoman from St Giles, Cripplegate (James Bernard) and a coppersmith of the same
parish (William[?] Myller) to the tune of £10 each. LMA MJ/SR/0523, 219; MJ/SR/0523, 221.

[76] TNA KB29/255, m. 84d.

[77] McMillin and MacLean, *The Queen's Men and Their Plays*, p. 43. See also Dave Kathman, 'London
Inns as Playing Venues for the Queen's Men', in *Locating the Queen's Men, 1583–1603*, ed. Helen
Ostovich, Holger Schott Syme and Andrew Griffin (Farnham: Ashgate, 2009), pp. 65–75. Dave

Bell in their case – the possibility was open that they could continue their
divided status at this time. This was also possible for the Jacobean Queen's
Servants.

From the records we have, Leigh must have possessed an imposing
and confident presence. Noted before as the eldest sharer among them,
he is equal with Thomas Greene in receiving court payments during
the period under study. Perhaps his open apathy towards Christopher
Beeston might be perceived as a little churlish in view of the fact that
Beeston had once helped Leigh. This was by bailing him on a rape charge
in 1605.[78] The accusation was that on 21 June of that year Leigh, along
with one Edward Norton, forcibly entered the house of Joan Hitchecocke
at 'Nortonfollgate' (an area near Shoreditch, just north of the City) and
attacked and raped her.[79] In a now well-known instance of a similar claim,
Christopher Beeston had also once been accused of rape and had apparently been acquitted.[80] Because of both players' known and continued
activity in the entertainment world after these events, it is obvious that
Leigh, too, was cleared of charges.

Apart from the Leigh/Swinnerton/Slatiar touring adventures we do
know of at least one instance of a legitimate-sounding Greene-led Queen's
Servants touring visit in England. However, on this occasion their experience of entertaining outside London was no more cheery. In Cambridge,
in July 1606, John Duke and Thomas Greene gained permission from the
Mayor to play in the Town Hall and to build a stage, responsibly taking
down the glass in the windows. Unfortunately the visit ended up with
the actors giving bond of £20 to the Chancellor of the University that
they would *not* act within five miles of either it or the town, whether by
themselves or in company.[81] Within the same period – and in no particular order – the 'Quenes players', or variations of the term, were paid

---

Kathman's work clarifies how one venue was intended for indoor performances and the other for
outdoor entertainment, but he sees no reason why the company, divided, could not perform at
both venues at the same time. Personal correspondence, February 2013.

[78] LMA MJ/SR/0429, 19. Three people gave Robert Leigh bail of £40 each. The two other than
Beeston were both Merchant Taylors – one William Patten of St Giles, Cripplegate, and William
Hart of St Botolph's, Aldgate.

[79] LMA MJ/SR/0430, 68.

[80] Bridewell Court Minute Books, LMA CLC/275/MS33011/004, 1597/8–1604, fos. 327v–332r. The
event was dated to June 1602. See Duncan Salkeld, 'Literary Traces in Bridewell and Bethlem,
1602–1624', *Review of English Studies*, n.s. 56, 379–85; Griffith, 'Christopher Beeston', pp. 610–11.

[81] Cambridge University Archives, Commissary Court Book, Comm. Ct. II.13, fo. 128v (*rev*) and fo.
107v (*rev*); Alan H. Nelson, ed., *Cambridge*, 2 vols., REED (University of Toronto Press, 1989), Vol.
I, pp. 403–4, and Vol. II, p. 1172. The original record carries the autograph signatures of John Duke
and Thomas Greene. The Queen's trumpeters were also paid 'v s' by St John's College in July.

at Dover, Faversham, Weymouth-Melcombe Regis, Exeter, Bath, Ludlow and Coventry. In 1606–7, similarly titled groups performed at Bridgwater, Bath, Oxford, Coventry, Shrewsbury and York, with Barnstaple and Coventry again recorded during 1607–8. They were paid at Faversham, Lydd, Folkestone, Canterbury, Dover, Dartmouth, Coventry and Shrewsbury in 1608–9; Norwich in 1609, and in Lydd and Maidstone in 1609–10. Finally, payments were made in New Romney, Dover and Norwich in 1610–11.[82] For the 1611–12 period we enter interesting times for the Queen's Servants, in that Thomas Greene died during the summer of 1612, with allusions to his demise allowing for the possibility that this occurred immediately he arrived back from a tour (possibly overseas). It also appears that Christopher Beeston could have taken over in a leadership or management role for the company stemming from this hiatus period. During 1611–12, touring records indicate that the company going by their name concentrated on the 'home counties': that is, those areas not far from London – primarily Kent and Sussex – from the records we have. To the west, Somerset and Shropshire figure, the Somerset visit demonstrated by a May payment of 20s (£1) in Bridgwater, and the Shropshire payment, in Shrewsbury, again for 20s.[83]

---

[82] For the following published touring records this book is almost entirely dependent on REED. A first touring date for Queen Anna's Men may be a 1603 Coventry one (*Coventry*, ed. R. W. Ingram (University of Toronto Press, 1981), p. 362). However, their listing has payments to Worcester's Men either side of it; therefore it is likely these are performances by Queen *Elizabeth's* Men. For the period from the 1604 draft patent, up to 1611–12, touring vists on the following pages should be considered. *Kent: Diocese of Canterbury*, ed. James M. Gibson, 3 vols. (University of Toronto Press, 2002), Vol. I, pp. 252–3 (Canterbury); and Vol. II, pp. 495, 498, 500 (Dover); 565, 566, 567 (Faversham); 585 (Folkestone); 707 (Lydd); 723 (Maidstone); 807 (New Romney). *Dorset*, ed. Rosalind Conklin Hays and C. E. McGee, in *Dorset/Cornwall*, ed. Sally L. Joyce, Evelyn S. Newlyn, Rosalind Conklin Hays and C. E. McGee (University of Toronto Press, 1999), pp. 3–367 (p. 278) (Weymouth-Melcombe Regis). *Devon*, ed. John M. Wasson (University of Toronto Press, 1986), pp. 180–1 (Exeter); 48 (Barnstaple); 69 (Dartmouth). *Somerset*, ed. James Stokes, *Including Bath*, ed. Robert J. Alexander, 2 vols. (University of Toronto Press, 1996), Vol. I, pp. 19 (Bath); 59 (Bridgwater). *Coventry*, ed. Ingram, pp. 370, 371, 373, 375–6. *Oxford*, 2 vols., ed. John R. Elliott, Jr and Alan H. Nelson (University), and Alexandra F. Johnston and Diana Wyatt (City) (University of Toronto Press, 2004), Vol. I, pp. 276 (Vol. II, p. 1016), 337, 381. *York*, ed. Alexandra F. Johnston and Margaret Rogerson, 2 vols. (University of Toronto Press, 1979), Vol. I, pp. 521 and 522. Galloway, *Norwich*, pp. 134 and 136. *Shropshire*, ed. J. Alan B. Somerset, 2 vols. (University of Toronto Press, 1994), Vol. I, p. 91 (Ludlow); pp. 290 and 293 (Shrewsbury). For entries of these visits with some refined dating go to the REED *Patrons and Performances* website, http://link.library.utoronto.ca/reed, accessed 12 June 2013.

[83] Stokes, *Somerset*, Vol. I, p. 59; and Somerset, *Shropshire*, Vol. I, p. 301. The other 1611–12 records are found in Gibson, *Kent*, Vol. II, pp. 502, 503 (Dover); 567 (Faversham); 586 (Folkestone); 634 (Hythe); 708 (Lydd); and 724 (Maidstone); as well as in the *Sussex* REED volume (ed. Cameron Louis (University of Toronto Press, 2000)), when they appeared at Rye (p. 147).

A company or companies named as associated with the Queen had been of a more northerly persuasion, probably venturing into York in 1606–7 and northern East Anglia by 1609, which they continued to visit thereafter, heading further afield to Newcastle by 1615. The Earl of Worcester's Men visited Newcastle three times during their Elizabethan touring days (in 1590, 1591 and 1593), so to some of the company, north-eastern climes may have been familiar.[84] Worcester's players were active touring performers with no other especially adventurous venues recorded during their travels in the earlier 1590s. There is an obvious slow-down in recorded touring *c.* 1597–1603, however, with only one touring date for Faversham during the period 1604–5 recorded, all this possibly indicating a period where the company was consolidating its new status centred on London and the court – amalgamating, regrouping and working towards the new playhouse.[85]

As for touring records from 1612–13 onwards until Queen Anna's death, we have now seen how problems with true status might vie with attempts at firmly stated knowledge. We know that – by insinuation – Martin Slatiar was accused of intending to perform with fewer than a handful of the Queens' Servants' members by 1606. After 1612 we have also seen in what ways records show that such practices – or accusations of such practice – had widened to include, for example, Thomas Swinnerton and Robert Leigh – hoarded paperwork in hand. With the actors taking Leigh to court for threatening to lease out the patents to itinerant companies, and warning letters from the Lord Chamberlain acknowledging this reprehensible kind of activity, the true identity of players travelling in the Queen's name can seem shaky. Nevertheless, true Queen's Servants, versions of them or fake ones, certainly toured during this time, and their visits can be traced through REED's published accounts of them.[86]

[84] J. J. Anderson, ed., *Newcastle upon Tyne*, REED (University of Toronto Press, 1982), pp. 73, 79, 91 and 148.

[85] A sum of 10s 'p*ai*d the Queenes playere*s*', Town Accounts, CKS: FA/FAc 35, Sheet 14 (Chamberlain's Allowances); Gibson, *Kent*, Vol. II, p. 565.

[86] See the following REED pages or their *Patrons and Performances* website for entries. Gibson, *Kent*, Vol. II, pp. 504–5, 508, 509, 511, 512, 516 (Dover); 568, 571 (Faversham); 588, 589 (Folkestone); 602–3 (Fordwich); 634, 635, 638 (Hythe); 708, 709, 710 (Lydd); 724–5, 807, 808, 810 (New Romney). Wasson, *Devon*, pp. 48–9 (Barnstaple); 189–90 (Exeter). *Bristol*, ed. Mark C. Pilkinton (University of Toronto Press, 1997), p. 173 (a company visiting Bristol is referred to as the 'Queenes ma*iesties* Revellers'; this may be another company – however, the payments coincide with Anna's visit to the city in 1613 with the earl of Worcester in attendance). Ingram, *Coventry*, pp. 386, 392, 397, 399, 405, 410, 414, 417, 421. Louis, *Sussex*, pp. 149 and 151; Elliott and Nelson, *Oxford*, Vol. I, pp. 405 (Vol. II, p. 1043), 422. Somerset, *Shropshire*, Vol. I, pp. 93, 104 (Ludlow); 303 and 306 (Shrewsbury). Galloway, *Norwich*, pp. 142, 145, 146, 148, 149, 150–1, 151–2, 157, 169, 171, 172, 175, 200. *Lincolnshire*, ed. James Stokes (University of Toronto Press, 2009), Vol. I, p. 42 (Boston). *Cheshire, Including*

Presumably the company took their great successes on tour with them – although it is hard to imagine the large-scale *Rape of Lucrece* being presented ad hoc at town halls of any nature. What is certain is that a play on this subject, if not Heywood's play, made it not simply to the provinces, but to the Continent. In contrast to the experiences recounted taking place in England, a successful company associated with the Queen's Servants certainly toured Europe, and it was, indeed, this company that performed the *Lucrece* play.

(ii)   European touring

'At the entertainement of the Cardinall *Alphonsus*, and the Infant of *Spaine* into the Low-countrye', writes Heywood in his *Apology for Actors*, 'they were presented at *Antwerpe*, with sundry pageants and playes' (E). In the margins here, Heywood notes that this person was also 'Archduke' Alphonsus; nobody, however, can make this Cardinal-Archduke's name 'Albert', the name of the Infanta's husband. Nor have I yet seen any identification of an 'Alphonsus' described in this way. Heywood goes on:

> the King of *Denmarke*, father to him that now reigneth, entertained into his seruice, a company of *English Comedians*, commended vnto him by the honourable the Earle of *Leicester:* the Duke of *Brounswicke*, and the *Landsgraue* of *Hessen* retaine in their Courts certaine of ours, of the same quality.

At the time of Heywood's writing, the King of Denmark was Queen Anna's brother, Christian IV, who had visited England while the Queen's Servants were performing, and who had also been visited in Denmark by the likes of Inigo Jones and John Dowland. The father referred to by Heywood was also Anna's – King Frederick II – and it is through Heywood, therefore, that we learn of one manifestation of the Danish court's early involvement with English entertainment.[87] For the 'Duke of *Brounswicke*' we should read Heinrich Julius, the duke of Braunschweig-

Chester, ed. Elizabeth Baldwin, Lawrence M. Clopper and David Mills, 2 vols. (University of Toronto Press, 2007), Vol. II, pp. 639, 642, 649 (Congleton). Conklin Hays and McGee, *Dorset*, p. 279 (Weymouth-Melcombe Regis). *Cumberland, Westmorland, Gloucestershire*, ed. Audrey Douglas and Peter Greenfield (University of Toronto Press, 1986), pp. 87 and 94 (Carlisle); 183, 184, 185 (Kendal). *Lancashire*, ed. David George (University of Toronto Press, 1991), p. 83 (Prescot); 177 (Gawthorpe); 186 (Dunkenhalgh). Anderson, *Newcastle upon Tyne*, p. 148. *Herefordshire*, ed. David N. Klausner (University of Toronto Press, 1990), p. 149 (Leominster). Stokes, *Somerset*, p. 26. Johnston and Rogerson, *York*, p. 564.
[87] At the period of Heywood's interest, the earl of Leicester was Sir Robert Dudley.

Lüneburg, husband to Elisabeth, Queen Anna's sister, who married this duke in 1590.[88] The town where the couple lived in Germany is known as Wolfenbüttel and is located in Lower Saxony, just south of Brunswick (as it is called in England). We shall hear about company visits to this example of 'the Dukes of *Saxony*' (*Apology*, G3) in this ensuing part of the chapter.

The '*Landsgraue* of Hessen' was Maurice 'the Learned', Landgrave of Hesse-Cassel, whose son, Otto, had visited London the year before the publication of Heywood's *Apology*. In the sixteenth century, the Landgrave, as it has been proved, used at least one actor – a Robert Browne – to carry letters to Robert Devereux, the then earl of Essex.[89] According to Willem Schrickx, this Browne was 'certainly a Landgrave's man by the beginning of 1595'.[90] It should be emphasised that this Robert Browne was not Robert Browne of the Boar's Head who died in 1603, but another Robert Browne, well known for travelling on the Continent, and who was associated with at least three actors who were certainly linked with the Queen's Servants, both at the Red Bull playhouse and at the Curtain in Shoreditch. The three actors were John Green, Robert Reynolds and John Thayer.[91]

In Chapter 3, mention was made of Thayer, present in Henslowe's records during Worcester's company's time at the Rose and then again present in 1608–9 as a half-sharer among the Queen's Servants at the Red Bull. He, like Thomas Greene, was to die in 1612. At this time, a sharer in the Queen's Servants company was a weighty thing to be. This was what Thayer was in terms of the English company's profits, yet he performed on the Continent too. Here we only push the boundaries of theatre history where we define what the term 'company' truly means. Thayer is just one representative player who demonstrates to what extent an off-shoot, splinter group or *version* of the company came to be playing in Europe – a Europe where Queen Anna's family and associates were contributing to the Continent's developing history. According to Schrickx, Thayer performed abroad, conveniently, in the latter half of 1603, demonstrating his

---

[88] See Mara R. Wade, 'The Queen's Courts: Anna of Denmark and Her Royal Sisters', p. 49.

[89] Willem Schrickx, *Foreign Envoys and Travelling Players in the Age of Shakespeare and Jonson* ([Gent]: Rijksuniversiteit te Gent, 1986), p. 122. A Cambridge University Press reader tells me that 'the Margrave Maurice' built a 'stone-made theatre for English players' in 1616 at Kassel. It was called the Ottoneum and can still be seen, functioning as a museum. For this information I thank this anonymous person.

[90] *Ibid.*, p. 193. For this section on Worcester's Men/Queen's Servants in Europe I am completely reliant on the work of Schrickx, and Jerzy Limon, *Gentlemen of a Company: English Players in Central and Eastern Europe, 1590–1660* (Cambridge University Press, 1985).

[91] The name of the actor 'Blackwood', present in Henslowe's records for the Earl of Worcester's Men, is also mentioned in the early European records when Robert Blackwood is named with Thayer at the Frankfurt autumn fair of 1603. See Schrickx, *Foreign Envoys*, p. 203.

easy movement between the Elizabethan earl of Worcester's company over to Europe and then back again to England and the Jacobean Queen Anna's troupe.[92] He, together with the two others associated with the Queen's Servants, is seen to play an important part in early English perform- ance history abroad. Countries they covered included France, Denmark, Germany, Poland, the area comprising the modern-day Czech Republic and Slovakia, Russia, Belgium and Austria.

Robert Reynolds is known to have come and gone in the Red Bull com- pany's history in a similar manner to Thayer. A hard-won and confused scholarship (faced with many Robert Brownes) concludes that Reynolds – married to Jane Browne, the sister of a Robert Browne who died in 1625 – is therefore the son-in-law of the Continental Robert Browne.[93] Much may be said about Reynolds and the Brownes. According to Jerzy Limon, Browne was in Leyden in 1590 but first visited Wolfenbüttel in 1592. This may be the Robert Browne who can be traced back to Worcester's Men in 1582/3.[94] Wolfenbüttel was where Elisabeth, Anna's sister, was residing as duchess of Brunswick, having married Duke Heinrich Julius two years before. Therefore we can begin to see in what further ways Heywood's European observations, about the retention of English players by the 'Duke of *Brounswicke*', as well as the King of Denmark and the Landgrave of Hesse, were true, as well as relevant to the Queen's Servants specifi- cally.[95] Schrickx, referring to 'The Howard Passport' of February 1592, which includes Browne, posits the actors' possible use of it with Maurice of Nassau at Arnhem while Maurice was resting during fighting.[96] Robert Browne's European movements in the decades after this include references to variations of his troupe in Prague in 1596, Strasburg and Munich in 1601; possibly Gdansk (Danzig) during 1601; Ulm and Frankfurt in 1606; Strasburg in 1618; and then again in Prague and Gdansk in 1619–20.[97]

[92] Thayer appears at Frankfurt in 1603 and again in the minutes of the Augsburg city council in December. *Ibid.*, p. 203.

[93] See, for instance, the will of the Robert Browne who died in 1625 in Honigmann and Brock, *Playhouse Wills*, pp. 129–30, where he mentions his sister, 'Iane Renaldes'.

[94] *JCS*, Vol. II, p. 391.

[95] Limon, *Gentlemen of a Company*, p. 12 (Leyden), and p. 8 (Wolfenbüttel); citing P. Zimmerman, 'Englische Komödianten am Hofe zu Wolfenbüttel', *Braunschweigisches Magazin* 4 (April 1902), 37–45, 53–7 (pp. 37–45 for Heinrich Julius' patronage). See Schrickx, *Foreign Envoys*, p. 199 for evidence of Wolfenbüttel/Hesse-Cassel swaps of artists. Heinrich Julius was also a playwright (see Schrickx, *Foreign Envoys*, pp. 189–90).

[96] This Maurice is different, it should be noted, from Maurice 'the Learned' mentioned earlier. See Schrickx, *Foreign Envoys*, pp. 113, 122, 186. In one footnote he points out, intriguingly, that 'Sir Francis Vere and Robert Sidney were in command of the English troops' at Arnhem at that time.

[97] Limon, *Gentlemen of a Company*, pp. 39 (Prague, Strasburg and Munich), 87 (Gdansk), 119 (Ulm and Frankfurt), 14 (Strasburg), 149–50 (table; Prague and Gdansk).

Reynolds, a later actor in European performance terms, especially after his marriage to Browne's daughter, has been linked to evidence concerning the comedic character 'Pickleherring', who is mentioned much in German records in particular. According to Honigmann and Brock in their book of *Playhouse Wills*, 'Iane Browne the daughter of Robert Browne', cited in William Sly's 1608 will, was the same who became the wife of Robert Reynolds. Moreover, Browne, her father, had married Cicely Sands, who is likely to have been the sister-in-law of Christopher Beeston through his marriage to Jane Sands.[98] This familial relationship between the Beestons, the Continental Browne and Reynolds makes sense in terms of the records we have of both Jane Beeston and the Reynolds family's many English indictments for non-attendance at church. On 1 January 1616, a Robert Reynolds along with Jane, his wife, appear in Middlesex sessions records with an Elizabeth Reynolds, Jane Beeston née Sands (wife of Christopher), and others to do with their theatrical community, and they do so again in March records of the following year, 1617 – on both occasions, for recusancy.[99] Reynolds is also recorded as not having signed a 1617 agreement to do with the *Worth* v. *Baskervile* case. Beeston, Thomas Drewe and Thomas Heywood remembered that Reynolds did not sign this agreement; however, they were vague concerning whether he, along with others, expressed any intention to sign or not. This would seem to indicate that they thought he might have known these agreements were pending, but were unsure whether he was present to take part in the debate about the signing. The talk of him, however, in questions put to the actors by the opposing side, definitely points to his share-owning status in the English troupe, as Susan Baskervile obviously thought his signing of the document was important.

Reynolds arrives in Europe in July 1616 (Gdansk) a few months after appearing in the Middlesex sessions lists, and is found under the leadership of his father-in law in Nuremberg in May 1618.[100] He is also found in Strasburg during June of the same year,[101] so unless he was travelling back and forth very regularly it could be assumed that he was abroad throughout the period, perhaps including the time of Queen Anna's death, which

---

[98] TNA PROB10/258. According to Schrickx (*ibid.*, p. 189) Cicely Sands married Browne on 7 March 1593/4 after the death of his first wife and family in August 1593, mentioned in a letter from Henslowe to Alleyn. Cicely was executor of Sly's will. See Honigmann and Brock, *Playhouse Wills*, pp. 80–1. John Astington believes that Reynolds married Jane Browne on 20 November 1614 at St Michael's, Cornhill (Astington, *Actors and Acting in Shakespeare's Time*, pp. 211–12).

[99] 1616: LMA MJ/SR/0550, 152. 1617: LMA MJ/SR/0558, 48 and LMA MJ/SR/0559, 141.

[100] Schrickx, *Foreign Envoys*, p. 224; Limon, *Gentlemen of a Company*, p. 47.

[101] Schrickx, *Foreign Envoys*, p. 225.

would explain his absence on the funeral lists. On the Continent, a work called *Engelische Comedien und Tragedien* published in Germany in 1620 and 1630 becomes important to discussions concerning 'Pickleherring', the Reynolds-related character. In the 1620 edition, this character's name is certainly mentioned, and in that of 1630 we find a play with eleven actors listed including '7. Pickelhering', who plays a prominent role.[102] Known for being able to configure his face so that he could look sad on one side of it and happy on the other, this character was part of a package of entertainment that brought a version of the Queen's Servants to the Continent.[103]

According to Limon, the 1616 records are the first evidence of Reynolds' presence in Europe, but the actor was to go on being recorded on the Continent well into the following decades. In the 1620s he is found in Torgau (north-west Saxony), the Netherlands and Germany; and in the 1630s in Amsterdam and Königsberg (now Kaliningrad, Russia).[104] He was to die in Warsaw in around 1642,[105] and the following comment and description was made by a travelling Englishman, Peter Mundy, while in Gdansk:

> Some Summers come here our English commedlens [*sic*] or players which represente in Netherlandishe Dutche [Low German], having bin att Coninxberg beffore the prince Elector of Brandenburge; Allsoe att Warsowe beffore the king of Poland. Among those Actors was one here Nicknamed pickled herring, much talked off and admired For his dexterity in the Jesters partt, Amo. Itt is said off him thatt hee could doe Frame his Face and countenance thatt to one halffe off the people on the one side hee would seeme heartily to laugh and to those on the other side bitterly to weepe and shedd teares – straunge. Hee died att Warsaw. His wife now liveth here in towne [and] hath allowance From the king For her Maynetenance.[106]

---

[102] In the 1620 edition, 'Pickelhering' is advertised in red on the title-page at the beginning of the book, and between Acts I and II of the third play the phrase 'Althier agiret Pickelhering' appears. In the 1630 edition, the Pickleherring play appears to be called *Comoedia und Prob getrewer Liebe* (*Comedy and Test of True* [faithful] *Love*), O6–XIV.

[103] See Schrickx, '"Pickleherring" and English Actors in Germany', *Shakespeare Survey* 36 (1983), 135–47 for a much more careful approach to the identity of 'Pickleherring', who could have been another actor called George Vincent, also associated with the Browne/Green troupe. It is also thought Robert Leigh could have been of the popular 'Pickleherring' type of performer, which would make sense in terms of the leadership role he could take up.

[104] Limon, *Gentlemen of a Company*, pp. 103, 52.

[105] *Ibid.*, pp. 81, 105.

[106] Peter Mundy, *The Travels of Peter Mundy in Europe and Asia, 1608–1667*, ed. R. C. Temple, 5 vols., Hakluyt Society Publications, Second Series 17, 35, 45–6, 55, 78 (Cambridge and London: Hakluyt Society, 1907–36), Vol. IV [55] (1925), pp. 181–2.

The King in question who gave a pension to Mrs Pickleherring was King Władysław IV of Poland. According to Schrickx, Władysław IV Vasa (1595–1648) was related through his mother, Anna, to the family of the Habsburg Archduke Charles of Styria and Bishop of Breslau who also gave the Green troupe patronage.[107] Władysław had certainly played patron to the John Green troupe (see below, p. 187) according to a petition of July 1619. Perhaps the King's pension was extra-fitting if Jane Reynolds was the wife in receipt of the pension, for her father, too, had been the enduringly Continental Robert Browne.[108]

The provenance of this touring company provides strong links with the Servants of Queen Anna, not just because of the personnel, but because of the European courts that they travelled to, and because of the plays that they performed. The evidence of this company's activity from 1603 is under the auspices of Browne, but there is also weighty and ubiquitous proof of the leadership of the actor John Green. It was Green who was in Gdansk when Reynolds arrived there by 28 July 1616. Among the Continental courts with which this company has been provably associated was that of Elisabeth, duchess of Brunswick, the sister of Queen Anna. Wolfenbüttel at that later time was ruled by Frederic Ulrich, Elisabeth's son, who married into the Brandenburg family in 1614 after the death of Heinrich Julius, the duchess' husband, in 1613. As a cousin through his mother, he had been warmly welcomed by Prince Henry on a visit to England in 1610.[109] The plays this company are known to have performed in Europe include the Queen's Servants' plays *No-body and Somebody* (anonymous, known in Germany as *Niemand und Jemand*), *The Rape of Lucrece* and Heywood's *Edward IV*.[110] Pre-empting his book, Schrickx brought a wealth of research together for a *Shakespeare Survey* article about this Continental touring company, and was to speculate on a possible family relationship between John Green and Thomas Greene.[111] This speculation proves correct; Thomas Greene of Romford did have a younger

[107] Schrickx, 'Pickleherring'; *Foreign Envoys*, p. 145.
[108] Limon, *Gentlemen of a Company*, p. 13. *JCS*, Vol. II, p. 543 notes another marriage possibility in 1626 to a Margery Powell.
[109] Schrickx, 'Pickleherring', pp. 139–40.
[110] *Ibid.*, pp. 142–3. Most of the plays were mentioned in a letter Archduchess Maria Magdalena wrote to her brother, Ferdinand II, except for 'Römischen Lucretia', which was mentioned in a petition made by Green to the council of Danzig dated 28 August 1619. The success of the play was used to try and persuade the powers that the company should be allowed to perform. For the others see Irene Morris, 'A Hapsburg Letter', *Modern Language Review* 69 (1974), 12–22; Schrickx, 'Pickleherring', p. 143.
[111] Schrickx, 'Pickleherring', p. 144.

brother called John, both being baptised at the Church of St Edward the Confessor in Romford: Thomas on 27 September 1573, and John on 14 December 1578. There was an older brother – in the Latin of the registers 'Galfridus', or Jeffrey in English – who was baptised in November 1563. All were the sons of another John, who may be the 'Johanes Grene' who married an 'Alicie Collyns' on 1 July 1563 in the same parish.[112] Thomas Greene, indeed, mentions both John and Jeffrey in his will; but it is Jeffrey, the elder, who is made overseer, along with Beeston and Richard Perkins, and Jeffrey witnesses the will without John too, indicating the possibility that John was away.[113] Further evidence that John Green was the brother of Thomas Greene emerges in the form of a subsidy record from St Leonard's, Shoreditch that lists a man going by his name as living 'at ye Curten' in 1628.[114] It will be remembered that Thomas Greene was described as holding the tenure of the playhouse in 1611, with the Curtain mentioned as the company's other playhouse from the first patents naming them.

In terms of Central European touring activity, the visits of Thomas Greene's brother John, as itemised by Limon, stretched from Gdansk in 1607 with stop-offs at Elbing (Poland again) and Graz (southern Austria); to 1608 visits to Graz and Passau (Lower Bavaria); to Gdansk again in 1612, 1613 and 1615; and again in 1616 with Robert Reynolds, also visiting Warsaw that year. He returned to Warsaw in 1617 as well as Neisse (Nysa, Poland) and Olmütz (Olomounc, Czech Republic), in addition to Prague and Vienna (Austria). In 1619 he visited Gdansk again, this time with Robert Browne. This is his last recorded appearance in Gdansk. For other areas of modern Europe he is also thought to have visited, for example, Lille (northern France) in 1603, Frankfurt in 1606 (with Robert Browne) and Brussels in 1608.[115] He is also likely to have led a company to Brussels again in 1609 and 1610, as well as Gent (also Belgium) in 1610. As a group calling itself the servants of the Elector of Brandenburg (Wolfenbüttel connections again), a troupe led by Green, was given permission to perform in Utrecht (Netherlands) in July 1620.[116] The Thirty Years War ended a lot of the movements of English players around Europe, with John Green disappearing from records in 1627, the year before he was noted

[112] Essex Record Office, Chelmsford, St Edward the Confessor Parish Registers, Romford, D/P 346/1/1.

[113] For the text of Greene's will see Honigmann and Brock, *Playhouse Wills*, pp. 90–2.

[114] TNA E179/142/307, m. 5. He paid £3 16s – the amount most people paid in St Leonard's parish. He is the only person listed who is separated out through his living at 'ye Curten', which may mean the playhouse or the estate.

[115] See, e.g., Schrickx, *Foreign Envoys*, p. 205.

[116] Limon, *Gentlemen of a Company*, pp. 42, 79–80.

paying his subsidy at the Curtain in Shoreditch. This was obviously after a long and adventurous Continental touring career. Reynolds, however, was to continue being noted in Europe until at least 1639, dying, as we know, in the early 1640s.[117]

Evidence of these actors abroad covers a spectrum of relevant facts and issues of which we should be aware. Heywood claimed, in his publication of 1612, that an English company was part of the retinue of the 'Cardinall of Bruxels'. The European scholars' identification of who this could be seems to be confused and hazy. However, a passport for an English company, emanating from the court of Archduke Albert, Governor of the Spanish Netherlands, and dated February 1607, appears to support the evidence of a company residing and touring in this area, and this company is likely to have been John Green's.[118] According to Willem Schrickx's belief, it was certainly a version of Queen Anna's men because of a 1605 reference to a royal touring company mentioned in a Brussels document, published in 1864 but now lost.[119] In 1607, when they went to Wolfenbüttel, it appears they arrived in time for the wedding of Duke Heinrich Julius' daughter, Sophia Hedwig, to Ernest Casimir, count of Orange-Nassau. Sophia Hedwig, as the daughter of Elisabeth, Queen Anna's sister, would have been the English Queen's niece.

John Green in Europe makes his presence known through personal appeals, letters and requests, and, on these occasions, we also learn about the company. When he approached the city council in Gdansk in 1615, for instance, he offered not only plays but 'music and other interesting things', and he said the performances would be given in 'pure German'.[120] This informs us about the company's considerable capabilities. The authorities could be very strict, however, and on that occasion, Green was told that he could only play if they saw a rehearsal first. It would seem that the company had already proved itself careful with profane actions and language, for Archduchess Maria Magdalena of Austria showed herself delightedly relieved when Green's company, performing at Graz in 1608, did so without 'the least little bit of love-making'.[121] Maria Magdalena was

[117] *Ibid.*, pp. 30, 150–1.
[118] Schrickx, *Foreign Envoys*, p. 205; Limon, *Gentlemen of a Company*, p. 10 (however, Limon has the 'Governor-General' as 'Archduke Charles', not Albert).
[119] Charles Ruelens, 'Notes pour l'histoire du théâtre à Anvers', *Revue d'histoire et d'archéologie* 4 (1864), 405; see Schrickx, *Foreign Envoys*, pp. 203–4.
[120] J. Bolte, *Das Danziger Theater im 16. und 17. Jahrhundert* (Hamburg and Leipzig: L. Voss, 1895), pp. 44–7; Limon, *Gentlemen of a Company*, p. 19.
[121] Limon, *Gentlemen of a Company*, p. 14. See Morris, 'A Hapsburg Letter' for Maria Magdalena's letter in both the original German and in translation; and also Orlene Murad, *The English Comedians*

the half-sister of the aforementioned King of Poland and, in a letter to another brother, Ferdinand, we hear about the repertoire and the character of the company, with the archduchess describing how the actors were particularly interested in watching the masques and dancing of the women of the court.[122] In an addendum, she also describes how there was a fight between one of the English players and a Frenchman. The English player was noted for being a fiddle-player and for having long red hair, and was particularly applauded as pious enough to go and receive the sacraments immediately when he was wounded (confession and communion).[123]

The fact that the founding of the Queen's Servants at the Red Bull was rooted in a Danish-European context has now been covered. Following on from Martin Slatiar's professed search for the duke of Holstein's wished-for 'company of Comedians' resident in the London area, these English players abroad – owning sharer links or status with the Queen's Servants, the company of the duke's sister – represented a useful foreign diplomatic entity as they travelled and performed around northern Europe. Perhaps these were, in effect, the duke of Holstein's men, packaged more flexibly for a trans-European market. Jerzy Limon saw, in the history and purpose of this company, connections with the Gdansk public theatre and the Fortune in Golding Lane. It is worth considering, however, that with the three-way union of Robert Browne, Green and Reynolds, with the extra Thayer as a certain sharer, what we are actually observing is more of a spin-off from the Queen's Servants at the Red Bull and the Curtain.

In a similar fashion to the way in which we know this version of the English company played abroad, we also know that the Red Bull seemed open to foreigners. As we have seen in *The Rape of Lucrece*, Valerius' songs include a Dutch-sounding drinking ballad, and Allan Holaday has the following to say about 'unusual' descriptions of the character in the text: 'In the second address To the Reader the unknown player is referred to as "The stranger that lately acted Valerius his part". Again, this time within the text of the piece, Valerius is said to be "Germanized" and to have been in the German wars. And a few lines later he sings a Dutch catch.'[124] Holaday theorises the possibility that the 'stranger' referred to is Continental Robert Browne, home from abroad but not quite a member

---

at the Habsburg Court in Graz 1607–1608 (Universität Salzburg, 1978) for a more sustained study in terms of the repertoire that the archduchess saw.

[122] Morris, 'A Hapsburg Letter', pp. 16–17.

[123] *Ibid.*, pp. 20–22.

[124] See Heywood, *The Rape of Lucrece* (London, 1608), E3v–E4; *The Rape of Lucrece*, ed. Holaday, pp. 16–17.

of the company. He backs up his argument by citing Browne's service to Maurice the Learned, Landgrave of Hesse-Cassel, and evidence of a mission to England for arms.[125] This is a good theory, and he is right to point out that to be 'Germanized' sounds like you had to be something other than German to begin with. If the English actors had brought back a foreigner to play the part, however, there is evidence to support their collaboration. Jerzy Limon mentions English players working with foreign performers abroad several times. For instance, the German, Bernard Sandt, was with one English troupe in 1600; Behrendt Holzhew and August Pflugbeil accompanied the acrobatic Peadle family in about the same year; and in 1617/18 the Elector of Brandenburg entitled a company associated with him 'comedians from England and the Netherlands'. In 1627, John Green himself included 'Jacob of Hesse' in his troupe, and the trend is said to have continued and been consolidated into the period beyond the thirty years war.[126]

Later, the Red Bull itself was proved not averse to welcoming foreign troupes. In 1629 it made room for French actors, including women performers. By this time, however, these players were able to perform at the Blackfriars and the Fortune as well.[127]

---

[125] Heywood, *The Rape of Lucrece*, ed. Holaday, pp. 17–18.
[126] Limon, *Gentlemen of a Company*, pp. 10–11.
[127] *EPT*, pp. 526–7 and 584.

CHAPTER 6

The company: 1605–1612

In 1612, Thomas Heywood, main actor-playwright of the Queen's Servants company, published the only contemporary complete text we have – by an early modern actor *about* early modern actors. It was called *An Apology for Actors*, and prefatory material included poetry by acting fellows among the Queen's Servants such as Christopher Beeston, Richard Perkins and Robert Pallant. John Webster also wrote a poem as did John Taylor, 'the water poet', who addressed it 'To my approued good friend M. THOMAS HEYVVOOD'.

Heywood wrote of the theatre of the classical world in response to Puritan disapproval of the stage. In the voice of Melpomene, the Muse of Tragedy, he wrote of Roman Seneca and Greek Sophocles, of the original Olympics and classical gods, as well as the inspiration derived from English kings 'Personated' as they fought with France. Early in the *Apology*, we learn as much about spectacle as drama, spectacle comprising the distinctive feature of much of Heywood's drama at the time of the *Apology's* inception. As the rhetoric moves forward, Heywood brings in Christian contexts and the Bible to show that ornament has always been as important as practicalities; he describes occasions when limits on entertainment have been attempted and have failed, of transvestism versus the cross-dressing of male actors playing female roles, and of university drama and its success as a student training device.

In 'THE SECOND BOOKE' he broaches, specifically, the building of classical theatres – both those of timber and those of stone – and itemises theatres on the Continent, particularly those in Italy. But on signature E1v, after mentioning contemporary European interest in English actors, he starts to write of more recent English actors performing specifically in the London area, alluding to the Revels Office particularly at 'S. *Iohnes*', where Edward IV once saw 'the Citty Actors'. It is here that Heywood describes the old 'Palace' as belonging to 'the office of the Reuels, where our Court playes haue beene in late daies yearely rehersed, perfected, and corrected before they come to the publike view of the Prince and the Nobility'. Then, in a grand build-up to Heywood's personal list of the best of the early modern English players, the actor-writer gives them classical weight by reeling off the names known from ancient Greece (*'Theodoretes'*) and many from Rome, especially *'Roscius'*. Of the earlier English comic actors he mentions *'Knell, Bently, Mils, Wilson, Crosse, Lanam'* (E2v) as those he has heard of but never seen. Of his own time he talks of *'Tarleton'* and *'VVil. Kemp'*, who 'succeeded' him 'as wel in the fauour of her Maiesty, as in the opinion & good thoughts of the generall audience'. He then mentions *'Gabriel, Singer, Pope, Phillips, Sly'* – as dead actors but also remembered, significantly (perhaps) tacking on to this list *'Edward Allen'* as one still living.

He prefaces what he has to say about the questionable behaviour of actors by stating what qualities make the preferred actor. They should be chosen – as 'men pick'd out personable' and suited to the roles they will play, or, in Heywood's words 'according to the parts they present'. They should be intelligent or rather 'schollers' so that they will have confidence enough to speak in public – 'or else have that volubility that they can speake well, though they vnderstand not what, & so both imperfections may by instructions be helped & amended' (E3).

On speech and comprehension matters, Heywood was adamant: 'where a good tongue & a good conceit both faile, there can neuer be good actor' (E3).

An Apology is a defence, and the whole text is, more accurately, a defence of the theatre rather than actors – although at this point in the text, it is interesting that he chose a book title that made it sound as if the actions of the player fraternity were his first concern. Here Heywood goes on to state a collection of issues about the behaviour of actors.

> I could also wish, that such as are condemned for their licentiousnesse, might by a generall consent bee quite excluded our society: for as we are men that stand in the broad eye of the world, so should our manners, gestures, and behauiours, sauour of such gouernment and modesty, to deserue the good thoughts and reports of all men, and to abide the sharpest censures euen of those that are the greatest opposites to the quality. Many amongst vs, I know, to be of substance, of gouernment, of sober liues, and temperate carriages, house-keepers, and contributary to all duties enioyned them, equally with them that are rank't with the most bountifull. (E3)

Heywood then returns to the thought of the licentious actor, but rather spoils his argument for a twenty-first-century reader by bringing in a quote from Ovid about the majority of women: 'and if amongst so many of sort, there be any few degenerate from the rest in that good demeanor, which is both requisite & expected at their hands, let me entreat you not to censure hardly of all for the misdeeds of some, but rather to excuse vs, as *Ouid* doth the generality of women' (E3).

In the text of the *Apology*, Heywood was not the only actor to take a defensive attitude when it came to actors and drama. Each of the players who wrote a poem for the publication had their own perspective on where things had gone awry for the reputation of drama. The irony of what these men had to say about the virtues of the theatre becomes evident when their actions as human beings are contemplated through the legal texts we have about them. For Heywood may well have seen with his own eyes the player licentiousness of which he wrote on sig. E3.

Christopher Beeston, for example, wrote his prefatory poem in honour of his 'good friend and fellow, THOMAS HEYWOOD'. Beeston claimed he was not a hypocrite or a pretender – he genuinely enjoyed plays as a pastime. Interestingly, for those of us who struggle to get through an early modern play in under three hours, he saw attendance at a drama as 'Two houres well spent', and finished his couplet with the line 'Whats good I follow, and whats bad I shun' (a3). Ten years before the publication of the *Apology*, Beeston had been accused of the rape of Margaret White, the event in question supposedly happening on 23 June 1602. Beeston was also married later that year on 10 September. The Bridewell justices were horrified at the behaviour of Beeston and his friends in attendance at court for the hearing later that autumn, noting that 'the said Beeston and other his Confederates plaiers did verie vnreverentlie demeane themselues to certen governors and muche abused the place'.[1] Somehow Beeston must have been released – the court, perhaps, believing Beeston's counter-accusation that Margaret White had accused the twenty-two-year-old maliciously. This was not the last rape allegation with which the Queen's Servants were involved, however, for, in 1605, the same year when the Red Bull was built, and when the company were no doubt also performing at the Curtain playhouse, Shoreditch, Robert Leigh was also accused, together with Edward Norton, of that rape assault on Joan Hitchecocke of Norton Folgate.[2] This area of the early modern suburbs is located just north of the boundaries of the City of London, and very close to Shoreditch. Beeston stood bail for Leigh, and again, it would appear, the actor got off

[1] See Griffith, 'Christopher Beeston', pp. 610–11.
[2] LMA MJ/SR/0429, 19 and 0430, 68.

the charge, for there is no evidence that the accusation curtailed Leigh's activities in any way.

The separated Leigh of 1612 is not seen to be offering any morally edifying words to the beginning of Heywood's *Apology* like Beeston, but Richard Perkins and Robert Pallant proffered thoughts, both promoting the virtues of playgoing in their own ways. Perkins was more subtly frank about behaviour in general than any of his fellows, arguing for drama over a whole range of possible activities including drinking, gambling and whoring:

> How wouldst thou haue me spend my idle houres?
> Wouldst haue me in a Tauerne drinke all day?
> Melt in the Sunnes heate? or walke out in showers?
>
> (a2v)

Perkins had been involved in court cases, once as a very young actor when he was the subject of a dispute concerning his commitment to the Henslowe–Alleyn enterprises.[3]

In 1605, at the time of the accusation of rape against Leigh, Aaron Holland was finishing the playhouse, while actors of the company, as well as others, were buying shares. These playhouse share-owning people included Thomas Swinnerton, who we know owned a one-eighteenth share. It is through this Swinnerton evidence that we learn the playhouse profits were accessed along these share proportions, at one time at least. Martin Slatiar, who, according to the petition of 1605, was part of the Holland enterprise at this time, had been made a member of the company from the year before. The beginning of his sworn membership should be dated somewhere between the royal procession of 15 March and August 1604. However, by 9 December that year, the company had become concerned about what kind of member he intended to be, as their new leader, Thomas Greene, came to an agreement with Slatiar about this secured on that date.[4] He was, in effect, given £12, in exchange for a promise only to advertise performances given by a fair representation of the company. It was essential that no fewer than six of them, including Slatiar, should perform in 'any the kinges Maiesties domynyons' in the Queen's Servants' name, and there was a penalty of £30 involved if he failed in this. We only know about this agreement because the actors believed Slatiar failed to live up to it. For in 1607, Greene was forced to take Slatiar to court, claiming he had endured losses to the value of £10 because Slatiar could not pay

---

[3] Mateer, 'Edward Alleyn, Richard Perkins and the Rivalry'.
[4] The following is detailed in Griffith, 'Martin Slatiar and the Red Bull Playhouse', pp. 561–2.

the £30. The writing out of a company patent in Southampton during 1606 is the evidence that Greene was right about Slatiar's aims. It mentions Slatiar, Robert Leigh and an actor so far unknown to the company called Roger Barfield – it is unlikely that this company's paperwork and activities included six Queen's Servants members. The patent, however, claimed to be authorised by the Queen, and called the actors permitted 'our Comedians'.[5]

By 1607, when Greene and the players took Slatiar to court over the 1604 agreement, Greene was in receipt of his playhouse shares, which included half the tiring house and yard. Since the Christmas just past he was also possessed of rooms at the Red Bull, which could have been located at the inn next door, which we know Aaron Holland also owned through lease. It is certainly possible that he lived on the playhouse site. The layout of what I have assumed must be the timber inn rather than its 'square court' (now theatre) yard, suggests an intimate set-up careered around smaller 'Yards' – going by the plot attached to the later seventeenth-century indenture. At this later time, when the inn structure was still made of timber, two of these smaller 'Yards' are shown as well as two gardens.

One 1620s description of note records the tiring house of the Red Bull in a defamation case that includes evidence from Mrs Dionisia Perry. She was the wife of William Perry – an exhausting person in early modern theatre history – who led many touring groups of players.[6] In 1629, when we know this court case was taking place, Perry was the leader of a troupe centring on the Red Bull.[7] It is not Perry, however, or his exotically named wife, who mentions the tiring house in this Consistory Court case, but John Buckley, a twenty-one-year-old from the parish of St Giles, Cripplegate, who was actually present in the 'tyring roome of the play house … commonly called and knowne by the signe of the Red Bull'

---

[5] See 'The Manuscripts of the Corporations of Southampton and King's Lynn', *Report of the Historical Manuscripts Commission* II, appendix, Part III, p. 26.

[6] See Astington, *Actors and Acting in Shakespeare's Time*, p. 209 concerning Perry's work. For his time in Ireland as well as references to his activities all over England, see Eva Griffith, 'James Shirley and the Earl of Kildare: Speculating Playhouses and Dwarves à la Mode', in *Dublin and the Pale in the Renaissance c. 1540–1660*, ed. Michael Potterton and Thomas Herron (Dublin: Four Courts Press, 2011), pp. 352–71 (p. 367 and note).

[7] N. H. Bawcutt, *The Control and Censorship of Caroline Drama: The Records of Sir Henry Herbert, Master of the Revels 1623–73* (Oxford: Clarendon Press, 1996), includes a record from Reading where 'William Perrye' and 'Richard Weekes' are described as 'his Majesties sworne servantes' and the rest of their company are named 'all of the Red Bull company' by the Master of Revels, dated 10 November 1629 (p. 169).

when he heard a commotion.[8] This was from a 'litle room' of a 'dwelling house' associated with a man called 'Evan Iones' and his wife, Anne, which was 'adioyning unto the said play house', and involved argumentative language between the plaintiff, a widow called Elizabeth Hambell and a man called William Hall. Hall, at that time, was, as Hambell claimed, defaming her good name. The name 'Hall' makes sense in terms of what we know of the inhabitants on the Seckford Estate, as in Seckford's will of 1587 – transcribed in Chapter 1 – Thomas Seckford mentions 'twoo acres and xxxij perches' demised to 'William Bowes esquier and Thomas Hall gent' for sixty years at that time. The new image from the Seckford Estate papers at Suffolk Record Office in Ipswich shows the divisions between these families. The portions included that allotted to an unnamed owner, who we know was Anne Bedingfeild, to the south; with 'mr Graves house that was once Bowes' some way to the north; and the land of William 'Gold', or Gould, at the north-east end. It also confirms the name 'Hall' as that associated with the area between Bedingfeild's and Bowes' land – that is, immediately adjoining Anne Bedingfeild's – next door to the Red Bull playhouse.[9]

William Hall was obviously an animated personality. Buckley heard him speaking 'as it were vnder the said tyring roome … in a very violent and angrie manner [to] Elizabeth Hambell', who was living with the Perrys according to Dionisia.[10] 'Thou art a Bawd', he said, 'with an intent and meaning (as much as he could) to slaunder the said Elizabeth Hambel in her good name'. Because we know that the house of Jones and his wife, where this conversation was heard, adjoined the playhouse, we may imagine the layout of this small area of St John Street if the straightforward location of the tiring house – as on the 1660s Gloucestershire sketch – is right for 1629. With Buckley standing upstairs in the tiring room of the theatre, facing towards the yard away from St John Street, he would have heard the argument coming from downstairs to the right of him. For the Jones' house could not have been to the left of him, as this is where the inn was located.[11]

[8] LMA DL/C/0231, fo. 615–615v. I am grateful to Jessica Freeman for directing me to this Consistory Court case.
[9] SROI FC25/L3/3/11.
[10] LMA DL/C/0231, fos. 605–605v.
[11] Evan Jones is mentioned in the St James' Parish Vestry Book as, for example, a sidesman in 1611, when Aaron Holland was voted an overseer for the poor (fo. 26). In 1616, as 'Evan ap Jones', he is a collector for the poor along with Holland and Beeston.

With reference to the buildings around the playhouse, therefore, we must be discussing an intimate area where people were living in close proximity and where raised voices, in these adjoining places, could have been heard clearly.

In 1607, when Thomas Greene was moving onto the Seckford Estate, he also made his one and only appearance in the vestry minute book of St James' parish, signing his name to record his attendance at a meeting concerning the working and living conditions of the then curate, John Preston. The meeting was held in the Christmas season on 27 December. Aaron Holland and Christopher Beeston can also be traced in these records, with Holland appearing many times – as a churchwarden, for instance, in 1619 – and with Beeston listed as a collector for the poor in 1616. Robert Leigh, as ever, appears, but in a separate time period, when Beeston had gone to the Cockpit-Phoenix. Leigh is a collector for the preacher in 1622 and a churchwarden in 1624, leaving a consideration for the poor of the parish in his will of 1629.[12] From these kinds of records we can only conclude that these actors were not always – while their Clerkenwell lives progressed – as licentious, either as they had appeared at an earlier time, or as the actors suggested by Heywood in his *Apology*. It would seem, in other words, that both of the one-time accused rapists were – at this time – leading responsible parish lives. Beeston is also recorded in 'March Anno domini 1616' as involved, with Aaron Holland, in two apprenticeships: of Alexander Jones as a cook and William Grace as a cordwainer.[13]

A court case of 1623 affords us more material with reference to the Queen's Servants' actors and – at least – their Clerkenwell domesticity, this time in the form of their addresses. However, the subject of the case itself leans us in the other direction, seeing to what extent they, among a whole group of people, might not have been trustworthy friends. The bill from which the information comes was one brought by Gervase Markham, one of several men going by that name with the most likely candidate being the poet and playwright described in the current *Oxford Dictionary of National Biography*.[14] This Markham wrote at least one play for the company at the Red Bull after the Queen's Servants' time there called *Herod and Antipater* (London, 1622).

[12] LMA DL/AL/C/003/MS09052/007, item 174. He left 40 shillings to be distributed 'in bread' the day after his burial.

[13] LMA P76/JS1/127, 10 and 11. See Griffith, 'Christopher Beeston', pp. 613–14.

[14] Matthew Steggle, 'Markham, Gervase (1568?–1637)', *Oxford Dictionary of National Biography*, www.oxforddnb.com/view/article/18065, accessed 31 July 2012.

C. W. Wallace found the 1623 'uncalendared' bill – which is still, unfortunately, uncalendared and currently lost – and published the material from it in 1910.[15] Markham had undertaken an ambitious feat – that of travelling from London to Berwick with only a leap-staff to aid him. In order to fund his trip, he acquired 'bills of adventure' from a large group of acquaintances, many of whom failed to pay up on his return. There were six named Clerkenwell residents among thirty-nine defendants in the ensuing case. Many of the thirty-nine were actors, although Wallace ascertained that two were publishers of the period with some unknown.[16] Some defendants did not give an address. The six who were willing to put up money for this venture and who gave addresses in Clerkenwell in 1623 included 'Roberte Leigh', who lived in 'Clarkenwell Close'. This Close, still known by this term, was a very select area, curving around the Church of St James, opposite the house owned by Sir Thomas Chaloner (d. 1615), adjacent to another residence owned by William Cavendish, earl of Newcastle by the 1630s.[17] Chaloner was, at one time, a governor of Prince Henry, and King James, knowing of his Clerkenwell residence, prompted him to communicate critical observations about the immediate state of the area.[18] 'Richard Perkins', the actor who won great praise from John Webster when he performed at the Red Bull in *The White Devil*, lived 'att the vpper end of St Iohns Streete', and John Blaney 'neare the Red Bull in St Iohns Streete'. Thomas Heywood resided 'neare Clarkenwell Hill'.

Many of the actors of the company settled and had families in the area. Evidence found in the parish registers of St Leonard's shows that Beeston children were both baptised and given burial in Shoreditch near the Curtain playhouse up to 1609.[19] However, Anne Beeston was baptised at St James' on 15 September 1611, and a servant to Beeston, Elizabeth Morier, was buried in the parish on 1 July 1615, showing that Beeston had moved to Clerkenwell by 1611.[20]

---

[15] C. W. Wallace, 'Gervase Markham, Dramatist', *Jahrbuch der deutschen Shakespeare Gesellschaft* 46 (1910), 345–50.

[16] *Ibid.*, p. 345.

[17] Pinks also mentions Richard de Burgh, fourth earl of Clanricarde, as a neighbour in the Close in 1619 (Pinks, *The History of Clerkenwell*, p. 94).

[18] This letter of 28 May, with no year given, was directed to Chaloner's 'verie loving friendes and good neighboures the Churchwardens, Constables and the rest of the vestrie', and it concerned the lack of cleanliness and the impassability of the area near the well that was behind Chaloner's house. See LMA P76/JS1/141.

[19] See LMA P91/LEN/A/001/MS07493. Augustine was baptised on 16 November 1604, Christopher on 1 December 1605 and Robert on 2 April 1609. Jane Beeston was buried in the parish, however, on 22 September 1607 (LMA P91/LEN/A/012/MS07499/ 001).

[20] LMA P76/JS1/001. The two-year-old son, Robert Beeston, was remembered in George Pulham's will of *c.* 1611 as his godchild, and the boy seems to have continued to live in Shoreditch after the

A Richard, son of Richard 'Parkins', was baptised at St James' on 25 October 1609. Perkins' wife Elizabeth, however, was buried on 31 March 1621.[21] This was a year or so after she gave evidence in the *Smith v. Beeston* case, where she spoke of Beeston's association with Emmanuel Reade, an actor who left for Ireland.[22] Several children were baptised as John Duke's in Shoreditch after his September 1596 marriage to Susan Mitten at St Helen's, Bishopsgate. This was with its attendant baptism of a daughter, Susan, the month after. Duke's son, also named John, was baptised at St Leonard's in 1601, as were William (buried 1607), Elizabeth, Thomas and Mary up to 1609. But Duke children are also recorded at St James' – with Elizabeth and Thomas buried in 1612 and 1614 respectively, and with their father dying between them in 1613.[23] A Susan Duke – presumably either his wife or eldest daughter – continued to live there and was buried in Clerkenwell in September 1637. Heywood's children – those baptised at both St Saviour's, Southwark and St James', Clerkenwell – seem numerous, with a Joseph, Alice and Richard christened south of the River Thames to 'Thomas a player' between 1603 and 1605, and six other children with a father Thomas Haywood/Hayward/Haywarde baptised at St James' between 1608 and 1615.[24] Compared to those of other players, very few of Heywood's children are found in burial records for either parish.[25] Heywood was certainly a Clerkenwell man from this time on, written down in the burial register for 16 August 1641 as 'Tho. Heywood, Poet, buried in ye Church'.

A Robert Leigh had three daughters baptised at St James' – Margaret, Joane and Helene – between 1608 and 1611. However, none of them is mentioned in his will of 1629 and no Clerkenwell burials can be found for these daughters, so it is not certain they were of the actor's family.

rest of his family had begun living in Clerkenwell, as his burial is recorded there on 26 December 1615. Pulham was a one-time sharer in the Queen's Servants' company, as the *Worth* v. *Baskervile* case showed.

[21] LMA P76/JS1/001.

[22] TNA REQ1/130, Elizabeth Perkins' affidavit, 27 June 1620. Emmanuel Reade was put into the Clink for the killing of Robert Dawes in 1615. See TNA KB29/259, m. 3.

[23] He is renounced by Suzanna Duke, relict, in an administrations record where he is described as 'histrio'. See Honigmann and Brock, *Playhouse Wills*, p. 230.

[24] LMA P92/SAV, item 3001 (Southwark); LMA P76/JS1/001 and 004 (Clerkenwell). The combined marriage/christening/burial Clerkenwell records of LMA P76/JS1/004, taking in most records to at least June 1616, will be used in most cases for these actors. In other instances, LMA P76/JS1/001–003, which are separate registers for each rite, will be used, particularly for later records.

[25] One child, Mary Hayward, christened the daughter of a Thomas on 8 March 1608/9, was buried on 11 September 1609.

No children or grandchildren are mentioned in the will – only a wife called Constance.[26] This document does confirm, however, his residence at St James' parish, Clerkenwell. It is through Leigh's will that we are able to identify the wife of Richard Baxter as Joan Ellit, who was married to Baxter at St James' on 2 October 1614 and was named a 'Cossen' of Robert Leigh in his will. The first noted baptism of a daughter to the Baxters was a Constance, possibly named after Constance Leigh. She was christened on Christmas Day 1616. She was to last less than a year, however, receiving burial on 21 October 1617. There are further children baptised to Richard and Joan Baxter between 1618 and 1631, with two – Robert and John –buried in 1625 within a month of one another. Leigh mentions two Baxter children still extant in his will of 1629 and remembered in his bequests, namely 'William and Richard'.

Two daughters are recorded for a James Hoult/Holt – a name occurring on the procession list of 15 March 1604, the draft patent of the same year and the official one of 1609: Anne, a daughter of a James 'Hott', christened on 29 November 1608, and an Alice 'Holte' on 20 September 1610. With Thomas Greene we have one daughter, baptised on 17 April 1609, who was named 'Honor'. We know she was his daughter, for she was buried in his grave in the chancel of St James' on 24 October 1618, six years after he died. There are other possible entries for the actors, but perhaps the most pleasing are those of the younger generation among them. Given that Ellis Worth is not that common a name, we learn that this actor was possessed of a servant, Alexander Scrogge, who was buried on 13 October 1616 in St James'. An Ellis Worth marries an Elizabeth Slead by licence in the parish on 8 October 1612, but she is buried there on 27 September 1623. A 'Marie, wid., mother to Mr Ellis Worth', was buried in Clerkenwell on 25 July 1634. However, Ellis Worth's own will locates him in the parish of St Giles, Cripplegate in 1659 – the Fortune playhouse's parish – where he had married Frances Holcomb, the widow of a King's Men's actor, on 13 January 1626. It appears Worth was possessed of two children by the time of his death: a Jane Alsopp who lived in Barbados with her husband, and a son, Elizeus Worth, baptised on 12 March 1628 at St Giles'. Jane was christened on 19 July 1613, not in Clerkenwell but also at St Giles', according to records.[27]

A Thomas Drewe married a Margarett Harte in Clerkenwell on 17 February 1612. Such a union brought about an Elizabeth Drewe, christened

[26] LMA DL/AL/C/003/MS09052/007, item 174.
[27] LMA P69/GIS/A/002/MS06419/002.

March 1613, who was buried within the month; a 'Francis Drew', baptised in 1614 and buried three years later; another Elizabeth of May 1617; and a Robert of 1618. The second Elizabeth seems to have survived, and may have married somebody of interest to the Red Bull's history – one Richard Gill. The scrivener, Gill, not only appears in the Red Bull's history in relation to the famed case of the accidental injury of a member of the audience by Richard Baxter, but he also appears, as the scrivener he said he was, as the person who signed off Robert Leigh's will.[28]

The name King is a familiar one in Clerkenwell history; however, in the *Worth* v. *Baskervile* case of 1623, John King claimed to be of the parish of St Sepulchre's 'without Newgate' – closer to Smithfield and nearer the City than Clerkenwell. John King also gives us cause to pause and contemplate his true function. In the 1623 suit he claims to have been a hired man of the company for thirty years, but at no point does he mention the term 'player', not even in his evidence in the *Smith* v. *Beeston* case of 1619.[29] A John King is noted in Caroline history as someone who found specialist leather masks for court entertainments.[30] King was forty-eight in 1623, and therefore approximately eighteen when he joined them in *c*. 1593. Could King have been the 'tiring man' who Henslowe refers to in his accounts of the company's time at the Rose? Similarly, Robert Pallant, an actor who took part in the procession as a Queen's Servant, and was named on the draft patent of 1604, as well as the official patent for the company of 1609 and also the funeral procession list of 1619, was never resident at Clerkenwell, but only ever mentioned in the registers of St Saviour's, Southwark. He was, it would seem, a core member in the Queen's Servants company, but chose to journey across the river from his Langley's rents' residence to travel yet further north to perform his Red Bull duties. His name also occurs in Henslowe's papers, and in Revels records in quite different capacities, so it seems the performer or performers going by that name preferred or led a varied work existence.[31]

---

[28] For the 1623 injury to a John Gill, feltmaker – sometimes identified as Richard, a scrivener's servant – see LMA MJ/SR/0617, 30 and MJ/SR/0616, 89; also *EPT*, p. 581 and note. A Richard Gill married an Elizabeth Drewe on 3 August 1635 when Thomas's daughter was eighteen years old. For Richard Gill's signature as a scrivener on Robert Leigh's will of 1629 see LMA DL/AL/C/003/007. The marriage took place twelve years after the incident at the playhouse.

[29] See Wallace, 'Three London Theatres of Shakespeare's Time', pp. 333–4.

[30] Ravelhofer, *The Early Stuart Masque*, p. 175.

[31] See BL, Additional MS 19256, item 8, fo. 44, where a Pallant is named among a group in a December 1624 record forbidding musicians and attendants to be arrested or detained during the Revels. Pallant had a son, also named Robert, who was an actor as well. See Astington, *Actors and Acting in Shakespeare's Time*, p. 207.

Pallant was another one of the actors, along with Perkins and Beeston, who wrote a prefatory poem for Heywood's *Apology:*

> Haue I not knowne a man that to be hyr'd,
> Would not for any treasure see a play,
> Reele from a Tauerne? Shall this be admir'd?
> When as another but the tother day,
> That held to weare a surplesse most vnmeet,
> Yet after stood at *Pauls-crosse* in a sheet.

(3v)

Pallant's poem is of interest because it directly addresses the public play-house audience to whom the Queen's Servants had long appealed. From the evidence of the words themselves, the actors' directive had been to counter attempts to put off audiences from coming to the playhouses. The presumed culprits for such an enterprise were those who had authority over audience members and who took the moral high ground concerning what could go wrong if they indulged in drama. This is clear from Pallant's first line where (to paraphrase) he says that for a man to get work ('to be hyr'd') he will claim that he will not be seen near a play ('not for any treasure'). Yet the same man is seen drunk later in the evening and made to do public penance ('Yet after stood at *Pauls-crosse* in a sheet'). 'Shall this be admir'd?'

I think the actors' prefatory poems are good, and argue for what Heywood said should be in the quality of an actor – a 'good tongue' and a 'good conceit' – clarity of speech and intelligence of purpose. Understanding what their domestic lives were like – mostly set around the theatre and Clerkenwell, with only a few journeying in or preferring a more detached or varied existence – urges us to comprehend what most people in and around London were having to confront: moral and intellectual demands, the yearly tragedy of plague and other diseases, thriving and dying children and wives, annoying communal highway expectations, friends who ask you to pay up, angry arguing neighbours, parochial expectations of service. When additions to this include the normal aggravations of the actors' workload – learning lines, fitting in rehearsals, re-rehearsal of old lines of a play reproduced – we begin to catch sight of the lives of this particular group of players existing to the north of Shakespeare's Globe and the Blackfriars theatre.

Although we are taught to remember that child death was common in the early modern period, and that mortality rates in London were high, the statistics still have the power to shock – particularly after 1612. Up to 1612, the company described above are known to have lost just two children – Jane Beeston and William Duke, both of St Leonard's, Shoreditch.

After 1612 an escalation is seen, where nine children and two wives are lost to the twelve men, most of the dead from the Clerkenwell parish. The numbers are not exhaustive. They represent the more certain of the company's family appearances in theatrical parish records. There may be more to add into the statistical mix. Three of the sharers or sworn members themselves were to die in the period up to 1613 – two of them important enough, at one time, to receive court payments: George Pulham in 1611, John Duke in 1613 and, of course, Thomas Greene between them in 1612. The effect of their deaths within this close-knit, interdependent community, living close to one another, must have been keenly felt.

While contemplating these approaching, unforeseen difficulties for the company, we should remind ourselves that the period up to the death of Greene was a golden time for the company's work, borne out by the evidence of the plays we know were performed by them. Among these we should certainly include *The Foure Prentises of London* (London, 1615) and *The Rape of Lucrece* (London, 1608) already discussed, described on their title-pages as Red Bull plays. *The Golden Age* (London, 1611) and *The Brazen Age* (London, 1613) should also be included as earlier Red Bull plays – *The Golden Age*, most certainly, owing to its title-page ascription 'As it hath bene diuerse times Acted, at the Red Bull, by the Queenes Maiesties Seruants'. For *The Silver Age*, published in 1613, we have that 1612 court performance date, and it is hard to believe that there would not have been follow-on playhouse performances as part of Heywood's *Ages* cycle, coming between *The Golden* and *The Brazen*. Indeed, in Heywood's address 'To the Reader' before the first of the *The Iron Age*'s two parts (London, 1632), which talks of the whole cycle, he says the following:

> *I desire thee to take notice, that these were the Playes often (and not with the least applause,) Publickely Acted by two Companies, vppon one Stage at once, and haue at sundry times thronged three seuerall Theaters, with numerous and mighty Auditories.* (A4v)

What Heywood describes as a multi-company venture working together is something we know was the case with *The Silver Age* at court, performed by the King's and Queen's men combined. Here we are told that company collaborations extended to the rest of the cycle, Parts I and II of *The Iron Age* coming (it is likely) after the mid-point of 1612. Heywood usefully writes of the Queen's Servants' multi-venue reality too.[32] Other

---

[32] The *Ages* plays are all distinctively expressive production pieces, although the two *Iron Age* plays (Parts I and II), published late in 1632, are not possessed of showy pyrotechnics, preferring fight scenes. Heywood was clear in his prefatory material that he saw these plays performed by several

plays to be included in the pre-1612 list would include Cooke's *Greene's Tu Quoque; or, The Cittie Gallant* (London, 1614), which we also know was performed at court, a vehicle for Thomas Greene; and the *The Travails of the Three English Brothers* (with an appearance by 'Will Kemp') by John Day, William Rowley and George Wilkins (London, 1607). One certain Red Bull play, Thomas Dekker's *If This Be Not a Good Play the Devil Is in It*, and the less certain but oft-times Red-Bull-interpreted play *The White Devil* by John Webster (both London, 1612) should also be considered.

These latter two have been useful to interpreters of the company and its ambience because both make reference to the company's playing spaces, the actors, the performance conditions for the texts and the audience at the playhouse. It is not unlikely that the prefatory material in one refers to what is found in the other.

Dekker and Webster had worked together prior to their separate ventures with the Queen's Servants and they were to come back into the Red Bull's history after the company ended its time working under that name. The two had collaborated (with others, including Heywood) on 'Lady Jane', recorded in Henslowe's accounts for Worcester's Men in 1602.[33] This is thought to be the same play as *The Famous History of Sir Thomas Wyat*, described as a Queen's Servants play when it was published in 1607, and another drama to add to the early Queen's Servants repertoire (if of uncertain original playhouse parentage).[34] Webster and Dekker also collaborated on two other dramas presented by the satirical Paul's Boys' company: *Westward Ho!* performed in 1604 and *Northward Ho!* performed in 1605.[35] Webster (since 1602 and *Lady Jane*) had also been involved in Marston's *The Malcontent*. This he adapted from the Blackfriars' Children's play it had been in 1602–3 to a 1603–4 King's Men's drama.[36]

Dekker's Red Bull devil play, *If This Be Not*, is described on the title-page as a 'A Nevv Play, AS IT HATH BIN lately Acted, vvith great applause, by the Queenes Maiesties Seruants: At the Red Bull'. It begins with an address entitled: 'To my Loving, and Loved Friends and Fellowes, the Queenes Maiesties Seruants'. With some affection and great humour, this preliminary tries to communicate (between Dekker's satirical lines) some thoughts

companies together in a number of venues over time. We know *The Golden, The Silver* and *The Brazen Ages* are of a piece because the address 'To the Reader' of *The Brazen Age* talks of it being a 'younger brother' – 'a third' – to 'the two elder'.

[33] Henry Chettle, Thomas Dekker and 'mr [Wentworth?] smythe' are also mentioned in relation to this play. Henslowe, *Henslowe's Diary*, ed. Foakes and Rickert, p. 218.

[34] Charles Forker, *Skull beneath the Skin: The Achievement of John Webster* (Carbondale: Southern Illinois University Press, 1986) p. 66.

[35] *Ibid.*, p. 81.   [36] *Ibid.*, pp. 73–4.

concerning financial troubles or payment difficulties.[37] '*Knowledge* and *Reward* dwell far a-sunder', it begins.

> *Greatnes* lay once betweene them. But (in his stead) *Couetousnes* now. An ill neighbour, a bad *Benefactor*, no paymaister to *Poets*.
>   By *This Hard Houskeeping*, (or rather, *Shutting* vp of *Liberalities Doores*,) *Merit* goes a *Begging*, and *Learning* starues.

Dekker is in a humorously complaining mode but wittily so, and the satire is deeply encoded. He follows with an itemisation of the characters available within an audience and what they have to offer: '*Lords*, look wel: *Knights*, *Thank* well; *Gentlemen*, promise well; *Citizens*, *Take* well; *Gulles*, *Sweare* well: but *None*, *Giue well*.'

With reference to the company to whom his text is addressed, Dekker acknowledges what he believes he has – their '*Loues*'. But again he refers to financial matters:

> *Acknowledgement* is part of payment sometimes, but it neither is, nor shall be (betweene you and me) a *Cancelling*. I haue cast mine eye vpon many, but find none more fit, none more worthy, to *Patronize this* [his play], than *you*, who haue *Protected it*. Your *Cost*, *Counsell*, and *Labour*, had bin ill spent, if a *Second* should by my hand snatch from you *This Glory*.

Dekker then goes on to discuss theatres and theatre buildings. He writes about theatres because it would appear that the Fortune playhouse had turned down the play before he took it to the Red Bull. Theatre buildings are alluded to where a swathe of architectural terminology is used. Here meaning slips between references to actual buildings and the 'building' that is the play:

> When *Fortune* (in her blinde pride) set her foote vpon *This imperfect Building*, (as scorning the *Foundation* and *Workmanship*:) you, gently raizd it vp (on the same *Columnes*,) the *Frontispiece* onely a little more *Garnished*: To you therefore deseruedly is the *Whole Frame* consecrated. For I durst sweare, if *Wishes* and *Curses* could haue become *Witches*, the necke of this *Harmles Diuell* had long a goe bin broken.

Although Dekker's prose would appear to be only referring to his play, the metaphors he uses are all about the fabric of a theatre building. Writing of '*This imperfect Building*' and 'the *Foundation* and *Workmanship*' of the same, how it was 'raizd' 'gently', including its '*Columnes*' with the '*Frontispiece*' or – in the context of a theatre – its 'frons' decorated more ornately, he makes it clear that this analogy is important to him. We have

---

[37] Thomas Dekker, *If This Be Not a Good Play the Devil Is in It* (London, 1612), A3–A3v.

already seen the term '*Frame*' used with reference to the Red Bull itself in Martin Slatiar's petition, and it was one that was in common usage for the timber skeleton that represented the first stage in an early modern building process. It is irresistible to suggest that Dekker's reference may have been not just poetic, but subtly referring, in some deliberate way, to the Red Bull too. The beginning of the play – or the '*Frontispiece*' that was more '*Garnished*' under the company's influence as Dekker describes it – is an amusing one, in that in it we see a scene where Charon, the waterman of Hades, is arguing with Pluto over the set fare to row souls to hell. He claims he will row no more:

> … Graues-end-barge has more,
> And caries as good as any are in hell;
> I feare th'infernall riuers are frozen or'e
> So few by water come: els the whores that dwell
> Next dore to hell goe about ; besides, tis thought,
> That men to find hell, now, new waies haue sought,
> As Spinirards [Spaniards] did to the Indies. *Pluto*, mend
> My wages, or row thy selfe.
>
> (B)

The scene is performed to '*hellish musick*', and later demons with names like 'Ruffman' and 'Shackle-soule' come 'up', indicating at least one trapdoor onstage, maybe more. The idea of a frozen Styx may refer back to the recent Great Frost of 1608 in London, where the Thames froze over sufficiently for the City to enjoy a 'frost fair' on the ice. Presumably at this time – and from the tenor of the text – the prostitutes of the Southwark stews could move more cheaply across the river without the aid of the watermen, or their clients could move more cheaply southwards towards them. One can only imagine in what ways the Red Bull company decided to 'garnish' these opening moments, possibly with the use of fireworks.

When it comes to the Prologue, given on stage, which follows the address in the book, Dekker returns to the subject of finances, this time in the context of receipts that were, perhaps, meant for the writer.

> A Play whose *Rudenes, Indians* would abhorre,
> Ift fill a house with Fishwiues, *Rare, They All Roare.*
> It is not Praise is sought for (Now) but *Pence,*
> Tho dropd, from Greasie-apron *Audience.*
>
> (A4)

What he is saying is that in the now seriously commercial world of the theatre, content and style are no longer what are held important, nor even applause, but the money that the auditors bring with them. And these auditors, too, are specified and despised for being what they are.

> Clapd may he [the author] bee with *Thunder*, that plucks *Bayes*,
> With such *Foule Hands*, and with *Squint-Eyes* does gaze
> On *Pallas Shield*; not caring (so hee *Gaines*,
> A Cramd *Third-Day*,) what *Filth* drops from his *Braynes*.

For Dekker, certain inferior playwrights – 'Bastards' of '*Phoebus*', as he calls them – do not care about the quality of their work, but rather concentrate on what they can gain financially from a hoped-for 'Cramd *Third-Day*'. Scholarship has suggested that certain printed Prologues at the beginning of plays may well represent speeches given on performance days where the playwright received a cut of the returns.[38] Perhaps, when it comes to these bad writers, Dekker was aiming at those playwrights whose work was chosen over his at the Fortune, in which case the '*Third-Day*' and the greasy audience may refer to lowered expectations at that theatre. Equally possible, however, with Dekker writing this spoken Prologue for his play performed at the Red Bull, is that he found himself bold and confident enough to look this audience in the eye and make fun of both them and his own needs derived from them.

Coming back to the Address, written for the published play-text and not for speaking in the theatre, on first sight it looks as if Dekker could have been disappointed in his third day, although what he is truly writing about is a future experience for somebody else.

> I wish a *Faire* and *Fortunate Day*, to your *Next New-Play* (for the *Makers-sake* and your *Owne*,) because such *Braue Triumphes* of *Poesie*, and *Elaborate Industry*, which my *Worthy Friends Muse* hath there set forth, deserue a *Theater* full of very *Muses* themselues to be *Spectators*. To that *Faire Day* I wish a *Full*, *Free*, and *Knowing Auditor*. And to that *Full Audience, One Honest Doore-Keeper*.[39]

Dekker was writing with his tongue in his cheek, wanting to warn the company that his friend's new play really needed a large and intelligent audience to understand and appreciate it, and suggesting that in view of this they really needed to ensure an '*Honest Doore-Keeper*' on a sunny '*Faire*' day for him, so that they could hand over appreciative returns.

If this publishable address was written soon after the performance of *If This Be Not*, there is a chance that Dekker was referring to his friend

[38] Tiffany Stern, 'A Small-Beer Health to His Second Day: Playwrights, Prologues, and First Performances in the Early Modern Theatre', *Studies in Philology* 101.2 (Spring 2004), 172–99.
[39] Dekker, *If This Be Not Good*, A3v.

John Webster, who, at about the same time, wrote *The White Devil* for performance by the Queen's Servants.[40] In fact, from the tenor of Dekker's humour in his address, the disaster of the first performance of *The White Devil* may have already happened, and his words could actually represent a jibe at Webster – knowing the nature of his preliminary complaints written into the print-prepared text.

The title-page for *The White Devil* does not refer to the Red Bull, only its performance by '*the Queenes Maiesties Seruants*' – and, since it was published in 1612, critics have assumed that the Red Bull was where it was performed. Since we now understand that the company's plays were performed at two venues, we are left with the possibility that what Webster describes is not the Red Bull at all but the Curtain in Shoreditch, although if the Dekker-the-Webster-teaser theory is correct, it is more likely it was performed in Clerkenwell. Wherever it was first performed, on reading Webster's address 'To the Reader' it is clear that no Dekker-like humour was intended as Webster sat down to write it. No double or metaphorically architectural meaning was used. His third day was not full of Muses. He penned his address in the context of his daring to publish his play:

> … not that I affect praise by it, for, *nos haec novimus esse nihil*, only since it was acted, in so dull a time of winter, presented in so open and black a theatre, that it wanted (that which is the only grace and setting out of a tragedy) a full and understanding auditory: and that since that time I have noted, most of the people that come to that playhouse, resemble those ignorant asses (who visiting stationers' shops, their use is not to enquire for good books, but new books) I present it to the general view with this confidence:
>
> > *Nec rhoncos metues, maligniorum,*
> > *Nec scombris tunicas, dabis molestas.*
>
> ['You [the poet's book] will not fear the sneers of the malicious, nor supply wrappers for mackerel.']⁴¹

Not content with describing the theatre in question as dark and open to the cold English weather, and the audience as a kind of nouveaux riches just wanting to add to their collection of new books rather than good-quality ones, Webster goes on:

---

⁴⁰ There are no earlier Stationers' Register entries recorded for either of these plays in W. W. Greg, *A Bibliography of the English Printed Drama to the Restoration*, 4 vols. (London: Oxford Universitiy Press, 1939), Vol. 1, pp. 445–8, so it is not possible to see which was the first to be printed in 1612.

⁴¹ Webster, *The White Devil*, ed. Luckyj, p. 5.

Should a man present to such an auditory, the most sententious tragedy that ever was written, observing all the critical laws, as height of style, and gravity of person; enrich it with the sententious *Chorus*, and as it were lifen death, in the passionate and weighty *Nuntius:* yet after all this divine rapture, *O dura messorum ilia* ['O strong stomachs of harvesters'], the breath that comes from the uncapable multitude is able to poison it, and ere it be acted, let the author resolve to fix to every scene, this of Horace, *Haec hodie porcis comedenda relinques* ['What you leave will go today to feed the pigs'].[42]

Webster, clearly, did not see himself as one of Dekker's bastards of Phoebus. He does not once show concern about money in his address, nor does he mention returns achieved from any '*Doore-Keeper*', honest or not.

Doorkeepers, however, were not the only workers in the Red Bull theatre building who brought in the money. For Thomas Swinnerton's gallery playhouse share, which we know he was given in 1605/6, Aaron Holland included in his agreement a 'gatherers place' in the galleries.[43] In the *Woodford* v. *Holland* case beginning in 1613, Woodford was angered by the fact that Thomas Swinnerton, through his lease agreement involving an eighteenth-part share, had been entitled to a gatherer's place worth 3d per day – or 18d per week – which was not passed on to Woodford through Philip Stone. This was when Stone bought it from Swinnerton in February 1609. Stone sold this Swinnerton share to Woodford in *c.* 1612, but without having made the right kind of agreement – or so Woodford believed. The right to the money from the gatherer's place had not been forthcoming.[44] Because we know the eventual decision over this long set of suits (Holland won and Woodford had to pay costs), we know that Woodford had to accept what Holland denied in 1623: that 'there is or ever was … incident or belonginge to the said eighteenth parte by anie vsuall Custome a Gatherers place'.

> Neither … anie such three pence a daie proffitt arysinge to the said Thomas Swynnerton or to such gatherers as he did appointe during the tyme of their playinge by reason of anie such Gatherers place as incident or belonginge to the said eighteenth parte as in the said Bill is alleadged, But saith if the said Swynnerton did receave anie such three pence a daie, he did not receave the same as incident to the said eighteenth parte, but rather in respect of some speciall wordes conteyned in his said graunte which are not mencioned or conteyned in the graunte afterwardes made to the said

---

[42] Quoting Horace, *Epistles* I.vii.19. Webster, *The White Devil*, ed. Luckyj, pp. 5–6.

[43] TNA REQ1/26, fo. 729v; Wallace, 'Three London Theatres of Shakespeare's Time', pp. 296–7.

[44] TNA REQ1/26, fo. 779v and REQ2/411, Box 2, item 149. See Wallace, 'Three London Theatres of Shakespeare's Time', pp. 297, 304–5 (proceedings of 1613 and 1619).

Phillipp Stone … Or if there were noe such speciall wordes in the said
graunte as this defendant remembreth not certenlie after soe longe tyme
and the deed beinge nowe cancelled, Then he saith he permitted him the
said Swynnerton to take the same oute of his love and favor towardes him;
in respect of the hard penny worth the said Swynnerton then afirmed he
had thereof.[45]

It seems there was a special extra arrangement for the actor that was not
included in the arrangements for Stone and therefore Woodford. Holland
was to go on to say that both Philip Stone and Thomas Woodford, believing that the 3d per day went with the share, claimed and received without
right anyway, and it was only when Holland confronted Stone about this
issue that Stone decided to sell it in 1609.[46] Both formal and informal
financial practice in the company will come up for more and more scru-
tiny as we enter discussion about the approaching difficult time for them,
particularly noticeable after the death of Thomas Greene.

Social mobility and northern playhouse audiences

To study what is actually implied about the Queen's Servants' audiences
by John Webster and Thomas Dekker is to look at something that is more
multiple than it would first appear.

Dekker speaks of fishwives and greasy aprons – but this may be the
resented Fortune theatre's audience in Dekker's mind in the context of
his complaint; Webster writes of the bad-smelling breath of the ignorant
crowds, but he also describes the people going to *The White Devil*'s theatre
as desiring – and therefore being able to afford – *new* books, rather than
the older, more intellectual classics. He imagines such people specifically in terms of the playhouse where *The White Devil* was performed. The
Red Bull was the new local playhouse for this man whose father's coach-
making yard was situated in Smithfield, at the junction of Cow Lane and
Hosier Lane at the bottom of St John Street.

The Websters belonged to the Merchant Taylors' company – one of the
'Twelve Great' livery companies of London – and they were engaged in
the manufacture of the latest travel technology. This was an attendant new
trade alongside the horses on sale in Smithfield – but still a trade. Webster,
from his better-off citizen family, would have enjoyed the benefit of a
Merchant Taylors' School education before his time at the inns of court.

[45] TNA C3/390/47 (Holland's Answer, 6 November 1623); Hotson, *The Commonwealth and Restoration
Stage*, pp. 336–7.
[46] TNA C3/390/47; Hotson, *The Commonwealth and Restoration Stage*, pp. 338–9.

At both institutions he would have derived learning from classical languages and texts, resulting in the pains he took to insert such texts into his works – noticeably in Latin. When Francis Beaumont referred to the Red Bull in his play, *The Knight of the Burning Pestle*, the Queen's Servants/Red Bull plays that were alluded to (including *The Foure Prentises of London*; *If You Know Not Me You Know Nobody*, Part II; *The Travails of the Three English Brothers*; and *The Rape of Lucrece*), were only laughable in the context of the comments and suggestions of the citizen couple and apprentice who preferred Queen's Servants fare. These imagined citizens were, however, affluent enough to *pay* for the private playhouse play given by the Children of the Queen's Revels in the first place. The fact that Beaumont chose to create a satire of civic life – at the expense of City people, very many of whom formed part of the economic structure of playgoing – is thought to be a reason – according to one theory – why the play had problems on its opening performance.[47]

Although we may guess that many of the indoor theatres were mainly patronised by the gentry, mixed-status gentry citizens, already discussed in Chapter 3 in the context of *The Foure Prentises* and Edmund Bolton's observations, are just as likely to have attended. They would have brought with them their anxieties concerning those inherent social mobility perceptions discussed, causing them embarrassment in the context of Beaumont's play. In tandem with this, and bearing in mind what was going on at the early Red Bull – masque-like spectacle, processions, song and fireworks – the entertainment on offer must have been as appealing to all sectors of the early modern audience, just as they still sound appealing to us today. It is, therefore, a mistake to come to easy conclusions about the Queen's Servants' audience at their open-air playhouse, going too eagerly on the evidence available among Dekker's, Webster's or Beaumont's impressions. On one hand we see the possibility of a noisy, bad-smelling labour-force

---

[47] See the publisher Walter Burre's letter to Robert Keysar, the Goldsmith citizen manager of the Children of the Queen's Revels, the company that acted the play. In this letter, published with the play, Burre describes the play's rejection by the audience on its first night (Beaumont, *The Knight of the Burning Pestle*, p. 3). Various critics have tried to tackle the subject of why *The Knight of the Burning Pestle* failed on its first night, especially with reference to the social makeup of its audience. See, for example, Leslie Thomson, 'Who's In, Who's Out? *The Knight of the Burning Pestle* on the Blackfriars Stage', in *Inside Shakespeare: Essays on the Blackfriars Stage*, ed. Paul Menzer (Selinsgrove: Susquehanna University Press, 2006), pp. 61–92; or, more recently, Brent E. Whitted, 'Staging Exchange: Why *The Knight of the Burning Pestle* Flopped at Blackfriars in 1607', *Early Theatre* 15.2 (2012), 111–30. Any critic who misses the fact that the majority of the dramas satirised are early Heywood/Worcester's/Queen's Servants plays, however, misses a vital component of the audience amusement attempted.

(Dekker); on another, ignorant rich people (Webster); on the last, an embarrassingly opinionated, if drama-savvy, middle class (Beaumont).[48]

In *An Apology for Actors*, Heywood turns his attention onto the children's companies – such as that which performed *The Knight of the Burning Pestle* – in no uncertain terms. Talking, in fact, of the evils of actors' impersonations of the living, he writes of those who express 'their bitternesse, and liberall inuectiues against all estates, to the mouthes of Children, supposing their iuniority to be a priuiledge for any rayling'. Taking the moral high ground Heywood becomes wisdom incarnate: 'be it neuer so violent, I could aduise all such, to curbe and limit this presumed liberty within the bands of discretion and gouernment'.[49]

Heywood's feelings may have acted as a retort to the thought of Beaumont's satire on the work of the Queen's adult players.

The Queen's Servants/Curtain/Red Bull audience, then, particularly before the death of Thomas Greene in 1612, was certainly perceived as a City one, attracted to plays treating citizens like heroes, examining social cohesiveness issues and enjoying adventure stories, as has been discussed here and in Chapter 3. A citizen, however, could stretch from a smelly fishwife with bad breath to a stylish young Goldsmith showing off his 'new' books. The rich leasehold-owner of the Red Bull Inn, married into England's nobility, was, after all, herself a brewer's daughter.

REPERTOIRE 5   *GREENE'S TU QUOQUE; OR, THE CITTIE GALLANT* (LONDON, 1614)

In the period before Thomas Greene's death, social mobility became a subject the company could finally find to be worthy of seventeenth-century wit. This was in a comedy we know to have been performed at court both late in 1611 and early in 1612, and it concerned a social world of class distinction – for perfectly believable reasons – turned upside down and studied in many different pie-bald kinds. It was also a vehicle for the company's central force at the time, the managerial clown and large shareowner, Thomas Greene.

The play was by 'Jo: Cooke' and published in 1614. This was two years after Greene's death, and the play came complete with an impressive title-page woodcut of the actor in what appears to be a jerkin made up in a

---

[48] The best representation of the Red Bull's audience seen as the 'apprentices and small tradesmen' of London is found in Wright's *Middle-Class Culture in Elizabethan England*. See, for example, p. 611.
[49] Heywood, *An Apology for Actors*, G3v.

diamond-striped style pattern (see figure 7 on p. 87). The overall appearance must have been of a piebald nature, but also like a backgammon board, with backgammon pieces as buttons. Greene, in character, wears a feather in his cap and sports a beard, and a similarity can be clearly detected between the face of the man in this image and that of the *No-body and Some-body* actor, possibly John Green. He was Thomas's family namesake of European company fame.[50] The effect of Greene's gaming woodcut sits well with the action of Cooke's play, where many games, including cards and various kinds of dicing, are played on stage. There are no weighty prefatory dedications with actors remembering Greene – just one simple two-line poem within the preliminaries. This was possibly written by William Rowley ('*W.R.*') referring to the colour inherent in the name.

> Vpon the death of Thomas Greene.
> *How fast bleake Autumne changeth Floraes dye,*
> *What yesterday was* (Greene) *now's seare & dry.*

The play, in fact, is full of local reference – to Greene, the Red Bull playhouse before 1612, and the area in which the play found itself performed. For although Greene died in the summer following the winter when the play was performed at court, because of internal references, we can be sure it was intended for the Red Bull.

The title, and the elaborate title-page with the image of Greene in the role of Bubble, point to his centrality in the comedy, playing the servant to a gentleman about town in the City of London. The main plot of the play is about what happens when servant and master change places and how things eventually right themselves; however, theirs are not the only social estates that are put under the microscope in this play. Indeed, a whole cocktail of societal representatives and their subtleties are studied around them, all in a London context. This plot has social mobility and its dangers as a central concern with two 'servants' who take up their masters' places – one, Bubble, as waiting-man to his master, Gervase, and the other, Frank Spendall, a prodigal journeyman who takes up his master's position in his mercer's shop. There is one lowering of social status in play, and one significant 'rising' of a citizen – this time achieved through the purchase of a knighthood.

The play opens with the journeyman character, Frank Spendall, selling wares at his master mercer's shop. Spendall's master is Lionell Rash, whose

---

[50] Picture appended to anon., *No-body and Some-body: With the true Chronicle Historie of Elydure …* *as it hath beene Acted by the Queenes Maiesties Seruants* (London, [1606?])

daughter, Gartred, also works in the shop. From the moment the play opens it deals with the relationship between them. Here we see a virtuous citizen daughter, Gartred, wooed by the gentleman character, Geraldine, who is greeted as 'sir' by his friend, another gentleman, 'master' Longfield. When warding off the attentions of the man she is eventually to marry, Gartred observes that he seems to 'rellish too much Courtier'. By this she means that his properties are too much like a courtier and out of tune with her own social level, while she puns at the same time on his ability to 'court'.[51] It is not long after this that Gartred's father enters, with a 'Boy' coming before him who tells Spendall to shut up shop to celebrate, for the now 'Sir' Lionell has been knighted. The mercer is excited at the event but honest about how it was achieved:

> O *Francke*! I have the worship now in the right kinde: the sword of Knighthood sticks stil upon my shoulders, and I feele the blow in my purse, it has cut two leather bagges asunder; but all's one, honour must be purchac'd.[52]

In ebullient mood Rash gives up his City life, giving Spendall responsibility for the shop:

> I will give over my Citty coate, and betake my selfe to the Court jacket; as for trade, I will deale in't no longer: I will seate thee in my shop, and it shall be thy care to aske men what they lacke; my stocke shall be summed up, and I will call thee to an account for it.

Sir Lionell is going to move to the Strand, by this time the fashionable, new area to live, beyond the civic jurisdiction that ended at Temple Bar, and in between the City and the court at Westminster. He says he is then going to move to Fulham for the next part of the year.

He that hath choice, may shift, and whilst shalt thou
Be maister of this house, and rent it free.

From the outset of this play, therefore, several situations presented are shown to be dependent on an awareness of different estates and how they relate to one another. However, the central 'rising' of the play is none of these. Set alongside the Rash–Spendall exchange, complicated by City and court manoeuvres, it is the main character of the play – the Greene comedy character, Bubble – who effects the straight swap when it comes to servant–master exchange.

[51] Cooke, *Greene's Tu Quoque*, B2r. See John Cooke, *Greene's Tu Quoque; or, The Cittie Gallant by J. Cooke: A Critical Edition*, ed. Alan J. Berman (New York: Garland Publishing, 1984), pp. 7, 125n.
[52] Cooke, *Greene's Tu Quoque* (1614), B3r.

Gervase Staines, Bubble's gentleman-master, has entered into financial difficulties through the agency of Bubble's uncle Whirlepit, who is a
usurer. At the beginning of the play, Whirlepit, whom we never see, dies,
leaving Bubble the money that he gained through ruining Staines. Staines
is therefore in a situation where his servant rises through his own fall, and
he is forced to take his servant's place, agreeing to tutor Bubble in the
ways of the gentry status he has obtained from Staines' own money. Up
until this point, Staines was planning to take to sea, much like Quicksilver
in Jonson, Chapman and Marston's *Eastward Ho!* (London, 1605). Here,
however, he is not thinking of travelling for adventure but for fear of being
punished for his debts:

> I dare not walke abroad to see my friends, for feare the Serjeants should
> take acquaintance of me: my refuge is *Ireland*, or *Virginia*; necessitie cries
> out, and I will presently to *Westchester*.[53]

Now that he is Bubble's servant, Staines sees a way of recovering his fortune and his status from him. As a servant, Staines turns into a cozening
gentleman gallant for the rest of the play. He manages to make Bubble
look foolish with his advice on how to be a gentleman, which is the main
source of the comedy, and he eventually tricks Bubble into the financial
ruin that results in Staines' recovery of both his money and his status. One
of the pieces of advice Staines gives to Bubble is that he launch into Latin,
so that when another gentleman greets him he should always answer 'Tu
quoque' – or, in English, 'Same to you' – advice which engenders some
embarrassing moments throughout. In this way Staines gains his fortune
back, as well as by a combination of disguise and trickery at the gaming
tables of London.

In this play, called, no doubt, *Tu Quoque; or, The Cittie Gallant* before
the death of Greene, it is Greene who certainly stars in more ways than
one. Surrounded by differing characters with their social statuses in flux –
the prodigal journeyman, Spendall; Will Rash, the citizen son (fresh from
university) of the knighted Sir Lionell; and Gervase, Bubble's one-time
master and now his servant – it is Bubble who is the central, satirically
observed student 'Gallant' who has no idea what he should do and what
is expected.

The local reference in the play to both Greene and the Red Bull is the
one oft-quoted, and demonstrates to what extent the author 'Jo:' Cooke
meant it to be played before a Red Bull audience alone. It comes at a

---

[53] *Ibid.*, B3v.

point when a group of the young people in the play, including 'Bubble', Greene's character, are deciding what to do, referring to some important life-decisions.

SCATT. ... if Mistris *Gartred* will, wee will be married to morrow.
BUB. S'fott, if Mistris *Joyce* will, wee'le be married to night.
RASH. Why you couragious Boyes, and worthy Wenches, made out of Waxe. But what shall's doe when wee haue dinde, shall's goe see a Play?
SCATT. Yes fayth Brother if it please you, let's goe see a Play at the Gloabe.
BUB. I care not; any whither, so the Clowne haue a part: For I fayth I am no body without a Foole.
GER. Why then wee'le goe to the Red Bull; they say *Green's* a good Clowne.
BUB. *Greene? Greene's* an Asse.
SCATT. Wherefore doe you say so?
BUB. Indeed I ha no reason: for they say, hee is as like mee as euer hee can looke.
SCATT. Well then, to the Bull ...[54]

The young people, including Bubble (played by Greene the clown), then go off to 'the Bull' to see Greene the clown; yet there is an intervening scene at a bawdy house where the young Spendall faces his downfall as the upstart mercer and no master. He all but spits on the prostitute he is with, cursing her as he leaves with the sergeants.

SPEND. ...
   Thou Strumpet, that wert borne to ruine men,
   My fame, and fortune : be subiect to my Cursse,
   And heare me speake it : May'st thou in thy youth,
   Feele the sharpe Whippe; and in thy Beldame age,
   The Cart: when thou art growne to bee
   An old Vpholster vnto *Venerie,*
   (A Bawd I meane, to liue by Fether-beds,)
   Mayst thou be driuen to sell all thou hast
   Vnto thy *Aqua vitae Bottle:* that's the last
   A Bawd will part withall ...
   May the *French* Canniball eate into thy flesh,
   And pick thy bones so cleane, that the report
   Of thy Calamitie, may draw resort
   Of all the common sinners in the towne,
   To see thy mangled Carcasse: and that then,
   They may vpon't, turne honest; Bawd, say Amen *Exit.*[55]

It is ironic that Spendall is taken away for his profligacy while he is with the prostitutes, for after this scene we are back with the young people,

[54] *Ibid.,* G2v.   [55] *Ibid.,* H1v.

and it is here that mention is made of 'Middlesex', the county outside the City walls where Clerkenwell, the Red Bull and many houses of ill repute (for example, in Turnmill Street) were located.[56] If their plans are to be believed, the Red Bull is where the characters have just attended a play.

Enter Rash, Stayns and Geraldine.
RASH. Well this Loue is a troublsome thing, *Iupiter* blesse
   mee out of his fingers: ther's no estate can rest for him:
   Hee runnes through all Countries, will trauell through the
   Ile of man in a minut, but neuer is quiet till hee came into
   Middle-sex, and there keepes his Christmas:
   Tis his habitation, his mantion; from whence,
   Heele neuer out, til hee be fierd.[57]

Sexual allusion is present in this speech when one once understands the meaning of 'Loue' juxtaposed with '*Middle-sex*', and perhaps we should not ignore the number of times the players are found associated with accused prostitutes in the Consistory Court books and other records. Christopher Beeston's brush with Margaret White accusing him of rape, recorded in the Bridewell books, may have resulted from a malicious accusation as he suggested; however, he did not deny that he had dealings with this woman, already in the Bridewell on prostitution charges. One obvious example in the church court books already discussed is that of William Perry's wife, Dionisia, claiming the widow Elizabeth Hambell's residence at her home in Clerkenwell. Hambell takes Hall to court for libel, as he has accused her of being a 'Bawd' in front of witnesses and without evidence – but it is possible that in this case there is 'no smoke without fire'.

   In these and other instances, however, we should hesitate before we curse players for having any closeness to the sex trade in the way of Spendall. Then as now – but surely worse then – there may have been instances where it was difficult for the early modern woman to take up more respectable trades in London. In a widow or single woman's situation for instance, without a man's wages, the female was in danger of all kinds of situations and perceptions.[58] The quick turnaround among

---

[56] See Ian Archer, *The Pursuit of Stability: Social Relations in Elizabethan London* (Cambridge University Press, 1991), p. 212 for his map of bawdy houses and the concentration of them around Turnmill Street in Clerkenwell. See also the more recent chapter on Clerkenwell and its entertainments in Duncan Salkeld, *Shakespeare among the Courtesans: Prostitution, Literature and Drama, 1500–1650* (Farnham: Ashgate, 2012), pp. 119–50.
[57] Cooke, *Greene's Tu Quoque* (1614), H2.
[58] Incidents are noted where women new to the area – those whose husbands were away, or those forced to find work – seemed vulnerable. See Laura Gowing, *Domestic Dangers: Women, Words, and Sex in Early Modern London* (Oxford: Clarendon Press, 1996), pp. 15, 17.

actors' wives, finding another player to marry soon after the death of the last, is evidence more of these kind of needs than of anything heartless. Witness the cases of Susan Browne-Greene-Baskervile or Cicely Browne-Robins, who remarried relatively quickly after the death of the last husband. The Consistory Court case of 1607 where we learned the little we know of Thomas Greene's provenance also concerned libellous accusations of prostitution. Mary Phillips was a playhouse doorkeeper at the Boar's Head, and her husband, Ellis, was told that there were 'no wome*n* that k*e*pt playehowses dores but weare whores'. Greene is recorded as going to the accuser personally to see if this was an accurate account of the matter and heard him abuse the woman again, which Greene deemed libellous.[59]

If we believe Greene's care here, we may see him as having concerns with both the reputation of the playhouses and also the workers associated with them. It is interesting that Mary Phillips went straight to see Greene about the incident, showing his managerial power and standing. It is of interest as well that Mary Phillips was also a worker associated with the Red Bull, for she is mentioned too in the *Woodford* v. *Holland* suit in that capacity.[60] When Dekker spoke of 'one honest door-keeper', perhaps he used the term 'honest' as meaning 'sexually virtuous' as well as 'truthful' when it came to money changing hands.

The year 1612 and Greene the good clown

In what I have dubbed the company's golden age, there is very little to show much actual misdemeanour. Indeed – apart from implied queries about returns on the author's 'third day', the records show that the Queen's Servants, at this time, were far more 'sinned against than sinning'. The records of these particular difficulties, however, again centre themselves around the managerial influence of Thomas Greene, and again they demonstrate what a central figure he was. Of Greene's management, the actors had several things to say when the subject came up for discussion during the *Worth* v. *Baskervile* case of 1623, most of them describing him as 'one of

---

[59] LMA DL/C/0217, pp. 216–19, fos. 108–10.
[60] When Leslie Hotson transcribed the 1623 plea of the case (TNA C3/390/47) he saw Woodford's claim that Aaron Holland 'procured one Marie Phillips for ten shillings to bring the said Phillip Stone vnto him'; Hotson, *The Commonwealth and Restoration Stage*, pp. 327–47. Unfortunately, part of this sentence that Hotson saw – the part that is located in the bottom right-hand corner of the original bill – is unreadable today, including Marie Phillips' name.

the cheef per*so*nes of the *sai*d Company'.[61] Thomas Heywood was to comment (albeit in parenthesis) that the company loved 'the *sai*d Thomas very
well in his lief tyme' (Int. 4). Others did not go quite that far. Christopher
Beeston, for instance, who took over Greene's managerial position in the
company, and who was accused of making off with the company's funds
and assets when he rejected them for the Cockpit, was to sound almost
churlish when it came to his appreciation of Greene. According to his
testimony, Greene was 'well respected by the *sai*d Company as anie of the
chiefest of them' (Int. 2).

The questions at stake with regard to Thomas Greene often centred on
his generosity with the company, and where funds came from, particularly just before his death in 1612. Christopher Beeston acknowledged that
Greene 'did sometymes lay out money for some necessarie pr*o*visions', and
believed that it was 'of his owne pr*o*pre moneys' (Int. 3). Robert Leigh
also acknowledged a sum of 'thirty & od Pownds', to which the company stood in debt to Greene before he died. Richard Perkins, in direct
opposition, was to say that he did not think Greene had spent any mon-
ies for the company that had not come out of 'the com*m*on purse of the
*sai*d Company' (Int. 3). In answer to the interrogatories for Worth's side,
he was to be yet more direct. Not only did he say that Greene was 'at his
death indebted unto the *sai*d Company', but that he had been drawing
on the finances of the company without accounting for it. He claimed
that: 'Greene had for certeine yeares the receivi*n*g of the pr*o*fitte*s* of the
half galleries at the ^*sai*d^ Red Bull for the *sai*d Companye and ... that
to his rem*em*brance he did never knowe or heare that the *sai*d Greene did
accompt to the *sai*d Company at any tyme for the same.'[62] Perkins, at the
time of the depositions of the court case, was not a member of the company. After a time away then briefly returning to the Revels, he joined the
King's Men for, possibly, two years (1623–5). After this he was soon a part
of Beeston's new enterprises at the Cockpit, and was fiercely supportive
of the once Chamberlain's, then Worcester's/Queen's Servants actor, now
maligned playhouse-owner and manager, in contrast to the other actors
who generally loved Greene. Perhaps his respect for Beeston is unsurpris-
ing in view of the fact that Perkins probably wished to stay friendly with
the now successful if somewhat ruthless impresario. There is evidence

[61] TNA C24/500/9, Robert Leigh, Int. 2. Thomas Drewe concurred with this opinion in answer
    to the same direct question, as did Gertrude Browne (friend of Susan Greene), Richard Perkins,
    Thomas Heywood and William Roberts, engrosser of covenants included in an agreement in the
    Worth v. *Baskervile* case.
[62] TNA C24/500/103, Int. 3.

that, as time went on, others were to join Perkins in newly found respect for Christopher Beeston.

During Greene's management, it was possibly the popularity of both the clown and the playhouse that brought about recorded instances of theft. For instance, in 1611, Greene was to put his name to an accusation against one William Sayer, who had stolen, so it was reported, a 'veluett Jerken', coloured 'purple', a pair of black 'satten breeches', ten shillings-worth of 'hatched sword' and a crimson 'vellvett Cloke ... lyned with Cloth of silver' worth £20.[63] These were of the goods and chattels of Thomas Greene of Clerkenwell. A related record makes it clear that the crime had occurred at the 'red bull' – but whether this was the playhouse or the inn where Greene may have owned rooms one cannot tell.[64] Two years earlier in 1608, a hatband was stolen 'att the redd Bull a playhouse', with one John Burton, of Clerkenwell, accused; although again it is not completely obvious whether the hatband in question was from the company's property stored at the playhouse, or belonged to one of the audience members attending – one assumes the former since no specific owner is communicated, just the venue.[65]

Of the most infamous instances where the playhouse was sinned against during this earlier time was in 1610 when a group of men, at least four of them feltmakers, were forced to appear at the Middlesex sessions because of a 'notable outrage at the playhouse called the Red Bull'.[66] Although no clue is given as to the nature of the outrage, no implication is made that the playhouse itself was at fault in this instance.

The year 1612 represented one of significant change for Clerkenwell, for Middlesex and, indeed, for the country – as well as for the company. According to Pinks, this was the year when Sir Baptist Hicks, a justice of Middlesex, completed his task of building an official Sessions House for the county, made of brick and stone and built at his own expense.[67] This happened early in the year, and 'Hicks Hall', as it was known, situated at the base of St John Street where it widens out before Smithfield, must have become a place of great activity as the century continued, dealing, as

[63] LMA MJ/SR/0499, 114.
[64] LMA MJ/SR/0499, 70.
[65] LMA MJ/SR/0466, 33.
[66] William Tedcastle, yeoman, along with John Fryne, Edward Brian, Edward Purfett and Thomas Williams, feltmakers. LMA MJ/SR/0489, 9, 11, 101, 103, 105; *EPT*, p. 569.
[67] John Stow, *Annales; or, A Generall Chronicle of England*, ed. Edmund Howe (London, 1631), p. 1003; Pinks, *The History of Clerkenwell*, p. 297.

it did, with the crime of most of London's suburbs, as well as the whole county of Middlesex.[68]

A series of terrible disasters were about to unfold for the company at the Red Bull, however, with the worst of happenings occurring during the summer.

As we know, on 7 August 1612, Thomas Greene, 'householder', was buried in the chancel of St James' Church.[69] The manager, thought by some to have laid out his own sums for their success, and the one whom workers provably turned to on matters to do with reputation, was no more. Speculation exists that the clown had just come back from a trip abroad because of a set of epitaphs included in a work entitled *Remains after Death*, written by one 'MVSOPHILVS' (believed to be R. Braithwaite) and published in 1618. This group of verses is intriguing, as they undoubtedly refer to Greene because of their references to '*Tu quoq*', but scholars usually only quote one of them.

> Vpon an Actor now of late deceased: and
>   vpon his Action *Tu quoq:* and first
>   vpon his Trauell.
> *Hee whom this mouldered clod of earth doth hide,*
> *New come from Sea, made but one face and dide.*
>   Vpon his Creditors.
> *His debtors now, no fault with him can finde,*
> *Sith he has paid to nature, all's behinde.*
>   Vnto his fellow Actors.
> *What can you craue of your poore fellow more?*
> *'He does but what* Tu quoque *did before:*
> *Then giue him dying, Actions second wreath,*
> *'That second'd him in Action and in death.*[70]

Debtors to Greene, along with his 'Creditors', were to become a theme in the story of the vacuum he created once gone. The word 'Action' could be given several meanings here. 'Action' as in acting; 'Action' as in court cases; and 'Action', along with the idea of 'second'd', as in sword-fighting. Quite what the term 'second wreath' means alongside the term 'Actions' cannot yet be stated with any certainty, but it may indicate more than one entertainment skill for which Greene was known, and the Red Bull repertoire,

---

[68] Prior to this, sessions were held at various inns, notably the Castle Inn in St John Street, where Ben Jonson's case of manslaughter was heard.

[69] LMA P76/JS1/004.

[70] R. B. ('Musophilus'), *Remains in Death*, in Patrick Hannay, *A Happy Husband; or, Directions for a Maide to Choose Her Mate* (London, 1618), G5v.

with its many fight scenes oft-times noted, should not be forgotten in this regard.

Thomas Heywood was obviously enamoured of Greene, calling him *'my entirely beloued Fellow, the Actor'*. This was in an address 'To the Reader' in the preliminaries to the successful play by Cooke, published in 1614, performed twice at court in 1611–12, which took on the clown's name. Heywood wrote of Greene that *'there was not an Actor of his nature in his time of better ability in performance of what he undertooke; more applaudent by the Audience, of greater grace at the Court, or of more general love in the Citty'*.[71]

The death of Greene was to cause untold confusion and misery for the actors as time went on; however, no doubt unaware of how things would pan out, they had more bad news to come with the autumn. On 1 October 1612 a 'Remarkable Order touching the Fortune Play-House' was made at a General Session of the Peace at Westminster, before Baptist Hicks as well as many other justices. It was 'An Order for suppressinge of Jigges att the ende of Playes':

> Whereas Complaynte have beene made at this last Generall Sessions that by reason of certayne lewde Jigges songes and daunces vsed and accustomed at the play-house called the Fortune in Gouldinglane divers cuttpurses and other lewde and ill disposed persons in greate multitudes doe resorte thither at th'end of euerye playe many tymes causinge tumultes and outrages wherebye His Majesties peace is often broke and much mischiefe like to ensue thereby, Itt was hereuppon expresselye commaunded and ordered by the Justices of the said benche That all Actors of euerye playehouse within this cittye and liberties thereof and in the Countye of Middlesex that they and euerie of them vtterlye abolishe all Jigges Rymes and Daunces after their playes And not to tollerate permitt or suffer anye of them to be used vpon payne of ymprisonment and puttinge down and suppressinge of theire playes.[72]

The term 'jig' has two meanings that may be confused here, both associated with the more extemporising kind of entertainer, such as Greene and Kemp. It can mean both a dance (such as the Morris dance used by Kemp on his famous 'nine daies wonder' journey to Norwich) and the short, light, post-play entertainments that could get a little too suggestive and out of hand. Both the entertainment kind of jig and dancing were prohibited by this edict. This kind of thing represented, no doubt, a popular extra part to the end of a day out at the playhouse, and although it was the

---

[71] Cooke, *Greene's Tu Quoque* (1614), A2.
[72] The original text of the edict is found at LMA MJ/SB/R/001, or published in *MCR*, Vol. 1.

Fortune's jigs that were specified in the complaint, the Red Bull and all the other playhouses came under this anti-jig edict as well. We know jigs were a popular extra at the Red Bull, however, because of the provable failure of the edict to stop them taking place. A play by one Thomas Goffe called *The Careles Shepherdess* (London, 1656) demonstrates this, containing, as it does, a mean citizen character called Thrift who, unable to acquire a cheaper seat at another venue says:

> I will hasten to the money Box,
> And take my shilling out again, for now
> I have considered that it is too much;
> I'll go to th'Bull, or Fortune, and there see
> A Play for two pense, with a Jig to boot.[73]

The Fortune playhouse was the theatre, built in 1600, for the Admiral's, later the Prince's, Men, given patronage by the heroically perceived and much adored Prince Henry Frederick, the Prince of Wales. At the beginning of the winter, however, something was to happen that was to prove devastating to both the Queen's Servants and the Prince's company alike, during what had been, already, a terrible year for the Clerkenwell company. For on 6 November Prince Henry died. Early in October the fever, diagnosed today as a likely typhoid, took hold of the nineteen-year-old prince who, at that time, was determinedly preparing for his sister Elizabeth's marriage to the protestant Palatinate Prince Frederick.

It was not just that the whole country went into mourning concerning the loss of what Roy Strong described as 'this athletic and masculine figure', casting a shadow over entertainment in general; the effect on Queen Anna and the rest of the royal family was acute, making court entertainment a difficult if not an impossible effort.[74] If it had not been for the entertainments for the marriage – many already in preparation – it is hard to imagine a way in which dramatic entertainment could have found a way back from the malaise. Queen Anna removed herself; masques were called off; much of what the company stood for must have been put in doubt with its foundations shaken. Yet worse and much more complex difficulties were to come.

---

[73] Gurr, *Shakespearean Stage*, p. 215.
[74] Roy Strong, *Henry, Prince of Wales and England's Lost Renaissance* (London: Thames & Hudson, 1986), p. 220.

CHAPTER 7

The company: 1612–1619

Springs of hope bubbled up to the surface for London in 1613, and it is worthwhile to note these before the examination of the spiral downwards for company interests from 1612 onwards. Just north of Clerkenwell, fresh water came into the suburbs from Hertfordshire through the man-made rivers and channels that Sir Hugh Myddelton had instigated – what we know today as London's 'New River'.[1] For the company, however, because of the troubles of 1612, trials and challenges were beginning that were to poison relations like a foolish waterway's lead pipes. By this time the company had proved their spectacle mettle with Heywood's *Ages* cycle, and it is, perhaps, a possibility that their efforts at pyrotechnics may have influenced the King's Men's decision to use a cannon for *All Is True*. This resulted in the famous destruction of the first Globe by fire, with William Shakespeare leaving soon after.

This chapter begins with thoughts about the years 1612–13, to show how the difficulties and disasters that happened to the company at about this time were to develop and affect all of them to the end of their Queen's Servants period. This was particularly so after the death of Greene, but not exclusively because of this. With the promise of another new venue – their indoor playhouse, the Cockpit – adjacent to the Queen at Somerset House on the Strand (renamed Denmark House in her honour), so much could have gone right for the company, but, in the end, much went wrong. If the unfolding story seems a little complex, then this is because what happened was complex, and the scholar's experience contemplating these things should somewhat reflect the confusions felt by the actors too.

---

[1] See G. C. Derry, 'Sir Hugh Myddelton and the New River', *Transactions of the Honorable Society of Cymmrodorion* (1956), 17–46.

The year 1612 and Christopher Beeston

If the rhymes made up about him were true, Thomas Greene was absent just prior to his illness and death in the summer of 1612, and this idea is backed up by evidence of the timings of Beeston's taking over Greene's role as manager in the company. In a 1619 case concerning earlier debts owed by the company, for example, Christopher Beeston was described as ultimately responsible. On 27 June 1612 Beeston empowered actors to buy things 'for the vse of the Company of players at the Redd Bull neere St Jones'.[2] The actors specified were 'Ellis Worth Richard Perkins and John Comber and others', who bought 'diverse tinsell stuff*es* and other stuff*es* for their vse in playing amounting in the wholl to ffourtie six pound*es* five shillings and eight pence or thereaboutes'. John Smith, the aggrieved trader, stated that 'the said Christofer Beeston did faithfully promis to make payment vnto your said subiect and to satisfie him for the said stuffes'.

It is from this case that we learn of William Freshwater, a Merchant Taylor of St Botolph's, Bishopsgate, who described himself as 'a workman to the s*ai*d company'. It was Freshwater's job to go to the house of Smith, who was of the Fishmongers' company, who was selling goods to the players. Freshwater went, 'some tymes by direcc*i*on from the sayd Beeston & some tymes as sent by others of the sayd Company, for diu*er*se stuffes, wh*i*ch they had occasion to vse.'[3] However, he had already confirmed that Beeston had promised Smith it was he, Beeston, who would be responsible for payment.[4] At such times as he went, Freshwater was directed by Smith to return to Beeston to get a 'token' from him, and either Beeston sent a token for Smith or Beeston sent another member of the company with Freshwater for the things (Int. 3).

John King, that long-term hired man of the company whose association with it stretched back to 1593, said that Beeston did come to an arrangement with Smith about the delivery of goods to the company at the Red Bull in 1612.[5] Beeston undertook to pay for those goods, and King remembered Smith insisting on tokens from Beeston. King also said that the company gave Beeston half of the gallery profits 'toward*es* the satisfyinge of the Compl*ainan*tes debt wh*i*ch he Received weekly accordingly',

[2] TNA REQ2/459, Box 1, Smith's bill.
[3] Freshwater's deposition of 5 May 1620, Int. 3; see Wallace, 'Three London Theatres of Shakespeare's Time', pp. 331–2 (p. 332).
[4] Freshwater's deposition, Int. 2; Wallace, 'Three London Theatres of Shakespeare's Time', p. 331.
[5] John King's deposition, also of 5 May 1620, Int. 2; see Wallace, 'Three London Theatres of Shakespeare's Time', pp. 333–4.

but he could not calculate how much Beeston received over that time or when exactly the company gave Beeston that allowance.[6] He also said that when the company separated in *c.* 1617, Beeston took much of the stuffs and apparel with him:

> at the sep*ara*cion of the *sai*d Company the sayd Beeston did take and Carry Away all the apparrell that was then amongst the *sai*d Company and Converted them to his owne vse/ and since disposed of them to other Companyes at his pleasure.[7]

In May 1612, several months prior to his death, Greene found he owed one Robert Livesey a debt of £7 10s for 7 yards of black satin, and for grosgrain and cloth that, with other transactions, eventually came to £9 5s 3d.[8] This situation came out in a suit that Livesey began against Susan Greene after her husband, Thomas, had died. Agreements were reached between Livesey and Greene about what was owed while Greene was in London (at the parish of St Mary le Bow). Greene's *Tu Quoque* was performed at court at Candlemas 1612, so if Greene went away, it would have to have been either between Candlemas and May or between May and August (the latter is likeliest given Beeston's activities in June). Even though it looks as if Beeston took Greene's place when he was first away and then – perhaps – when he became ill, in the *Smith* v. *Beeston* case the impresario was to deny that he had ever been given more powers than anyone else, claiming equality among them: 'Their vsuall manner was, that sometymes one, and sometymes another of the said Company Did provide Clothes and [other] necessaries for the setting forth of the actors of that Company.'[9]

He was again to say that this was the case during the *Worth* v. *Baskervile* case of 1623:

> He thinketh That the now compl*aina*ntes and the rest of their Company ~~did put~~ bothe before and after the dece*a*sse of the *sai*d Tho*mas* Greene, did put such Trust & Confidence in him this dep*one*nt, concerninge the Managing of their seu*er*all affayers of Playing or Acting, As they did repose in other Sharers of the *sai*d Company, And not otherwise.[10]

After her husband's death, with debt-seekers at her tail, Susan, Thomas Greene's widow, began her endeavour to get the money that she felt the actors owed her back from the company.[11] With her background in

[6] King's deposition, Int. 4; see Wallace, 'Three London Theatres of Shakespeare's Time', p. 334.
[7] King's deposition, Int. 5; see Wallace, 'Three London Theatres of Shakespeare's Time', p. 334.
[8] TNA KB27/1439, Part 1, m. 955; see also Eccles, 'Elizabethan Actors II', p. 457.
[9] TNA REQ2/459, Box 1, Beeston's answer.
[10] TNA C24/500/9, Beeston's deposition, Int. 33.
[11] Because of the Livesey debt, it would appear that Susan may have been sent to the Marshalsea.

playhouses stretching back over many years, and her knowledge of the licensing of companies to perform at particular venues, we can start to understand the motivations behind tying up these matters in the way she did. We can also understand something of the actors' response to her approach. Susan's actions are made evident because of the court case of 1623, when Ellis Worth took her to court over her claims on the company finances. Without the knowledge of her *playhouse* share-ownership, what happened has been impossible for critics to comprehend fully, even though the case was centrally much more about company shares and sharers.

Susan Greene's 1612 claims and a succession of subsequent agreements

Susan Greene's claims concerned two sums. One was for £37, which she said her husband had laid out for the company shortly before his death. It was this amount that the other actors either remembered was owing or was part of what Greene was permitted to take from the receipts to make payments on their behalf. In the case of Richard Perkins, it was never owing because it came out of the 'com*m*on purse' of the company. Perkins was one of two witnesses who was to depose how he thought that Greene rather owed the company money, and not the other way round.

The other amount under dispute concerned Greene's company share, valued at £80. This claim led to a great deal of discussion about the nature of a company share – the amount contributed by a member of the company to become a sharer with them – which went towards the props, costumes, books and other necessaries of a troupe, and was what entitled them to profits. Was such a share reclaimable when a member left the company or died, or was it not reclaimable? Susan Greene pointed to the case of George Pulham, an unfortunate half-sharer who had died soon after investing in the company in 1610–11. Susan said that Pulham's executors had received his £40 back after his death, and that therefore she should be repaid the whole £80 of Greene's full share.[12] Beeston said he was not sure about Pulham's share – whether Worth paid the company or Pulham's executors for it – for the sum was not paid 'absolutely in respect of his s*ai*d half share … But … in considerac*i*on of … ^a^ greater Sum*m*e w*h*ich he had payd for his s*ai*d place wherin he lived but a shorte tyme and was indebted for a great parte therof at the tyme of his death.'[13]

---

[12] TNA C2/JASI/W2/67; Fleay, *A Chronicle History of the London Stage*, p. 280.
[13] TNA C24/500/9, Beeston's evidence, Int. 5.

Beeston claimed that Pulham's share had actually cost Pulham £60 including something towards his accommodation, and that Ellis Worth had paid £40 – either to the company or to Pulham's executors – he could not remember which.[14] One has to comment that Beeston's hesitation concerning the details of the receipt of Pulham's money by his executors is truly curious, because, in truth, Christopher Beeston *was* George Pulham's sole executor. Moreover, 90 per cent of the beneficiaries of Pulham's will were from Beeston's family – a situation highly beneficial to Beeston, and not wholly understood before.[15]

Thomas Drewe said that he had 'heard it rumored amongst the *said* Company, That there was an agreem*ent* made … That yf any of the *said* Company dyed being a full Sharer, his wife should haue fowerscore pownds payd hir … yf a half Sharer, fortie pownds, and yf a three quarters Sharer, then threescore pownds, ratably'.[16] He also added, however, that he did not know whether anyone had been paid that way. Heywood gave evidence that the company had been willing to pay Susan because of their love for Greene. This would have been paid 'out of their Gettinge*s* by the name, & way of a half share'.[17] In other words, they would have given her this money back gradually over time – now and again, as it turned out – through granting her a percentage of the profits as if she were a sharer herself.[18]

Other members of the company were not to confess such graciousness at the time of the court case. Perkins pointed to John Thayer, who died in the same year as Greene and who had been a half-sharer, as well as Thomas Albany, who was a three-quarters-sharer and had died in 1617/18.[19] The executors of neither of these actors had claimed the value of their shares. Christopher Beeston denied that he had ever considered paying Susan the money she claimed, owing both to losing Greene (which impoverished them), and to fears of losing any more of the company after Greene's death. What with losing Greene, their audience-drawing clown, who had also paid their expenses for them as he 'tooke up the *said* Companyes

---

[14] *Ibid.*

[15] I gave the details of this in a paper at the *Managing Shakespeare and the Early Modern Theater Business* seminar, led by Christopher Matusiak at the Forty-First Annual Meeting of the Shakespeare Association of America, Toronto, 28–30 March 2013. The paper circulated was called 'Managing Queen Anna's Men and the Single-Parent Mother: Viscount Lisle, Thomas Greene, Christopher Beeston and Susan Baskervile'.

[16] TNA C24/500/9, Drewe, Int. 4.

[17] TNA C24/500/9, Heywood, Int. 4.

[18] Heywood also thought, however, that it was more likely that Greene owed the company at his death, not the other way around (Int. 3).

[19] TNA C24/500/103, Perkins, Int. 2.

Galery Moneys, for the paym*en*t of necessarie debtes', they were now in some financial straits. Moreover, to pay Susan the share equivalent would have set a dangerous precedent they could not afford to repeat.[20] In this he had a point. They had already lost Pulham, Greene and Thayer, and were to lose John Duke in 1613. Beeston also emphatically declared his belief that 'eu*er*ie mans share ends, whensoeuer the Company dissolveth'.[21] This is likely to have been the belief that Susan Greene feared most with regard to the company, as her actions and the actors' responses subsequent to 1612 shall testify.

Having no luck, in the first instance, with going directly to the company with her claims, it would seem that Susan Greene went to that official of the Queen's court who had the most immediate hold over the royal consort's entertainers: Sir Robert Sidney, at that time Viscount Lisle. As we know, Lisle took her part, somewhat impatient with the company. Beeston, remembering this action with the utmost clarity, described her as 'so violent, and so forward to peticion' him (the term 'so violent' was later deleted from the text), yet out of this move came the company offer of that occasional half-share.[22] Susan graciously acquiesced to this, a method of payment for the sums she felt were due to her, accepting it 'from tyme to tyme as it came in' from the actors in view of their 'pou*er*tie'.[23] In June 1613, Susan married James Baskervile, and by that time (as her answer to the bill records), only £6 of the debt had been paid, which she had received by April of that year.[24] At some point during this period, too, after their 1613 marriage, Susan and James Baskervile were blessed with the birth of a son, Francis. Two years later, in June 1615, the Baskerviles were drawn into the company's finances to the tune of £57 10s, which they gave to them in exchange for 20d per day out of the profits.

Gertrude Browne, a friend of Susan's, told the court hearing in the *Worth* v. *Baskervile* case how this happened.

> It was hir chaunce after the end of a play, at the red Bull … to be in Company w*i*th the now compl*ainan*te Worth, James Baskervile… the s*ai*d def*endan*tes Susan & W*illia*m Browne hir sonne drinking a cup of wyne together, at a Tauerne on Clarkenwell Greene./ And this dep*onen*t sayth That at the same tyme, Amongst other words that they passed amongst them, shee this dep*onen*t heard the compl*ainan*te Worthe say unto the s*ai*d

[20] TNA C24/500/9, Beeston, Int. 9.
[21] TNA C24/500/9, Beeston, Int. 10.
[22] *Ibid.*
[23] TNA C2/JASI/W2/67; Fleay, *A Chronicle History of the London Stage*, p. 281.
[24] TNA C2/JASI/W2/67; Fleay, *A Chronicle History of the London Stage*, pp. 281–2.

James Baskervile to this or like effect, vizt ffather Baskervile, why doe yow not buy some things amongest us; I pray yow buy some thing amongest us, And I will see That yow shall haue *your* Right. And this dep*onen*t sayth that afterwards ^by reporte^ there was some penc*i*on of twenty pence by the day, bought by the *sa*id mr Baskervile of the *sa*id then Company, or some other penc*i*on, w*hi*ch was afterwards payd by the *sa*id Company.[25]

The answer of the Baskerviles in the case describes how the couple paid the company 'seu*er*all somes of monie amounting to ffiftie seauen pound*es* tenne shilling*es*'.[26] This was to be in exchange for the 20d per day, and agreements were signed to that effect on 7 July 1615. However, the 20d per day was only paid for twenty days, for the answer to the bill specifies that it was on 27 July 1615 that the covenants were broken. With the company in debt to the Baskerviles 'in the som*m*e of threescore and twelue pound*es*, or therabout*es*', it is hard to believe but reportedly true that a further investment of £38 was forthcoming from them.[27] With this the company came to terms with everything they owed the Baskerviles (£110), and the figure of 3s 8d per day for the debt was agreed to be paid while Susan and her son, Francis, lived. On 26 July 1616, this agreement, with its attendant bonds, was also broken. Little Francis was to die shortly afterwards, during the Michaelmas of that year.[28] His father left for Ireland. Some believed that he left in a hurry. Thomas Basse deposed evidence – which was, at some hasty point, deleted – implying that Baskervile had married Susan bigamously. Baskervile, according to Basse, 'having taken up diuerse commodityes in & about London upon Creditt, and being taxed for hauing two wieues lyving both at one tyme did about vij yeares agone ^did goe^ into Ireland'.[29]

It was then, according to Thomas Drewe's memory of the time, that Susan began to press suits and costs on the company. These not only included all the debts that had gone before, but sums concerning the wages of her son, William Browne (the son of Robert Browne of the Boar's Head), who was a hired man among them.[30] Francis Walpole deposed that it was in the regnal year 1617/18 that an indenture was sealed by some of the company, including himself. This was for the 3s 8d per day, to be paid to Susan Baskervile and William Browne instead of the deceased Francis.

[25] TNA C24/500/9, 'Gartrude' Browne, Int. 12.
[26] TNA C2/JASI/W2/67; Fleay, *A Chronicle History of the London Stage*, p. 282.
[27] TNA C2/JASI/W2/67; Fleay, *A Chronicle History of the London Stage*, p. 283.
[28] TNA C2/JASI/W2/67; Fleay, *A Chronicle History of the London Stage*, pp. 283, 285.
[29] TNA C24/500/9, Basse, Int. 22.
[30] TNA C24/500/9, Drewe, Int. 23.

The arrangements were brought about through an action of William Jordan, who was to receive the money from the company.[31]

At this point it would be well to raise a question that has been posed – by inference – before. Why did Susan Baskervile and her husband continue to invest in a company that so consistently failed to give them returns? Kathleen McLuskie and Felicity Dunsworth put the puzzle concerning the Baskerviles' payments in this way: 'were the sums put forward loans that the Baskerviles might expect to be repaid, or were they investments in which the couple would have to take their chance on profits? ... In the event, the company did not pay.'[32]

Why did Susan and James invest, and why did the company not pay? There is enough evidence from the actors to show that they felt they were not rich enough to make the payments. Beeston was crystal-clear about this, when he described the 'great debtes' of the company that had accrued around the death of Greene, and also when he said the company was 'very poore' at the time they agreed to give Susan a half-share.[33] Certainly there was a great deal of resentment expressed among the hired men of the company about the claim for William Browne's wages arrears. John King, who had worked for the company for over thirty years, said that he had an informal arrangement with the company whereby he was to be given certain weekly wages. However, 'if at any tyme it should happen the gettinges of the *said* Companie to bee but small & to decrease, that then hee should not haue his whole wages agreed to bee paide unto him but to beare his part of the losse thereof'.[34] He estimated that the company owed him over £100 in wages.

Richard Baxter said he kept records concerning the arrears of his 'ten shillinges a weeke', that 'divers tymes it fell so out that the gettinges of the Company was so small as ... [the] hiered ^men or servants [received] no wages, and sometymes lesse', and that he 'did recon the same uppe from tyme to tyme' with no luck in getting remuneration.[35] Roger Clarke, too, gave evidence concerning his lack of agreed income, but he also

31 TNA C2/JASI/W2/67, Susan Baskervile's answer; Fleay, *A Chronicle History of the London Stage*, p. 284. TNA C24/500/103, Francis Walpole, Int. 6.
32 Kathleen McLuskie and Felicity Dunsworth, 'Patronage and the Economics of Theater', in *A New History of Early English Drama*, ed. John D. Cox and David Scott Kastan (New York: Columbia University Press, 1997), pp. 423–40 (pp. 435–6).
33 TNA C24/500/9, Beeston, Ints. 9 and 10.
34 TNA C24/500/103, King, Int. 5.
35 TNA C24/500/103, Baxter, Int. 5.

described the normality of such informal arrangements among companies throughout the adult company world.[36]

Despite the claims she made on the behalf of her son, there were reasons other than simple maternal pride why it was in Susan Baskervile's best interests to see that the company was well maintained. Above all, she wanted to ensure that the players would remain together, tied up with both her and the Red Bull. The agreements she made the company sign tell us much about her anxieties concerning them and what they might do if they were given a chance. When William Roberts engrossed the covenants made in 1615 they were to be enforced while the company played at the Red Bull 'or els where. ^within two myles of London^'.[37] According to Francis Walpole, the differently worded indenture of 3 June 1617 stipulated that it was in force 'for six dayes in the weeke so long as the *said* Company or any ffower or three of them should playe together'.[38] Within these agreements it was important, for some reason, that a set number of them were playing together, preferably at the Red Bull. By 1615 the company was teetering on the brink of a new way of working, with an indoor playhouse to perform in as well as at Clerkenwell. As we know, there were to be splinter groups who toured, like the separate Leigh company, possibly coming in to the Curtain playhouse, the company's other venue. Where would the anxious Susan stand in relation to these activities while she owned shares in a playhouse in which only the Queen's Servants were licensed to play? What would it mean if they went anywhere else?

The further interesting question is, did they eventually divide in the way they did because they had to, or did at least some of them divide knowing that once they were smaller groups playing 'els where', Susan could no longer make claims upon them within the terms of her ever-burgeoning agreements? There is yet more to say.

Christopher Beeston, the Cockpit playhouse and further Susan Baskervile considerations

It is possible that in 1615–17, with the opportunity to follow in the footsteps of the King's Men – not only possessing their own yard playhouse but an indoor private house as well – paying off the Baskerviles seemed something the company could do. Unfortunately, things were not to turn

[36] TNA C24/500/103, Clarke, Int. 5.
[37] TNA C24/500/9, Roberts, Int. 12.
[38] TNA C24/500/9, Walpole, Int. 6; see also TNA C2/JASI/W2/67 (Fleay, *A Chronicle History of the London Stage*, pp. 277, 284).

out the way they thought, because their combined association with the Cockpit was illusory. Although Beeston, as a member of the company, had rented the land to build the Cockpit at £45 per year for the next thirty-one years, it was Beeston who had done this and not the company.[39] He was also responsible for the building works. At the beginning of September 1616, when the builder-artisans of the theatre were arrested because of objections, they were only given bail with the proviso that the person bailing them appear before the Lords at Whitehall at their 'first sitting', that he disallow the continuation of the building and use 'his best endeavoure' to bring forth Beeston the following day in court. Beeston was even to be bound over because of his responsibility for the playhouse.[40]

Beeston's sole responsibility for the Cockpit was to lead him to feel able to desert the Queen's Servants and commandeer the theatre, which the others presumably expected to be shared out among them. In the *Worth* v. *Baskervile* case, the actors, in retrospect, saw that the hold Susan had over the company when they played 'ffower or three of them … together' would not include Beeston once he had left, making him, suspiciously, no longer liable. This would explain why the younger actors who remained seemed to accuse Beeston and Baskervile of acting in combination, and of bribing the actors to sign the 1617 indenture. Worth's bill alleges that Susan 'begann to insinuate with the said Christopher Hutchinson alias Beeston' in order to get him to prompt the others to sign.[41] Thomas Drewe deposed that he had heard from Susan that 'the said Beeston ^and other of the said Company haue^ receiued gratuiityes of hir in money, Beaver hattes & silk stockins, to drawe the Rest of the said Company, to allow of hir demaunds'.[42] Beeston, of course, denied any persuasive force or the company taking money, except the 'gratuities' that were given 'some unto this deponent in particular', but how much these gratuities came to he could not remember.[43] It would seem that Susan's own rights to money had to be written into legal agreements that ensured the company stayed together. However, bribes and buying into the company still seem a little extreme, especially when she derived so little back.

An important matter to consider when it comes to the 1617 indenture, and how the younger actors felt about it, was the attempted device within it regarding replacement actors. Such replacements should also

[39] See TNA C2/CHAS1/H28/26. It was a sublease acquired on 9 August 1616.
[40] LMA MJ/SB/R/002, p. 344; *MSR*, Vol. III, p. 310.
[41] TNA C2/JAS1/W2/67; Fleay, *A Chronicle History of the London Stage*, p. 274.
[42] TNA C24/500/9, Drewe, Int. 34.
[43] TNA C24/500/9, Beeston, Int. 34.

be made liable to pay the Baskervile sums, and should be bound over like the others to this effect. This was to lead some actors to refuse to sign, and created further divisions and disagreements. Another factor was Susan's substantial *playhouse* shares – the ones that she had owned alongside her husband Greene. These shares, it will be remembered, consisted of half the tiring house and yard minus the eighth or ninth part that had been given to Beeston, which meant that her returns on this working venue alone must have represented a good sum. She owned nothing in respect of the Cockpit theatre; she only – with respect to this company – owned shares in the Red Bull, and it was this playhouse that was the main one licensed to the Queen's Servants, so technically no other company could perform in it. With the threat of the company part-leaving the site where they and only they were licensed to perform – her capital-earning enterprise (and home) – her anxiety must have been considerable. This would explain the need she felt to tie the company to herself both legally and financially, as preferably a Red Bull entity, and even – as the possibility of their divided playhouse loyalties remained and developed – as the Queen's Servants at the Cockpit. William Jourdan's indenture of 1617 stipulated that the company were to pay what they owed 'att the play howse called the Cockpitt in Drurie Lane, or att such other place or play howse within two miles of London' where any four of them should play together. It would seem that all concerned expected them to be playing there in the long term; thus Susan needed to enshrine their commitment in writing wherever they played.

Her Red Bull share-ownership, which would have been nominally owned by Baskervile once they were – even tenuously – married, also explains why she and Baskervile went on investing in the company itself. The company had to be maintained no matter what they owed her in return, because if they failed as a going concern, so would her profits from both theatre-ownership and the company payments in the context of the actors' patent. If she could access funds from the company's profits independently from what she received from their theatre, so much the better – she could gain from them no matter where they played.

The above scenario concerning her playhouse shares would also explain a number of remarks made by the actors. For example, Thomas Drewe stated that between 1617 and Christmas 1618, the company had become so exasperated with the outgoings that they 'would haue put downe the fflag, being weary of the *said* payment ... wherupon the *said* Susan not of courtesie as this dep*onen*t beleveth ... did agree to accept fro*m* the *said*

Company, only two shillings six pence a day'.[44] Susan was frightened of them finishing with the Red Bull. This new arrangement of a decreased sum was supposed to begin at Christmas 1618 and, although intended as an interim measure, it lasted for four years according to Ellis Worth's bill.[45]

Richard Perkins was the most direct in his assessment of Susan's anxieties. In his deposition he described how when the company found the payments 'to be t*oo* heavy', they were 'determined to have played at another house unles the said Susanna would abate something of that daylie pay-m*ent* for if they had left that house then the s*ai*d Susanna should have lost a greater p*ro*fit by the benefite she made of the s*ai*d house'.[46] Indeed, we have it loud and true with Perkins. Susan needed the company at the Red Bull playhouse because she thought she would have lost the greater amount of money from her playhouse shares. This was the reason for all her financial efforts to keep them in place, and the reason the company knew they were better off dividing – or, at least, seeming to divide.

Attitudes to Beeston after 1612

Perceptions of Beeston were certainly mixed. Between 27 June 1612 and 23 February 1616 the company gained goods from John Smith with Beeston in charge. The company (as far as Smith was concerned) included 'Ellis Worth Richard Perkins and John Comber'.[47]

Protesting that Beeston well knew that the things were brought to him by his order and for his use, Smith claimed that despite 'most kinde and frendly' conversations and promises from Beeston to see that it was paid, no money had been forthcoming. Moreover, Smith said that the actors, under the cunning contrivance of 'combyning themselves' with one another, had 'intised' his one witness, Thomas Chambers, who was his servant, 'beyond the Seas or into some vnkowne & remote place' so that he could not give evidence. According to Smith, the actors had claimed at a time previously that Beeston had paid the debt either to Smith or to his absent servant on behalf of the company. However, since that period, Smith said, the company had fallen 'at variance and strife amongst themselves', and now they claimed that the debt was true but 'questioned

[44] TNA C24/500/9, Drewe, Int. 31.
[45] TNA C2/JASI/W2/67; Fleay, *A Chronicle History of the London Stage*, p. 275.
[46] TNA C24/500/103, Perkins, Int. 11.
[47] TNA REQ2/459, Box 1; Wallace, 'Three London Theatres of Shakespeare's Time', p. 318.

betweene themselves w*h*ich of them should paie and discharge your said Subiect'.[48]

The answer of the actors Worth, Cumber and Perkins is revealing about their view of Beeston and the company structure at this time in 1619, and explains the 'variance and strife' that Smith detected. According to the actors, for the best organisation during their time together, the company required 'divers officers' among them. All of the actors were expected to 'take vpon them some place & charge', but for the greater 'prouision of the furniture & apparrell' they needed 'a thriueing man & one that was of abilitie & meanes'. That man, so they thought, should be Beeston, who would 'defaulke outt of the collec*c*ions and gatheringes w*h*ich were made continually whensoeuer any playe was acted a certen some of money as acomon stock towardes the buyeing and defraying of the charges of the furniture & apparrell aforesaid'.[49]

They were clear about the role Beeston had been assigned, describing at some length how nobody else 'should be troubled or ymployed in this busines' but him, how he should only use what was needed, and 'if there did fall outt any surplusage or remainder of the Com*m*on stocke & money soe by him to be gathered, that then the said Beeston should give a true accompt vnto the company & that every one of them should haue a share & part according to there place & qualitie'.[50]

Beeston filled this role for seven or eight years according to the actors, presumably from about the time when Greene was away, ill or dying.[51] This case began to be heard in 1619, the year after Beeston's departure to fulfil his destiny at the Cockpit and the year when the company had lost their royal patron, Queen Anna. The actors were still undoubtedly smarting from his separation, having 'giuen over his coate' (perhaps meaning his livery) and 'condic*i*on', obviously in favour of the indoor playhouse, 'carriing awaie … all the furniture and app*a*rell'. They claimed that during the period when Beeston was the man in charge of major expenditure he had 'deducted & defaulked divers greate somes of money outt of the collec*c*ions & gatheringes aforesaid & hath w*i*th the said moneyes much enriched himself as these def*enda*ntes conceaue'.

[48] TNA REQ2/459, Box 1; Wallace, 'Three London Theatres of Shakespeare's Time', p. 319.
[49] TNA REQ2/459, Box1, 'The ioynt and seue*r*all answers of Ellis Worth, Richard Perkins, and John Cumber …'; Wallace, 'Three London Theatres of Shakespeare's Time', p. 321.
[50] TNA REQ2/459, Box 1; Wallace, 'Three London Theatres of Shakespeare's Time', p. 322.
[51] See TNA REQ2/459, Box 1; Wallace, 'Three London Theatres of Shakespeare's Time', p. 322. For Int. 31 in the *Worth* v. *Baskervile* case (TNA C24/500/9), Beeston said he left at the end of 1618; for his answer to this case he said he joined Prince Charles' Men *after* the death of Queen Anna.

Considering the period with hindsight, the actors accused Beeston of embezzlement, citing an instance where he gave the company what they now took to be 'a falce [*sic*] accompte of fower hundred poundes'.[52] On reflection they realised that, having believed him when he said all the money had been used, they had no way of proving if this were the case or what arrangements he had made with the tradesmen involved. Moreover, although they did not state this, £400 would be enough to start work on a new theatre, which was just what Beeston did. Just as Smith had accused the actors of being in league with Beeston, so the actors also accused Beeston of being in cahoots with Smith. This was in order 'to trouble & molest these defend*an*tes hopeing thereby either to come by some composition or otherwise some couller for the said Beeston to exclayme on these defend*an*tes & the rest of the companie'.[53]

Beeston even denied that he had ever had dealings with Smith on behalf of the company, but only admitted buying things from him for his 'Children', for which, he claimed, 'he allwayes payd ready money'.[54] Moreover, he denied – as he did in the later *Worth* v. *Baskervile* case – that he had ever had a significant managerial role among the actors. At that time, he said, there were ten sharers in the company, of whom the defendants represented only four, and their 'vsuall manner was … that sometymes one, and sometymes another of the said Company Did provide Clothes and other necessaries for the setting forth of the actors of that Company'.[55] In other words, he did not know what the other sharers had bought for provisions, but he absolutely denied responsibility for the payment of them.

A very different set of things happened when Beeston was later approached for more debts concerning the company, and it is interesting to contemplate the passage of time between the two occasions. In a case of 1633, Richard Holden, a Haberdasher of the City of London, took Beeston, Worth and Perkins to court over the sale of some hats that had taken place in 1617.[56] The hats were to the value of £7 17s 6d, and the reason why it took Holden so long to file a suit against the players was because first he was put in prison and then he went abroad. Holden claimed that on the occasion of the sale, 'Christopher Beeston, Ellis Worth and Richard Perkins did then faithfully *p*romise' that he would be paid for the hats 'by

⁵² TNA REQ2/459, Box 1; Wallace, 'Three London Theatres of Shakespeare's Time', p. 322.
⁵³ TNA REQ2/459, Box 1; Wallace, 'Three London Theatres of Shakespeare's Time', p. 323.
⁵⁴ TNA REQ2/459, Box 1; Wallace, 'Three London Theatres of Shakespeare's Time', p. 327.
⁵⁵ TNA REQ2/459, Box 1; Wallace, 'Three London Theatres of Shakespeare's Time', p. 326.
⁵⁶ TNA REQ2/655, Box 2.

the handes of Mr Houker then paymaster under the then right honor-able the then Lord Carew'. Sir George Carew, baron of Clopton, was, as we have learned previously, Queen Anna's Vice-Chamberlain and Receiver General. Carew was in charge of the Queen's revenues and was therefore the person who could be a channel for company funds if the Queen so desired. However, the money did not come, and this debt, together with others, resulted in Mr Holden being thrown into Ludgate Prison because of his own mounting debts. Here he stayed 'a long tyme',

> and presentlie after his deliuerie your said subiect went into the partes beyond the Seas hoping to recouer his owne debtes from such of his debt-ors as were fledd thither and from thence your saide Subiect is but late-lie returned, In which long continewance of tyme all the witnesses which should proue the sale of the said hattes are dead and departed this life which the said Christopher Beeston Ellis Worth and Richard Perkins well know-ing doe nowe utterlie deny and refuse to giue your said subiect anie satisfac-cion for the said hattes Contrary to all right Equitie and good Conscience.

The actors, for various reasons, were able to avoid retribution in terms of this suit. They simply denied knowledge of the transaction and took Holden's bill apart as a faulty piece of legal work, not specifying times and periods in the way that it should. What the actors did not do during this suit, however, was deny that they had been working together as a group or had been procuring things together at the time – and this included Beeston. As I indicated before, the 1619 John Smith case was brought at a time when the company was still reacting to Beeston's departure for the Cockpit. It seems that in their opinion he took with him a substantial amount of company property, along with their good faith that he had paid their debts; however, by the 1630s, with Beeston now a very powerful figure, they chose to see the situation very differently. Beeston saw things differently too.

This is where the picture becomes confusing concerning Beeston because of the considerable number of building projects that he had apparently entered into, all in 1616. Research now suggests that he had more building interests throughout his life than was previously thought, but in 1616 he became a developer of a very risky order. Not only did he get into trouble for starting foundation work on the Cockpit at the beginning of September because it was a new building 'Contrary to the law & his Majesties proclamacions', but Beeston was also accused of building a 'base Tenement, not of Bricke' in Clerkenwell.[57] This was recorded in a letter from the Privy

---

[57] Cockpit building: LMA MJ/SB/R/002, p. 347; Clerkenwell building: TNA PC2/28, pp. 399–400, Privy Council meeting, 18 September 1616.

Council to the High Sheriff of Middlesex about the extent of prohibited new building. Beeston was named among others as one of 'such persons as are greate Offendors in Building', and the letter noted that his venture, although formerly prohibited, was supposed to be erected as 'an Addition to his owne dwelling howse'. Instead he had made 'a Tenement of it, distant from his howse, and neere to his *Majesties* passage'.

The letter ended 'To be pulled downe.'[58]

Later, a note was made in 'The Reporte of William Gore and John Gore late Sheriffes of London & Midd' that Christopher Beeston's house was indeed 'for the most *parte* puld downe not to be inhabited'.[59] In the autumn of the year of the famous Shrovetide riot, 1617, which saw Beeston's house in Drury Lane and his playhouse all but destroyed by the rioters, the Privy Council was to write another letter to the High Sheriff. This time it complained that Beeston had re-erected the disallowed tenement in Clerkenwell that had been rightly 'pulled downe and demolished' in respect of the order made concerning it before:

> and his Majesty of late passing that way hath taken speciall notice thereof, being highly offended with the presumption. Yow shall therefore by vertue of this our letter make *your* present repaire unto the place, and to Cause the sayd Buylding ymediatly and without delay, before to morrow at night at the furthest, being the last of this Moneth, to be pulled downe to the grownde and utterly demolished, And to take sufficient Bond*es* of the owner to his Majestie's use that neyther in that place, nor in any other he shall Erect any Buylding hereafter contrary to his Ma*jest*ies Proclamac*i*ons on that behalfe. Or ells in case of Refusall, to Com*m*itt him to Prison till hee submitt himselfe.[60]

Despite his dissociation from the company and his ruthless, brave or foolhardy commitment to proceed with, for example, his building in Clerkenwell, all the accusations concerning Beeston and the company with whom he was licensed to play should be carefully contextualised. The character of Beeston, the Queen's Servants' bad debtor, the thief of the company's funds and the disloyal company fellow, should not, I suggest, be read only in the light of his dissociation and supposed absolute separation from the company to become an independent theatre-owner. From the *Baskervile* v. *Beeston* case of 1632, we learn that not only did Beeston own a share of the tiring house and yard of the Red Bull from 1607, but that, according to Susan, he was still entitled to it until 1633.[61]

---

58 *Ibid.*, p. 400.
59 *Ibid*, p. 422.
60 TNA PC2/29, p. 334. See Chapter 6, n. 18, concerning King James' visit to Clerkenwell and Thomas Chaloner's subsequent letter to the authories.
61 TNA REQ2/709.

It was probably because of this continued relationship with the play-house building that Beeston stayed linked with the company who played there, especially in the minds of those approaching the actors for financial redress of one kind or another, but also in the mind of Beeston himself, who can be shown to have had a hand in shuffling companies to and from the playhouse. Beeston, just like Susan Baskervile, still made sure he saw returns on his investment in the Red Bull. He had absolutely no reason to want to see that venture fail. Indeed, as well as getting out of a difficult problem for himself when he left the company at the end of 1618 (along with Drewe and, for a time, Perkins), Beeston may have believed that by leaving he was usefully helping to reduce the numbers to below four. By doing this, he would be helping the company divest themselves of their payments to Susan Baskervile.

Following on from what is known of Beeston's Red Bull involvement, the next mistake is to assume that with his departure to, and success in, a private indoor venue, Beeston would no longer have seen the continued potential of inn-yard venues generally. There does exist some evidence for a contrary view.

On 7 July 1635, an indenture was made that was recorded in the Close Rolls of the time, describing an agreement Beeston made with one Samuel Sandys concerning an inn in Shoreditch. The inn was 'knowne by the name and signe of the kinges head', and it was in St Leonard's parish, Beeston's old stomping ground during the time when he had lived near the Curtain theatre. The property consisted of 'Two partes in three partes already devided of and in one mesuage' that the King's Head represented. The two parts of three came with tenements and cottages, as well as:

> all buildinges stables gardens yardes backsides easementes waies lightes and comodities whatsoeuer thereunto belonging or therewith all used enioyed or reputed as parcell thereof And also one ancient passage or entrie from the streete and the next Court yard with the well and the yard beyond the well called the stable yard and the Shedd of boardes in the same stable yard which last mencioned premisses are yet undevided.[62]

In truth, Beeston's involvement with the King's Head stretched back much further to 1605. It is certainly Christopher Beeston who is referred to in the relevant document because he uses his alias, which helps to define him. The agreement was between Alice Burnell of St Leonard's, Shoreditch; 'Edwine Sandes of Furnesfells' in Lancashire, gentleman; and

---

[62] TNA C54/3060, no. 3.

'Christopher Hitchinson al*ia*s Beeston, gentleman'.[63] It is believed that the Sandes family were relatives of Beeston's wife Jane Sands, along with her sister Cicely Sands, wife of Continental Robert Browne – the women held up to the authorities many times because of their recusancy.[64] With reference to Beeston's continued involvement in this inn in 1635, despite old difficulties experienced with the Red Bull, and the continued assumption that this must have been to do with the unfashionable outlook for inn-yard theatre spaces at that time, Beeston's readiness to continue to invest in an inn is telling. Referring to his will of 1638 where he leaves some property in Shoreditch to his son, William, this inn property must have been included in his bequests, as in William's will the King's Head was specified as something he could leave to others.

Robert Leigh's 'leaving' and changes for the Queen's Servants

Of all the information that comes out of the 1623 depositions for the *Worth* v. *Baskervile* case, the most practical in terms of the company's history is the data concerning Ellis Worth. Worth was to be a successful actor into the succeeding Caroline era, associated with Andrew Cane at the Fortune for instance, as well as the Red Bull.[65] Because he was a main complainant in this important 1623 Chancery case for the company, each deponent who gave a statement was asked to disclose how long they had known him, and in this way we are given a chronology that pinpoints Worth's relationships and share-holding involvement with the company.

The dates that we are given for Worth's first meetings with the actors range over an extensive period. Richard Perkins is the first in 1603, when Perkins was twenty-four years old, and Worth only sixteen.[66] It would

---

[63] LMA O/257/001.

[64] See Christopher M. Matusiak, 'The Beestons and the Art of Theatrical Management in Seventeenth-Century London', Ph.D. thesis, University of Toronto, 2009 (available online at www.google.co.uk/u rl?sa=t&rct=j&q=&esrc=s&source=web&cd=1&ved=0CDIQFjAA&url=https%3A%2F%2Ftspace. library.utoronto.ca%2Fbitstream%2F1807%2F19203%2F6%2FMatusiak_Christopher_M_200911_ PhD_thesis.pdf.pdf&ei=KP1jUaKrA-KOoAWjtIDYAQ&usg=AFQjCNEFzyXl1G-HWEHx7XL GiKZQENt9Kw&sig2=7EA2BzlupLkXWmvXoEHS-A&bvm=bv.44990110,d.d2k&cad=rja; accessed 19 May 2013), Appendix D, 'Lancashire Record Office: DDSA 30/2/1': the 1591 will of Anthony Sandys, father of Cicely, Jane and Edwin.

[65] See Gerald Eades Bentley, 'The Troubles of a Caroline Acting Troupe: Prince Charles's Company', *Huntington Library Quarterly* 41 (1977–8), 217–49 for something of the Ellis Worth–Andrew Cane working relationship.

[66] TNA C24/500/103. Worth's age is taken from the *Cane* v. *Wintershall* case of 1654: TNA C24/785, Box 1.

be easy to assume that perhaps Worth was taken on as an apprentice with the company at that time. However, this possibility seems to be belied by the different years when other long-term members of the company say that they met him. Robert Leigh, for instance, claimed he met Worth in about 1605, when Leigh was thirty-six and Worth eighteen.[67] Thomas Heywood, thirty-four years old in 1607, met Worth in that year when Worth himself was twenty.[68] Perhaps the best latest date for Worth's first involvement with the company would be 1609. This could be indicated by the evidence of Richard Baxter, hired man among the players, who claimed in his deposition that he met both sides of the 1623 dispute in 1609–10 when he (Baxter) was sixteen or seventeen.[69] This may show that Baxter arrived in around 1609–10 as an apprentice, and so met the litigants all at once, where others of the company may have met Worth before he joined them. However, a 'Baxter' is also part of a group of young actors listed coming into the company some years later. What we can be sure of is that on the evidence of Christopher Beeston, the unfortunate actor, George Pulham, became a half-sharer in the 1610–11 period and, when he died soon after, his share, once bought for £60 (including a place to live), was acquired by Worth for £40.[70] Worth therefore became a sharer in the company at this time when he was between twenty-four and twenty-five years old, although he may have been a hired player with them before this period.

Worth's first share-holding involvement with the company in c. 1611 is perhaps indicative of the start of a change. Roger Clarke, who was only twelve in 1611, claimed that he first knew Worth and the Baskervile side in this year, pointing to the possibility that he was first associated with the company then. He said he knew John Blaney, another of the main complainants in the 1623 case, for even longer, and William Browne 'from his Childhood'.[71] Blaney was certainly a child actor, for he is named as one of the players in Jonson's *Epicoene*. This play was published in Jonson's folio of 1616, where the author stated that 'the Children of her Maiesties REVELLS' gave the first performance of it in 1609.[72] That the very young

---

[67] TNA C24/500/9, Int. 1.
[68] TNA C24/500/103, Int. 1.
[69] *Ibid.*
[70] TNA C24/500/9, Int. 5. Beeston clarified things by saying the £40 was not absolutely paid for the share, but for the 'said place wherin [Pulham] lived but a short tyme', and concerning which his family then found themselves in debt.
[71] TNA C24/500/103, Int. 1.
[72] Ben Jonson, *Epicoene*, ed. R. V. Holdsworth (London: Ernest Benn, 1979), pp. xvi–xvii.

Clarke knew Blaney before 1611 may well show that he could have been a child actor or of the Queen's Revels too. Thomas Drewe, twenty-five in 1611, deposed that he first knew both Worth and Blaney from this time. He also emphasised that he had nothing to do with the company while George Pulham was alive, which indicates his association began later than Pulham's death in 1611.[73]

One last actor who would seem to have been associated with the actors since *c.* 1611 – Francis Walpole – was twenty-six when he met the Baskerviles for the first time, but he also said that he had already met Worth and Blaney in 1606–7 when he was about twenty-one.[74] Walpole and Worth were of an age, as was Drewe. If not child actors, they were certainly a younger generation of actor among the Queen's Servants, knowing one another, it would seem, from before Thomas Greene's death. The possibility that these actors – entering the annals of Queen's Servants history *c.* 1610–13 – were perhaps children's company-related is intriguing, as this is the recognised period when the activities of the children's companies were at least in a state of flux if not coming to a kind of end. With such a situation the actors involved may have slotted into other, more 'adult' companies.[75] The market for the children's company style of play may also have seemed open, and perhaps the number of court-room drama plays that came into the Queen's Servants' repertoire – outlined below – may be seen as written in order to appeal to inns-of-court audiences, for example.

Coinciding with this possible injection of new blood into the company at this time was the departure of the oldest member of the Jacobean Queen's men – Robert Leigh.[76] Leigh would have been significantly older than these younger actors coming in, although he had always seemed of a somewhat wandering intention. Leigh's name was on that performing permission of 1606, recorded in Southampton, along with Martin Slatiar and Roger Barfield, and, as E. K. Chambers points out, there are records of a touring company going by the name of the Queen's Men at times when the London playhouses were open and working.[77] This confirms simply, and from an older theatre history perspective, what becomes

[73] TNA C24/500/9, Ints. 1 and 5. The first record for Drewe in Clerkenwell is when he was married in February 1612.
[74] TNA C24/500/103, Int. 1.
[75] See Munro, *Children of the Queen's Revels*, pp. 23–5; and various actors given biographical entries in her Appendices C and D, pp. 179–86.
[76] TNA C24/500/9, Ints. 1, 5 and 31.
[77] *ES*, Vol. II, pp. 233–4.

plainer and plainer today – that there was a separate touring version or versions of the Queen's Servants, one possibly led by Leigh at the time when he declared he had 'left the *said* Company, and disposed of himself elsewhere'.[78]

There is further evidence of Leigh's 'leaving' in around 1611–12 – an exemplification granted him in January, for instance, which cost him 20s 4d (seemingly the going rate for such permissions at that time).[79] However, even if this was intended for immediate touring (it was recorded as presented in a City of Norwich record of 1617 – see below), we know that Leigh accepted payments for Queen's Servants performances at court during the period 1613–16. During this period, a meeting took place when a group of actors from all the main London companies were called before the Privy Council. This meeting was held in April 1615 and concerned performing during Lent. Both Leigh and Beeston were named to appear, and one wonders how comfortable the two actors were on this occasion, at this time heading, apparently, two different kinds of Queen's Servants company.[80]

A matter also already discussed is the occasion when Leigh tried to give up the profession of playing, and his right to call himself a Servant of the Queen. This was in *c.* 1616 and is recorded in that case of *c.* 1618 where the actors were affronted by his attempt to rob them, in fact, not only of their name and their properties, but also of their younger actors. Despite their financial difficulties after the Cockpit riot, Leigh, contrary to his stated wish that he did not want to be a party to them again and wished to give back various 'cloaths^ book*es* of playes, & other good*es*', called in some bonds and tried to make off with their trainees.[81]

The actors claimed they had made losses to the tune of £500 'in the Riffling of their house'. This house was most likely the Cockpit, which ended up Beeston's rather than the company's. However, as already discussed, on the National Archives document itself, the name of the theatre is non-existent.

---

[78] TNA C24/500/9, Leigh, Int. 5. It is in Int. 31 that he reveals he did not return until Christmas 1618.

[79] TNA AO3/379/3, p. 26; Wallace papers, Box 2, File B1, 11.

[80] The date the warrant was issued was 29 March 1615. The following were ordered to appear: 'John Hemming*es*, Richard Burbidge, Christopher Beeston, Robert Lee, William Rowley, John Newton, Thomas Downton, Humphry Jeffe*s*'; TNA PC2/27, fos. 283–283v.

[81] TNA C2/JASI/P16/14.

Repertoire considerations, the Cockpit riot and
Robert Leigh's 'return'

Despite all the horrors since 1612, the Queen's Servants did produce plays and publish them, some of them with specialist woodcuts, such as *The Foure Prentises of London* (London, 1615) and *Swetnam the Woman-Hater* (London, 1620). Both of these are specified Red Bull plays. Some care should be taken when actually believing the evidence of actors who claimed the company was poor at this time. Firstly, there would hardly have been so many legal wranglings such as with the *Woodford* v. *Holland* series of suits or Susan Baskervile's insistence on her payments if there was no money to be made from them. The Worth side of the *Worth* v. *Baskervile* case put questions to actors designed to demonstrate how poor they were, but this was representative of their argument in the case – that they could not pay Susan Baskervile any more. Something that was struck from Thomas Heywood's evidence concerned Beeston's management over an approximate three-year period, claiming there was no 'accompt therof by him made' while at the time there was 'eight or nyne pownds in a day received at the doors & Galleries'.[82] Heywood, it seems, did not believe the company was so poor.

More court-room drama is certainly evident in the Queen's Servants' repertoire from *c*. 1612, with Webster's *The White Devil* and Dekker's *If This Be Not a Good Play the Devil Is in It* – a comedy that ends with a court scene and punishment in hell. Then there was a play called *The Honest Lawyer* (London, 1616) and Webster's *The Devil's Law Case* (London, 1623), the latter possibly performed at the Cockpit.[83] There may be several other component reasons for this perceived change, one being that with jigs – at that time – banned, and Greene dead, a more formal type of drama could have seemed the direction to take. As time went on, with the Cockpit more and more a possibility, the proximity of the inns of court to Holborn and the Strand may have made this type of drama seem a more sensible repertoire approach. The Cockpit did not provably present all this legally interested drama in the brief time the company performed there, however, for we should not forget that *Swetnam the Woman-Hater* has multiple court-room scenes, and was firmly advertised as a Red Bull play.

[82] TNA C24/500/9, Heywood, Int. 33.
[83] It was advertised, on its title-page, 'As it was approouedly well Acted / by her Maiesties Seruants' when there was, as yet, no other Queen to give it patronage.

It would have made good sense for the company to repeat their already proven successes during this time: for example, the *If You Know Not Me You Know Nobody* plays, which went on being published in the period after their first editions (Part I in 1606, 1608, 1610, 1613 and beyond; Part II in 1609 and beyond), and *The Rape of Lucrece*, which also continued to be printed after 1608 with the songs swelling in number (1609, 1614 and beyond).

In whatever way the plays of the repertoire were apportioned, according to what we know of the Queen's Servants' history, their indoor playhouse dreams proved short-lived. It was during Shrovetide 1617 that the Cockpit was all but destroyed by rioting apprentices.[84] There is an account of this recorded by Edward Sherbourne dated 8 March:

> The Prentizes on Shrove Tewsday last, to the nomber of 3. or 4000 comitted extreame insolencies; part of this nomber, taking their course for Wapping, did there pull downe to the grownd 4 houses, spoiled all the goods therein, defaced many others, & a Justice of the Peace coming to appease them, while he was reading a Proclamation, had his head broken with a brick batt. Th' other part, making for Drury Lane, where lately a newe play-house is erected, they besett the house round, broke in, wounded divers of the players, broke open their trunckes, & whatt apparrell, bookes, or other things they found, they burnt & cutt in peeces; & not content herewith, gott on the top of the house, & untiled it, & had not the Justices of Peace & Sherife levied an aide & hindred their purpose, they would have laid that house likewise even with the grownd. In this skyrmishe one prentise was slaine, being shott throughe the head with a pistoll, & many other of their fellowes were sore hurt, & such of them as are taken his Majestie hath commaunded shal be executed for example sake.[85]

It is likely this account denotes the 'Riffling', then, which cost the company £500 according to the court case with Leigh, who had professed wanting to give up his Queen's man status in 1616. Was it the success of Beeston that in some way prompted this desire? The two men had to meet when they were part of that group of representatives from companies called in to discuss playing in Lent in 1615.[86] In whatever way one looks at this, Leigh, as we know, did not give up the profession of acting. He set up a children's company, purloining many of the company's things including their trainees (according to the actors) – 'calling them by the name

---

[84] Shrove Tuesday fell on 4 March that year.
[85] *JCS*, Vol. VI, p. 54; Gurr, *Shakespearean Stage*, p. 14.
[86] TNA PC2/27, warrant calling actors together, ordered 29 March 1615 for a meeting the following Friday, fos. 283–283v.

of the children [of her/his] Ma*jesti*es Revells' – and took their ' *Lette*res Patente*s*', or licences. He also made impossible demands.

There are a number of questions or comments still arising out of that decaying document at The National Archives.[87] Firstly, because of the reductive state of the text, no one can be certain whether the words originally written concerned 'the children [of her] Ma*jesti*es Revells' or '[of his]', hinting that it is just as likely that it was the King's children's troupe as it was Queen Anna's. However, there are indications that Leigh may have involved himself with such a troupe, as there is some evidence that he joined with William Perry, Philip Rosseter and Nicholas Longe as leaders of a patented Children of the Revels company, the possible licence dated to 31 October 1617 on evidence. On 31 May that year, 'Robe*rt* Lee' is recorded coming into the Norwich offices with his exemplification of 1612, a copy of the official patent of 1609. Although it named all the other Queen's Servants not present, the city's authorities allowed this man's company to play the following week.[88] A few days later, on 4 June, the letter from the Lord Chamberlain – William Herbert, earl of Pembroke – dated 16 July the previous year, was recorded in Norwich. This concerned companies who should not be trusted, with William Perry named as one who had acquired a warrant under the name of 'the Children of hir Ma*iesti*es Revelle*s*'.[89] According to the Records of Early English Drama for Norwich, by 29 August 1618, 'Lee' came into the offices again, this time with 'Philip Rossiter will*ia*m Percy & Nicholas Longe', with a 31 October 1617 'Commission', not naming the company.[90] Although this, as a piece of evidence possibly linking Leigh with a children's company, is appealing – thus potentially connecting him with such a company on tour – there is an initial difficulty with a Perry linked to a children's company mentioned in a letter of July 1616, carrying a patent, according to the later entry, dated to the last day of October 1617.[91] This must have been yet another patent. As already stated, with Leigh accused of farming out licences, any record naming him should be treated with a measure of insecurity in terms of identity. On *some* occasions, hard to identify, a

[87] TNA C2/JASI/P16/14.
[88] See NRO, Mayors' Court Books XV, 16.a, fo. 132v; Galloway, *Norwich 1540–1642*, pp. 150–1.
[89] NRO, Mayors' Court Books XV, 16.a, fo. 133; Galloway, *Norwich 1540–1642*, pp. 151–2.
[90] NRO, Mayors' Court Books XV, 16.a, fo. 204; Galloway, *Norwich 1540–1642*, p. 157.
[91] Longe brought back the patent involving 'the yuthes & Children of the Revelles of Quene Ann' on 9 June 1619, but was rejected because, by this time, the Queen had died. NRO, Mayors' Court Books XV, 16.a, fo. 240v; Galloway, *Norwich 1540–1642*, p. 159.

recorded Leigh presence may well have been someone pretending to be Leigh.[92]

In the context of the Queen's interests, seeking redress from Sir Francis Bacon with the case against Leigh might not have been as much of a foregone conclusion as it at first seems. Not only was Bacon made Lord Chancellor in 1618, and therefore the correct person to whom this case should have been addressed, but he was also, according to the Queen's Accounts of 1615/16, a 'Serjeant at Law' in her household.[93] This meant he inherently had a more direct relationship with the difficulties of the Queen's players as a legal adviser to their patron. Bacon was also mentioned by Christopher Beeston during his deposition for the *Worth* v. *Baskervile* case. In an apparent, no doubt exasperated, response to Susan's successful approach to the Queen's Chamberlain, Sir Robert Sidney, Beeston managed to secure a 'Referrance' from Bacon, 'then Lord Keeper of the great seale', for them to go to 'Sr Charles Caesar, ^Knt^' – one of the masters of Chancery according to Beeston – to 'consider of the matter and therupon to certefie' Sidney. In the end they did not pursue the contact. Instead,

> for Quietnes sake and bycause they could not follow their Imploymentes & Studye, wherupon their Livinges depended, They yeilded to pay the said defendente Susan, the said Summe of xviili xs at seuerall paymentes.[94]

He took the decision, in other words, that the actors were better off learning their lines and concentrating on rehearsals etc., rather than going through the anxiety of approaches to powerful people who might help them with Susan Baskervile's claims.

A matter worthy of comment concerns the number of 'young men' specified whom the actors had 'trayned up & fitted for that quallety' – namely the '7 or more' – that Leigh tried to take from the company. Seven 'or more' would seem to be quite a large quota of trainees. Speculation as to who these players could have been involves relating a range of information. Thomas Basse gave evidence about seven new members accepted into the company since 1617 in answer to a question about whether arriving players had given security to Susan Baskervile and William Browne for the payments expected from the company. Basse replied to this in the negative. This interrogatory question in the *Worth* v. *Baskervile* case

---

[92] A later licence under the 'Sygnet' is recorded 'to Robert Lee and Nicholas Longe with the rest of their Companie to play Comedies histories Interludes & Subscribed by the lo: Chamberlaine', dated 'the 24th ffebruary' 1619/20. It cost '6–8'. See TNA SO 3/7, unpaginated.

[93] TNA SC6/JASI/1650, fo. 18v. He is also described as one of her 'Counsellors at Lawe' in the incomplete accounts; E101/437/8, fo. 30.

[94] TNA C24/500/9, Int. 23.

represents a difficulty that the Queen's Servants had with reference to a specific clause in the 1617 agreement. This clause indicated that whoever joined the company after the signing of the indenture should be liable for the payments agreed in it. Indeed, it insisted that the company should actively 'procure' replacements to be equally bound to the agreement.

Because of this clause, some company members initially refused to sign; those that signed did so on the understanding that the covenants were only in force while four of those that signed played together.[95] Some actors still refused to sign. These included Thomas Basse, who deposed in a passage containing some deletions that: 'this dep*onen*t ^Robert Reynolde*s*, Emanuell Read^, & Richard Parkins being named for partyes unto the *s*aid *p*roduced deed did forbeare to seale & deliuer the same And this dep*onen*t for his owne parte would not be acquainted therwith, ~~as not well liking of the Busines therin conteyned~~.[96]

Emmanuel Reade was with the Lady Elizabeth's company before he became a servant of the Queen. We know this because he appeared in the cast lists of both *The Coxcomb* and *The Honest Man's Fortune*. He was with the Queen's Servants at the time of Susan Baskervile's agreement of 1616 but, as was stated, he was not involved in the June 1617 indenture. Reade stayed with the company only until he went to Ireland in about 1617, and in this way he missed out on signing the document. Indeed, it may have seemed best for Reade to go to Ireland. Two years before, it was Emmanuel Reade who had been detained at the Clink prison for the killing of Robert Dawes.[97] Dawes was that actor who had been associated with a Thomas Greene in the hanaper accounts. He was also someone who was linked with Martin Slatiar on the occasion of that assault on a waterman called Edmund Chambers. This occurred at the door of the Curtain playhouse in 1613.[98] A year after this, in 1614, we have a record of a detailed contract between Philip Henslowe and Robert Dawes, ensuring his sobriety and requiring his care with a company's costumes and properties after performances.[99] During 1615, however – it seems – he was killed.

Emmanuel Reade, the accused perpetrator, was, according to Elizabeth Perkins (wife of Richard Perkins), a particular friend of Christopher Beeston. Mrs Perkins claimed that when Reade returned to England in

[95] TNA C2/JASI/W2/67; Fleay, *A Chronicle History of the London Stage*, pp. 276–7.
[96] TNA C24/500/9, Basse, Int. 35.
[97] TNA KB29/259, m. 43.
[98] LMA MJ/SR/0523/219, 220, 221; TNA KB29/255, m. 84d.
[99] For the text of this contract and another interesting Dulwich item mentioning Dawes, see *EPT*, pp. 219, 282–4.

1620 he had 'made his abode in Jreland by the space of two or three yeares last past or thearabout*es* with his wife & familie and about Easter last did come into England and did lye often tymes in the howse of the said xpofer Beeston & was much in his company whilest he was in England'.[100]

Robert Reynolds, the other actor who did not sign the 1617 indenture, although named in Worth's bill as involved in the one of 1616, was the player discussed concerning the touring company evident in records of Europe.[101] He was the one who has been linked to the comedic character 'Pickleherring', who is mentioned in these records, although other scholarship has questioned whether Reynolds was the original comedian who introduced this character.[102] The provenance of this touring company, as has been demonstrated, provides strong links with the Servants of Queen Anna, because of the actors involved, the European courts that they travelled to and the plays they performed.

Robert Leigh's seven 'young men'?

Back in England, the seven actors whom Basse named for having joined since the signing of the 1617 agreement, but who had not made themselves parties to it, were listed as 'Rowley, Newton, Hobbs, Hamlett, Mathew Smyth, Anth*ony* Smyth [and] Baxter'.[103] Richard Baxter we have come across before as another deponent in the *Worth* v. *Baskervile* case, and we know from this that he had known both sides of the case since 1609. Most of the others whom Basse listed have – up until now – only been associated in research with Prince Charles' Men. However, their now known involvement with Queen Anna's company is worthy of note and is also interesting in the context of other puzzles to do with inter-company associations. Bentley wrote about these in his entries on the Lady Elizabeth's and this company.[104]

In essence, according to Bentley, it would seem that Lady Elizabeth's company, including Thomas Basse and Emmanuel Reade until about 1615–17, also included Robert Hamlen, or 'Hamlett'. Hamlen signed the company's bond with Henslowe in 1611 when Basse was also associated

---

[100] 27 June 1620. TNA REQ 1/130; Wallace, 'Three London Theatres of Shakespeare's Time', p. 336. According to Mrs Perkins, when Reade left this time he said he would not return to England again.
[101] TNA C2/JASI/W2/67; Fleay, *A Chronicle History of the London Stage*, p. 275.
[102] Schrickx, 'Pickleherring'; Eccles, 'Elizabethan Actors III', pp. 302–3.
[103] TNA C24/500/9, Basse, Int. 40.
[104] *JCS*, Vol. I, pp. 176, 199–217.

with them.[105] In March 1613, Philip Rosseter combined the Lady Elizabeth's with the then Queen's Revels' children's company to work under Philip Henslowe and, it would seem, because of difficulties experienced after this time, grievances were issued against Henslowe by this amalgamated company.[106] At around that time, Bentley surmises, the Lady Elizabeth's actors made some kind of agreement with the Prince's Men, and he cites four reasons why this should have been so. Firstly, William Rowley and John Newton, ostensibly of the Prince's company, were present to represent both companies before the Privy Council in that meeting of early April 1615, along with representatives of all the companies to consider Lent playing.[107] Secondly, Alexander Foster, a one-time Lady Elizabeth's man, received payments at court for four Prince's Men plays during the next winter. Thirdly, Philip Rosseter was given a patent to build a playhouse in the Blackfriars ('Porters Hall') to house the three companies – the Lady Elizabeth's, the Prince's and the Queen's Revels – in June 1615 (although this ultimately failed). Lastly, Nathan Field's *Amends for Ladies* (1618) states on the title-page that it was played by two companies – the Lady Elizabeth's and the Prince's Men.[108]

Bentley, I feel, was right to call this a 'co-operation' rather than an 'amalgamation', for the association became even more complicated into the next period. What we see is that many of the same new actors who came to be part of the Red Bull company post-1617 had been of a group who owed Henslowe money and signed articles of agreement in 1616 concerning this ('William Rowley, John Newton, Thomas Hobbes, Joseph Taylor, Robert Hamlen, William Barksted, Robert Pallant, Hugh Attwell, William Penn, and Anthony Smith').[109] Perhaps, when trying to isolate a period when these young actors arrived, we should take into account how Christopher Beeston, claiming he was himself a Prince's Man by early 1619, apparently took Prince Charles' Men into the Cockpit after ousting the Queen's Servants – whom he had left shortly before. We should also consider that it could have been for a period after May 1622 when these Prince's Men arrived at the Red Bull to be taken in as part of the new company.

[105] *Ibid.*, pp. 360, 459.
[106] *Ibid.*, p. 176; Gurr, *Shakespearean Stage*, pp. 58–60.
[107] TNA PC2/27, fos. 283–283v.
[108] *JCS*, Vol. I, pp. 176, 198.
[109] *Ibid.*, p. 199. 'Robert Pallant' may well be the son of the original core member of Queen Anna's men.

We know Beeston became a Prince's Man from his evidence in the *Smith* v. *Beeston* case of 1619–20, where he states that after he had left the company he 'entred into the service of the most noble Prince Charles'.[110] Bentley describes how the Prince's Men only lasted with Beeston until May 1622, relating how they moved to the Curtain when he took in the Lady Elizabeth's.[111]

These questions about the presence of these actors represent puzzles about possible Prince's Men at the Red Bull after 1617 that have existed before. Bentley muses on the possibility that, when the Prince's company wrote to Edward Alleyn about their lack of a theatre to play in during the winter of 1616/17, Alleyn somehow got them into the Clerkenwell playhouse. Bentley stated that this suggestion 'cannot be definitely established as a fact', but now, with Basse's evidence, it can be presented as a possibility.[112] Bentley went on to describe how Alleyn must have wanted his £200 gallery takings owed to him by the Prince's company, and that this was the reason why he continued to take an interest in them. Pointing to the supposed vacancy of the Red Bull when the Queen's Servants company moved to the Cockpit in early 1617 (before the riot), he speculates that Alleyn could have moved them into Clerkenwell, where they could have played in their own name and right. However, Basse claimed that these players were accepted into the Queen's Servants/Revels company, not that they played as the Prince's Men in any isolated way.

The last piece of evidence that Bentley mentions with reference to the Prince's Men at the Red Bull at this time is how on 1 October 1617 Alleyn 'came to London in ye coach & went to ye red bull'. Two days later he went again 'to ye red bull & R/ for ye younger brother, but 3. 6. 4.'. This visit Bentley sees as evidence of Alleyn claiming his cut in the Prince's Men's takings while at the playhouse, but I know no proof of this idea today.

There is certainly evidence, little articulated, that actors' affiliations with companies during this period represented shifting phenomena. By this I mean that when you were a patented member of a company this did not mean that you had to perform under that company name for the whole duration of your patron's life or that you could not feel able to 'co-operate' at will. Pallant was on both the draft patent for the Queen's

---

[110] TNA REQ2/459, Part 1 (or see Wallace, 'Three London Theatres of Shakespeare's Time', p. 40; *JCS*, Vol. VI, p. 58). Beeston says he waited until after Queen Anna's death to do this; yet in the *Worth* v. *Baskervile* suit he makes it clear that he left her company before this, at Christmas 1618.

[111] *JCS*, Vol. VI, pp. 58–9.

[112] See *JCS*, Vol. VI, p. 201.

company in 1604 and the official one of 1609, but there is very little evidence of his actual presence in Clerkenwell. Pallant's name, however, was included in the funeral list for the Queen's Servants' attendance in 1619, as was that of Christopher Beeston, who was a Prince's Man (or so he said) at this time. Similarly, although Rowley, Newton, Hobbes and co. were members of the actors' company in 1623 according to Thomas Basse, this did not prevent them from being included in the funeral arrangements for King James in 1625 as the 'Comaedians' of 'The Chamber of our Dread Soueraigne Lord King Charles'.[113]

What is probably true is that these extra actors were not the trainee players that Robert Leigh filched from the company, for they were clearly already experienced. The identities of Robert Leigh's trainee actors – seven or more of them – remain, for now, a mystery.

The players up to 1622

Whoever the itinerant trainee actors might have been that Robert Leigh tried to take from the Queen's Servants, it would appear that quarrels were resolved by 1618 for long enough for him to return to the company and help them reduce Susan Baskervile's payments to 2 s 6d per day. He then, self-confessedly, left them again after disagreements, probably to do with the problems set before Sir Francis Bacon. Leigh was enough of a Queen's Servants member to be listed for the funeral procession of 1619, however.

This must have been a very strange gathering of old associates: the now patronless company together with Leigh the difficult, and Beeston the erring ex-leader. The company had just taken Leigh to court, and, resentful of Beeston's exit, the actors were about to give evidence against him in the *Smith* v. *Beeston* court case of that year. Thomas Drewe had left the company at Christmas 1618 according to his *Worth* v. *Baskervile* evidence, although he, like Beeston, was listed for the funeral.[114] James Holt was non-existent in the court cases; Swinnerton and Slatiar had been more involved with touring. Perkins thought himself away from the troupe from about 1618; he was a Revels Player for a time and then, all too briefly, with the King's Men from 1623 to 1625, before returning to the Cockpit and Beeston as one of Queen Henrietta Maria's men in 1626.[115] The career of

---

[113] TNA LC2/6, fo.73r; Wallace papers, Box 3, File B1, 20. 'Robert Hamlett', 'Anthonie Smith', 'William Rowley', 'William Carpenter', 'William Penn', 'John Newton', 'Gilbert Raison' and 'Thomas Hobbs' as a group are all given 4 yards of black cloth.

[114] TNA C24/500/9.

[115] He is in the cast list for James Shirley's *The Wedding* (London, 1629).

Heywood followed a similar trajectory, in that he became one of Beeston's circle. The full list at the funeral, in order, was:

> Robert Leigh, Richard Parkins, Christopher Beeston, Robert Pallant, Thomas Heywood, James Hoult, Thomas Swin*n*erton, Martin Slater, Ellis Wroth [*sic*], John Cumber, Thomas Basse, John Blany, William Robinson, John Edmonds, ^b^ Gregorie Saunderson, a Thomas Drewe.[116]

The actors who appear on this list but who have so far not been mentioned have little to offer us in the way of further knowledge about them. A John Edmonds was given clothes in the will of Thomas Pope, the particular friend of William Kemp, and, living south of the river, he married into a half-share of the Globe theatre via Mary Clarke, another Pope beneficiary. In April 1618, a 'Letter of Assistance' from the Privy Council was written. It was shown at Exeter in June, citing Martin Slatiar, John Edmonds and Nathaniel Clay, giving them permission to perform 'in Bristol or any city, &c. under the power of the patent to John Daniel'.[117] William Robinson, or Robbins, stuck with the Red Bull into its next period. He was to become a long-term Servant of Queen Henrietta Maria at the Cockpit and died during the Civil War, the victim of a war crime in today's parlance.[118] Very little is known of Gregorie Saunderson at this time.

The ordering of the list is of interest. For some reason the person who wrote it wanted to change the ordering of the last two actors (Drewe had to come before Saunderson, and the terms 'a' and 'b' reversed them as listed). Quite what this means is hard to tell; however, the less familiar names come towards the end, and Drewe had been a Queen's man for a good amount of time by 1619.[119]

Meanwhile, the problems with Susan Baskervile's expectations of returns continued, but there had been good news for the company at Christmas 1618. As Thomas Drewe explained in his deposition for the Baskervile side, by this time the players were getting tired of paying the 3s 8d per day '^without abatem*ent*^'. However, 'Susan not of courtesie as this dep*onent* beleeveth, But rather for hir owne ends, did agree to accept fro*m* the *s*aid Company, onely two shillings six pence a day.'[120]

---

[116] TNA LC2/5, fo. 39. Each was given 4 yards of black cloth for the occasion.

[117] *JCS*, Vol. II, p. 431.

[118] A parliamentarian called Harrison refused quarter to the royalist Robbins 'and shot him in the head when he had laid down his Arms'. See *JCS*, Vol. II, pp. 547–9 (p. 549).

[119] Chambers, after Collier, included John Garret in the list. In the original he is not there. See *ES*, Vol. II, pp. 236, 240.

[120] TNA C24/500/9, Drewe, Int. 31.

Robert Leigh's evidence suggests that initially this reduction was only supposed to be in force for a year, however: 'afterwarde*s*, the s*ai*d year being expired The s*ai*d def*en*dan*t* ^Susan^ continued the Receipt or Receiuing of the s*ai*d Company, onely the s*ai*d Sum*me* of two shillinge*s* six pence by the day, for the space of three yeares after'.[121] This means that between 1618 and 1622, the company was granted a reduction in payments; however, Leigh also claimed he knew nothing more of other things because, soon after the agreement of 1618, he left the company again 'upon some discontents falling out amongst them'.[122] This was, presumably, around the time of the court case involving him. By this time, of course, they were no longer the Queen's Servants.

The Revels Players at the Red Bull and beyond

During this period, the company, now nominated the 'Revels Players', are known to have performed plays, but throughout the advertisements they offered concerning them it is notable how diffident they were about where they were playing. The plays of this time included '*A Pleasant Comedie*' by 'I. C.', entitled *The Two Merry Milke-Maids; or, The Best Words Weare the Garland* (Q. 1620). The title-page describes how it was 'Acted before the King, with generall Approbation, by the Com-*panie of the Reuels*'. Another play, 'Written by Phillip Messenger and Thomas Deker', was a tragedy called *The Virgin Martir*, and was licensed on 6 October 1620. It was published in 1622 'AS IT HATH BIN DIVERS times publickely Acted with great Applause, *By the seruants of his Maiesties Reuels*'. Also in 1622, Thomas May's comedy *The Heire* was published, advertising that it was 'lately Acted by the Company of the Reuels', and in a later edition of 1633 the first performance was pinpointed: 'As it was Acted by the Company of the Revels. 1620'. None of the above plays advertised that the company performed them at the Red Bull. It is not until the publication of *The true Tragedy of Herod and Antipater* by Gervase Markham and William Sampson in 1622, that the title-page advertises itself as '*late divers times publiquely Acted* (with great Applause) at the Red Bull, by the Company of his Maiesties REVELS'. Bentley also alluded to the title-page of a manuscript copy of a play called *The Two Noble Ladys and the Converted Coniurer*. This play was described as 'A Tragecomicall Historie often tymes acted with approbation

[121] TNA C24/500/9, Leigh, Int. 31.
[122] TNA C24/500/9, Leigh, Int. 34.

At the Red Bull in St Johns Street By the Company of the Reuells'. There is no date on the document, however.[123]

It is possible, then, that the company played, not only at the Red Bull but at other venues, in an effort, perhaps, to escape the Baskervile payments. For as Robert Leigh stated, the company only paid Susan Baskervile her 2s 6d per day 'for any day that they played at the *said* red Bull during these 4. yeares'.[124] The problems must have crescendoed by the time of John Cumber's death at Whitsuntide 1623, as Richard Perkins deposed.[125] For it was from that time onwards that the company decided they no longer needed to pay, presumably in view of the fact that their numbers had gone down below the original three or four members stipulated in the agreement.

The players were permitted a licence to train up child actors. A warrant was made to the Signet Office for the King's signature on 8 July 1622, which was signed by 'Mr Windebank' on 22 July. This was an enterprise Robert Leigh seems to have cherished. The relevant part of the warrant was thus worded:

> Robert Lee Richard Perkins Ellis woorth Thomas Bass^e. John Blany John Cumber and Will: Robins late Commedians to Queene Ann^e. deceased to bring vp Children in the quallitie and exercise of playing Commedyes Histories Enterludes Morralle pastoralls Stage playes and such other like aswell for the Sollace and pleasure of his Maj*es*^tie as for the honest recreacion of such as shall desier to see themto be called by the name of the Children of the Revells.[126]

By November the players had returned to wanting to perform themselves:

[123] Anon., *The Two Noble Ladies*, ed. Rebecca G. Rhoads, Malone Society Reprints (Oxford: Malone Society, 1930). See *JCS*, Vol. I, p. 166.

[124] TNA C24/500/9, Int. 32.

[125] TNA C24/500/103, Int. 11.

[126] Inner Temple Library, The Petyt Collection, MS 515, Vol. VII, found between fos. 20 and 53v. This manuscript is taken to be the 'Lord Chamberlain's Entry Book, 1 October 1621 to 30 September 1622'. On the original flyleaf it says 'A Book containing several particulars with relation to the King's servants, petitions, warrants, bills etc. and may be supposed to be a copy of some part of the Lord Chamberlain of the Household's Book in and about the year 1622'. See J. Conway Davies, ed., *Catalogue of Manuscripts in the Library of the Honourable Society of the Inner Temple*, 3 vols. (Oxford University Press for the Masters of the Bench of the Inner Temple, 1972), Vol. I, p. 316 for a record of Ellis Worth's collecting 20 nobles as well as a reward of £3 6s 8d, for a play called *Gramercy* on the previous 30 December. This is found alongside a Prince's Men payment of the same sum for two plays a few days earlier. My transcript here is taken from John Tucker Murray, *The English Dramatic Companies, 1558–1642*, 2 vols. (London: Constable, 1910), Vol. II, pp. 193–4.

A Warra*n*t: vnder the Signet to licence Robert Lee Richard Perkins and others Comedians to the late Queene Anne to exercise the quality & Arte of Stage players as they haue bin heretofore accoustomed.[127]

In that year, Sir John Astley listed the members of the company playing at the Red Bull:

The names of the chiefe players at the Red Bull, called the players of the Revells. Robert Lee, Richard Perkings, Ellis Woorth, Thomas Basse, John Blany, John Cumber, William Robbins.[128]

So – we assume – with many of the company back together again in 1622 (excluding, noticeably, Drewe, Heywood and Beeston), a percentage of the inter-company problems should have been resolved, if their direction seemed somewhat insecure. During 1623, things seemed to change again, particularly by the summer. So at the time of the opening addresses in the *Worth* v. *Baskervile* suit, attitudes hung in the balance, with some of those involved perhaps confused, vague, or all too angled towards one opinion or another – or, more tellingly, towards one powerful playhouse impresario in particular.

The Revels Players – according to records – were no longer playing at the Red Bull during the 1623 part of the court case, as the conclusion to this book will relate.

[127] TNA SO3/7, unpaginated. It was subscribed by the 'L: Chamb*e*rlaine and by order from him'.
[128] Bawcutt, *The Control and Censorship of Caroline Drama*, p. 136.

Conclusion: St John's Day at night

Although we could proceed further with this history up until 1626, when the *Worth* v. *Baskervile* court case finished, it would be well to end this company's story at 1623. This is because much of the evidence from the case has already been used to tell us about the Queen's Servants company – a *Jacobean* entity – our main concern. The 1620s Red Bull becomes of interest with the intimation of playhouse yard development and expansion – and we should not forget this as we contemplate the different companies that came into the playhouse at this time, excluding the Revels Players, by 1623. When it comes to company history, evidence demonstrates the determinedly fractured nature (perhaps helpfully fractured) that the one-time multi-venue entity represented.

In contrast to Astley's description of the Revels Players of 1622, Nigel Bawcutt presented entries taken from versions of Sir Henry Herbert's office-book concerning both the theatre and the company that played there in 1623, like this:

> The Princes Players – A french Tragedy of the Belman of <Paris contayning 40> sheetes written by Thomas Drickers & John <Day, for the company> of the Read-bull this 30 July 1623. Ili. o[1]
>
> For the Princes servants of the Rede Bull – An oulde <play called the> Peacable Kinge or the lord Mendall former<ly allowed of by Sir> George Bucke & likewise by mee & because <itt was free from adition> or reformation I tooke no fee this 19th Augt. <1623>[2]
>
> For the lady Eliz:s Players. September
>
> A new Comedy called the Cra Marchant <or come to my Cuntry> houss contayninge 9 sheetes may be acted <this 12th Septr. 1623> Written by William Bonen.

---

[1] Bawcutt, *The Control and Censorship of Caroline Drama*, p. 141. Angle brackets, for Bawcutt, are used for 'text that is in varying degrees problematic'. They are also used when Halliwell-Phillips edited transcripts and 'wrote in the missing words himself'. See *ibid.*, p. 124.

[2] *Ibid.*, p. 142.

It was acted at the Red Bull & licensed without <my hande to itt because> they were none of the foure companys[3]

According to Bentley, the company at the Curtain in August 1623 were allowed to perform 'A Tragedy of *the Plantation of Virginia*' – as long as the 'profaneness' was left out.[4] Companies of 'Strangers' performed in the autumn to winter of 1623 without licence from Herbert – for they were 'none of the *four* companys', according to him.[5] One play that we know was performed at the Red Bull by a company of 'Strangers' was John Day's 'Come see a wonder', which was dated to 18 September. The Prince's company presented a new comedy called 'a *Fault in Friendship*', written by 'Young Johnson, and Broome', on 2 October – venue not mentioned – which cost them a pound, and then another record of a Red Bull 'Strangers' company exists concerning a play called 'The *Fayre Fowle One: or the Baytinge of Jealous Knight*, written by Smithe', costing £2 for a 28 November performance.[6]

In 1632, Susan Baskervile had her court case with Christopher Beeston, which told us much of the playhouse-ownership of her one-time husband, Thomas Greene, and, indeed, of Beeston's ownership of a part of Greene's half of the tiring house. Baskervile described how Beeston had agreed to pay £5 per term (£20 per year) as rent for his share, which he had duly paid over both before and since the death of Thomas Greene. However, Susan accused him of underhandedly acquiring the documented agreement that he had made with her husband Greene, and of not paying her his rent since. Further:

> the said Christopher haueinge conceiued some uniust and causeles displeasure against your subiect he hath for these fiue years last past deteined the saide Rent and foreborne to pay the same or any parte thereof to your subiect as formerly he had ^did^ done to your subiects said Husband and since to your subiect her selfe contrary to all right equity and good conscience albeit your subiect hath ^often^ both by her selfe and others in frendly manner demaunded the same of him and albeit he knoweth in his conscience the saide rent is truly due.[7]

[3] *Ibid.*, pp. 144–5. Bawcutt believes this permission must have been erroneously appended, as 'the Lady Elizabeth's players were definitely one of the four companies, and did not play at the Red Bull'. The speculative thinking is that this may be a play called *The Crafty Merchant* that was entered into the Stationers' Register in 1653.

[4] *JCS*, Vols. V, pp. 1495–6; and VI, p. 137.

[5] Bawcutt, *The Control and Censorship of Caroline Drama*, p. 144.

[6] *Ibid.*, p. 147.   [7] TNA REQ2/709.

He had not paid his rent despite the fact that he still enjoyed 'his saide *par*te and share of the p*ro*fitts and benefitts of the saide Playhouse truely'.

Five years before 1632 takes us back to 1627, the year after the *Worth* v. *Baskervile* suit of 1623–6. Could it be that in the aftermath of the case Beeston was to find himself turning against the old clown's wife who had caused the company such difficulties? With the death of Sir Robert Sidney, the earl of Leicester, in 1626, Beeston, seeing Susan's significant champion dead, may have realised that she was now a woman of straw where her rights were concerned. He was fast becoming a powerful theatre person, and, having a main hand in moving companies between venues, perhaps it seemed to Beeston that Susan was much more dependent on him than he – or the companies he moved – were in any way dependent on her.

With reference to the main venue, the Red Bull, this book has achieved a sweep of new information as far as its concept, its building and all its contexts as a project are concerned, including the all-important ground beneath it. Set in Clerkenwell, a place that the City of London had always associated with entertainment from medieval times, the playhouse, like a fair few others, was built on ex-monastic property – but this time developed within a Reformation charitable context. The woman responsible for handing over the lease of the inn-yard built on St Mary's nunnery land was a City of London brewer's daughter who had married well – into a family of England's nobility. This family had most famously served England during Queen Mary's time; however, their service went on with the changing orders. One of their number had been associated with that other piece of monastic land in Clerkenwell at St John's, where the Office of the Revels was located until *c.* 1608.

Perhaps the simplest, most useful issue that can emerge from information about the actors who played at the Red Bull in its earliest years concerns to what extent shifting movements of players took place across the board during the rise of the commercial playhouse. This movement of players occurred despite patented company allegiance. Take, for example, the evidence explored concerning the Oxford's/Worcester's amalgamation of 1602, where it cannot be explained unequivocally which players were originally from what company. Firstly, we can either assume that patented members of companies could simply combine in the period running up to royal patronage with the new reign. Alternatively, we can understand, with the use of later evidence concerning Stuart patented members moving into other companies (but retaining their licensed status with an original company), that movement between companies was an accepted custom, whether specifically permitted or not. The evidence derived from the *Worth* v. *Baskervile* case of 1623 is considerable, as is the new information obtained via the use of C. W. Wallace's papers.

The impression that is gained of Christopher Beeston is one that requires patient rethinking, as do a number of perceptions. It would appear that the theatre impresario of the succeeding period did, indeed, escape from the Queen's Servants, carrying what they thought to be their private indoor theatre in tow. There was nothing illegal about what he did, as he built and paid for the Cockpit – but it seems likely that he built it with a suspicious amount of Red Bull money, as the actors clearly thought. Perhaps he held the money legitimately, believing the company would find a home at the Cockpit. The company and their associates clearly believed it too – that the Cockpit would be their theatre in the future, as the stipulation of making payments to Baskervile and her son via the Drury Lane venue makes clear. Either this was the case or, with changing fortunes, Christopher Beeston steered an alternative course. Perhaps he, Drewe and even Perkins knew that a Red Bull company reduced meant escaping Susan Baskervile's demands.

Beeston's now provable involvement with the Red Bull playhouse as a sharer in the building contextualises his attempt at firm separation from the company, and complicates and informs knowledge that had before seemed straightforward, if incomplete. At odds with the impression we have had of Beeston previously, it would appear that he was prepared to assist his old company with problems – with the Holden case of 1633, for example – as someone who still profited from their work. He was not averse to taking a continued interest in further inn or inn-yard projects, as the evidence of his involvement with the King's Head, Shoreditch shows. This interest would seem to counter the idea of Beeston as solely the investor in the indoor venue for more reasons than drama alone. Catering, too, was a Beeston family interest, as disputes over plans for a tavern near the Cockpit show, and it should be remembered that access to further profits through the drinking and socialising associated with entertainment would always have been a consideration.[8]

A better understanding of Martin Slatiar has been achieved, and Thomas Greene the clown emerges as a vibrant personality who appeared

---

[8] See, e.g., TNA PC2/50, pp. 271, 280 (records of 1639); and TNA C2/CHASI/H28/26 concerning the George Tavern, retrospectively, from 1647.

to shoulder management with both energy and sensitivity. He came from nowhere that we (currently) know of in theatre history terms, prior to his appearance in records beginning in 1603–4 with the fading away of Will Kemp. We now have the benefit of some contextualisation concerning Queen Anna and her circle, and the performances that the company presented both before the King's court and that of the Queen, alongside some evidence of multiple versions of the company, playing both in England and in Queen Anna's Europe. Equally it is understood that the company was licensed to perform at more than one venue in the Middlesex area (the Boar's Head, the Curtain and – because Beeston was among them – the Cockpit near Drury Lane). Although 'citizen fare' is often invoked and may be perceived as an important element of the Queen's Servants/Red Bull repertoire, more than one targeted audience can be perceived once the plays are put into a chronological perspective. We also start to appreciate the generic scope of what these actors truly played – with sophisticated tragedy and tragi-comedy thrown into the mix.

The job of a true repertoire appreciation has yet to be completed, however, and it is hoped that alongside, for example, the Heywood work of Richard Rowland, and that begun by Grace Ioppolo, an understanding of the whole context of an author's works within the economic group where they belonged may be achieved. The flavour of the early Red Bull repertoire was one that relished spectacle, battle scenes, fireworks, song and special effects, as well as morally edifying thought for citizen men and women. The later Queen's Servants appear more thoughtful in approach with the presentation of new works, while carrying on the job (no doubt) of producing old favourites. I have perceived a division between the Queen's Servants' history pre-1612 and post-1612, both in the context of management – with the death of Thomas Greene and Christopher Beeston's taking over – and in a developing personnel. The agency of Robert Leigh still seems one that is important; however, the sense of his part remains as yet incomplete. The situation feels like one where he acted as an important catalyst within the chemistry of the company. What becomes clear is that – as a group, for some reason – these players took both the activity of training actors, and the value of the young actors themselves, very seriously indeed.

Where valuable pointers concerning the company and its playhouse come together is with the near location of the Red Bull to St John's Priory. Time and again the term 'St John' is brought into the Queen's Servants' history. The Red Bull was located in St John Street, a stone's

throw from the Revels Office located within the St John's Priory buildings. Thomas Heywood, in his *Apology for Actors* – a work that mentions
so much that is relevant to this company in particular – goes out of his
way to describe how all actors would lately repair to 'the office of the
Reuels', where 'our Court playes haue beene … yearely rehersed, perfected, and corrected before they come to the publike view of the Prince
and the Nobility'.

The specific relevance of St John as an emblem that the court associated with this company is curiously demonstrated with the tradition,
provable year-on-year early during the Jacobean period, of the Queen's
Servants performing their plays on St John's Day. At the beginning of
Chapter 5, it seemed inescapably noticeable that where a date is stipulated, the company gave court performances on 27 December in 1605,
1609, 1610 and 1611, with 'St John's Day at night' specified on many of the
entries. Although the Priory of St John of Jerusalem originally referred
to St John the Baptist, the feast day of 27 December was dedicated to St
John the Apostle: by tradition also the Evangelist; also by tradition the
'disciple Jesus loved', the innocent among Christ's friends. This, perhaps,
marks out the company as one that appealed with a special style of affection from the court.

All this, however, happened before 1612. After this time everything
changed, with no more central, famous clown, and a perceptibly different repertoire approach. Where the association continued with St John's,
perhaps, is when the company's name changed to that of 'the Revels' – a
possible reference to court contexts that should be explored further in the
future.

In the Introduction to this book I described the way in which
assumptions have been made about this company's work, much of the
time based on warped perceptions of its history. A new and detailed set
of contexts has been achieved for the Queen's Servants and their main
playhouse, filling a gap in that important period for the development
of drama: those first, Shakespearean years of public amphitheatre playhouse profit-making. Yet, in truth, this much-needed data, here interpreted into story – palatable to the human mind, but always flawed by
nature – can only last as long as the time between now and the discovery of the next relevant record or the next important observation
in this field. The future will clarify, perfect and correct in theatre history's own office of England's Revels – or, at least, it will suggest further
matters for consideration. With a newly revitalised attitude, however,

afforded to us by contemplating the data we have now, we can look to discover the all-important plays of this company with fresh eyes, appreciating the Queen's Servants' repertoire, and that of subsequent Red Bull companies, for what they represented as plays individually, and as the all-important economic group.

Select bibliography

THE NATIONAL ARCHIVES, KEW

AO3/377/3	Audit Office, Comptroller's Accounts (Greene payments)
AO3/377/4	Audit Office, Comptroller's Accounts (Greene payments)
AO3/379/3, p. 26	Robert Leigh's 1612 licence
AO3/908, Part 14	Jacobean Revels accounts
C2/CHASI/H28/26	Beeston, the Cockpit and the George Tavern
C2/JASI/P16/14	Richard Perkins v. Robert Leigh
C2/JASI/W2/67	*Worth* v. *Baskervile* (bill and answer)
C3/390/47	*Woodford* v. *Holland* (1623 bill and answer)
C24/497	Aaron Holland's age (*Bingham v. Bonham*)
C24/500/9	*Worth* v. *Baskervile* case, depositions (for Baskervile side)
C24/500/103	*Worth* v. *Baskervile* case, depositions (for Worth's side)
C33/146, fo. 948	*Woodford* v. *Holland* (1624 court result)
C54/2075, no. 17	Greene's tenure of Curtain, etc.
C54/3060, no. 3	Beeston and the King's Head, Shoreditch
C66/1137, mm. 32–3	Thomas Bedingfeld, sharer in playing cards
C66/1291, mm. 37–9	Establishment of Seckford's almshouse (patent, 1588)
C66/1827, no. 29	Company's official licence, 1609
C66/3040, no. 10	Anne Bedingfeld's permission to build (1663)
C142/261/51	Eustace Bedingfeld's inquisition post mortem (1)
E101/437/8	Queen Anna's household accounts (incomplete)
E179/69/82, m. 11	Thomas Bedingfeld, Gentleman Pensioner
E179/142/307, m. 5.	John Green at the Curtain
E179/269/41	Aaron Holland in Gray's Inn Lane
E351/543	Court payments to players
E351/543, m. 113b	Payment to players as Grooms of the Chamber
E351/544	More court payments to players
E407/1, 4–35	Thomas Bedingfeld, Gentleman Pensioner
KB9/685/14	Aaron Holland's bowling alley in Drury Lane (1594)

KB27/1439/1, m. 955	Greene indebted to Robert Livesey, May 1612
KB29/242, m. 25d	Aaron Holland, a Clerkenwell inn-holder by the end of 1602
KB 29/255, m. 84d	Martin Slatiar and Robert Dawes outlawed
KB 29/259, m. 43	Emmanuel Reade detained in the Clink for killing Robert Dawes
LC2/4/5, p. 84	Procession list of March 1604
LC2/5, fo. 39	Queen Anna's funeral (Queen's Servants)
LC2/6, fo.73r	King James' funeral (Prince Charles' players)
PC2/26, fos. 84v, 90v	Penelope Rich in Clerkenwell
PC2/27, fos. 283–283v	Privy Council meeting of April 1615 re performing in Lent
PC2/28, 29	Privy Council meetings re Beeston's building
PC2/50, pp. 271, 280	Elizabeth Beeston and the George Tavern
PROB 11/58/119, fos. 56v–57v	John Draper's will (1576)
PROB 11/72/51, fos. 25–26v	Thomas Seckford's will (1587)
PROB 11/103/138, fos. 95–7	Thomas Pope's will (1604)
PROB 11/125/67, fos. 42–3	Henry Draper's will (1614)
REQ1/26, fos. 729v–730, 779v–780	*Woodford* v. *Holland* (1613 proceedings)
REQ1/130	*Smith* v. *Beeston* (affidavits)
REQ2/78/56	*Thomas Hobson* v. *Margery Draper*
REQ2/411, Box 2, 148	*Woodford* v. *Holland* (answer of 1619)
REQ2/411, Box 2, 149	*Woodford* v. *Holland* (bill of 1619)
REQ2/459, Box 1	*Smith* v. *Beeston* (bill and answer)
REQ2/655, Box 2	Mr Holden's hats
REQ2/709	*Baskervile* v. *Beeston* case (1632)
SC6/JASI/1646, 1648, 1650, 1653	Queen Anna's household accounts
SO3/7	Desire to return to adult playing (November 1622)
SP14/2, fos. 246v–247	Draft licence for the Queen's Servants, undated (1603–4)
Ward 7/24/153, Box 2	Eustace Bedingfeld's inquisition post mortem (2)

LONDON METROPOLITAN ARCHIVES

CLC/275/MS 33011/004	Beeston's rape charge of 1602 (Bridewell Court minutes)

COL/CC/01/01/027 fo. 143v — Martin Slatiar, a Court of Common Council bond

COL/RMD/PA/01/002, no. 189 — Privy Council request re third company (at the Boar's Head)

DL/AL/C/003/MS 09052/007, item 174 — Robert Leigh's will

DL/C/0217, pp.216–19, fos. 108–10 — Thomas Greene and the Mary Phillips case

DL/C/0231, fos. 605r–v, 615r–v — The intimacy of the Red Bull playhouse (when unfit: X079/051) (*Hambell* v. *Hall*, Consistory Court)

MJ/SB/P/001 (microfilm X071/003) — Process Register Book of Indictments (Highways)

MJ/SB/R/001 (1 October 1612) — Middlesex edict forbidding jigs

MJ/SB/R/002 (microfilm X071/24) — Sessions of the Peace Register (Highways, 1617)

MJ/SB/R/002, pp. 344, 347 — Beeston in trouble about the Cockpit

MJ/SB/R/003 (microfilm X071/25) — Sessions of the Peace Register (Highways, 1622)

MJ/SR/0355, 38 — Aaron Holland's inn at the Savoy (1598)

MJ/SR/0410, 3, 4, 9, 10 — Troubles at the Boar's Head

MJ/SR/0416, 55 — Martin Slatiar in prison

MJ/SR/0429, 19 — Robert Leigh and the Norton Folgate rape charge (1605)

MJ/SR/0430, 68 — Robert Leigh and the Norton Folgate rape charge (1605)

MJ/SR/0466, 33 — John Burton stealing a hatband

MJ/SR/0489, 9, 11,101, 103, 105 — The 'notable outrage' at the Red Bull playhouse (1610)

MJ/SR/0499, 70 — The theft of goods from the Red Bull (Sayer, 1611)

MJ/SR/0499, 114 — Theft from Thomas Greene (Sayer, 1611)

MJ/SR/0519, 53 — Pickpocketing incident, Fulsis and Sweete (1613)

MJ/SR/0523, 219, 220, 221 — Robert Dawes, Martin Slatiar: the assault on Chambers

MJ/SR/0550, 152 — Recusancy and the Queen's Servants

MJ/SR/0558, 48 — Recusancy and the Queen's Servants

MJ/SR/0559, 141 — Recusancy and the Queen's Servants

MJ/SR/0561, 30 — Beeston in trouble re Highways (1617)

MJ/SR/0616, 89	The wounding of John/Richard Gill (1623)
MJ/SR/0617, 30	Gill's threat against Richard Baxter (1623)
O/257/001	Beeston and the King's Head, Shoreditch
P69/BOT2/A/001/MS 09220	St Botolph's parish, baptisms, 1558–1625
P69/BOT2/A/019/MS 09234/002	St Botolph, Aldgate, memoranda book, 1591–2
P69/GIS/A/002/MS 06419/002	St Giles, Cripplegate, parish register
P76/JS1/001, 002, 003, 004	St James, Clerkenwell, parish registers
P76/JS1/127, 10, 11	Beeston and Holland support two apprenticeships
P76/JS1/141	Sir Thomas Chaloner's letter
P91/LEN/A/001/MS 07493	St Leonard, Shoreditch, parish registers
P91/LEN/A/012/MS 07499/001	St Leonard, Shoreditch, parish registers
P92/SAV/3001	'Kempe a man' buried, St Saviour's, Southwark
P93/MRY1/001 (microfilm X024/090)	St Mary, Whitechapel, parish register
SKCS/018 (microfilm X067/001)	Surrey and Kent Sewer Commission

OTHER MANUSCRIPT SOURCES
British Library
BL Additional MS 19256, item 8, fo. 44

'Robert Pallant', 1624

BL Additional MS 34563

Princess Elizabeth (Tudor) and the Bedingfeld family

Hatfield House, Cecil Papers, MS 197, fo. 91(2)

Martin Slatiar's petition, available on BL microfilm M485/52/91(2)

Cambridge University Archives
Commissary Court Book, Comm. Ct. II.13, fo. 128v (rev) and fo. 107v (rev)

The visit of Thomas Greene and the Queen's Servants on tour

College of Arms

College of Arms MS 116/416

Eustace Bedingfeld's funeral certificate

Dulwich College, London

Dulwich College MS 1

Letters and papers of Philip Henslowe and Edward Alleyn on English drama and the stage at the Fortune Theatre, 1559–1662

Essex Record Office, Chelmsford

St Edward the Confessor Parish Registers, Romford, D/P 346/1/1

Records of the Greens/Greenes

Gloucestershire Archives, Gloucester

Gloucestershire Archives, D1799/P12

Sketch of outside of Red Bull playhouse (*c.* 1664)

Gloucestershire Archives, Dyrham papers

Blathwaite family

Guildhall Library

Brewers Company, Court Minute Books: CLC/L/BF/B/001/MS 05445/007 (1582–6)
and CLC/L/BF/B/001/012 (1604–12)

Henry Draper, brewer

Huntington Library, San Marino, California

Wallace papers, Box 2, File BI 11

Wallace papers, Box 3, File BI 20

Wallace papers, Box 9, File BV, 11b

Islington Local History Centre, Finsbury Library, St John Street

St James' Parish Vestry Book, 1590–1683

Kent History and Library Centre, Maidstone
De L'Isle papers, CKS-U1475/A62/4

Sir Robert Sidney in debt (1607)

De L'Isle papers, CKS-U1475/C81/91–165, nos. 144–5, 144

A Thomas Greene mentioned

Lambeth Palace Library
LPL 3201, fos. 182v–183

Worcester's letter describing Queen Anna's ladies of the household

Oxburgh Hall, Norfolk
Wooden Box, Household Inventories

Suffolk Record Office, Ipswich
SROI FC25/L3/3/8

Anne Bedingfeild's deposition (1633)

SROI FC25/L3/3/11

Document showing division of Thomas Seckford's Clerkenwell Estate (cf. will)

SROI HB10/427/214

Indenture of lease with survey (1679/80)

SROI HD21/480

Sketch of Seckford Estate (seventeenth century, undated)

Surrey History Centre, Woking
Loseley MS SHC LM/348/125

Eustace Bedingfeld property (1578)

Loseley MS SHC LM/COR/3/707

A letter from Anthony Bedingfeld

Westminster City Archives

St Clement Danes Parish Records B1, Surveyor's Accounts 1581–1621
Poor rates paid by Eustace Bedingfeld and Anne Bedingfeild

St Mary le Strand Churchwardens' Accounts
Poor rates paid by Aaron Holland

PUBLISHED WORKS

Allegations for Marriage Licences Issued by the Bishop of London 1520 to 1610, 2 vols. (London: Harleian Society, 1887)

Arber, Edward, ed., *Transcript of the Registers of the Company of Stationers 1554–1640*, 5 vols. (London, 1875–94)

Archer, Ian, *The Pursuit of Stability: Social Relations in Elizabethan London* (Cambridge University Press, 1991)

Ashbee, Andrew, *Records of English Court Music, 9 vols., Vol. iv: 1603–1625* (Snodland: Ashbee, 1991)

Astington, John H., *Actors and Acting in Shakespeare's Time: The Art of Stage Playing* (Cambridge University Press, 2010)
  'Playing the Man: Acting at the Red Bull and the Fortune', *Early Theatre* 9 (2006), 130–43

Baldwyn, Charles, ed., *The Old English Drama*, 2 vols. (London: Hurst, Robinson, 1825)

Barroll, Leeds, *Anna of Denmark, Queen of England: A Cultural Biography* (Philadelphia: University of Pennsylvania Press, 2001)
  'Defining "Dramatic Documents"', *Medieval and Renaissance Drama in England* 9 (1997), 112–26

Bawcutt, N. H., *The Control and Censorship of Caroline Drama: The Records of Sir Henry Herbert, Master of the Revels 1623–73* (Oxford: Clarendon Press, 1996)

Beaumont, Francis, *The Knight of the Burning Pestle*, ed. Michael Hattaway (New York: Norton, 1995)

Bedingfeld, Katherine, *The Bedingfelds of Oxburgh* (Privately printed, 1912)

Bennett, Judith M., *Ale, Beer and Brewsters in England: Women's Work in a Changing World 1300–1600* (Oxford University Press, 1996)

Bentley, Gerald Eades, 'The Troubles of a Caroline Acting Troupe: Prince Charles's Company', *Huntington Library Quarterly* 41 (1977–8), 217–49

Berry, Herbert, *The Boar's Head Playhouse* (Washington, DC: Folger Library, 1986)

Berry, Herbert,, 'Building Playhouses, the Accession of James I, and the Red Bull', *Medieval and Renaissance Drama in England* 18 (2005), 61–74

Brennan, Michael G., 'Sir Charles Somerset's Music Books (1622)', *Music and Letters* 74 (1993), 501–18

Briscoe, A. Daly, *A Tudor Worthy: Thomas Seckford of Woodbridge* (Ipswich: *East Anglian Magazine*, 1979)

Butler, Martin, 'Entertaining the Palatine Prince: Plays on Foreign Affairs 1635–1637', *English Literary Renaissance* 13 (1983), 319–44

Chambers, E. K. and W. W. Greg, eds., *Dramatic Records of the City of London: The Remembrancia*, MSC 1.1 (Oxford: Malone Society, 1907)

Clifford, Anne, *The Diary of Anne Clifford: 1616–1619*, ed. Katherine O. Acheson (New York: Garland, 1995)

Cook, David and F. P. Wilson, eds., *Dramatic Records in the Declared Accounts of the Treasurer of the Chamber, 1558–1642*, MSC 6 (Oxford: Malone Society, 1962 [1961])

Cox, John D. and David Scott Kastan, eds., *A New History of Early English Drama* (New York: Columbia University Press, 1997)

Davies, J. Conway, *Catalogue of Manuscripts in the Library of the Honourable Society of the Inner Temple*, 3 vols. (Oxford University Press for the Masters of the Bench of the Inner Temple, 1972)

Doran, Susan and Thomas S. Freeman, eds., *The Myth of Elizabeth* (Basingstoke: Palgrave Macmillan, 2003)

Duncan-Jones, Katherine, 'Shakespeare's Dancing Fool', *Times Literary Supplement*, 11 August 2010

Dutton, Richard, ed., *The Oxford Handbook of Early Modern Theatre* (Oxford University Press, 2009)

Eccles, Mark, 'Elizabethan Actors I: A–D', *Notes and Queries* 236 [n.s. 38] (1991), 38–49

  'Elizabethan Actors II: E–J', *Notes and Queries* 236 [n.s. 38] (1991), 454–61

  'Elizabethan Actors III: K–R', *Notes and Queries* 237 [n.s. 39] (1992), 293–303

  'Elizabethan Actors IV: S to End', *Notes and Queries* 238 [n.s. 40] (1993), 165–76

Feuillerat, Albert, *Documents Relating to the Office of the Revels in the Time of Queen Elizabeth* (Louvain: A. Uystpruyst, 1908)

Fisher, N. R. R., 'The Queenes Courte in Her Councell Chamber at Westminster', *The English Historical Review*, 108.427 (April, 1993), 314–37

Fleay, Frederick Gard, *A Chronicle History of the London Stage, 1559–1642* (London: Reeves and Turner, 1890)

Foakes, R. A., *Illustrations of the English Stage, 1580–1642* (London: Scolar Press, 1985)

Foucault, Michel, 'What is an Author?', trans. Josue V. Harari, in *Textual Strategies: Perspectives in Post-Structuralist Criticism*, ed. Josue V. Harari (London: Methuen, 1980), pp. 141–60

Foxe, John, *Actes and Monuments of these Latter and Perillous Dayes ...* (London: John Day, 1563)

Galloway, David, ed., *Records of Early English Drama: Norwich 1540–1642* (University of Toronto Press, 1984)

Golland, Jim, 'Anne Bedingfeld: The Brasses in Pinner Church', *Pinner Local History Society Newsletter: Silver Jubilee 1972–1977*, 25

Gowing, Laura, *Domestic Dangers: Women, Words, and Sex in Early Modern London* (Oxford: Clarendon Press, 1996)

Griffith, Eva, 'Martin Slatiar and the Red Bull Playhouse', *Huntington Library Quarterly* 74 (2011), 553–74

'New Material for a Jacobean Playhouse: The Red Bull Theatre on the Seckford Estate', *Theatre Notebook* 55 (2001), 5–23

'Playhouse, Company, Repertoire: The Queen's Servants at the Red Bull Theatre, Clerkenwell (*c.* 1605–1619)', Ph.D. thesis, University of London, 2003

Gurr, Andrew, *Playgoing in Shakespeare's London*, 2nd edn (Cambridge University Press, 1996)

Shakespeare's Opposites: The Admiral's Company 1594–1625 (Cambridge University Press, 2009)

The Shakespearean Stage 1574–1642, 3rd edn (Cambridge University Press, 1992)

Henslowe, Philip, *Henslowe's Diary*, ed. W. W. Greg, 2 vols. (London: A. H. Bullen, 1904–8)

Henslowe's Diary, ed. R. A. Foakes and R. T. Rickert (Cambridge University Press, 1961)

Henslowe's Diary, ed. R. A. Foakes, 2nd edn (Cambridge University Press, 2002)

Heywood, Thomas, *An Apology for Actors* (London, 1612)

The First and Second Parts of King Edward IV, ed. Richard Rowland (Manchester University Press, 2005)

A Woman Killed with Kindness, in '*A Woman Killed with Kindness' and Other Domestic Plays*, ed. Martin Wiggins (Oxford University Press, 2008)

Thomas Heywood's "The Rape of Lucrece", ed. Allan Holaday (Urbana: University of Illinois Press, 1950)

Honigmann, E. A. J. and Susan Brock, eds., *Playhouse Wills 1558–1642: An Edition of Wills by Shakespeare and His Contemporaries in the London Theatre* (Manchester University Press, 1993)

Hotson, Leslie, *The Commonwealth and Restoration Stage* (Cambridge, MA: Harvard University Press, 1928)

Ingram, William, *The Business of Playing: The Beginnings of the Adult Professional Theater in Elizabethan London* (Ithaca, NY: Cornell University Press, 1992)

'Playhouses Make Strange Bedfellows: The Case of Aaron and Martin', *Shakespeare Studies* 30 (2002), 118–27

Jonson, Ben, *Ben Jonson: The Complete Masques*, ed. Stephen Orgel (New Haven: Yale University Press, 1969)

The Cambridge Edition of the Works of Ben Jonson, ed. David Bevington, Martin Butler and Ian Donaldson, 7 vols. (Cambridge University Press, 2012)

Jonson, Ben, George Chapman and John Marston, *Eastward Ho!*, ed. C. G. Petter (London: Black; New York: Norton, 1994)

Kathman, David, 'Reconsidering *The Seven Deadly Sins*', *Early Theatre* 7.1 (2004), 13–44

Kirkman, Francis, *The Wits; or, Sport upon Sport* (London, 1673)

Knutson, Roslyn Lander, *The Repertory of Shakespeare's Company, 1594–1613* (Fayetteville: University of Arkansas Press, 1991)

Lancashire, Anne, 'Multi-Day Performance and the London Clerkenwell Play', *Early Theatre* 9 (2006), 114–29

Lewalski, Barbara Kiefer, *The Polemics and Poems of Rachel Speght* (Oxford University Press, 1996)

Limon, Jerzy, *Gentlemen of a Company: English Players in Central and Eastern Europe, 1590–1660* (Cambridge University Press, 1985)

McManus, Clare, ed., *Women and Culture at the Courts of the Stuart Queens* (Basingstoke: Palgrave Macmillan, 2003)

    ed., *Women on the Renaissance Stage: Anna of Denmark and Female Masquing in the Stuart Court (1590–1619)* (Manchester University Press, 2002)

Madge, Sidney J., 'Worcester House in the Strand', *Archaeologia or Miscellaneous Tracts Relating to Antiquity* 91 (1945), 157–80

McMillin, Scott and Sally-Beth MacLean, *The Queen's Men and Their Plays* (Cambridge University Press, 1998)

Manning, C. R., 'State Papers Relating to the Custody of the Princess Elizabeth at Woodstock, in 1554', *Norfolk Archaeology* 4 (1855), 133–231

Mateer, David, 'Edward Alleyn, Richard Perkins and the Rivalry between the Swan and Rose Playhouses', *Review of English Studies* 60 (2007), 64–77

Matusiak, Christopher M., 'The Beestons and the Art of Theatrical Management in Seventeenth-Century London', Ph.D. thesis, University of Toronto, 2009.

Mullaney, Steven, *The Place of the Stage: License, Play, and Power in Renaissance England* (University of Chicago Press, 1988)

Munro, Lucy, 'Governing the Pen to the Capacity of the Stage: Reading the Red Bull and Clerkenwell', *Early Theatre* 9 (2006), 99–113

Murray, John Tucker, *The English Dramatic Companies, 1558–1642*, 2 vols. (London: Constable, 1910)

Nelson, Alan H., *Monstrous Adversary: The Life of Edward de Vere, 17th Earl of Oxford*, Liverpool English Texts and Studies 40 (Liverpool University Press, 2003)

Nelson, Alan H.ed., *Cambridge*, 2 vols., Records of Early English Drama [REED] (University of Toronto Press, 1989)

Payne, Helen, 'Aristocratic Women and the Jacobean Court 1603–1625', Ph.D. thesis, University of London, 2001

Peck, Linda Levy, ed., *The Mental World of the Jacobean Court* (Cambridge University Press, 1991)

Pepys, Samuel, *The Diary of Samuel Pepys*, ed. Robert Latham and William Matthews, 11 vols. (London: Bell, 1970)

Pinks, William J., *The History of Clerkenwell*, ed. Edward J. Wood, 2nd edn (London: Charles Herbert, 1881)

Resl, Brigitte and Linda Kalof, eds., *The Cultural History of Animals*, 6 vols. (Oxford: Berg, 2007)

Reynolds, George Fullmer, *The Staging of Elizabethan Plays at the Red Bull Theater 1605–1625* (New York: Modern Language Association of America, 1940)

Rowland, Richard, *Thomas Heywood's Theatre 1599–1639: Locations, Translations and Conflict* (Farnham: Ashgate, 2010)

Schrickx, Willem, *Foreign Envoys and Travelling Players in the Age of Shakespeare and Jonson* ([Gent]: Rijksuniversiteit te Gent, 1986)

'"Pickleherring" and English Actors in Germany', *Shakespeare Survey* 36 (1983), 135–47

Shakespeare, William, *Hamlet* ed. Harold Jenkins (London: Methuen, 1982)

Sisson, Charles J., 'The Red Bull Company and the Importunate Widow', *Shakespeare Survey* 7 (1954), 57–68

Smith, David L., Richard Strier and David Bevington, eds., *The Theatrical City: Culture, Theatre and Politics in London, 1576–1649* (Cambridge University Press, 1995)

Stern, Tiffany, 'A Small-Beer Health to His Second Day: Playwrights, Prologues, and First Performances in the Early Modern Theatre', *Studies in Philology* 101.2 (Spring 2004), 172–99

Stow, John, *Annales; or, A Generall Chronicle of England*, ed. Edmund Howe (London, 1631)

A Survey of London: Reprinted from the Text of 1603, ed. Charles Lethbridge Kingsford, 2 vols. (Oxford: Clarendon Press, 1909)

A Survey of the Cities of London and Westminster: Containing the Original, Antiquity, Increase, Modern Estate and Government of Those Cities, ed. John Strype, 2 vols. (London, 1720)

Straznicky, Marta, 'The Red Bull Repertory in Print', *Early Theatre* 9 (2006), 144–56

Streitberger, W. R., ed., *Jacobean and Caroline Revels Accounts, 1603–1642*, MSC 13 (Oxford: Malone Society, 1986)

Strong, Roy, *Henry, Prince of Wales and England's Lost Renaissance* (London: Thames & Hudson, 1986)

Suckling, Alfred, *The History and Antiquities of the County of Suffolk with Genealogical and Architectural Notices of Several of Its Towns and Villages*, 2 vols. (London: John Weale, 1846–8)

Temple, Philip, ed., *Survey of London Vol. XLVI: South and East Clerkenwell* (New Haven: Yale University Press, 2008)

Tighe, William Joseph, 'Gentlemen Pensioners in Elizabethan Politics and Government', Ph.D. thesis, University of Cambridge, 1983

Wade, Mara R., 'Duke Ulrik (1578–1624) as Agent, Patron, Artist: Reframing Danish Court Culture in the International Perspective *c.*1600', in *Reframing the Danish Renaissance: Problems and Prospects in a European Perspective*, ed. Michael Andersen, Birgitte Bøggild Johannsen and Hugo Johannsen, Studies in Archaeology and History 16 (Copenhagen: National Museum of Denmark, 2011)

'Entries in Denmark and Norway', in *Speculum Europaeum [Theatre and Spectacle in Europe (1580–1750)]*, ed. Pierre Béhar and Helen Watanabe-O'Kelly (Wiesbaden: Harrassowitz, 1999), pp.744–9

Triumphus nuptialis danicus. German Court Culture and Denmark: The 'Great Wedding' of 1634 (Wiesbaden: Harrassowitz, 1996)

Wallace, C. W., 'Three London Theatres of Shakespeare's Time', *University of Nebraska Studies* 9 (1909), 291–397

Weaver, Carol and Michael Weaver, *The Seckford Foundation: Four Hundred Years of a Tudor Charity* (Woodbridge: Seckford Foundation, 1987)

Webster, John, *The White Devil*, ed. Christina Luckyj, 2nd edn (London: A. & C. Black, 1996)

Weever, John, *Ancient Funerall Monuments Within the United Monarchie of Great Britaine, Ireland, and the Islands adjacent* ... (London, 1631)

Wickham, Glynne, *Early English Stages*, 4 vols. (London: Routledge, 1959–2002)

Wright, Louis B., *Middle-Class Culture in Elizabethan England* (Ithaca, NY: Cornell University Press, 1958)

Index

Grooms of the Chamber, 63, 65, 85
investors, loans, 230, 231, 234
patents, permissions, licences,
    exemplifications and warrants, 9, 62,
    63, 65, 68, 69, 73, 81, 83, 85, 86, 89, 91,
    172–3, 175–7, 187, 200, 201, 232, 234,
    239, 244, 247, 252, 256–7, 260
performing with the King's Men, 154, 155,
    163, 166, 170, 203
playbooks and scripts, 174–5, 227, 244, 246
'versions of' this company, 68, 72, 100,
    171–5, 177, 180, 182, 188, 194–5, 232,
    244, 262
warrants *see* patents, permissions, licences,
    exemplifications and warrants
Strange's Men, 80
Worcester's Men, 6, 58–63, 70–4, 79–83,
    84, 85, 91, 107, 108, 111, 120–3, 125, 180,
    182–3, 204, 219
    court payments, 85
    court performances, 72
company amalgamations and co-operations, 60,
    62, 71–3, 81–2, 84, 180, 250–1, 252, 260
company shares and sharers, 6, 10–11, 79, 81, 82,
    89, 148, 178, 182, 184, 189, 203, 226–9,
    237, 241–2
Cooke, 'Jo:', *Greene's Tu Quoque; or, The Cittie
    Gallant*, 87, 149, 213–16, 222
Cope, Sir Walter, 151
corral, corralling, 101–2
Corral de Comedias, Almargo, Spain, 101–2
Corte, Claudio, 56
costumes *see* clothes
court cases, 221
    Baskervile v. *Beeston*, 13, 69, 239
    Greene v. *Slatiar*, 65, 66, 68
    Livesey v. *Greene*, 226
    Perkins etc. v. *Leigh*, 174–6, 255
    Smith v. *Beeston*, 12, 14, 199, 201, 225, 226, 235,
        237, 252, 253, 259
    Woodford v. *Holland*, 12, 14, 67, 102, 209,
        230, 245
    Worth v. *Baskervile*, 10–12, 70, 73, 79, 100,
        107, 119, 148, 152, 171, 176, 184, 201,
        218–9, 226–32, 233, 235, 237, 241–4, 248,
        250, 253, 257, 258, 260,
        261
Courts of Law
    Consistory Court, 195–6, 217–8
    Court of Chancery, 12, 47, 241, 248
    Court of Common Pleas, 21, 23, 35
    Court of Requests, 32, 34, 46, 54, 69, 90
    Court of Marshalsea, 34
    Court of Wards and Liveries, 34
court-room writing and drama, 135–40, 144,
    243, 245

Cow Lane, 2, 210
Cowcross Street, 3
Crashaw, William, 99, 100
crime, 15, 21, 22, 23, 25
    and drama (treason, rape etc.), 127, 161, 166,
        168–70
    and the Red Bull playhouse and inn, 15,
        220, 222
    and the Red Bull's actors and associates, 91,
        194, 197, 218, 230
    bigamy, 11, 81, 230
    defamation, 86, 90, 217
    embezzlement, 237, 239
    manslaughter, 12
    rape, 12, 178, 193, 217
    theft, 12
    wounding, 12, 15
    and theatre history, 15, 16, 99, 233
critics, 4, 5, 7, 9, 12, 14, 16, 19, 27, 94, 110, 112,
    161, 163
    anti-acting, 202
cross-dressing, 137–9, 142–3, 191
Cumber, John, 152, 174, 225, 235, 236, 254,
    256, 257
Curtain estate, 9, 88, 90, 187

dancing, 189, 222
Daniel, John, 254
Daniel, Samuel, 122, 129
Danish royal family, 17, 111, 115, 160
    Augusta of Schleswig-Holstein at Dottorf,
        110
    Christian IV, 110, 112–13, 155, 158, 181
    Elisabeth of Braunschweig-Lüneburg, 110, 115,
        182, 183, 186, 188
    Frederick II, 110, 112, 181, 183
    Hans, duke of Schleswig-Holstein, 110
    Hedevig of Saxony, 110
    Sophia Hedwig of Braunschweig-
        Lüneburg, 188
    Sophia of Mecklenburg, 110, 111, 160
    Ulrik, duke of Schleswig-Holstein, 65, 66, 67,
        110, 111, 114, 158, 189
Danzig *see* Gdansk
Darsham (Suffolk), 41, 64
Dawes, Robert, 88, 177, 199
de Burgh, Richard, fourth earl of
    Clanricarde, 198
de Vere, Edward, seventeenth earl of Oxford,
    120, 122
de Vere, Elizabeth *see* Stanley, Elizabeth,
    countess of Derby
de Vere, Susan *see* Herbert, Susan, countess of
    Montgomery
debt, 73, 82, 202, 205, 215, 216, 219, 221, 225–6,
    227, 230, 231, 235, 237–8, 239